LLA

An I...
F

By the same author:

A Practical Course of English Pronunciation: a perceptual approach
(Edward Arnold, 1975)

An Introduction to the Pronunciation of English

FOURTH EDITION

A. C. GIMSON

formerly Professor of Phonetics
University College London

Revised by
SUSAN RAMSARAN
Lecturer in Phonetics,
University College London

Edward Arnold
A division of Hodder & Stoughton
LONDON NEW YORK MELBOURNE AUCKLAND

© 1962, 1970, 1980, 1989 A. C. Gimson
Revisions for the 4th edition © 1989 Edward Arnold

First published in Great Britain 1962
Second edition 1970
Third edition 1980
Fourth edition 1989

Reprinted 1989

Distributed in the USA by Routledge, Chapman and Hall, Inc.
29 West 35th Street, New York, NY 10001

British Library Cataloguing in Publication Data

Gimson, A.C. (Alfred Charles), *1917–1985*
  An introduction to the pronunciation
  of English. — 4th ed.
  1. English language. Pronunciation
  I. Title   II. Ramsaran, Susan
  421'.52

  ISBN 0–7131–6594–4
  ISBN 0–7131–6588–X   pbk

Library of Congress Cataloging in Publication Data

Gimson, A. C.
    An introduction to the pronunciation of English/A. C. Gimson.—
  4th ed. / revised for the fourth edition by Susan Ramsaran.
      p.   cm.
    Bibliography: p.
    Includes index.
    ISBN 0–7131–6594–4.—ISBN 0–7131–6588–X (pbk.)
    1. English language—Phonetics.   2. English language-
  -Pronunciation.   3. English language—Great Britain.
  I. Ramsaran, Susan.   II. Title.
  PE1135.G5   1989
  421'55—dc19   88–34068
                                                          CIP

Typeset in 10/11 pt English Times by Colset Private Limited, Singapore
Printed and bound in Great Britain for Edward Arnold, the educational, academic
and medical publishing division of Hodder and Stoughton Limited, 41 Bedford
Square, London WC1B 3DQ by Richard Clay Limited, Bungay, Suffolk

Foreword

The phonetic detail of the pronunciation of British English has already been described in several excellent works, notably those of Daniel Jones. This present book, written after a number of years of teaching the spoken language both to English students and to foreign learners, sets out to place the phonetics of British English in a larger framework than has been customary. For this reason, emphasis is given to the function of the spoken medium as a form of communication. Some treatment of the historical background and the linguistic implications of the present sound system is included, as well as information concerning the acoustic nature of English sounds. Those sections in Part II, in which detailed descriptions of the realizations of phonemes are given, deal with spelling forms, articulatory and acoustic features, variants and chief historical sources. In addition, throughout Parts II and III, general advice to the foreign learner is included.

The book is intended to serve as a general introduction to the subject which will encourage the reader to consult more specialized works on particular aspects. Though my own views and observations intrude both in the material and in its presentation, much of the information given is derived from the numerous sources quoted in the Bibliography. In particular, new evaluations, which seem to me to reflect more nearly the current trend of RP forms, are made of the phonetic characteristics of certain phonemes. In the acoustic field, where so much remains to be investigated and where research proceeds so rapidly, an attempt has been made to sum up the results of work done in the post-war period, though many of the conclusions must as yet be regarded as tentative. It was tempting to apply to British English a logical, elegant, and economical phonemic analysis such as is now commonplace in the United States, involving a very much simplified phonemic notation. If this has not been done, it is mainly because a type of analysis was required which was explicit on the phonetic level as well as reasonably tidy on the phonemic level; it seemed easier, for instance, to deal with phonetic developments and variants in terms of the largely traditional (for British English) transcription which has been used.

Throughout the book, the influence of my teachers, Professor Daniel

Jones and Dr. H. N. Coustenoble, will be obvious. To them my sincere thanks are due, not only for their teaching over the past twenty-five years but also for the example of dedication which they gave me. My gratitude is also due to Professor D. B. Fry and all my colleagues of the Department of Phonetics, University College, London, whose brains I have constantly picked during the writing of this book. In particular, I have valued the help of Mr. J. D. O'Connor and Dr. A. J. Fourcin, who have read sections of the book, made corrections, and suggested improvements. I am also much indebted to Professor Randolph Quirk for his helpful comments on several points of Old English phonology. I am most grateful, too, to Mr. J. C. Wells, who has generously allowed me to use unpublished figures resulting from his work on the formants of RP vowels.

A. C. GIMSON,
  University College,
    London.
December, 1961.

Preface to Second Impression

A number of mistakes have been corrected in this second impression. My grateful thanks go to all those who have pointed out errors, particularly to Mrs. H. J. Uldall and Mr. J. C. Wells for their corrections and comments, and to Mr. G. Perren of the British Council, London, who has kindly allowed me to use on p. 219 his amended figures for the English consonant frequencies.

A. C. G.
November, 1963.

Preface to the Second Edition

In this revised edition, a number of sections have been modified or expanded in the light of evidence which has appeared since the first publication of this book. The changing status of RP, especially amongst young people, has necessitated the re-writing of the pages dealing with this matter, and it has seemed to me worthwhile to add a section on the current problems of the intelligibility of spoken English in the world. The chief additions, however, are concerned with the phonotactic possibilities of English, the permissible variations in the phonemic components of English words and the frequency of occurrence of monosyllables and polysyllables in continuous speech. Finally, the bibliography, while remaining selective, has been considerably extended.

A. C. G.
March, 1970.

Preface to the Third Edition

Ten years after the appearance of the second edition, I have been able in this new version to introduce a number of small amendments. More significantly, I have added a new chapter which is concerned with the problems of teaching the pronunciation of English to foreign learners. This addition reflects the widespread use of the book as a text in the teaching of English as a foreign language. The style of the appended chapter inevitably differs from that of the rest of the book. The first eleven chapters remain essentially descriptive within a given theoretical framework. The new chapter is much more speculative, since it contains opinions and frequently offers advice to the reader. The opinions and advice are, however, the result of my experience gained in some thirty-five years of teaching foreign students and may therefore be found to be of some value to others.

A. C. G.
January, 1980.

Preface to the Fourth Edition

Despite the increasing number of books concerning phonetics and phonology, none has been published to supersede this volume which has been the most comprehensive and authoritative work on the pronunciation of English for almost thirty years. Clearly, it can remain so only if it is regularly updated; and in this fourth edition I have tried to be thorough whilst respecting the original spirit of the work, a task which I have undertaken as one who over seventeen years was successively a student, colleague and collaborator of Professor Gimson.

General updating is to be found in every chapter with regard to recent research and current terminology, the former being reflected in the revised bibliography. More particularly, I have expanded Section 3 (on the Word and Connected Speech) to include explicit accounts of some of the rules concerning such topics as suffix formation, stress shift, smoothing and elision. The book has always dealt with these implicitly and still provides ample exemplification, but it seemed that summaries of certain processes and patterning would enhance its usefulness as an important reference work. It also seemed appropriate that I should add some information in this section on stylistic variation in RP, as I was asked to carry out research in this field by Professor Gimson who then supervised my doctoral thesis. The generalizations that I feel able to make here are based on recorded data taken from twenty hours of spontaneous conversation and have not previously been published in any detail.

Similarly, the tentative comments that I have felt able to add to Chapter 6 on current changes in RP are based on pronunciations observed and elicited in connection with lexicographical work carried out by Professor Gimson and myself. The replacement of the symbol /aʊ/ by /aʊ/ in this edition brings the transcription in line with the *English Pronouncing Dictionary*.

It is to be hoped that any changes and additions that I have made will serve to provide such clear and up-to-date information as is needed by another generation of readers who hope to find comprehensive introductory coverage of the pronunciation of English within a single volume.

Susan Ramsaran
   University College,
      London
August, 1988.

The publishers wish to thank Dr Alan Cruttenden for his invaluable assistance in the production of this new edition.

List of Phonetic Symbols and Signs

a   Cardinal Vowel no. 4 (approximately as in French *patte*); used for first element of Eng. diphthong [aɪ]

æ   front vowel between open and half-open (Eng. vowel in *cat*)

ɑ   Cardinal Vowel no. 5 (approximately as in French *pas*); used for Eng. [ɑː] in *car*

ɒ   open rounded Cardinal Vowel no. 5 (Eng. vowel in *dog*)

b   voiced bilabial plosive (Eng. *b* in *labour*)

ɓ   voiced ingressive bilabial plosive

β   voiced bilabial fricative

c   voiceless palatal plosive

ç   voiceless palatal fricative

ɔ   Cardinal Vowel no. 6 (approximately as in German *Sonne*); used for Eng. [ɔː] in *saw*, and first element of diphthong [ɔɪ]

d   voiced alveolar plosive (Eng. *d* in *lady*)

ɗ   voiced ingressive alveolar plosive

ð   voiced dental fricative (Eng. *th* in *other*)

e   Cardinal Vowel no. 2 (approximately as in French *thé*); used for Eng. [e] in *bed*, and first element of diphthong [eɪ]

ə   unrounded central vowel (Eng. initial and final vowels in *another*)

ɚ   retroflexed central vowel (American *er* in *water*)

ɛ   Cardinal Vowel no. 3 (approximately as in French *père*); used for first element of diphthong [ɛə]

ɜ   unrounded central vowel (Eng. vowel in *bird*)

f   voiceless labio-dental fricative (Eng. *f* in *four*)

ɟ   voiced palatal plosive

g   voiced velar plosive (Eng. *g* in *eager*)

ɠ   voiced ingressive velar plosive

h   voiceless glottal fricative (Eng. *h* in *house*)

ɦ   voiced glottal fricative (sometimes Eng. *h* in *behind*)

i   Cardinal Vowel no. 1 (approximately as in French *si*); used for Eng. [iː] in *see*

ɨ   unrounded central close vowel

ɪ   centralized unrounded half-close vowel (Eng. vowel in *sit*)

j   palatal unrounded semi-vowel (Eng. *y* in *you*)

ɾ   linguo-alveolar tap (sometimes *r* in Eng. *very*)

k   voiceless velar plosive (Eng. *c* in *car*)

l   voiced alveolar lateral continuant (Eng. *l* in *lay*)

ɫ   voiced alveolar lateral continuant with velarization (Eng. *ll* in *ill*)

ɬ   voiceless alveolar lateral fricative (Welsh *ll*)

m   voiced bilabial nasal (Eng. *m* in *me*)

ɱ   voiced labio-dental nasal (Eng. *m* in *comfort*)

ɯ   unrounded Cardinal Vowel no. 8

n   voiced alveolar nasal (Eng. *n* in *no*)

ŋ   voiced velar nasal (Eng. *ng* in *sing*)

ɲ   voiced palatal nasal (French *gn* in *vigne*)

o   Cardinal Vowel no. 7 (approximately as in French *eau*)

ø   rounded Cardinal Vowel no. 2 (approximately as in French *peu*)

œ   open rounded Cardinal Vowel no. 3 (approximately as in French *peur*)

θ   voiceless dental fricative (Eng. *th* in *thing*)

p   voiceless bilabial plosive (Eng. *p* in *pea*)

r   linguo-alveolar trill (Scottish, Italian *r*); also used for Eng. *r* in *red*

ɹ   voiced post-alveolar approximant (Eng. *r* in *red*)

ɻ   voiced retroflex approximant

ʀ   voiced uvular trill

ʁ   voiced uvular fricative or approximant

s   voiceless alveolar fricative (Eng. *s* in *see*)

ʃ   voiceless palato-alveolar fricative (Eng. *sh* in *she*)

t   voiceless alveolar plosive (Eng. *t* in *tea*)

ʇ   voiceless alveolar click

u   Cardinal Vowel no. 8 (approximately as in French *doux*); used for Eng [u:] in *do*

ʉ   central rounded close vowel

ʊ   centralized rounded half-close vowel (Eng. *u* in *put*)

v   voiced labio-dental fricative (Eng. *v* in *ever*)

ʌ   unrounded Cardinal Vowel no. 6; used for Eng. vowel in *cup*

ʋ   labio-dental approximant

w   labial-velar semi-vowel (Eng. *w* in *we*)

ʍ   voiceless labial-velar fricative (sometimes Eng. *wh* in *why*)

x   voiceless velar fricative (Scottish *ch* in *loch*)

y   rounded Cardinal Vowel no. 1 (approximately as in French *du*)

ʎ   voiced palatal lateral continuant (Italian *gl* in *egli*)

ɤ   unrounded Cardinal Vowel no. 7

ɣ   voiced velar fricative

z   voiced alveolar fricative (Eng. *z* in *lazy*)

ʒ   voiced palato-alveolar fricative (Eng. *s* in *measure*)

ɸ   voiceless bilabial fricative

ʖ   voiceless alveolar lateral click

ʔ   glottal plosive (stop)

: indicates full length of preceding vowel
˙ indicates half length of preceding vowel
ˈ main accentual stress or pitch prominence on following syllable
ˌ secondary accentual stress on following syllable
‾ high unaccented pre-nuclear syllable
\ high falling pitch
\ low falling pitch
/ high rising pitch
/ low rising pitch
ˇ falling-rising pitch
ˆ rising-falling pitch
• syllable carrying secondary accent
ₒ syllable, immediately following nucleus, carrying secondary accent based on quality/quantity
❟ syllable carrying primary (nuclear) accent
. unaccented syllable
˜ nasalization, e.g. [õ]
¨ centralization, e.g. [ö]
ˏ more open quality, e.g. [ǫ]
. closer quality, e.g. [ɔ̣]
ₒ devoiced lenis consonant, e.g. [z̥] (above in the case of [ŋ̊, ʒ̊, g̊])
ı syllabic consonant, e.g. [n̩] (above in the case of [ŋ̍])
̪ dental articulation, e.g. [t̪]
[ ] phonetic transcription
/ / phonemic transcription

Other Symbols

> changed to
< developed from
†† RP (figs. 9–27)

Contents

Part III The Word and Connected Speech

Part I
Speech and Language

1

Communication

1.1 Speech

One of the chief characteristics of the human being is his ability to communicate to his fellows complicated messages concerning every aspect of his activity. A man possessing the normal human faculties achieves this exchange of information mainly by means of two types of sensory stimulation, auditory and visual. The child will learn from a very early age to respond to the sounds and tunes which his elders habitually use in talking to him; and, in due course, from a need to communicate, he will himself begin to imitate the recurrent sound patterns with which he has become familiar. In other words, he begins to make use of *speech*; and his constant exposure to the spoken form of his own language, together with his need to convey increasingly subtle types of information, leads to a rapid acquisition of the framework of his spoken language. Nevertheless, with all the conditions in his favour, a number of years will pass before he has mastered not only the sound system used in his community but also has at his disposal a vocabulary of any extent or is entirely familiar with the syntactical arrangements in force in his language system. It is no wonder, therefore, that the learning of another language later in life, acquired artificially in brief and sporadic spells of activity and without the stimulus arising from an immediate need for communication, will tend to be tedious and rarely more than partially successful. In addition, the more firmly consolidated the basis of a first language becomes or, in other words, the later in life that a second language is begun, the more the learner will be subject to resistances and prejudices deriving from the framework of his original language. It may be said that, as we grow older, the acquisition of a new language will normally entail a great deal of conscious, analytical effort, instead of the child's ready and facile imitation.

1.2 Writing

Later in life the child will be taught the conventional visual representation of speech—he will learn to use *writing*. To-day, in considering those languages which have long possessed a written form, we are apt to forget that the written form is originally an attempt at reflecting the spoken language and that the latter precedes the former for both the individual and the community. Indeed, in many languages, so parallel are the two forms felt to be that the written form may be responsible for changes in pronunciation or may at least tend to impose restraints upon its development. In the case of English, this sense of parallelism, rather than of derivation, may be encouraged by the obvious lack of consistent relationship between sound and spelling. A written form of English, based on the Latin alphabet, has existed for more than 1,000 years and, though the pronunciation of English has been constantly changing during this time, few basic changes of spelling have been made since the fifteenth century. The result is that written English is often an inadequate and misleading representation of the spoken language of to-day. Clearly it would be unwise, to say the least, to base our judgments concerning the spoken language on prejudices derived from the orthography. Moreover, if we are to examine the essence of the English language, we must make our approach through the spoken rather than the written form. Our primary concern will be the production, transmission, and reception of the sounds of English—in other words, the *phonetics* of English.

1.3   Language

From the moment that we abandon orthography as our starting point, it is clear that the analysis of the spoken form of English is by no means simple. Each of us uses an infinite number of different speech sounds when we speak English. Indeed, it is true to say that it is difficult to produce two sounds which are precisely identical from the point of view of instrumental measurement: two utterances by the same person of the word *cat* may well show quite marked differences when measured instrumentally. Yet we are likely to say that the same sound sequence has been repeated. In fact we may hear clear and considerable differences of quality in the vowel of *cat* as, for instance, in the London and Manchester pronunciations of the word; yet, though we recognize differences of vowel quality, we are likely to feel that we are dealing with a 'variant' of the 'same' vowel. It seems, then, that we are concerned with two kinds of reality: the concrete, measurable reality of the sounds uttered, and another kind of reality, an abstraction made in our minds, which appears to reduce this infinite number of different sounds to a 'manageable' number of categories. In the first, concrete, approach, we are dealing with sounds in relation to *speech*; at the second, abstract, level, our concern is the behaviour of sounds in a particular *language*. A language is a system of conventional signals used for communication by a whole community. This pattern of conventions covers a system of significant sound units (the *phonemes*), the inflexion and arrangement of 'words', and the association of meaning with words. An utterance, an act of speech, is a single concrete manifestation of the system at work. As we have seen, several utterances which are plainly different on the concrete, phonetic level may fulfil the same function, i.e. are the 'same', on the systematic language level. It is important in any analysis of spoken language to keep this distinction in mind and we shall later be considering in some detail how this dual approach to the utterance is to be made. It is not, however, always possible or desirable to keep the two levels of analysis entirely separate: thus, as we shall see, we will draw upon our knowledge of the linguistically significant units to help us in determining how the speech continuum shall be divided up on the concrete, phonetic level; and again, our classification of linguistic units will be helped by our knowledge of their phonetic features.

1.4 Redundancy

Finally, it is well to remember that, although the sound system of our spoken languages serves us primarily as a medium of communication, its efficiency as such an instrument of communication does not depend upon the perfect production and reception of every single element of speech. A speaker will, in almost any utterance, provide the listener with far more cues than he needs for easy comprehension. In the first place, the situation, or context, will itself delimit very largely the purport of an utterance. Thus, in any discussion about a zoo, involving a statement such as 'We saw the lions and tigers', we are predisposed by the context to understand *lions*, even if the *n* is omitted and the word actually said is *liars*. Or again, we are conditioned by grammatical probabilities, so that a particular sound may lose much of its significance, e.g. in the phrase 'These men are working', the quality of the vowel in *men* is not as vitally important for deciding whether it is a question of *men* or *man* as it would be if the word were said in isolation, since here the plurality is determined in addition by the demonstrative adjective preceding *men* and the verb form following. Then again, there are particular probabilities in every language as to the different combinations of sounds which will occur. Thus in English, if we hear an initial *th* sound [ð], we expect a vowel to follow, and of the vowels some are much more likely than the others. We distinguish such sequences as -*gl* and -*dl* in final positions, e.g. in *beagle* and *beadle*; but this distinction is not relevant initially, so that even if *dloves* is said, we understand *gloves*. Or again, the total rhythmic shape of a word may provide an important cue to its recognition: thus, in a word such as *become*, the general rhythmic pattern may be said to contribute as much to the recognition of the word as the precise quality of the vowel in the first, weakly accented syllable. Indeed, we may come to doubt the relative importance of vowels as a help to intelligibility, since we can replace our twenty English vowels by the single vowel [ə] in any utterance and still, if the rhythmic pattern is kept, retain a high degree of intelligibility. An utterance, therefore, will provide a large complex of cues for the listener to interpret, but a greal deal of this information will be unnecessary, or *redundant*, as far as the listener's needs are concerned. On the other hand, such an over-proliferation of cues will serve to offset any disturbance such as noise or to counteract the sound quality divergences which may exist between speakers of two dialects of the same language. But to insist, for instance, upon exaggerated articulation in order to achieve clarity may well be to go beyond the requirements of speech as a means of communication; indeed, certain obscurations of quality are, and have been for many centuries, characteristic of English. Aesthetic judgments on speech, such as those which deplore the use of the 'intrusive' *r*, take into account social considerations of a somewhat different order from those involved in a study of speech as communication.

1.5   Phonetics and Linguistics

This book is primarily concerned with the sound system of English and it is proper, as we have seen, that phonetic and phonemic analysis should occupy an important place in the study of any language. Indeed, when it is a question of a language which is being subjected for the first time to scientific analysis, it is necessary that some statement of the sound system should be made at the very outset, so that a notation can be devised for the recording of the language in a written form. Nevertheless, it should be remembered that phonetic analysis constitutes but one step in a linguistic investigation.

A complete description of the current state of a language must provide information on several interrelated levels:—

(1) *Phonology.*—The concrete *phonetic* characteristics (articulatory, auditory, acoustic) of the sounds used in the language; the concrete *phonetic* level is often separated from the more abstract *phonological* level which analyses the patterning of sounds in language and includes the functional, *phonemic* behaviour of these sounds for distinctive purposes; the combinatory possibilities (*syllabic structure* or *phonotactics*) of the phonemes; the nature and use of such *prosodic* features as pitch, stress and length. A study of the phonic substance of the language may be accompanied by a description of the written form of the language (*graphology*).

(2) *Lexis.*—The total number of word forms which exist.

(3) *Morphology.*—The structure of words.

(4) *Syntax.*—The system of rules governing the structure of phrases, clauses and sentences consisting of words contained in the lexicon.

Note. Statements may be made which combine phonemic and morphemic features (*morphophonemics* or *morphophonology*), e.g. the phonemes /s/ and /z/ in *cats* and *dogs* are exponents of the same morpheme of plurality which might be symbolized as |s|.

(5) *Semantics*.—The relation of meaning to the signs and symbols of language.

Other aspects of language which would require investigation include the variation of the same language in different regions and social classes (*dialectology*); the influence of *context* and *style* upon the form and substance of the language; the influence of situation on the interpretation of utterances (*pragmatics*); the behaviour of human beings in their production and perception of the language (*psycholinguistics*); the interaction of the language and the society in which it is spoken (*sociolinguistics*).

Finally, it is clear that the phonology, lexis, syntax and semantics of a language are always undergoing change in time. The state of a language at any (*synchronic*) moment must be seen against a background of its historical (*diachronic*) evolution. It is for this reason that this book includes information on earlier states of the sound system of English, with some speculation on possible developments in the future.

2

The Production of Speech
The Physiological Aspect

2.1 The Speech Chain

Any manifestation of language by means of speech is the result of a highly complicated series of events. The communication in sound of such a simple concept as 'It's raining' involves a number of activities on the part of the speaker. In the first place, the formulation of the concept will take place at a linguistic level, i.e. in the brain; the first stage may, therefore, be said to be *psychological*. The nervous system transmits this message to the so-called 'organs of speech' and these in turn behave in a conventional manner, which, as we have learned by experience, will have the effect of producing a particular pattern of sound; the second important stage for our purposes may thus be said to be articulatory or *physiological*. The movement of our organs of speech will create disturbances in the air, or whatever the medium may be through which we are talking; these varying air pressures may be investigated and they constitute the third stage in our chain, the *physical* or acoustic. Since communication generally requires a listener as well as a speaker, these stages will be reversed at the listening end: the reception of the sound waves by the hearing apparatus (physiological) and the transmission of the information along the nervous system to the brain, where the linguistic interpretation of the message takes place (psychological). Phonetic analysis has often ignored the role of the listener. But any investigation of speech as communication must ultimately be concerned with both the production and the reception ends. A number of phonetic features, e.g. stress, must be defined in different terms according to whether the emphasis is laid on the speaker's feeling for his own speech activity or on the listener's appreciation of significant features.

Our immediate concern, however, is with the speaker's behaviour and more especially, on the concrete speech level, with the activity involved in the production of sounds. For this reason, we must now examine the speaker's articulatory stage (his speech mechanism) to discover how the various organs behave in order to produce the sounds of speech.

2.2 The Speech Mechanism

Man possesses, in common with many other animals, the ability to produce sounds by using certain of his body's mechanisms. The human being differs from other animals in that he has been able to organize the range of sounds which he can emit into a highly efficient system of communication. Non-human animals rarely progress beyond the stage of using the sounds they produce as a reflex of certain basic stimuli to signal fear, hunger, sexual excitement, and the like. Nevertheless, like other animals, man when he speaks makes use of organs whose primary physiological function is unconnected with vocal communication, namely, those situated in the respiratory tract.

2.2.1 Thus, the most usual *source of energy* for our vocal activity is provided by an air-stream expelled from the *lungs*. There are languages which possess sounds not requiring lung (pulmonic) air for their articulation, and, indeed, in English we have one or two extra-linguistic sounds, such as that we write as *Tut-tut* and the noise of encouragement made to horses, which are produced without the aid of the lungs; but all the essential sounds of English need lung air for their production. Our utterances are, therefore, largely shaped by the physiological limitations imposed by the capacity of our lungs and by the muscles which control their action. We are obliged to pause in articulation in order to refill our lungs with air and the number of energetic peaks of exhalation which we make will to some extent condition the length of any breath group. Syllabic pulses and dynamic stress, both typical of English, are directly related to the behaviour of the muscles which activate the lungs. In those cases where the lung air-stream is not available for the upper organs of speech, as when, after the removal of the larynx, lung air does not reach the mouth but escapes from an artificial aperture in the neck, a new source of energy, such as stomach air, has to be employed; a new source of this kind imposes restrictions of quite a different nature from those exerted by the lungs, so that the organization of the utterance into groups is changed and variation of energy is less efficiently controlled.

A number of techniques are available for the investigation of the activity in speech of the lungs and their controlling muscles. It is, for instance, possible to measure air pressures within the lungs by observing the reaction of an air-filled balloon placed in the stomach; X-ray photography reveals the gross movements of the ribs and muscles; and the technique of electromyography has demonstrated[1] the electrical activity of those respiratory muscles most concerned in speech, notably the internal intercostals.

2.2.2 The air-stream provided by the lungs undergoes important

[1] P. Ladefoged, M. H. Draper, and D. Whitteridge, 'Syllables and Stress,' *Miscellanea Phonetica III*, 1958 (International Phonetic Association).

modifications in the upper stages of the respiratory tract before it acquires the quality of a speech sound. First of all, in the *trachea* or windpipe, it passes through the *larynx*, containing the so-called *vocal folds* (see Fig. 1).

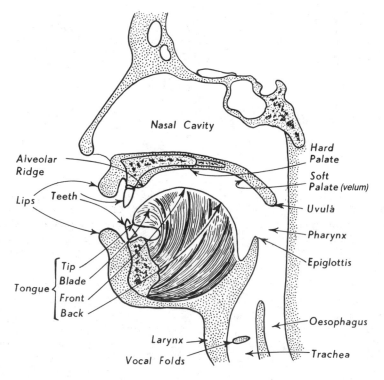

FIG. 1.—Organs of speech (schematic diagram).

The larynx is a casing, formed of cartilage and muscle, situated in the upper part of the trachea. Its forward portion is prominent in the neck below the chin and is commonly called the 'Adam's apple'. Housed within this structure from back to front are the vocal folds, two folds of ligament and elastic tissue which may be brought together or parted by the rotation of the arytenoid cartilages (attached at the posterior end of the folds) through muscular action. The inner edge of these folds has a length of about 23 mm. in adult men and about 18 mm. in women. The opening between the folds is known as the *glottis*. Biologically, the vocal folds act as a valve which is able to prevent the entry into the trachea and lungs of any foreign body or which may have the effect of enclosing the air within the lungs to assist in muscular effort on the part of the arms or the abdomen. In using the vocal folds for speech, the human being has adapted and elaborated upon this original open-or-shut function in the following ways (see Fig. 2):—

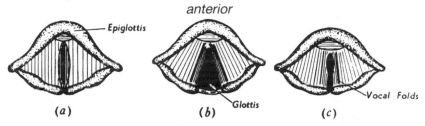

FIG. 2.—Diagrams of the vocal folds as seen from above: (a) tightly closed as for [ʔ];   (b) wide open as for breath;   (c) loosely together and vibrating as for voice.

a. The glottis may be held tightly closed, with the lung air pent up below it. This 'glottal stop' [ʔ] frequently occurs in English, e.g. when it precedes the energetic articulation of a vowel or when it reinforces or even replaces *p*, *t*, *k*. It may also be heard in defective speech, such as that arising from cleft palate, when [ʔ] may be substituted for the stop consonants, which, because of the nasal air escape, cannot be articulated with proper compression in the mouth cavity.

b. The glottis may be held open as for normal breathing.

c. The action of the vocal folds which is most characteristically a function of speech consists in their role as a *vibrator* set in motion by lung air—the production of *voice*, or *phonation*; this vocal fold vibration is a normal feature of all vowels or of such a consonant as *z* compared with voiceless *s*. In order to achieve the effect of voice, the vocal folds are brought sufficiently close together that they vibrate when subjected to air pressure from the lungs. This vibration, of a somewhat undulatory character, is caused[1] by compressed air forcing an opening of the glottis and the resultant reduced air pressure permitting the elastic folds to come together once more; the vibratory effect may easily be felt by touching the neck in the region of the larynx when saying *ah* or *z*, for instance, on a low note. In the typical speaking voice of a man,

---

[1]The theory of vocal fold vibration here described is known as the aerodynamic-myoelastic or tonic theory. Since the war, however, the experimental work of R. Husson and his associates has introduced a new explanation of the vibrations, in neuro-muscular (or clonic) terms. According to this theory, the vibrations of the vocal folds in speech are activated directly by the laryngeal recurrent nerve independently of sub-glottal air-pressure (although this latter will always be present if 'voice' is to be produced). The frequency of vibration (pitch) is also explained as dependent on direct innervation (rather than as the result largely of variations of air-pressure) and only the intensity of the larynx note as dependent on the force of sub-glottal air.

this opening and closing action is likely to be repeated between 100 and 150 times in a second, i.e. there are that number of vibration *cycles per second* (cps)[1]; in the case of a woman's voice, this *frequency* of vibration might well be between 200 and 325 cps. We are able, within limits, to vary the speed of vibration of our vocal folds or, in other words, are able consciously to change the *pitch* of the voice produced in the larynx; the more rapid the rate of vibration, the higher is the pitch (an extremely low rate of vibration being partly responsible for the 'grunting, creaky' type of voice). Normally the vocal folds come together rapidly and part more slowly, the opening phase of each cycle thus being longer than the closing phase. This gives rise to 'modal' (or 'normal') voice which is used for most of English speech. Other modes of vibration result in other *voice qualities*, most notably breathy and creaky voice which are used contrastively in a number of languages. (See also Chapter 5, §5.8.) Moreover, we are able, by means of variations in pressure from the lungs, to modify the size of the puff of air which escapes at each vibration of the vocal folds; in other words, we can alter the *amplitude* of the vibration, with a corresponding change of loudness of the sound heard by a listener. The normal human being soon learns to manipulate his glottal mechanism so that most delicate changes of pitch and loudness are achieved. Control of this mechanism is, however, very largely exercised by the ear, so that such variations are exceedingly difficult to teach to those who are born deaf, and a derangement of pitch and loudness control is liable to occur among those who become totally deaf later in life.

d. One other action of the larynx should be mentioned. A very quiet whisper may result merely from holding the glottis in the 'voiceless' position. But the more normal whisper, by means of which we are able to communicate with some ease, can be felt to involve energetic articulation and considerable stricture in the glottal region. Such a whisper may in fact be uttered with an almost total closure of the glottis and an escape of air in the region of the arytenoids. Once the vibrations of the vocal folds are lost, however, variations of pitch can be only of the grossest kind.

For our purposes in the analysis of English, the most important of these four activities are those which result in the production of *voiced* or *voiceless* sounds and that which produces the *glottal stop*.

The behaviour of the vocal folds may be observed in several ways. In particular, it is possible by means of the *laryngoscope* to have a stationary mirrored image of the glottis. Using stroboscopic techniques, it is possible to obtain a moving record and high-speed films have been made of the vocal folds, showing their action in ordinary

---

[1] The term *hertz* (Hz) is now generally applied to such a unit of frequency; 'cps', a more explicit abbreviation, is retained in this book.

breathing, producing voice and whisper, and closed as for a glottal stop. The situation of the folds renders them difficult to photograph with X-rays other than by tomographic techniques.

2.2.3 The Resonating Cavities The air-stream, having passed through the larynx, is now subject to further modification according to the shape assumed by the upper cavities of the *pharynx* and *mouth* and according to whether the *nasal cavity* is brought into use or not. These cavities function as the principal *resonators* of the note produced in the larynx.

2.2.3.1 The *pharyngeal cavity* (see Fig. 1) extends from the top of the larynx and oesophagus, past the epiglottis and the root of the tongue, to the region in the rear of the soft palate. It is convenient to identify these sections of the pharynx by naming them: laryngo-pharynx, oropharynx, nasopharynx. The shape and volume of this long chamber may be considerably modified by the constrictive action of the muscles enclosing the pharynx, by the movement of the back of the tongue, by the position of the soft palate which may, when raised, exclude the nasopharynx, and by the raising of the larynx itself. The position of the tongue in the mouth, whether it is advanced or retracted, will affect the size of the oropharyngeal cavity; the modifications in shape of this cavity should, therefore, be included in the description of any vowel. It is a characteristic of some kinds of English pronunciation that certain vowels are articulated with a strong pharyngeal contraction; in addition, a constriction may be made between the lower rear part of the tongue and the wall of the pharynx so that friction, with or without voice, is produced, such fricative sounds being a feature of a number of languages.

The pharynx may be observed by means of a laryngoscope or nasendoscopy and its constrictive actions are revealed by lateral X-ray photography.

The escape of air from the pharynx may be effected in one of three ways:—

a. The soft palate may be lowered, as in normal breathing, in which case the air may escape through the nose and the mouth. This is the position taken up by the soft palate in articulation of the French nasalized vowels in such a phrase as *un bon vin blanc* [œ̃ bõ væ̃ blɑ̃], the particular quality of such vowels being achieved through the function of the nasopharyngeal cavity.

b. The soft palate may be lowered so that a nasal outlet is afforded to the air stream, but a complete obstruction is made at some point in the mouth, with the result that, although air enters all or part of the mouth cavity, no oral escape is possible. A purely nasal escape of this sort occurs in such nasal consonants as [m, n, ŋ] in the English words *ram, ran, rang*. In a snore and some kinds of defective speech, this nasal escape may be accompanied by friction between the rear side of the soft palate and the pharyngeal wall.

c. The soft palate may be held in its raised position, eliminating the action of the nasopharynx, so that the air escape is solely through the mouth. All normal English sounds, with the exception of the nasal consonants mentioned, have this oral escape. Moreover, if for any reason the lowering of the soft palate cannot be effected, or if there is an enlargement of the organs enclosing the nasopharynx or a blockage brought about by mucus, it is often difficult to articulate either nasalized vowels or nasal consonants. In such speech, typical of adenoidal enlargement or obstruction caused by a cold, the French phrase mentioned above would have its nasalized vowels turned into their oral equivalents and the English word *morning* would have its nasal consonants replaced by [b, d, g]. On the other hand, an inability to make an effective closure by means of the raising of the soft palate —either because the soft palate itself is defective or because an abnormal opening in the roof of the mouth gives access to the nasal cavity— will result in the general nasalization of vowels and the failure to articulate such oral stop consonants as [b, d, g]. This excessive nasalization (or hypernasality) is typical of such a condition as cleft palate.

It is evident that the action of the soft palate is accessible to observation by direct means, as well as by lateral X-ray photography; the pressure of the air passing through the nasal cavities may be measured at the nostrils or within the cavities themselves.

2.2.3.2 *The Mouth*   Although all the cavities so far mentioned play an essential part in the production of speech sounds, most attention has traditionally been paid to the behaviour of the cavity formed by the mouth. Indeed, in many languages the word *tongue* is used to refer to our speech and language activity. Such a preoccupation with the oral cavity is doubtless due to the fact that it is the most readily accessible and easily observed section of the vocal tract; but there is in such an attitude a danger of gross over-simplification. Nevertheless, it is true that the shape of the mouth determines finally the quality of the majority of our speech sounds. Far more finely controlled variations of shape are possible in the mouth than in any other part of the speech mechanism.

The only boundaries of this oral chamber which may be regarded as relatively fixed are, in the front, the teeth; in the upper part, the hard palate; and, in the rear, the pharyngeal wall. The remaining organs are movable: the lips, the various parts of the tongue, and the soft palate with its pendent uvula (see Fig. 1). The lower jaw, too, is capable of very considerable movement; its movement will control the gap between the upper and lower teeth and also to a large extent the disposition of the lips. The space between the upper and lower teeth will often enter into our description of the articulation of sounds; in all such cases, it is clear that the movement of the lower jaw is ultimately responsible for the variation described.

It is convenient for our descriptive purposes to divide the roof of the mouth into three parts: moving backwards from the upper teeth, first, the *alveolar* or teeth ridge which can be clearly felt behind the teeth; secondly, the bony arch which forms the *hard palate* and which varies in size and arching from one individual to another; and finally, the soft palate or *velum* which, as we have seen, is capable of being raised or lowered, and at the extremity of which is the uvula. All these parts can be readily observed by means of a mirror. The main divisions will be referred to as: dental, alveolar, palatal (the hard palate), and velar (the soft palate).

(a) Of the movable parts, the *lips*, whenever the nasal passage is shut off, constitute the final orifice of the mouth cavity. The shape which they assume will, therefore, affect very considerably the shape of the total cavity. They may be shut or held apart in various ways. When they are held tightly shut, they form a complete obstruction or occlusion to the air-stream, which may either be momentarily prevented from escaping at all, as in the initial sounds of *pat* and *bat*, or may be directed through the nose by the lowering of the soft palate, as in the initial sound of *mat*. If the lips are held apart, the positions they assume may be summarized under six headings:—

1. held sufficiently close together over all their length that friction occurs between them. Fricative sounds of this sort, with or without voice, occur in many languages and the voiced variety [β] is sometimes wrongly used by foreign speakers of English for the first sound in *word*;

2. held sufficiently far apart for no friction to be heard, yet remaining fairly close together and energetically spread. This shape is taken up for a tense variety of the vowel in *see* and is known as the *spread* lip position;

3. held in a relaxed position with a medium lowering of the lower jaw. This is the position taken up for the vowel of *get* and is known as the *neutral* position;

4. held relatively wide apart, without any marked rounding, as for the vowel in *card*. This is the *open* position;

5. tightly pursed, so that the aperture is small and rounded, as in the vowel of *do*, or more markedly so in the French vowel of *doux*. This is the *close rounded* position;

6. held wide apart, but with slight projection and rounding, as in the vowel of *got*. This is the *open rounded* position.

Variations of these six positions may be encountered, e.g. in the vowel of *saw*, for which a type of lip rounding between open and close is commonly used. It will be seen from the examples given that lip position is particularly significant in the formation of vowel quality. English consonants, on the other hand, with the exception of such sounds as [p, b, m, w] whose primary articulation involves lip action, will tend to share the lip position of the adjacent vowel. In addition, the lower lip is an active articulator in the pronunciation of [f, v], a light contact being made between the lower lip and the upper teeth.

(b) Of all the movable organs within the mouth, the *tongue* is by far the most flexible and is capable of assuming a great variety of positions in the articulation of both vowels and consonants. The tongue is a complex muscular structure which does not show obvious sections; yet, since its position must often be described in considerable detail, certain arbitrary divisions are made. When the tongue is at rest, with its tip lying behind the lower teeth, that part which lies opposite the hard palate is called the *front* and that which faces the soft palate is called the *back*, with the region where the front and back meet known as the *centre*. This whole upper area of the tongue is sometimes referred to as the *dorsum*. The tapering section facing the teeth ridge is called the *blade* and its extremity the *tip*. The tip and blade region is sometimes known as the *apex*. The edges of the tongue are known as the *rims*.

Generally, in the articulation of vowels, the tongue-tip remains low behind the lower teeth. The body of the tongue may, however, be 'bunched up' in different ways, e.g. the front may be the highest part as when we say the vowel of *he*; or the back may be most prominent as in the case of the vowel in *who*; or the whole surface may be relatively low and flat as in the case of the vowel in *ah*. Such changes of shape can easily be felt if the above words are said in succession. These changes, moreover, together with the variations in lip position, have the effect of modifying very considerably the size of the mouth cavity and of dividing this chamber into two parts: that cavity which is in the forward part of the mouth behind the lips and that which is in the rear in the region of the pharynx.

The various parts of the tongue may also come into contact with the roof of the mouth. Thus, the tip, blade, and rims may articulate with the teeth as for the *th* sounds in English, or with the upper alveolar ridge as in the case of *t*, *d*, *s*, *z*, *n*; or the apical contact may be only partial as in the case of *l* (where the tip/blade makes firm contact whilst the rims make none) or intermittent as in a rolled *r*. In some languages, notably those of India, the tip contact may be retracted to the very back of the teeth ridge or even slightly behind it; the same kind of retroflexion, without the tip contact, is typical of some kinds of English *r*, e.g. those used in South-West England and America.

The front of the tongue may articulate against or near to the hard palate. Such a raising of the front of the tongue towards the palate (palatalization) is an essential part of the [ʃ, ʒ] sounds in English words such as *she* and *measure*, being additional to an articulation made between the blade and the alveolar ridge; or again, it is the main feature of the [j] sound initially in *yield*.

The back of the tongue can form a total obstruction by its contact with the soft palate, raised in the case of [k, g] and lowered for [ŋ] as in *sing*; or again, there may merely be a narrowing between the soft palate and the back of the tongue, so that friction of the type occurring finally in the Scottish *loch* is heard. And finally, the uvula may vibrate against the back of the tongue, or there may be a narrowing in this region which causes uvular friction.

It will be seen from these few examples that, whereas for vowels the tongue is generally held in a position which is convex in relation to the roof of the mouth, some consonant articulations, such as the Southern English *r* in *red* and the *l* in *table*, will involve the 'hollowing' of the body of the tongue so that it has, at least partially, a concave relationship with the roof of the mouth.

Moreover, the surface of the tongue, viewed from the front, may take on various forms: there may be a narrow groove running from back to front down the centre line as for *s*; or the grooving may be very much more diffuse as in the case of a *sh* [ʃ] sound; or again, the whole tongue may be laterally contracted, with or without a depression in the centre (sulcalization), as is the case with various kinds of *r* sounds.

(c) The oral speech mechanism is readily accessible to direct observation as far as the lip movements are concerned and also many of the tongue movements which take place in the forward part of the mouth. A lateral view of the shape of the tongue over all its length and its relationship with the palate and the velum may be obtained by means of still and moving X-ray photography. Formerly, it was thought to be necessary for a thin metal chain to be laid along the surface of the tongue in order to make its contours visible under X-rays; but, to-day, a coating of barium solution would be sufficient to make its lateral outline visible. Such a procedure permits photography of tongue positions not only of vowels but also of many consonant articulations. It is not, however, to be expected that an X-ray photograph of the articulation of, say, the vowel in *cat* will show an identical tongue position for the pronunciation of a number of individuals. Not only is the sound itself likely to be different from one individual to another, but, even if the sound is for all practical purposes the 'same', the tongue positions may be different, since the boundaries of the mouth cavity are not identical for two speakers; and, in any case, two sounds judged to be the same may be produced by the same individual with different articulations. When, therefore, we describe an articulation in detail, it should be understood that such an articulation is typical for the sound in question, but that variations are to be expected.

It is often important to know the extent of the area of contact between the tongue and the roof of the mouth. Formerly, such information was obtained by means of a false palate, of metal or plastic, made to fit exactly over the human palate and covered with a powder which would be removed by any contact from the tongue. This false palate could be removed after articulation and the contact pattern observed and photographed. Such a procedure was superseded by a technique of direct photography of the palate, which was itself covered with a powdery substance to show tongue contact. This direct photography was not only more rapid than the former method but also had the advantage that the articulation was not deformed to the extent it may well be after the insertion of even the best fitting false palate. More recently the development of the electropalatograph has allowed a series of representations to be made of the changing contacts between the tongue and the palate during speech. Electrodes on a false palate respond to any tongue contact, the contact points being simultaneously registered on a visual display.

2.3 Articulatory Description

We have now reviewed briefly the complex modifications which are made to the original air-stream by a mechanism which extends from the lungs to the mouth and nose. The *description* of any sound necessitates the provision of certain basic information:—

1. The nature of the *air-stream*; usually, this will be expelled by direct action of the lungs, but we shall later consider cases where this is not so. It may also be relevant to assess the force of exhalation.

2. The action of the *vocal folds*; in particular, whether they are closed, wide apart, or vibrating.

3. The position of the *soft palate*, which will decide whether or not the sound has nasal resonances.

4. The disposition of the various *movable organs* of the mouth, i.e. the shape of the lips and tongue, in order to determine the nature of the related oral and upper pharyngeal cavities.

In addition, it may be necessary to provide other information concerning, for instance, a particular secondary stricture or tenseness which may accompany the primary articulation; or again, when it is a question of a sound with no steady state to describe, an indication of the kind of movement which is taking place.

3
The Sounds of Speech—The Acoustic and Auditory Aspects

3.1 Sound Quality

To complete an act of communication, it is not normally sufficient that our speech mechanism should simply function in such a way as to produce sounds; these in turn must be received by a hearing mechanism and interpreted, after having been transmitted through a medium, such as the air, which is capable of conveying sounds. We must now, therefore, examine briefly the nature of the sounds which we hear, the characteristics of the transmission phase of these sounds, and the way in which these sounds are perceived by a listener.

3.1.1   When we listen to a continuous utterance, we perceive an everchanging pattern of sound. As we have seen, when it is a question of our own language, we are not conscious of all the complexities of pattern which reach our ears: we tend consciously to perceive and interpret only those sound features which are relevant to the intelligibility of our language. Nevertheless, despite this linguistic selection which we ultimately make, we are aware that this changing pattern consists of variations of different kinds: of *sound quality*—we hear a variety of vowels and consonants; of *pitch*—we appreciate the melody, or intonation, of the utterance; of *loudness*—we will agree that some sounds or syllables sound 'louder' than others; and of *length*—some sounds will be appreciably longer to our ears than others. These are judgments made by a listener in respect of a sound continuum emitted by a speaker and, if the sound stimulus from the speaker and response from the listener are made in terms of the same linguistic system, then the utterance will be meaningful for speaker and listener alike. It is reasonable to assume, therefore, that there is some constant relationship between the speaker's articulation and the listener's reception of sound variations. In other words, it should be possible to link through the transmission phase the listener's impressions of changes of quality, pitch, loudness, and length to some articulatory activity on the part of the speaker. It will in fact be seen that an exact parallelism or correlation between the production, transmission, and reception phases of speech is not always easy to establish, the investigation of such relationships being one of the tasks of present-day phonetic studies.

19

3.1.2   The formation of any sound requires that a vibrating medium should be set in motion by some kind of energy. We have seen that in the case of the human speech mechanism the function of vibrator is often fulfilled by the vocal folds and that these are activated by air pressure from the lungs. In addition, any such sound produced in the larynx is modified by the resonating chambers of the pharynx, mouth and, in certain cases, the nasal cavity. The listener's impression of *sound quality* will be determined by the way in which the speaker's vibrator and resonators function together.

3.1.3   Speech sounds, like other sounds, are conveyed to our ears by means of waves of compression and rarefaction of the air particles (the commonest medium of communication). These variations in pressure, initiated by the action of the vibrator, are propagated in all directions from the source, the air particles themselves vibrating at the same rate (or frequency) as the original vibrator. In speech, these vibrations may be of a complex but regular pattern, producing 'tone' such as may be heard in a vowel sound; or they may be of an irregular kind, producing 'noise', such as we have in the consonant *s*; or there may be both regular and irregular vibrations present, i.e. a combination of tone and noise, as in *z*. In the production of normal vowels, the vibrator is normally provided by the vocal folds; in the case of many consonant articulations, however, a source of air disturbance is provided by constriction at a point above the larynx, with or without accompanying vocal fold vibrations.

Despite the fact that the basis of all normal vowels is the glottal tone, we are all capable of distinguishing a large number of vowel qualities. Yet there is no reason to suppose that the glottal vibrations in the case of [ɑː] are very different from those for [iː], when both vowels are said with the same pitch. The modifications in quality which we perceive are due to the action of the supra-glottal resonators which we have previously described. To understand this action, it is necessary to consider a little more closely the nature of the glottal vibrations.

3.1.4   It has already been mentioned that the glottal tone is the result of a complex, but mainly regular, vibratory motion. In fact, the vocal folds vibrate in such a way as to produce, in addition to a basic vibration over their whole length (the *fundamental* frequency), a number of overtones or *harmonics* having frequencies which are simple multiples of the fundamental or first harmonic. Thus, if there is a fundamental frequency of vibration of 100 cycles per second (cps), the upper harmonics will be of the order of 200, 300, 400, etc., cps. Indeed, there may be no energy at the fundamental frequency, but merely the harmonics of higher frequency such as 200, 300, 400 cps. Nevertheless, we still perceive a pitch which is appropriate to a fundamental frequency of 100 cps, i.e. the fundamental frequency is the highest common factor of all the frequencies present, whether or not it is present itself.

The number and strength of the component frequencies of this complex glottal tone will differ from one individual to another and this accounts at least in part for the differences of voice quality by which we are able to recognize speakers. But we can all modify the glottal tone so as to produce at will vowels as different as [iː] and [ɑː], so that despite our divergences of voice quality we can convey the distinction between two words such as *key* and *car*. This variation of *quality*, or timbre, of the glottal tone is achieved by the shapes which we give the resonators above the larynx—the pharynx, mouth, and nasal cavity. These chambers are capable of assuming an infinite number of shapes, each of which will have a characteristic vibrating resonance of its own. Those harmonics of the glottal tone which coincide with the chamber's own resonance are very considerably amplified. Thus, certain bands of strongly reinforced harmonics are characteristic of a particular arrangement of the resonating chambers which produces, for instance, a certain vowel sound. Moreover, these bands of frequencies will be reinforced whatever the fundamental frequency. In other words, whatever the pitch on which we say, for instance, the vowel [ɑː], the shaping of the resonators and their resonances will be very much the same, so that it is still possible, except on extremely high or low pitches, to recognize the quality intended. It is found that the vowel [ɑː] has one such characteristic band of strong components in the region of 800 cps and another at about 1,100 cps. The vowel [iː] has bands of energy at about 280 and 2,500 cps.

3.2 Acoustic Spectrum

This complex range of frequencies of varying intensity which go to make up the quality of a sound is known as the *acoustic spectrum*; those bands of energy which are characteristic of a particular sound are known as the sound's *formants*. Thus, formants of [ɑː] are said to occur in the region 800 and 1,100 cps. Such a complex wave pattern may be analysed by means of a number of instrumental techniques, most of which involve lengthy calculations; e.g. the number of fundamental vibrations may be counted on an oscillographic tracing. But the instrument known as the *sound spectrograph*, originally designed to render speech patterns visible to the deaf, makes possible a relatively rapid and visual presentation of the spectrum and the various intensities of sound contained in it. In an instrument of this sort in common use, a number of filters, covering a range of frequencies from 0–8,000 cps, respond to the varying sound intensities at different frequencies and ultimately produce a length of paper giving a three-dimensional display of the acoustic spectrum: frequency is shown on the vertical axis, time on the horizontal, and the energy at any frequency level by means of the degree of blackening made by the tracing pen on the paper. Thus, the

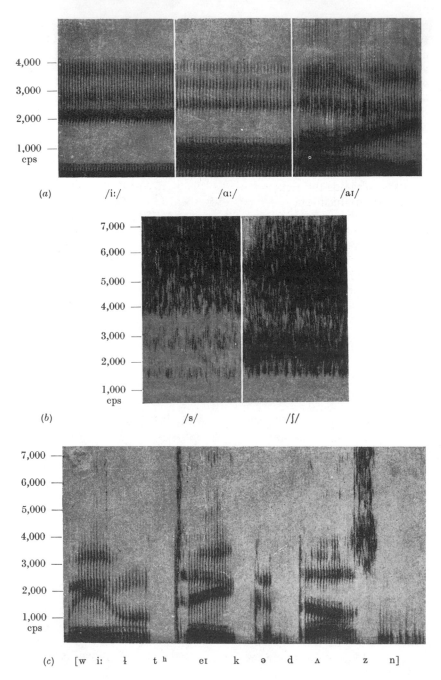

(a)   /iː/   /ɑː/   /aɪ/

(b)   /s/   /ʃ/

(c)   [w iː ɫ t ʰ eɪ k ə d ʌ z n]

Fɪɢ. 3.—Spectrograms of /iː/, /ɑː/, /aɪ/, /s/, /ʃ/, and *We'll take a dozen.*

concentrations of energy at particular frequency bands (the formants) stand out very clearly (see Fig. 3 for the spectrogram of the vowels [ɑː] and [iː]). Moreover, since the machine permits the analysis of an utterance lasting up to about $2\frac{1}{2}$ seconds, the everchanging pattern of the spectrum of continuous speech (see Fig. 3) and the difficulty of dividing up an utterance into separate (discrete) segments are made obvious. Such spectrographic analysis provides a great deal of acoustic information in a convenient form and, in addition, the instrument itself is relatively simple for a phonetician without special training to operate. Nevertheless, much of the information given is, in fact, irrelevant to our understanding of speech and the phonetician is obliged to establish by other methods the elements of the spectrum which are essential to speech communication.

Although there remain a number of problems to be solved by spectrographic analysis, much is already known about the acoustic structure of *vowels*. For instance, two, or at the most three, formants appear to be sufficient for their correct identification. As far as the English vowels are concerned, the first three formants are all included in the frequency range 0−4,000 cps, so that the spectrum above 4,000 cps would appear to be largely irrelevant to the recognition of our vowels. It is true that on a telephone system, which may have a frequency range of about 300−3,000 cps, we find little difficulty in identifying the sound patterns used by a speaker and are even able to recognize voice qualities. Indeed, when we are dealing with a complete utterance in a given context, where, as we have seen above (pp. 5−6), there is a multiplicity of cues to help our understanding, a high degree of intelligibility may be retained even when there are no frequencies above 1,500 cps.

As one would suspect, there appear to be certain relationships between the formants of vowels and the cavities of the vocal tract (i.e. the shapes taken on by the resonators, notably the relation of the oral and pharyngeal cavities). Thus, the 1st formant appears to be low when the tongue is high in the mouth: e.g. [iː] and [uː], having high tongue positions, have 1st formants of the order of 280−300 cps, whereas [ɑː] and [ɒ] have their 1st formants in the region 600−800 cps, their tongue positions being relatively low. On the other hand, the 2nd formant seems to be inversely related to the length of the front cavity: thus [iː], where the tongue is raised high in the front of the mouth, has a 2nd formant at about 2,500 cps, whereas [uː], where the tongue is raised at the back of the mouth and lips are rounded, has a relatively low 2nd formant around 900 cps.

It is also confirmed from spectrographic analysis that a diphthong, such as that in *my*, is indeed a glide between two vowel elements (besides involving a perceptible articulatory movement), since the formants bend from those positions typical of one vowel to those characteristic of another (see Fig. 3).

For many *consonant* articulations (e.g. the initial sounds in *pin*, *tin*, *kin*, *thin*, *fin*, *sin*, *shin*, in which the glottal vibrations play no part) there is an essential noise component, deriving from an obstruction or constriction within the mouth, approximately within the range 2,000–8,000 cps (see Fig. 3). This noise component is also present in analogous articulations in which the vocal note is present, as in the final sounds of *ruse* and *rouge* where, as we have seen, we are dealing with sounds which consist of a combination of glottal tone and noise. Relevant acoustic data concerning both vowel and consonant articulations will be given in the sections dealing with individual English sounds (Chapters 7 and 8).

Spectrographic analysis also reveals the way in which there tends, on the acoustic level, to be a merging of features of units which, linguistically, we treat separately. Thus, our discrimination of [f] and [θ] sounds would appear to depend not only on the frequency and duration of the noise component but also upon a characteristic bending of the formants of the adjacent vowel. Indeed, in the case of such consonants as [p, t, k], which involve a complete obstruction of the air-stream and whose release is characterized acoustically by a relatively brief burst of noise, the vowel *transition* between the noise and the steady state of the vowel appears to be of prime importance for our recognition of the consonant. This overlapping of vowels and consonants would suggest that an analysis of speech based solely upon acoustic data would find it convenient to operate with units larger than the sound segment.

3.2.1   Our perception of the *pitch* of a speech sound depends directly upon the frequency of vibration of the vocal folds. Thus, we are normally conscious of the pitch caused by the 'voiced' sounds, especially vowels; pitch judgments made on voiceless or whispered sounds, without the glottal tone, are limited in comparison with those made on voiced sounds, and are induced mainly by variations of intensity or by the dominance of certain harmonics brought about by the dispositions of the resonating cavities.

The higher the glottal fundamental frequency, the higher our impression of pitch. A male voice may have an average pitch level of about 150 cps and a female voice a level in the region of 240 cps. The pitch level of voices, however, will vary a great deal between individuals and also within the speech of one speaker, the total range of a speaking voice being liable to have a range as extensive as 80–350 cps. Yet our perception of pitch change extends further than the limits of glottal fundamental frequency, since our recognition of quality depends upon frequencies of a much higher order. In fact, the human ear perceives frequencies from as low as 16 cps to about 20,000 and in some cases even higher. As one becomes older, this upper limit may fall considerably, so that at the age of fifty it may extend no higher than about 10,000 cps. As we have seen, such a reduced range is no impediment to perfect understanding of speech, since a high percentage of acoustic cues for speech recognition fall within the range 0–4,000 cps.

Our perception of pitch is not, however, solely dependent upon fundamental frequency. Variations of intensity on the same frequency may induce impressions of a change of pitch; and again, tones of very high or very low frequency, if they are to be audible at all, require greater intensity than those in a middle range of frequencies.

As far as the variation of pitch in speech is concerned, it is by no means easy to measure the continuous changes. It is, of course, possible to count the fundamental vibrations within a selected segment in a trace such as is provided by an oscillograph. But, besides being a laborious process, such a method is likely to give us a pattern which is much more complicated than our auditory impression of pitch change. Our impression of pitch changes in speech results largely from fundamental frequencies carried by vowels and other voiced sounds, the voiceless sounds being discounted. With pitch, as with quality, an instrumental analysis does not make this human linguistic discrimination and may, therefore, provide us with a good deal of irrelevant information. Several instrumental procedures do, however, exist which go far towards showing us the grosser pattern which is relevant to linguistic work, e.g. a general pitch curve can be seen by tracing a harmonic on an expanded spectrographic display. The second harmonic is a convenient one to choose, since this is low enough usually not to be obscured by formant intensity nor very much deformed by formant transitions.

Since then, a technique making use of the *laryngograph* (Abberton and Fourcin, 1983) has been developed which provides immediate visual feedback of fundamental frequency contours which correspond essentially to our impression of a pitch pattern.

3.2.2 Our sensation of the relative *loudness* of sounds may depend on several factors. A sound or syllable may appear to stand out from its neighbours—be 'louder'—because a marked pitch change is associated with it or because it is longer than its neighbours. It is better to use a term such as *prominence* to cover these general listener-impressions of variations in the perceptibility of sounds. More strictly, what is 'loudness' at the receiving end should be related to *intensity* at the production stage, which in turn is related to the size or *amplitude* of the vibration and the speaker's feeling for 'stress'. Generally speaking, it may be said that an increase in amplitude of vibration, with its resultant impression of greater loudness, is brought about by an increase of air-pressure from the lungs. When a sound or syllable is stressed, it is being uttered with more muscular effort, increased air pressure, and greater amplitude of vibration. As we shall see (§9.2), this greater intensity is not in itself usually the most important factor in rendering a sound prominent in English. Moreover, all other things being equal, some sounds appear by their nature to be louder or more sonorous than others: e.g. the vowel in *barn* has more carrying power than that in *bean*, and vowels generally are more powerful than consonants.

The judgments we make concerning loudness are not as fine as those made for either quality or pitch. We may judge which of two sounds is the louder, but we find it difficult to express the extent of the difference. Indeed, in terms of our linguistic system, we need perceive and interpret only gross differences of loudness, despite the fact that when we judge quality we are, in recognizing the formant structure of a sound, reacting to characteristic regions of strong intensity in the spectrum.

3.2.3   In addition to affording different auditory impressions of quality, pitch, and loudness, sounds may appear to a listener to be of different *length*. Clearly, whenever it is possible to establish the boundaries of sounds or syllables, it will be possible to measure their duration by means of such traces as are provided by oscillograms or spectrograms. Such delimitation of units, in both the articulatory and acoustic sense, may be difficult, as we shall see when we deal with the segmentation of the utterance. But, even when it can be done, variations of duration in acoustic terms may not correspond to our linguistic judgments of length. We shall, for instance, refer later to the 'long' vowels of English such as those of *bean* and *barn*, as compared with the 'short' vowel in *bin*. But, in making such statements, we shall not be referring to absolute duration values, since the vowel of *barn* may in fact, in any given utterance, be very considerably longer than that of *bean*. In the English system, however, we know that only two degrees of length are linguistically significant and all absolute durations will be interpreted in terms of this relationship. This distinction between measurable duration and linguistic length provides another example of the way in which our linguistic sense interprets from the acoustic material only that which is significant.

The sounds comprising any utterance will have varying durations and, notably in English, we will have the impression that some syllables are longer than others. Such variations of length within the utterance constitute one manifestation of the dynamic rhythmic delivery which is characteristic of English and so is fundamentally different from the flow of other languages, such as French, where syllables tend to be of much more even length.

The absolute duration of sounds or syllables will, of course, depend upon the speed of utterance. An average rate of delivery might contain anything from about 6 to 20 sounds per second, but lower and much higher speeds are frequently used without loss of intelligibility. The time required for the recognition of a sound will depend upon the nature of the sound and the pitch, vowels and consonants differing considerably in this respect, but it seems that a vowel lasting only about 4 msecs may have a good chance of being recognized.

3.3 Hearing

Our *hearing mechanism* must be thought of in two ways: the physiological mechanism which reacts to the acoustic stimuli—the varying pressures in the air which constitute sound; and the psychological activity which, at the level of the brain, selects from the gross acoustic information that which is relevant in terms of the linguistic system involved. In this way, measurably different acoustic stimuli may be interpreted as being the 'same' sound unit. As we have seen, only part of the total acoustic information seems to be necessary for the perception of particular sound values. One of the tasks which confront the phonetician at the moment is the disentanglement of these relevant features from the mass of acoustic material, such as modern methods of sound analysis make available. The most fruitful technique of discovering the significant acoustic cues is that of *speech synthesis*, controlled by listeners' judgments. After all, the sounds [ɑː] and [s] are [ɑː] and [s] only if listeners recognize them as such. Thus, it has been established that only two formants are necessary for the recognition of vowels, because machines which generate sound of the appropriate frequency bands and intensity produce vowels which are correctly identified by listeners.

Listeners, without any phonetic training, can, therefore, frequently give valuable guidance by their judgments of synthetic qualities. But it is important to be aware of the limitations of such listeners, so as to be able to make a proper evaluation of their judgments. A listener's reactions are normally conditioned by his experience of handling his own language. Thus, if there are only five significant vowel units in his language, he is liable to allow a great deal more latitude in his assessment of what is the 'same' vowel sound than if he has twenty. An Englishman, for instance, having a complex vowel system and being accustomed to distinguishing such vowels as those in *sit, set, sat*, will be fairly precise in his judgment of an *e* type of vowel. A Spaniard, however, whose vowel system is made up of fewer significant units, is likely for this reason to be disposed to be more tolerant of variation of quality, while still identifying a sound of the *e* type. Or again, if a listener is presented with a system of synthetic vowels which is numerically the same as his own, he is able to make allowance for considerable variations of quality between his and the synthetic system and still identify the vowels correctly—by their 'place' in a system rather than by their precise quality; this is what he does when he listens to and understands his language as used by a speaker of a different dialect. Tests involving synthetic speech and concerned with the recognition of absolute vowel qualities would have, therefore, to be presented to a listener in such a way that his own linguistic prejudices have the least possible influence on his judgments.

Our hearing mechanism also plays an important part in monitoring our own speech; it places a control upon our speech production which is complementary to our motor, articulatory habits. If this 'feed-back' control is disturbed, e.g. by the imposition of an artificial delay upon our reception of our own speech, disturbance in the production of our utterance is likely to result. Those who are born deaf or who become deaf before the acquisition of speech habits are rarely able to learn normal speech; similarly, a severe hearing loss later in life is likely to lead eventually to a deterioration of speech.

4

Description and Classification of Speech Sounds

4.1 Phonetic Description

We have considered briefly both the mechanism which produces speech sounds and also some of the acoustic and auditory characteristics of the sounds themselves. It is now important to formulate a method of description and classification of the sound types which occur in speech and, more particularly, in English. We have seen that a speech sound has at least three stages available for investigations—the production, transmission, and reception stages. A complete description of a sound should, therefore, include information concerning all three stages. To describe the first sound in the word *ten* merely in terms of the movements of the organs of speech is to ignore the nature of the sound which is produced and the features perceived by a listener. Nevertheless, to provide all the information in respect of all phases entails a lengthy description, much of which may be irrelevant to a particular purpose. For example, since the description of the sounds of a language has in the past been most commonly used in the teaching of the language to foreigners, the emphasis has always been laid on the articulatory event. Moreover, it is only comparatively recently that there has existed any considerable body of acoustic information concerning speech. In the future, it is likely that acoustic analysis will provide a general descriptive framework applicable to all speech sounds. But, at the moment, the most convenient and brief descriptive technique relies either on articulatory criteria or on auditory judgments, or on a combination of both. Thus, those sounds which are commonly known as 'consonants' are most easily described mainly in terms of their articulation, whereas 'vowel' sounds require for their description a predominance of auditory impressions.

4.2 Vowel and Consonant

The terms 'vowel' and 'consonant' have been in use for many centuries. But it is clear that, if we are to distinguish between a purely phonetic investigation of concrete, measurable material and a linguistic analysis

29

in terms of abstractions from this material, any attempt to use 'vowel' and 'consonant' to cover categories at both levels may well be embarrassing, as will be shown in the next chapter when we consider linguistic analysis. In the past, when such a distinction was not generally made and the terms served to denote sometimes phonetic, sometimes linguistic categories, vowel and consonant tended to have a predominantly linguistic significance, 'vowel' having typically a central syllabic function, whereas 'consonant' was marginal in the syllable. When vowel and consonant have been defined phonetically, the criterion of distinction has generally been one of stricture, i.e. the articulation of vowels is not accompanied by any closure or narrowing in the speech tract which would prevent the escape of the air stream through the mouth or give rise to audible friction; all other sounds (necessitating a closure or a narrowing which involves friction) are consonants. Such a definition entails difficulty with such sounds as Southern British [l, r], which are traditionally consonants but which are more characteristically vowel-like in the terms of the definition; the difficulty has sometimes been avoided by calling such sounds semi-vowels or semi-consonants. It is clearly helpful if vowel and consonant are kept as terms to denote linguistic categories, whereas, if a phonetic division of sound types is required, other terms should be used to name them (cf. the use by K. L. Pike[1] of *vocoid/contoid* for the phonetic types and *vowel/consonant* for the linguistic categories).

From the practical phonetic standpoint, it is convenient to distinguish two types of speech sound, simply because the majority of sounds may be described and classified most appropriately according to one of two techniques:—

1. the type of sound which is most easily described in terms of articulation, since we can generally feel the contacts and movements involved. Such sounds may be produced with or without vocal fold vibration (voice) and very often have a 'noise' component in the acoustic sense; these sounds fall generally into the traditional category of consonants and will be known here as the *consonantal type*.

2. the type of sound, depending largely on very slight variations of tongue position, which is most easily described in terms of auditory relationships, since there are not contacts or strictures which we can feel with any precision. Such sounds are generally voiced, having no noise component but rather a characteristic patterning of formants; these sounds fall generally into the traditional category of vowels and will be known here as the *vowel type*.

We shall be able to assign the sounds of English to one or other of these phonetic classes but, as we shall see (Chapter 5), the linguistic

---

[1] As, for instance, in his *Phonemics*, University of Michigan, 1947.

categorization of sound units will not always correspond to the phonetic one.

4.3   The Consonantal Type (described in mainly articulatory terms)

We have seen, in the preceding chapters, that the production of a speech sound may involve the action of a source of energy, a vibrator, and the movement of certain supra-glottal organs. In the case of consonantal articulations, a description must provide answers to the following questions:—

(1) Is the air-stream set in motion by the lungs or by some other means? (pulmonic or non-pulmonic).

(2) Is the air-stream forced outwards or sucked inwards? (egressive or ingressive).

(3) Do the vocal folds vibrate or not? (voiced or voiceless).

(4) Is the soft palate raised, directing the air-stream through the mouth, or lowered, allowing the passage of air through the nose? (oral, or nasal or nasalized).

(5) At what point or points and between what organs does the closure or narrowing take place? (place of articulation).

(6) What is the type of closure or narrowing at the point of articulation? (manner of articulation).

In the case of the sound [z], occurring medially in the word *easy*, the following answers would be given:—

(1) pulmonic;   (2) egressive;   (3) voiced;   (4) oral;   (5) tongue blade—alveolar; (6) fricative.

These answers provide a concise phonetic label for the sound; a more detailed description would include additional information concerning, for instance, the shape of the remainder of the tongue, the relative position of the jaws, the lip position, etc.

4.3.1   Egressive Pulmonic Consonantal Sounds

Most speech sounds, and all normal English sounds, are made with egressive lung air. At any point of articulation, a consonantal articulation may be voiceless or voiced.

4.3.2   Place of Articulation

The chief points of articulation, with special reference to the sounds of English, are the following:—

Bilabial.—The two lips are the primary articulators, e.g. [p, b, m].

Labio-dental.—The lower lip articulates with the upper teeth, e.g. [f, v].

Dental.—The tongue tip and rims articulate with the upper teeth, e.g. [θ, ð].

Alveolar.—The blade, or tip and blade, of the tongue articulates with the alveolar ridge, e.g. [t, d, l, n, s, z].

Post-alveolar.—The tip (and rims) of the tongue articulate with the rear part of the alveolar ridge, e.g. [ɹ, tɹ, dɹ].

Retroflex.—The tip of the tongue is curled back to articulate with the part of the hard palate immediately behind the alveolar ridge, e.g. a retracted [ɻ] such as is found in South-West British and American English.

Palato-alveolar.—The blade, or the tip and blade, of the tongue articulates with the alveolar ridge and there is at the same time a raising of the front of the tongue towards the hard palate, e.g. [ʃ, ʒ, tʃ, dʒ].

Palatal.—The front of the tongue articulates with the hard palate, e.g. [j] or [ç] as in *queue* [kjuː] or [kçuː], or a very advanced type of [k, g]° = [c, ɟ].

Velar.—The back of the tongue articulates with the soft palate, e.g. [k, g, ŋ].

Uvular.—The back of the tongue articulates with the uvula, e.g. [ʁ, ʀ].

Glottal.—An obstruction, or a narrowing causing friction but not vibration, between the vocal folds, e.g. [ʔ, h].

In the case of some consonantal sounds, there may be a secondary place of articulation in addition to the primary. Thus, in the so-called 'dark' [ɫ], in addition to the partial alveolar contact, there is an essential raising of the back of the tongue towards the velum (velarization); or, again, some post-alveolar articulations of [ɹ] are accompanied by slight lip-rounding (labialization). The place of *primary articulation* is that of the greatest stricture, that which gives rise to the greatest obstruction to the airflow. The *secondary articulation* exhibits a stricture of lesser rank. Where there are two co-extensive strictures of equal rank an example of *double articulation* results. (See §8.9.2.)

4.3.3   Manner of Articulation

The obstruction made by the organs may be total, intermittent, partial, or may merely constitute a narrowing sufficient to cause friction. The chief types of articulation, in decreasing degrees of closure, are as follows:—

(1) *Complete Closure*

Plosive.—A complete closure at some point in the vocal tract, behind which the air pressure builds up and can be released explosively, e.g. [p, b, t, d, k, g, ʔ].

Affricate.—A complete closure at some point in the mouth, behind which the air pressure builds up; the separation of the organs is slow compared with that of a plosive, so that friction is a characteristic second element of the sound, e.g. [tʃ, dʒ, tɹ, dɹ].

Nasal.—A complete closure at some point in the mouth but, the soft palate being lowered, the air escapes through the nose. These sounds are continuants and, in the voiced form, have no noise component; they are, to this extent, vowel-like (see §4.3.5), e.g. [m, n, ŋ].

(2) *Intermittent Closure*

Trill or Roll.—A series of rapid intermittent closures or taps made by a flexible organ on a firmer surface, e.g. [r], where the tongue tip taps against the alveolar ridge, or [ʀ] where the uvula taps against the back of tongue.

Tap.—A single tap made by a flexible organ on a firmer surface, e.g. [ɾ] where the tongue tip taps once against the teeth ridge.

(3) *Partial Closure* (i.e. median)

Lateral.—A partial (but firm) closure is made at some point in the mouth, the air-stream being allowed to escape on one or both sides of the contact. These sounds may be continuant and non-fricative and therefore vowel-like, as in [l, ɫ], or they may be accompanied by a little friction [l̥] or by considerable friction [ɬ].

(4) *Narrowing*

Fricative.—Two organs approximate to such an extent that the air-stream passes between them with friction, e.g. [f, v, θ, ð, s, z, ʃ, ʒ, ç, x, h]. In the bilabial region, a distinction is to be made between those purely bilabial such as [ɸ, β] where the friction occurs between spread lips, and a labial-velar sound like [ʍ] where the friction occurs between rounded lips and is accompanied by a characteristic modification of the mouth cavity brought about by the raising of the back of the tongue towards the velum.

4.3.4 Approximants

Approximants (or *frictionless continuants*), such as the common variety of Southern British [ɹ], have neither the closure nor the noise component characteristic of consonantal articulations; they are, however, frequently variants of consonantal types, as well as having the functional status of consonants and may therefore be included under this heading.

[w] and [j] (also referred to as *semi-vowels*) are usually included in the consonantal category on functional grounds, but from the point of

view of phonetic description they are more properly treated as vowel glides.

4.3.5 Obstruents and Sonorants

It is sometimes found useful to classify categories of sounds according to their noise component. Those in whose production the constriction impeding the airflow through the vocal tract is sufficient to cause noise are known as *obstruents*. This category comprises plosives, fricatives and affricates. *Sonorants* are those voiced sounds in which there is no noise component (i.e. nasals, approximants and vowels).

4.3.6 Fortis and Lenis

A voiceless/voiced pair such as [s, z] are distinguished not only by the presence or absence of voice but also by the degree of breath and muscular effort involved in the articulation. Indeed, we shall see that on the linguistic level, in certain situations, the voice opposition may be lost, so that the energy of articulation becomes a significant factor. Those English consonants which are usually voiced tend to be articulated with relatively weak energy, whereas those which are always voiceless are relatively strong. Thus, it may be important to define [s], for instance, as strong or *fortis* and [z] as weak or *lenis*. But see §8.5 for a discussion of fortis and lenis as phonological categories.

4.3.7 Classification of Egressive Pulmonic Consonantal Articulations

The essential factors to be included in any classificatory chart refer to:—

(1) The place of articulation.
(2) The manner of articulation.
(3) The presence or absence of voice.
(4) The position of the soft palate.

The customary chart is based on a vertical axis showing *manner* of articulation; a horizontal axis showing *place* of articulation; a pairing of consonantal types to show the voiceless (or fortis) variety on the left and the voiced (or lenis) variety on the right; and an extra column under 'manner' to include the relatively few consonantal types which require the lowered position of the soft palate. The chart, shown in Fig. 4, includes the symbols of the sound types of British English.

PHONETIC TABLE
CHIEF ENGLISH CONSONANTAL ARTICULATIONS
Place of Articulation

Manner of Articulation	Bilabial	Labio-dental	Dental	Alveolar	Post-alveolar	Retroflex	Palato-alveolar	Palatal	Velar	Uvular	Glottal
Complete Oral Closure Plosive	p b		t̪ d̪	t d				c ɟ	k g		ʔ
Affricate					tɹ dɹ		tʃ dʒ				—
Nasal	m̥ m	ɱ	n̪	n̥ n					ŋ̊ ŋ		
Intermittent Closure Trill				r						R	
Tap (Flap)				ɾ							
Partial Closure Lateral				l̥ (lɬ)		ɭ			(ɫ)		
Narrowing Fricative	ʍ	f v	θ ð	s z (ɬ)	ɹ̥ ɹ¹		ʃ ʒ	ç ʝ	x ɣ (ʍ)	ʁ	h ɦ
Frictionless Continuant or Glide or Approximant	w	ʋ		l ɫ	ɹ¹			j	(w ʍ)	ʁ	

FIG. 4

¹The symbol [ɹ], used to differentiate the post-alveolar type of English *r* from other varieties, will normally be replaced by [r] when no such comparison is required.

4.3.8   Egressive Consonants made with the Glottalic (or Pharyngeal) Airstream Mechanism

Speech sounds may be articulated without the passage of lung air into the upper speech tract. In the production of these sounds, known as *ejective*, the glottis is closed, so that lung air is contained beneath it. A closure or narrowing is made at some point above the glottis (the soft palate being raised) and the air between this point and the glottis is compressed by a general muscular constriction of the chamber and a raising of the larynx. Thus, a bilabial ejective plosive sound [p'] may be made by compressing the air in this way behind the lips. However, it is not only plosives which may be ejective; affricates and fricatives commonly have this type of compression in a number of languages, e.g. [ts', tl', s', x', etc.]. If the glottis is tightly closed, it follows that this type of articulation can apply only to voiceless sounds. [p', t', k'] occur sometimes in final positions. These are not to be confused with the more common variants of final [p, t, k] which are frequently (e.g. in London English) replaced or reinforced by a glottal stop, e.g. the final sound in the word *stop* may be replaced by a glottal stop or have a glottal closure accompanying the bilabial one, but there is no compression between the glottal and bilabial closures.

4.3.9   Sounds Made with an Ingressive Air-stream

A common method of expressing surprise or pain involves the energetic inspiration of air accompanied by bilabial friction. It is also possible to produce sounds with an ingressive air-stream in the articulation of which a complete closure is made at some point in the mouth. Thus, a bilabial stop may be made, with the soft palate raised, as for [b]; but, instead of air pressure from the lungs being compressed behind the closure, the almost completely closed larynx is lowered so that the air in the mouth and pharyngeal cavities is rarefied. The result is that the outside air is sucked in once the mouth closure is released; at the same time, there is sufficient leakage of lung air through the glottis to produce voice. It will be seen that the resulting sound is made by means of a combined airstream mechanism, namely a pulmonic airstream in combination with ingressive glottalic (or pharyngeal) air. Such ingressive stops (generally voiced) are known as *implosives* and occur with bilabial [ɓ], dental or alveolar [ɗ], or velar [ɠ] mouth closures. Though such sounds occur in a number of languages, sometimes in the speech of the deaf and in types of stammering, they are not found in normal English.

   Another set of sounds involving an ingressive air-stream, this time an ingressive velaric (or oral) airstream mechanism, is produced entirely by means of closures within the mouth cavity; normal breathing through the nose may continue quite independently if the soft palate is lowered. Thus, the sound made to indicate irritation or sympathy (often written as 'Tut-tut') is articulated by means of a double closure, the back of the tongue against the velum and the tip, blade, and sides against the alveolar ridge and side teeth. The cavity contained within these closures is then enlarged mainly by tongue movement, so that the air is rarefied. The release of the forward closure causes the outer air to be sucked in; the release may be crisp in which case a sound of a plosive type is heard, or relatively slow, in which case an affricated sound is produced. These sounds are known as *clicks*, the one referred to above being a dental or alveolar click [ǀ]. The sound made to encourage horses is a lateral click, i.e. the air is sucked in by releasing one side of the tongue [ʖ]. These clicks, extralinguistic in English, and several others occur as significant sounds in a number of languages.[1]

4.4 The Vowel Type (described in mainly auditory terms)

This category of sounds is normally made with a voiced egressive air-stream, without any closure or narrowing such as would result in the noise component characteristic of many consonantal sounds; more-over, the escape of the air is characteristically accomplished in an unimpeded way over the centre line of the tongue. We are now con-cerned with a glottal tone modified by the action of the upper resonators of the mouth, pharyngeal and nasal cavities. As we have seen (Chapters 2 and 3), the movable organs mainly responsible for shaping these resonators are the soft palate, lips, and tongue. A descrip-tion of vowel-like sounds must, therefore, note:—

(1) the position of the soft palate—raised for oral vowels, lowered for nasalized vowels;
(2) the kind of aperture formed by the lips—degrees of spreading or rounding;
(3) the part of tongue which is raised and the degree of raising.

Of these three factors, only the second—the lip position— can be easily described by visual or tactile means. Our judgment of the action of the soft palate depends less on our feeling for its position than on our perception of the presence or absence of nasality in the sound produced. Again, the movements of the tongue, which so largely deter-mine the shape of the mouth and pharyngeal cavities, may be so minute that it is impossible to assess them by any simple means in terms of positions; moreover, there being normally no contact of the tongue with the roof of the mouth, no help is given by any tactile sensation. A

[1] See pp. 340–1 for the Chart of the International Phonetic Alphabet which provides symbols to denote the sound types occurring in languages.

vowel description will usually, therefore, be based mainly on *auditory judgments* of sound relationships, together with some articulatory information, especially as regards the position of the lips. In addition, an acoustic description can be given in terms of the disposition of the characteristic formants of the sound.

4.4.1   Difficulties of Description

The description of vowel sounds, especially by means of the written word, has always presented considerable difficulty. Certain positions and gross movements of the tongue can be felt. We are, for instance, aware that when we pronounce most vowel sounds the tongue tip lies behind the lower teeth; moreover, in comparing two such vowels as [i:] (*key*) and [ɑ:] (*car*) (Fig. 5), we can feel that, in the case of the former, the front of the tongue is the part which is mainly raised, whereas, in the case of the latter, such raising as there is is accomplished by the back part of the tongue. Therefore, it can be stated in articulatory terms that some vowel sounds require the raising of the front of the tongue, while others are articulated with a typical 'hump' at the back; and these statements can be confirmed by means of X-ray photography. But the actual point and degree of raising is more difficult to judge. It is not, for instance, helpful to say that a certain vowel is articulated with the front part of the tongue raised to within 5 mm of the hard palate. This may be a statement of fact for one person's pronunciation, but an identical sound may be produced by another speaker with a different relationship between the tongue and palate. Moreover, we would not find it easy to judge whether our tongue was at 4 or 5 mm from the palate. It is no more helpful to relate the vowel quality to a value used in a particular language, as is still so often done. A statement such as 'a vowel quality similar to that in the English word *cat*' is meaningless, since the vowel in *cat* may have a wide range of values in English. The statement becomes

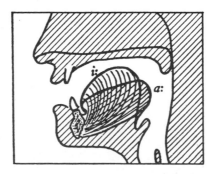

FIG. 5.—Tongue positions of [i:], [ɑ:].

more useful if the type of English is specified, but even then a number of variant interpretations will always be possible.

4.4.2 The Cardinal Vowel Scale

It is clear that a finer and more independent system of description is needed, on the auditory and articulatory levels. The most satisfactory scheme is that devised by Daniel Jones and known as the *Cardinal Vowel* system. The basis of the system is physiological, i.e. the two qualities upon which all the others were 'hinged' were produced with the tongue in certain easily felt positions: the front of the tongue raised as close as possible to the palate without friction being produced, for the cardinal vowel [i]; and the whole of the tongue as low as possible in the mouth, with very slight raising at the extreme back, for the cardinal vowel [ɑ]. Starting from the [i] position, the front of the tongue was lowered gradually, the lips remaining spread or neutrally open and the soft palate raised. The lowering of the tongue was halted at three points at which the vowel qualities seemed, from an auditory standpoint, to be equi-distant. The tongue positions of these qualities were X-rayed and were found to be fairly equi-distant from a spatial point of view. The symbols [e, ɛ, a] were assigned to these vowel values. The same procedure was applied to vowel qualities depending on the height of the back of the tongue, this raising the back of the tongue from the [ɑ] position; the lips were changed progressively from a wide open shape (for [ɑ]) to a closely rounded one and the soft palate remained raised. Again, three auditorily equi-distant points were established from the lowest to the highest position; the corresponding tongue positions were photographed and the spatial relationships confirmed as for the front vowels. These values were given the symbols [ɔ, o, u]. Thus, a scale of eight primary cardinal vowels was set up, denoted by the following numbers and symbols: 1, [i]; 2, [e]; 3, [ɛ]; 4, [a]; 5, [ɑ]; 6, [ɔ]; 7, [o]; 8, [u].

It is to be noticed that the front series [i, e, ɛ, a] and [ɑ] of the back series are pronounced with spread or open lips, whereas the remaining three members of the back series have varying degrees of lip-rounding. A secondary series can be obtained by reversing the lip position, e.g. close lip-rounding applied to the [i] tongue position, or lip spreading applied to the [u] position. Such a secondary series is denoted by the following numbers and symbols: 9, [y]; 10, [ø]; 11, [œ]; 12, [ɶ]; 13, [ɒ]; 14, [ʌ]; 15, [ɤ]; 16, [ɯ]. In addition, a pair of cardinal vowels, unrounded and rounded, have been established, for which the centre of the tongue has the highest point of raising; these are: 17 (unrounded), [ɨ]; 18 (rounded), [ʉ]. This complete series of eighteen cardinal vowel values may be divided into two lip shape categories, with corresponding tongue positions:—

Unrounded—[i, e, ɛ, a, ɑ, ʌ, ɤ, ɯ, ɨ].
Rounded— [y, ø, œ, Œ, ɒ, ɔ, o, u, ʉ].

Such a scale is useful because (*a*) the vowel qualities are unrelated to particular values in languages, though many may occur in various languages, and (*b*) the set is recorded,[1] so that reference may always be made to a standard, invariable scale. Thus, a vowel quality might be described as being, for instance, similar to that of cardinal 2 ([e]), or another as being a type half-way between cardinal 6 ([ɔ]) and cardinal 7 ([o]), but somewhat centralized. Diacritics are available to show modifications of cardinal values, e.g. a subscript hook ˛ to mean more open, a subscript dot ˌ meaning closer, and raised dots ¨ to mean centralized.[2] The last example given above might in this way be symbolized as [ɔ̣] or [ọ̈]. Other recorded cardinal values might be useful, especially for those types of vowel sound made by raising the centre part of the tongue, but the present scale is sufficient for most practical purposes.

It is, moreover, possible to give a visual representation of these vowel relationships on a chart which is based on the cardinal vowel tongue positions. The simplified diagram shown in Fig. 6 is obtained by plotting the highest point of tongue raising for each of the primary cardinal vowels and joining the points together. The internal triangle, corresponding to the region of central or [ə]-type vowel sounds, is made by dividing the top line into three approximately equal sections and drawing lines parallel to the two sides, so that they meet near the base of

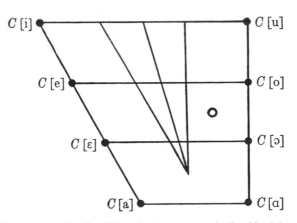

FIG. 6.—The primary Cardinal Vowels; the area symbolized by [ɔ̣] or [ọ̈] shown as a black circle.

---

[1] Two records (Eng. 252–3 and 254–5) are obtainable from the Linguaphone Institute.
[2] For details of such diacritics and other modifiers, see *The Principles of the International Phonetic Association*, obtainable from the Secretary of the Association, Department of Linguistics and Phonetics, University of Leeds.

the figure. On such a figure, the sound symbolized by [ɔ] or [ø̨] may have its relationship to the cardinal scale shown visually (see the black circle on Fig. 6).

It must be understood that this diagram is a highly conventionalized one which shows, above all, quality relationships. Some attempt is, however, made to relate the shape of the figure to actual tongue positions: thus, the range of movement is greater at the top of the figure, and the tongue raising of front vowels becomes more retracted as the tongue position lowers. Nevertheless, it has been shown that it is possible to articulate vowel qualities without the tongue and lip positions which this diagram seems to postulate as necessary. It is, for instance, possible to produce a sound of the cardinal 7 ([o]) type without the lip-tongue relationship suggested. But, on the whole, it may be assumed that a certain auditorily identified vowel quality will be produced by an articulation of the kind presupposed by the cardinal vowel diagram. Moreover, it is a remarkable fact that the auditory judgments as to vowel relationships made by Daniel Jones half a century ago have been largely supported by recent acoustic analysis; in fact, a chart based on an acoustic analysis of cardinal vowel qualities corresponds very well with the traditional cardinal vowel figure.

4.4.3 Nasality

Besides the information concerning lip and tongue positions which the above chart and symbolization denote, a vowel description must also indicate whether the vowel is purely oral or whether it is nasalized. The eighteen cardinal vowels mentioned may all be transformed into their nasalized counterparts if the soft palate is lowered. It is not normally necessary, however, to have such an extensive series of nasalized cardinal vowels, since it is unusual (though not unknown) for languages to make such fine, significant distinctions of nasalized qualities as are common in the case of the purely oral values.

4.4.4 Relatively Pure Vowels and Gliding Vowels

It is clearly not possible for the quality of a vowel to remain absolutely constant (or, in other words, for the organs of speech to function for any length of time in an unchanging way). Nevertheless, we may distinguish between those vowels which are relatively pure (or unchanging), such as the vowel in *learn*, and those which have a considerable and voluntary glide, such as the gliding vowel in *line*. The so-called pure vowels will be marked on the diagram as a dot, showing the highest point of the tongue or, better, a ring, since it would be inadvisable to attempt to be over-precise in the matter of these auditory judgments; the gliding (or diphthongal) vowel sound will be shown as an arrow,

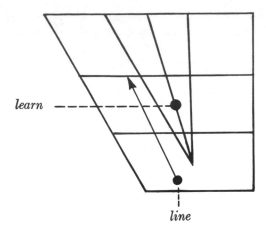

learn

line

FIG. 7.—The vowels of *learn* and *line*.

which indicates the quality of the starting point and the direction in which the quality change is made (corresponding to a movement of the tongue). Fig. 7 shows the way in which the vowels of *learn* and *line* will be marked.

We are now in a position to give a practical and comprehensive description of a vowel sound, partly in articulatory terms, partly in auditory terms. The vowel which we have symbolized above as [ɔ] or [ọ] might be described in this way: 'A vowel quality between cardinal vowels nos. 6 and 7, but having a somewhat centralized value; the lips are fairly closely rounded; and the soft palate is raised.' Such a written description will have a meaning in terms of sound for anyone who is familiar with the cardinal vowel scale. There may, of course, be other features of the sound to mention, e.g. a breathy quality, or the fact that the vowel is articulated with the tongue tip retroflexed, rather than with the tongue tip in its more usual position behind the lower teeth.

4.4.5   The Classification of Vowel Type Articulations

In describing vowel sounds, we have taken into account especially the positions of the lips, tongue, and soft palate. A system of classification should include, but not confuse, all three factors. A distinction between description and classification was not always made and early attempts at systematic description often established only general classificatory categories. A typical seventeenth-century system is based on tongue positions, since the vertical axis of a two-dimensional chart deals with open, medium, and close types of articulation; but the horizontal plane, with its divisions of guttural, palatal, and labial, introduces a lip dimension which only confuses the categorization. As in the case of

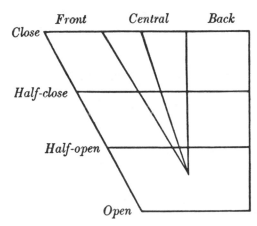

FIG. 8.—Classification labels combined with the Cardinal Vowel diagram.

consonants, it is, in fact, difficult to incorporate all factors in a two-dimensional chart and it is found most convenient to base classification on the tongue position. Our present system is not very different from that used in the nineteenth century, when such divisions as Back, Mixed, and Front referred to the part of the tongue raised, and High, Mid, and Low to the degree of raising. To-day, we combine our classificatory chart with the descriptive figure, naming those vowels in which the main raising is made by the front of the tongue towards the hard palate *front* vowels, those in which the back of the tongue is raised towards the soft palate *back* vowels, and those in which the centre is raised towards the juncture of the hard and soft palates *central* vowels. Instead of the threefold vertical division as regards degree of raising, it is customary to refer to four regions corresponding to the four cardinal degrees of raising; thus, the [i—u] level is known as the *close* region; the [e—o] level as the *half-close*, the [ɛ—ɔ] level as the *half-open*, and the [a—ɑ] level as the *open* (see Fig. 8).

On a chart of this type, the factors of lip and soft palate positions have to be indicated separately. A vowel in the general region of cardinal 2 ([e]) would, therefore, be classified briefly as an oral, front, unrounded, half-close vowel. Very often, when it is a question simply of identifying the significant vowel units in terms of the system of a particular language, such a brief classificatory label will serve also as an adequate description.

5

Sounds in Language

5.1 Speech Sounds and Linguistic Units

We have now considered a method of describing and classifying the sounds capable of being produced by the speech organs. Speech is, however, a manifestation of language and spoken language is normally a continuum of sound. A speech sound, produced in isolation and without the meaningfulness imposed by a linguistic system, may be described in purely phonetic terms; but any purely phonetic approach to the sounds of language encounters considerable difficulties. Two initial problems concern, firstly, the identification and delimitation of the sound unit (or segment) to be described and, secondly, the way in which different sounds are treated, for the purpose of linguistic analysis, as if they were the same.

As we have seen, in any investigation of speech, it is on the physiological and acoustic levels that most information is available to us. Yet, especially on the articulatory level, as is revealed by moving X-ray photography, any utterance consists of apparently continuous movements by a very large number of organs; it is well-nigh impossible to say, simply from an X-ray film of the speech organs at work, how many speech sounds have been uttered. A display of acoustic information is easier to handle (see illustration on p. 22), but even here it is not always possible, because of the way in which many sounds merge into one another, to delimit exactly the beginning and end of sound segments. Moreover, even if it were possible to identify the main characteristics of certain sounds without being sure of their limits, it would not follow that the phonetic statement we might accordingly make concerning the sequence of sound segments would be a useful one in terms of the language which we were investigating. Thus, the word *tot* is frequently pronounced in the London region in such a way that it is possible to identify five sound segments: [t], [s], [h], [ɒ], [t]. Yet much of this phonetic reality may be discarded as irrelevant when it is a question of the structure of the word *tot* in terms of the sound system of English. Indeed, the speaker himself will probably feel that the utterance *tot* consists of only three 'sounds' (not only because of the influence of the

44

spelling), such a judgment on his part being a highly sophisticated one which results from his experience in hearing and speaking English. In other words, the [s] and [h] segments are to be treated as part of the linguistic unit /t/.[1] The phonetic sequence [tsh] does not, in an initial position in this type of English, consist of three meaningful units; in other languages, on the other hand, such a sequence might well constitute three linguistic units as well as three phonetic segments.

This same example illustrates how different sounds may count, in respect of their function in a language, as the same linguistic unit. In such a pronunciation of *tot* as is noted above, the first realization of /t/ might be described as consisting of:—

(1) a voiceless stop made by the tongue tip and rims against the alveolar ridge and side teeth;

(2) a slow release of the compressed air, so that friction is heard—[s];

(3) the complete disengagement of the tongue from the roof of the mouth, so that no friction is caused in the mouth; but an interval before the beginning of the next sound, during which there is friction in the glottis (and voiceless resonance in the supra-glottal cavities)—[h].

The second manifestation of /t/, on the other hand, might have an articulation which could be described phonetically as follows:—

(1) an alveolar stop made as before, but with a simultaneous stop made in the glottis;

(2) the glottal closure is released, but the oral stop is retained slightly longer, during which time the air escapes (and respiration continues) through the nasal passage, the soft palate being lowered.

The first [t] might be briefly described as a voiceless alveolar plosive, released with affrication and aspiration; the second as an unexploded voiceless alveolar plosive made with a simultaneous glottal stop. These two different articulations, with the resultant difference of sound, function, nevertheless, as the same linguistic unit, the first sound occurring predictably under strong stress initially in a syllable and the second being a typical manifestation of the unit in a final position. Such an abstract linguistic unit, which will include sounds of different types, is called a *phoneme*; the different phonetic realizations of a phoneme are known as its *allophones*.

---

[1] Note that it is customary to distinguish sound segments from linguistic sound units (phonemes) by using [ ] to enclose the former and / / to enclose the latter.

5.2   The Linguistic Hierarchy

It is clear, as we hinted in Chapter 1, that speech and language require in their analysis different orders of units. An utterance, on the concrete speech level, will consist of the continuous physiological activity which results in a continuum of sound; the largest unit will, therefore, be the span of sound occurring between two silences. Within this unit of varying extent it may be possible to find smaller segments. It is, however, from the abstract, linguistic level of analysis that we receive guidance as to how the utterance may be usefully segmented in the case of any particular language. We might find, for instance, that an utterance such as 'The boys ran quickly away and were soon out of sight' is spoken without a pause or interruption for breath; it might be said to constitute a single breath group on the articulatory level. But, on the linguistic level, we know that this utterance is capable of being analysed as a sentence consisting of two clauses. Moreover, certain extensive sequences occurring within the utterance might be meaningfully replaced by other sound sequences, e.g. *boys* might be replaced by *dogs*, *ran* by *walked*, *quickly* by *slowly*, etc. These replaceable sound sequences are able to stand by themselves and are called *words*. In written forms of language, it usually happens that words are separated from each other by spaces, this being a sophisticated convention which is not reflected in speech. (We shall see, however, in Chapter 11, that words may retain at their boundaries certain characteristics in connected speech, so that their presence and span is signalled on a phonetic as well as a linguistic level.) Yet there are meaningful units smaller than the word. The word *boys* may be divided into *boy* and *s* ([z]), where the presence or absence of [z] indicates the plural or singular form; *quickly* may be said to consist of *quick* and the adverbial suffix *ly*. There are smaller sound sequences which may be interchanged meaningfully, but which may or may not be capable of standing by themselves. These smaller units, known as *morphemes*, may correspond with words (root morphemes), e.g. *boy*, in which case they may stand alone, or exist at a level lower than the word, e.g. [z], in which case they will not normally occur other than in association with a word. There is, however, yet a lower level at which meaningful commutation is possible. The word *ran* is also a morpheme; but, if instead of saying [ræn] we say [rʌn], we have, by changing an element on a lower level than the morpheme, changed the meaning and function of the word. This basic linguistic element, beyond which it is not necessary to go for practical purposes, is what we have already referred to as a *phoneme*. A phoneme may, therefore, be thought of as the smallest contrastive linguistic unit which may bring about a change of meaning.

5.3 The Phoneme, a Contrastive Unit

It is possible to establish the phonemes of a language by means of a process of commutation or the discovery of *minimal pairs*, i.e. pairs of words which are different in respect of only one sound segment. The series of words *pin, bin, tin, din, kin, chin, gin, fin, thin, sin, shin, win* supplies us with twelve words which are distinguished simply by a change in the first (consonantal) element of the sound sequence. These elements of contrastive significance, or phonemes, we may symbolize as /p, b, t, d, k, tʃ, dʒ, f, θ, s, ʃ, w/. But other sound sequences will show other consonantal oppositions, e.g.:—

(1) *tame, dame, game, lame, maim, name*, adding /g, l, m, n/ to our inventory;

(2) *pot, tot, cot, lot, yacht, hot, rot*, adding /j, h, r/;

(3) *pie, tie, buy, thigh, thy, vie*, adding /ð, v/;

(4) *two, do, who, woo, zoo*, adding /z/.

Such comparative procedures reveal twenty-two consonantal phonemes capable of contrastive function initially in a word.

5.3.1 It is not sufficient, however, to consider merely one position in the word. Possibilities of phonemic opposition have to be investigated in medial and final positions as well as in the initial. If this is done in English, we discover in medial positions another consonantal phoneme, /ʒ/, cf. the word oppositions *letter, leather, leisure* or *seater, seeker, Caesar, seizure*. This phoneme /ʒ/ does not occur in initial positions and is rare (e.g. in *rouge*) in final positions. Moreover, in final positions, we do not find /h/ or /r/, and it is questionable whether we should consider /w, j/ as separate, final contrastive units (see §§7.2, 7.5). We do, however, find one more phoneme that is common in medial and final positions but unknown initially, viz. /ŋ/, cf. *simmer, sinner, singer* or *some, son, sung*.

Such an analysis of the consonantal phonemes of English will give us a total of twenty-four phonemes, of which four (/h, r, ʒ, ŋ/) are of *restricted occurrence*—or six, if /w, j/ are not admitted finally. Similar procedures may be used to establish the vowel phonemes of English (see Chapter 7).

The final inventories of vowel and consonant phonemes will constitute a statement of the total oppositions in all positions in the word or syllable; when any particular place in the word or syllable is taken into consideration, the number of terms in the series of oppositions is likely to be more restricted.

5.3.2 Diversity of Phonemic Solutions

It is important to emphasize the fact that it is frequently possible to make several different statements of the phonemic structure of a language, all of which may be equally valid from a logical standpoint. The solution chosen will be the one which is most convenient as regards the use to which the phonemic analysis is to be put. Thus, one solution might be appropriate when it is a question of teaching a language to a particular group of foreigners, when similarities and differences between two languages may need to be underlined; another solution might be appropriate if it is a question of using the phonemic analysis as a basis for an orthography, when social considerations (i.e., for example, relations of the people with other countries having particular orthographic conventions) have to be taken into account. Even without such considerations, discrepancies in analysis frequently arise in the case of such sound combinations as affricates (e.g. [tʃ, dʒ, tr, dr]) and diphthongs (e.g. [eɪ, əʊ, aɪ, aʊ]), which may be treated as single phonemes or combinations of two. Such problems concerning English will be dealt with briefly when vowels and consonants are considered in detail.

5.3.3   Relevant Features of Phonemes

Up to now we have obtained an inventory of phonemes for English which is no more than a set of relationships of oppositions. The essence of the phoneme /p/, for instance, is that it is not /t/ or /k/ or /s/, etc. This is a negative definition, which it is desirable to amplify by means of positive information of a phonetic type. Thus, we may say that /p/ is, from a phonetic point of view, characteristically fortis and voiceless (compared with such lenis, voiced sounds as /b/ or /d/); bilabial (compared with the places of articulation of such sounds as /t/ or /k/); oral (as compared with /m/ or /n/); a stop or plosive (compared with /l/ or /r/ or /f/). The /p/ phoneme may, therefore, be identified positively by stating the combination of features which are significant within the English system: fortis, voiceless, bilabial, oral stop. This is a label which will be applicable to the phoneme in most of its realizations ('most', because in such a word as *cup-full* /p/ may well be realized as a labio-dental stop. Such a case is covered if the term 'labial' is used rather than 'bilabial').[1]

---

[1] It is possible, by extracting from the phonemes of a language the *distinctive features* which combine to form such phonemes, to account more economically for the sound system in operation in terms of fundamental phonological elements. For an elaboration of such 'distinctive feature' analysis in articulatory and acoustic terms, see particularly R. Jakobson, C. G. M. Fant and M. Halle, *Preliminaries to Speech Analysis*, 4th ed., Cambridge, Mass., 1963; C. G. M. Fant, *Theory of Distinctive Features*, Speech Transmission Lab. K.T.H., 1966; N. Chomsky and M. Halle, *The Sound Pattern of English*, New York, 1968.

5.3.4 Allophonic Variants

No two realizations of a phoneme (its *allophones*) are the same. This is true even when the same word is repeated; thus, when the word *cat* is said twice, there are likely to be slight phonetic variations in the two realizations of the phoneme sequence /k + æ + t/. Nevertheless, the phonetic similarities between the utterances will probably be more striking than the differences. Allophones of the same phoneme occurring in different words or in different situations in a word will, however, frequently show considerable phonetic differences. We have seen (§5.1) how different the initial and final allophones of /t/ in the word *tot* may be. Or again, the [k] sounds which occur initially in the words *key* and *car* are phonetically clearly different: the first can be felt to be a forward articulation, near the hard palate, whereas the second is made further back on the velum. This difference of articulation is brought about by the nature of the following vowel, [iː] having a more advanced articulation than [ɑː]; the allophonic variation is in this case conditioned by the context. The two [l] sounds of *lull* [lʌɫ] show a variation of a different kind. The first [l], the so-called 'clear' [l] with a front vowel resonance, has a quality very different from that of the final [ɫ], the 'dark' [ɫ] with a back vowel resonance. Here, however, the difference of quality is related to the position of the phoneme in the word or syllable and is not dependent upon the phonetic context, i.e. the adjacent sounds. It is possible, therefore, to predict in a given language which allophones of a phoneme will occur in any particular context or situation: they are said to have a *complementary distribution*, no two realizations of the same phoneme which have a markedly different phonetic quality occurring in the same situation. Such a generalization does not take into account those variant realizations of the same phoneme in the same situation which may constitute the difference between two utterances of the same word. When the same speaker produces slightly different pronunciations of the word *cat*, the different realizations of the phonemes are said to be 'free variants'. But, if both [l] and [ɫ] occurred in the same situation or context and had the function of distinguishing words, the two sounds would have to be treated as realizations (allophones) of different phonemes.

It is usually the case that there remains some phonetic similarity between the allophones of a phoneme: both the [l] sounds discussed above, as well as the voiceless fricative variety which follows /p/ or /k/ in words such as *please* and *clean*, are lateral articulations. But the Cockney realization of dark [ɫ] is often [o] (as in *little* [lɪʔo]), in which case, the distribution of the sounds still being complementary, we have to envisage the possibility of allophones belonging to the vocalic and consonantal types or are obliged to reorganize our phonemic analysis. Again, it sometimes happens that two sounds occur in complementary distribution, but are not treated as allophones of the same phoneme because of their total phonetic dissimilarity. This is the case of [h] and [ŋ] in English; they are never significantly opposed, since [h] occurs typically in initial positions in the syllable or word, and [ŋ] in final positions. A purely logical arrangement might include these two sounds within the same phoneme, so that *hung* might be transcribed phonemically as either /hʌh/ or /ŋʌŋ/; but such a solution would ignore the total lack of phonetic similarity and also the feeling of native speakers. The ordinary native speaker is, in fact, often unaware of the allophonic variations of his phonemes and will, for instance, say that the various [l] allophones we have discussed are the 'same' sound; [h] and [ŋ], however, he will always consider to be 'different' sounds. When he makes a statement of this kind, he is usually referring to the function of the sounds in the language system and can thereby offer helpful, intuitive information regarding the phonemic organization of his language, especially when it is a question of the first phonemic analysis of a language which has no written form. In the case of a language such as English, which already has an alphabetic orthography (however inconsistent), prejudices induced by the existence of such a written form have naturally to be taken into account in evaluating the native speaker's reaction.

5.3.5　Neutralization of Phonemes

It sometimes happens that a sound may be assigned to either of two phonemes with equal validity. In English, examples of this kind are to be found in the plosive series. The main contrastive feature between the pairs *pin/bin*, *team/deem*, *come/gum* resides in the presence of aspiration in /p, t, k/ and its absence in /b, d, g/, presence or absence of voice being usually irrelevant in this initial, accented position, where /b, d, g/ are largely or totally devoiced. When /p, t, k/ follow an initial /s/, however, they are realized with no aspiration even when stressed. Thus, in the case of such words as *spin*, *steam*, *scum*, we have three plosive phonemes which lack the aspiration often characteristic of /p, t, k/, but which do not have the voice which sometimes accompanies /b, d, g/. Since /p, t, k/ are never opposed to /b, d, g/ following /s/ in this position, the words might, therefore, be transcribed phonemically either as /spɪn, stiːm, skʌm/ or as /sbɪn, sdiːm, sgʌm/ without ambiguity.[1]

Another case concerns the allophones of /m/ and /n/ before /f/ or

---

[1] Experimental investigations suggest that perceptually and, to some extent, acoustically /p, t, k/ following /s/ have more in common with initial /b, d, g/ than with initial /p, t, k/ (see N. Davidsen-Nielsen, 'English Stops after initial /s/', *English Studies*, no. 4, August, 1969).

/v/, in words like *symphony* and *infant*. The nasal consonant in each case is likely to be [ɱ] in rapid speech, i.e. a labio-dental sound anticipating the labio-dental [f]. Here again, /m/ and /n/ are not opposed, so that the sound could be allocated to either the /m/ or the /n/ phoneme. In practice, since in a slow pronunciation the [m] sound would tend to be used in *symphony* and the [n] sound in *infant*, a phonemic differentiation is usually made.

5.3.6 Conditions of Phonemic Analysis

Statements concerning phonemic categories and allophonic variants can usually be made in respect of only one variety of one language. It does not follow, because, for instance, [l] and [ɫ] are not contrastive in English and belong to the same phoneme, that this is so in other languages—in some kinds of Polish [l] and [ɫ] constitute separate phonemes. Or again, although /ŋ/ is a phoneme in English, in Italian the velar nasal [ŋ] is an allophone of /n/ which occurs before /k/ and /g/. Indeed, in English, too, /ŋ/ has not always had phonemic status. Nowadays, [ŋ] might be considered an allophone of /n/ before /k/ and /g/, as in *sink* and *finger*, were it not for the fact that the /g/ in words such as *sing* was lost about 400 years ago; once this situation had arisen, a phonemic opposition existed between *sin* and *sing*.

It should also be noted that the number of phonemes may differ as between various types of the same language. Thus, in present-day Southern British English, the words *cat, half, cart* contain the phonemes /æ/, /ɑː/, and /ɑː/ respectively. But another type of English may have only one vowel phoneme for all three words, the words being phonemically /kat, haf, kart/ (the post-vocalic [r] being pronounced). Such a dialect[1] of English would have one phoneme less than Southern British English, since the opposition *Sam/psalm* is lost. On the other hand, this deficiency in number might be made up by the regular opposition of the first elements of such a pair as *witch/which*, which would establish a phonemic contrast between /w/ and /ʍ/.

It should not, however, be assumed that the phonemic systems of two dialects are different merely because the phonetic realizations of the phonemes are dissimilar. The sound sequence [sɛt], i.e. with a vowel in the region of cardinal 3, may be a realization of *sat* in one dialect and of *set* in another; the phonemic categories commonly represented as /iː, ɪ, e, æ, ɑː,* etc., may nevertheless be present in both dialects, the vowel system in the first dialect being somewhat more 'closed' than that of the second. Or again, the diphthong [əʊ] is a realization of the phoneme of *boat* in educated Southern British, but is frequently a realization of the

---

[1]Note that 'dialect' includes pronunciation, grammar and vocabulary; 'accent' is confined to pronunciation.

vowel in *boot* in a type of London popular speech; the same number of vowel phonemes occurs in both kinds of English. Moreover, two speakers of the same dialect may distribute the same number of phonemes differently among the words they use. In Southern British English, some will say *off, cloth, cross* with /ɔː/, others with /ɒ/; some will say *elastic* with /æ/ in the second syllable, others /ɑː/; some will say /ˈjuːnɪzn/ for *unison*, others /ˈjuːnɪsn/, etc. Ideally, phonemic analysis should be applied to the speech of one person (to one *idiolect*). Individuals are, however, inconsistent; in certain situations, they may change the number of their phonemes, e.g. the occasional use of /ʌ/; they may not always use the same phoneme in a particular word or group of words, e.g. the erratic use, in the same person's speech, of /ɒ/, or /ɔː/ in words of the *off* group.

To sum up, we may conclude that a phonemic analysis of a number of varieties of one language is likely to reveal: different coexistent phonemic systems; considerable phonetic discrepancies in the realizations of the phonemes of systems which have an equal number of phonemic categories; variation in the distribution of phonemes in words, even within a community using the same phonemic system; and variation of phoneme distribution, even within the speech of one individual, according to the situation. It is important to remember this likelihood of complication in both the system and its realization, not only in the present situation but also when it is a question of investigating past states of the language.

5.3.7 The Word as Basis for Phonemic Analysis

It frequently happens that a phonemic analysis is based on a unit not larger than the word. If any larger section of the utterance is used, the analysis becomes a great deal more complicated. As Daniel Jones has pointed out,[1] the two phrases *plum pie* and *plump eye* exemplify the sort of complication which will arise. The two phrases differ principally in the aspiration which accompanies the /p/ of *pie* but which is absent from the final /p/ of *plump*. A phonemic analysis which is based on such an extensive sound sequence would require the establishment of two /p/ phonemes, one with, one without aspiration. The difficulty is avoided if the word is treated as a complex phonetic and phonemic entity, special consideration being given to word boundaries in the utterance. If, however, the linguistic analysis is based on a sequence more extensive than the word, a mark of contrast has to be established in order to deal with the behaviour of phoneme sequences at word or morpheme boundaries (see 'Juncture', Chapter 11, §11.3.8).

[1] Daniel Jones, 'Some Thoughts on the Phoneme,' *Transactions of the Philological Society*, 1944.

5.4 The Syllable

The concept of a unit at a higher level than that of the phoneme or sound segment, yet distinct from that of the word or morpheme, has existed since ancient times. It is significant that most alphabets, such as our own, which have as their basis the representation of phonemes by letters (however approximately), have reached this state by way of a form of writing which symbolized a group of sounds—a syllabary. Indeed, the basis of the writing of many languages, e.g. that of the Semitic group, remains syllabic in this sense. The notion that there exists at this higher level a unit known as the syllable has led to many attempts in recent times to define the term. These attempts fall into two main categories: those which seek a universal definition in phonetic terms and those which look for a specific functional definition in terms of a particular language. In the following sections, some of the many approaches are outlined.

5.4.1 The Phonetic Approach

(1) *The Prominence Theory.*—In any utterance some sounds are said to be more 'prominent' or 'sonorous' than others, i.e. they are felt by listeners to stand out from their neighbours. In the word *sonority* /sə'nɒrətɪ/, such 'peaks' of prominence are carried by /ə, ɒ, ə, ɪ/. The number of syllables being determined by the number of peaks of prominence, there are in this case four syllables. Syllable boundaries occur at the points of relatively weak prominence ('valleys'), i.e. at /s, n, r, t/. This theory, which is based mainly on auditory judgments, does not determine to which syllable the weak sound, constituting the boundary between two syllables, is to be attributed. Moreover, difficulties are encountered in the case of languages such as English which permit consonant clusters. The word *extra*, for instance, transcribed as /'ekstrə/, would show by the same procedure three peaks of prominence on /e, s, ə/, thus forming three syllables. Such a solution is at variance with the native feeling for a division at a higher level than the phoneme, which tends to be interpreted as /ek-strə/ or /eks-trə/.

(2) *The Pulse Theory.*—A more fundamental approach to the syllable is concerned with the muscular activity controlling lung movement which takes place during speech and which is capable of being investigated by experimental methods. It is claimed that in any utterance there are a number of chest pulses, accompanied by increases in air pressure, which determine the number of syllables uttered. Such a theory suggests that the syllable rather than the sound is the basic unit of speech, consonantal sounds acting typically at the onset (releasing factor) and closure (arresting factor) of the syllable, while vowel sounds are nuclear to the syllable and render the chest pulse audible. Again,

such a unit on the speech level may prove to be irrelevant or misleading on the linguistic level. Particularly when it is a question of the juxtaposition of two vowel sounds, the second being weakly stressed as in the case of *seeing* /'siː ɪŋ/, it is doubtful whether a double chest pulse will be evident, although it is clear that the word is to be divided linguistically into two units.

5.4.2 The Linguistic Approach

A unit of greater magnitude than the phoneme or sound segment is more usefully defined in linguistic terms, i.e. with reference to the structure of one particular language rather than in general, phonetic terms with universal application. It may be found appropriate to divide a similar sound sequence differently in different languages; e.g. such an utterance as [ŋgɑː] might be found to consist of three units in one language -/ŋ-gɑ-ɑ/, two in another /ŋ-gɑː/, and even one in another -/ŋgɑː/. The divisions to be made might be indicated by the extent of the sequence covered by different tones or stress, in which case the syllable would correspond to a unit of tone or stress. Alternatively, a statement concerning the syllables of a language may refer to the particular way in which phonemes are found to combine in that language (the earliest meaning of the term), so that certain phonemes are shown to have a typically central situation in the permissible groups, whereas others are more typically marginal in their position. Such a procedure would not, however, decide in the case of the English word /'ekstrə/ the point at which the syllabic division is to be made, since /k/ is a possible final phoneme and /str/ a permissible initial cluster, and yet /ks/ is also possible finally and /tr/ initially; both solutions would be valid in the light of the English distributional system. (See §§9.8, 9.9 for details of the combinatory possibilities of English phonemes in the word.)

A term need not, of course, be defined simply because it has existed for two thousand years. If experimental procedures provide evidence of a unit above the sound segment at the physiological or acoustic levels of speech, or if, at the linguistic, structural level, a unit consisting of groups of phonemes is found to be useful, then the term 'syllable' may well be applied to such a unit. It is doubtful, however, whether the term can be applied to a unit both of speech and language, any more than 'sound' can cover, without ambiguity, both a phonetic segment and a linguistic, constrastive unit.

5.5 Vowel and Consonant

It was seen in the previous chapter that attempts to arrive at a universal phonetic definition of the two terms, from an articulatory or an auditory standpoint, encountered difficulties as regards certain border-line sounds as [l, r, j, w] in English. If, however, the syllable is defined linguistically, i.e. from the point of view of distribution of phonemes, a solution can be given to most of these problems. It will be found that the phonemes of a language usually fall into two classes, those which are typically central (or nuclear) in the syllable and those which are non-central (or marginal). The term 'vowel' can then be applied to those phonemes having the former function and 'consonant' to those having the latter. The frictionless English sounds /j, w, r/, for instance, which according to most phonetic descriptions are of a vowel-like (vocoid) type, function in the language as consonants, i.e. are marginal in the syllable. The English voiced lateral and nasal sounds are commonly classed phonetically as of the consonantal (contoid) type because of the complete or partial mouth closure with which they are articulated. From a functional viewpoint, too, they behave as consonants, since they are usually marginal in the syllable. Nevertheless, they sometimes seem to fulfil a syllabic function without the presence of a vowel, e.g. in *middle, button* ['mɪdl̩, 'bʌtn̩]. These /l/ and /n/ phonemes can be said to be syllabic here in terms of the prominence and pulse theories; they also function as separate units in the intonation structure of English. Yet there is some difficulty in establishing their syllabic nature in distributional terms, since it is possible to compare such word endings as /-dz/ and /-ts/, in which /z/ and /s/ are not usually considered to have syllabic function. This difficulty is sometimes avoided by equating [l̩, n̩] with /əl, ən/ both on logical grounds and also because /'mɪdəl/, for instance, is a possible pronunciation of *middle*. However, if the equation with /ə/ + /l, n/ is not admitted, the cases of consonant + /s/ or /z/ are not strictly parallel even on distributional grounds. Both /l/ and /n/ pattern in such a final situation very much as vowels in that they may follow the great majority of consonants; /s/ and /z/, on the other hand, have a much more restricted occurrence in this position and are, therefore, less vowel-like.

A further illustration of the consonantal function of /j/ and /w/ is provided by the behaviour of the English articles when they combine with words beginning with these phonemes. *The* is pronounced /ðiː/ or /ðɪ/ before a vowel and /ðə/ before a consonant, whenever it precedes the other English phonemes; we also have the forms *a* or an *an* according to whether a consonant or vowel follows. Since it is normal to pronounce *the yacht, the watch* with /ðə/ and to prefix *a* to *yacht* and *watch* rather than *an*, /j/ and /w/ may be said to behave as if they belong to the consonant class of phonemes, despite their vocalic quality.

It is clear that if the elements of the utterance are divided in two categories, some units which are assigned to one class according to speech (phonetic) criteria may fall into the other class when it is a question of linguistic (functional) analysis.

5.6   Notation

The symbolization of an utterance (analysed in terms of a linear sequence of sounds) will naturally differ according to whether the aim is to indicate detailed sound values—an *allophonic* (or 'narrow') transcription—or the sequence of significant functional elements—a *phonemic* (or 'broad') transcription.

(1) In the former, allophonic, type of notation, an attempt is made to include a considerable amount of information concerning our knowledge of articulatory activity or our auditory perception of allophonic features. The alphabet of the *International Phonetic Association* provides numerous diacritics for a purpose such as this; e.g. the word *titles* might have its phonetic features transcribed as [ˈtˢʰä· ëtᵻɬz]. Such a notation would show the affrication and aspiration of the initial [t], the fact that the first element of the diphthong is retracted from cardinal 4 and is long compared with the second element, which is a retracted cardinal 2 vowel, that the [ɬ] has a back vowel resonance and is partly devoiced in its first stage, and that the final [z] is completely devoiced. Such a notation is relatively explicit and detailed, but gives no more than an impression of the complexity of the utterance as revealed by the various methods of physiological and acoustic investigation. Nevertheless, an allophonic transcription of this kind can be useful for comparative purposes, e.g. for the comparison of different types of pronunciation, and is a necessary first step in the notation of a language for which no phonological system has been worked out.

(2) In the second type of notation—the phonemic, symbols are allocated only to the strictly contrastive sound categories of the language; a phonemic transcription is highly sophisticated, since a number of conventions are implicit in each symbol. The word *titles*, for instance, would be written /ˈtaɪtlz/, it being assumed that the phonemes occurring in such a context would have the predictable phonetic realizations noted in the preceding paragraph. The number and type of symbols used will, of course, depend upon the kind of phonemic solution which has been arrived at for the language. As far as English is concerned, and notably the English vowel system, several phonemic solutions are current and a corresponding number of notation systems exist, all of which are justifiable, although the choice of symbols and the conventions attached to them differ.[1] The striking discrepancies to be found among present-day phonemic transcriptions of British English are often due to the varying significance which is attached to vowel quantity and to the degree to which the symbols are made to coincide with the ordinary Latin alphabet. Thus, in the various phonemic

---

[1] For a discussion of the problems of phonetic transcription, see Daniel Jones, *Outline of English Phonetics*, 1956, Appendix A.

transcriptions of Southern British English, the vowels of *cot* and *caught* are symbolized as /ɒ, ɔ/ or /ɒ, ɔ:/ or /ɔ, ɔ:/ or /o, o:/ or /o, oo/, the last three solutions emphasizing the quantitative contrast (see Chapter 7 for a discussion of such solutions).

A phonemic transcription, with its implicit conventions, is the most common and least cumbersome method of indicating unambiguously the spoken realization of a language. It may happen that it has a form which is close to that of the language's orthography, e.g. Spanish or Serbo-Croat; it is particularly useful as a corrective instrument in the case of a language such as English where the orthography fails to mirror consistently the present-day pronunciation. A phonemic notation may also be used as a basis for teaching the pronunciation of a foreign language, the allophonic conventions to be related to a phonemic symbol being easily learnt. Sometimes, however, it may be helpful, at least in the early stages, to include symbols representing allophones in order to emphasize a particular feature of the language, e.g. in teaching English, it is often necessary to insist upon the variety of [l] sounds by using not only [l] but also [ɫ].

5.7 Prosodic Features

We have so far dealt almost entirely with the description and organization of the qualitative features of an utterance. As we have seen in Chapters 2 and 3, a sound has not only quality, whose phonetic nature can be described and function in the language determined, but also length, pitch, and a degree of stress. Such features may extend in time beyond the limits of the phoneme and embrace much higher units of the utterance. Indeed, in the case of the pitch variation characteristic of an intonation pattern, analysis may involve the whole of a lengthy utterance. In this sense, such features are *prosodic*, or supra-segmental.

All three features may be measured physiologically or acoustically: length, as duration; pitch, as the frequency of the fundamental; and stress, as a measure of intensity, muscular activity, or air-pressure. Once again, as with qualities, the absolute measurements are less useful than an assessment of relative function. It is, for instance, irrelevant to attempt to measure the precise duration of a sound, unless the language in question makes some use of length variation as a distinctive feature. If, in a language, there appears to be a significant opposition between a long and short [a], then it may be worth determining what the distinction is in absolute terms; or, if the length of sounds appears to vary considerably according to the context in which they occur, it is worth establishing the facts by measurement. But, in a phonemic notation, it is not normally necessary to take into account more than two (or sometimes three) significant degrees of length. Similarly, the absolute pitches used in speech are less important linguistically than the pitch relationships which a native speaker distinguishes as significant. And again, stress, which in the strict sense the listener hears as loudness, rarely requires more than two or three degrees to be shown, although the speaker's intensity will show an infinite number of degrees of variation. Thus, as with qualities, a preliminary transcription may indicate as many shades of duration, pitch, and loudness as possible, but the ultimate notation will present functional categories, abstracted from the concrete expression. Pitch will be described linguistically in terms of an intonation or tone system and duration in terms of contrastive oppositions of quantity; as far as stress is concerned, it will have to be established whether it has a linguistic reality independent of the other three features of quality, quantity and pitch, and, if it has, whether it is necessary to take into account more degrees than its simple presence or absence (see Part III for some discussion of the prosodic features of English).

5.8   Paralinguistic Features

In addition to the prosodic features concerned with pitch, rhythm, tempo, loudness, etc., there are other characteristics of the utterance which are involved in the speech communication process and which are categorized as *paralinguistic*. In the first place, an identification of the speaker relies largely on our recognition of his own peculiar voice quality (or 'voice set') which itself is the result of the anatomical structure of his vocal organs and of his articulatory habits. Secondly, he may make special modifications of his voice quality for a particular effect: e.g., he may use a whisper or a breathy or creaky voice or falsetto; or again, he may be stimulated to accompany his utterance with a laughing or sobbing or whining feature. This second category differs from the first in that the features involved are ones which are universally used in his own language (and in most others) as signals denoting particular mental or emotional states and which are therefore capable of classification (to the extent that such mental or emotional states can be categorized).[1]

---

[1]See entries in bibliography under Crystal, Quirk, Catford, Trager, Laver.

Part II
The Sounds of English

6

The Historical Background

6.1 Phonetic Studies in England

Although linguistic science has made rapid and spectacular progress in the present century, it is not merely in modern times that speech and language have been the object of serious study. Extensive accounts of the pronunciation of Greek and Latin were written two thousand years ago and, in India, at about the same time, there appeared detailed phonological analyses of Sanskrit, which reveal remarkable affinities with modern ways of thought—'These early phoneticians speak in fact to the twentieth century rather than to the Middle Ages or even to the mid-nineteenth century . . .'[1] In this country, too, printed works containing information of a phonetic kind extend back for at least four hundred years. It is true that the very earliest writers in England rarely had as their main interest a purely phonetic investigation; and the descriptive accounts which they provided are less rigorous and satisfactory, by modern standards, than those of the Indian grammarians. But, by the seventeenth century, we find a considerable body of published work, which is already entirely phonetic in character and which contains observations and theories still adhered to to-day.

6.1.1 Some of the first writers whose work we possess were concerned with the relation between the sounds of English and those of another language. Thus, John Palsgrave's French grammar *Lesclarcissement de la Langue Francoyse* (1530) includes a section which deals with the pronunciation of French, much as any modern grammar would. In order to explain the values of the French sounds, Palsgrave compares them with the English. This is done in no objective fashion, and it is not easy for us now to know what precise sound is indicated in either language. But this difficulty of communicating sound values in print—especially those of vowels—is one which will be shared by all writers until some system of objective evaluation, such as that of the Cardinal Vowels, is devised. At least, John Palsgrave was sufficiently aware of divergent associations of letters and sound to provide some

[1] W. S. Allen, *Phonetics in Ancient India*, Oxford University Press, 1953, p. 7.

passages of French in a kind of phonetic transcription. Another early writer concerned with pronunciation is William Salesbury, a Welshman, whose *Dictionary in Englyshe and Welshe* (1547) contained comments on the sounds of English. Sound values are indicated by means of a method of transliteration in Welsh or English. Indeed, though grammars of foreign languages published during the next three centuries will increasingly attempt more exact description and comparison of sounds, for the great majority of them the section devoted to pronunciation will rely mainly on transliteration for indicating approximate values. Even to-day, grammars of foreign languages frequently make use of this approximate method of 'simulated' pronunciation.

6.1.2 A more important type of phonetic inquiry stemmed from the activities of those who, particularly in the sixteenth and seventeenth centuries, were concerned at the increasing inconsistency of the relationship of Latin letters and the sounds which they represented, especially in English. There had been during the previous five or six centuries great changes of pronunciation, particularly as far as the vowel sounds were concerned, so that letters no longer had their original Latin values. The same sound could be written in a number of ways, or the same spelling do service for several sounds; moreover, the same word might be spelt in different ways by different writers. Thus, four hundred years before the activities of Bernard Shaw and the Simplified Spelling Society of to-day, men were aware of the need to bring some order into English spelling. During the four centuries that have elapsed since these early efforts, our pronunciation has continued to evolve without any radical changes of spelling having been made, with the result that to-day discrepancies between sound and spelling are greater than they have ever been. It can, however, be said that for more than two hundred years our spelling forms, inconsistent though they may be as far as sound symbolization is concerned, have been standardized.

The early *spelling reformers* were obliged, if they were to propose a more logical relationship of sound and spelling, to investigate the sounds of English. A writer such as Thomas Smith, *De recta et emendata linguae anglicae scriptione* (1568), makes many pertinent phonetic comments on such matters as the aspiration of English plosives and the syllabic nature of /n/ and /l/, as well as providing correct descriptions of the articulation of consonants. Yet, he, as a phonetician, is overshadowed in the sixteenth century by John Hart, whose most important work, the *Orthographie*, was published in 1569. Besides making out his case for spelling reform and proposing a revised system, Hart describes the organs of speech, defines vowels and consonants (distinguishing between front and back vowels and between voiced and voiceless consonants), and notes the aspiration of voiceless plosives. Of the numerous seventeenth-century orthoepists, only Alexander Gil, *Logonomia Anglica* (1619, 1621), can be compared with Hart on the phonetic level, though even his observations lack the objectivity of Hart's.

6.1.3 If the writers mentioned above used phonetic methods of analysis and transcription as a means to their end of devising an improved spelling, there emerged in the seventeenth century a group of writers who were interested in speech and language for their own sake. Because of their preoccupation with detailed analysis of speech activity, the comparative study of the sounds of various languages, the classification of sound types, and the establishment of systematic relationships between the English sounds, they can be said to be the true precursors of modern scientific phoneticians. Two of the most celebrated, John Wallis and Bishop Wilkins, were among the founders of the Royal Society; and, indeed, Isaac Newton, the greatest of the early members of the Society, was interested in phonetic analysis and has left notes of his own linguistic observations. Language was considered a proper object of the attention of the writers of this new scientific age, their view of speech and pronunciation being set against a framework of the universal nature and characteristics of language.

The linguistic fame of John Wallis, primarily a mathematician, spread throughout Europe and lasted into the eighteenth century, his work being copied long after his death. His principal linguistic work, *Grammatica Linguae Anglicanae*, was first published in 1653 and the last authoritative edition appeared in 1699; but other, unauthorized, editions continued to appear in the eighteenth century, the last being dated 1765. Wallis intended his *Grammar* to help foreigners to learn English more easily and also to enable Englishmen to understand more thoroughly the true nature of their language. He admits in his preface that he is not the first to undertake such a task, but claims that he does not seek to fit English into a Latin mould, as most of his predecessors had done, but rather to examine the sounds of English as constituting a system in their own right. By his methods, he says, he has succeeded in teaching not only foreigners to pronounce English correctly but also the deaf and dumb to speak. The introductory part of the work (*Tractatus de Loquela*), besides giving a short history of English, describes in detail the organs of speech and attempts to establish a general system of sound classification which will do service for all languages (illustrations of qualities are taken from French, Welsh, German, Greek, and Hebrew as well as English). Vowels are classified in *Guttural, Palatal*, and *Labial* categories, subdivided into *Wide, Medium*, and *Narrow* classes. The degrees of aperture are similar to those which are used even to-day, but the divisions Guttural, Palatal, and Labial, which take into account both the area of raising of the tongue and also lip action, show a confusion of dimensions not to be found in more modern analyses.

Consonants, like vowels, are divided into three classes: *Labial, Palatal,* and *Guttural,* being different from vowels in that the air-stream from the lungs is obstructed or constricted at some point. Wallis remarks that the air-stream may pass entirely through the mouth, almost completely through the nose, or almost equally divided between the mouth and the nose, the position of the uvula determining the difference of direction. Thus, nine basic consonantal articulations are postulated. In addition, the air-stream may be completely shut off (*Closed* or *Primitive*) or merely constricted (*Open, Derivative,* or *Aspirate*), the latter being articulated with a narrow aperture or with a wider, rounder, opening. The 'closed' consonants (stops) consist of the *mutes* [p, t, k],[1] the *semi-mutes* [b, d, g], and the *semi-vowels* [m, n, ŋ]. The corresponding 'open' or 'aspirated' consonants are: mute [f, s, x], semi-mutes [v, z, x] or [ɣ]; and those with a wider opening: mute [f] (again), [θ, h], semi-mutes [w, ð, j]; [l, r] are related to the [d] or [n] articulations; [ʃ, ʒ] are regarded as compound sounds. Wallis's detailed remarks on the pronunciation of English are made in terms of this general system stated in the *Loquela.* It will be seen that such a classification, despite errors and inadequacies which are apparent to-day, represents a serious attempt at the establishment of universal sound categories. Although the elements of Wallis's system have been quoted briefly here, it should be pointed out that his is merely the most celebrated of a number of similar analyses made at about the same time.

His fellow member of the Royal Society, Bishop John Wilkins, published in 1668 an *Essay towards a Real Character and a Philosophical Language.* Written in English, this work of 454 pages, with a dictionary appended, is of much wider scope than that of Wallis, since it aims at no less than the creation of a universal language, expressed by means of 'marks, which should signifie things, and not words'. Wilkins acknowledges his debt to his contemporary linguists, especially in respect of the account of pronunciation which forms a comparatively small part of the *Essay.* Wallis, he says, 'seems to me, with greatest Accurateness and subtlety to have considered the Philosophy of Articulate sounds.' Wilkins, too, describes the functions of the speech organs and gives a general classification of the sounds articulated by them; his treatment of consonants is in fact more satisfactory than that of Wallis. He claims that the thirty-four letters which he proposes for his alphabet are sufficient 'to express all those articulate sounds which are commonly known and used in these parts of the world'. In his

---

[1] Wallis's own symbols are here replaced by IPA equivalents, but it is not always clear from Wallis's description which sounds are intended: thus, his description of *ch* and *gh* would seem to indicate [x] for both, though in the system one would expect *gh* to mean [ɣ].

account of the values of the letters, reference is made not only to European sound systems but also to such little known languages as Mexican, Armenian, Arabic, Japanese, and Chinese.

Any account of seventeenth-century phoneticians should include the name of Christopher Cooper. Though he did not achieve the great European reputation of Wallis, he is considered by many to be the greatest English phonetician of the century. His work on English pronunciation was first published in 1685 (*Grammatica Linguae Anglicanae*), with an English edition appearing in 1687 (*The English Teacher, or The Discovery of the Art of Teaching and Learning the English Tongue*). A schoolmaster rather than a member of the Royal Society, Cooper was less concerned than many of his contemporaries with the establishment of universal systems. His aim was to describe and give rules for the pronunciation of English for 'Gentlemen, Ladies, Merchants, Tradesmen, Schools and Strangers', rather than to devise a logical system into which the sounds of English and other languages might be fitted. Moreover, he deals with the spelling of English as it exists and does not seek to reform it. The first section of his book is concerned with the description of speech sounds ('The Principles of Speech') and the second part gives rules for the relation of spelling and pronunciation in different contexts. Cooper describes the organs of speech and names those sections of the upper speech tract which are mainly responsible for the articulation of the 'breath': 'guttural, lingual, palatine, dental, labial, lingua-palatine, lingua-dental.' Those sounds in the production of which the air-stream is 'straitned or intercepted' are consonants (classified as semi-vowels, aspirated, semi mutes, and mutes), while those in which the air-stream is 'freely emitted through the nostrils or the lips' are vowels. He notes that voice, 'made by a tremulous concussion of the larynx,' is a characteristic of vowels, semi-vowels, and semi-mutes. His classification of vowels is in terms of *lingual*, *labial*, and *guttural* categories, a somewhat confusing distinction being made between the English long and short vowels. Diphthongs are defined properly as 'a joyning of two vowels in the same syllable, wherein the power of both is kept'. His consonantal classification, with IPA equivalents here, shows: *labial* sounds, subdivided into semi-vowels [w, v, m], aspirated [ʍ, f, m̥], semi-mute [b], mute [p]; *lingual* sounds, subdivided into semi-vowels [z, ʒ, ð, n, l, r, j], aspirated [s, ʃ, θ, n̥, l̥, r̥, ç], semi-mute [d], mute [t]; *guttural* sounds, subdivided into semi-vowels [ɣ, ŋ, h], aspirated [x, ŋ̊, h], semi-mute [g], mute [k]. The second part of the work, dealing with the pronunciation of various English spelling forms, provides more specific information about the pronunciation of English than is to be found in the work of any other writer in this period. Numerous examples are given, e.g. more than three hundred cases of the *-tion* suffix pronounced with [ʃ]; words are listed which have either the same pronunciation with different spellings or the same spellings with different pronunciation; and rules are given for the accentuation of words.

It will be seen from the mention of these few names, chosen from the many who were writing on matters of pronunciation in the seventeenth century and omitting those who were composing spelling books and grammars for foreigners, compiling lists of homophones and devising systems of shorthand, that there was at this time a surge of scientific and analytical interest in speech and pronunciation such as was not to be repeated until the nineteenth century. It is true that the judgments made were largely intuitive, but this was to remain the case in phonetic research until the second half of the nineteenth century. In their theoretical approach, however, many of these early writers show a preoccupation with classification, systematization, and problems of distribution which is paralleled in the activities of modern linguists.

6.1.4 The spirit of general scientific inquiry into speech which characterized a large proportion of the phonetic work of the seventeenth century had, by the eighteenth century, lost much of its original enthusiasm. Prescriptive grammars containing rules for pronunciation continued to be produced in large numbers and provide us with information concerning the contemporary forms of pronunciation; shorthand systems, too, which show an undiminished popularity, necessitated the analysis of English into its constituent sounds. Yet the main achievement of the century lies in its successful attempt to fix the spelling and pronunciation of the language. Dictionaries had been published in the seventeenth century, but the works having the main stabilizing and standardizing influence on the language were to be the Dictionaries of Samuel Johnson (1755), Thomas Sheridan (1780), and John Walker (1791), the last two writers being particularly concerned with the standardization of pronunciation. John Walker, whose dictionary is called by the *Dictionary of National Biography* 'the statute book of English orthoepy', exerted a great influence on the teaching of English not only in this country but also in America. Moreover, he pays considerable attention in his work to the analysis of intonation, treated but perfunctorily by most earlier writers. In this respect, however, he owes much to Joshua Steele's remarkable *Prosodia Rationalis* (1775−79), in which there is presented a system of notation capable of expressing pitch changes, stress, and rate of delivery. (Steele is celebrated for his detailed analysis of a soliloquy delivered by David Garrick.)

We have, in fact, been dealing up to now with two types of work on pronunciation, which, especially in the eighteenth century, came to be confused: on the one hand, and in the minority, the books which laid emphasis on description, analysis, and classification; on the other, the books which were mainly normative and continue the tradition of 'rhetoric'. That part of rhetoric known as 'elocution' originally referred to the style and form of speech, 'the garnishing of Speech,' but in the eighteenth century the term was increasingly applied to the method of delivery. It is not until the nineteenth century that a clear distinction will be made between the aesthetic judgments upon which elocution largely relies and the objective descriptive statements which form the basis of phonetic analysis. Until such a distinction is explicitly made, advances in phonetic techniques have to be disentangled from a mass of irrelevant opinion.

6.1.5 In the nineteenth century the English traditional preoccupation with phonetic notation and the simplification of English spelling continues. Isaac Pitman (1813–97), whose system of shorthand is so widely used to-day, and Alexander J. Ellis (1814–90), concerned at the difficulties which our spelling presented to English children as well as to foreigners, devised an alphabet (*Phonotype*, 1847) which conformed to a phonetic analysis of English and yet remained based upon the Latin characters. They were supported by the *Phonographic Society* and published a journal which eventually (1848) was named the *Fonetic Jurnal*. Ellis, however, developed other types of alphabet, notably *Glossic*, which is essentially an adaptation of traditional spelling, and *Palaeotype*, which used conventional letter shapes but in a great variety of type, so that fine shades of sound could be symbolized. This latter alphabet was put to good use by Ellis in his historical and dialectal studies; but not only is the precise value to be attached to a letter not always easily determined—because of the method of reference to sounds in languages—but also the complexity of the system renders it difficult for the reader to assimilate. Ellis's work on notation, however, largely inspired the 'Broad' and 'Narrow' Romic transcriptions of the great Henry Sweet (1845–1912). In 1867 Alexander Melville Bell, father of Alexander Graham Bell (an inventor of the telephone), published his book *Visible Speech*, while a lecturer on speech in the University of London. This remarkable work set out to classify all the sounds capable of being articulated by the human speech organs and to allot a systematic and related series of symbols to the sounds. The unfamiliarity of the invented symbol shapes was no doubt responsible for the fact that this means of notation has never been widely used in purely phonetic work, but its value was for many years demonstrated, especially in America, as a system applied to the teaching of the deaf.

Although, in referring to these writers, emphasis has been laid on their contribution to the development of phonetic transcription, their published work covers every aspect of speech activity. Bell's interests, in his forty-nine publications, lay mainly in the field of elocution and the description of articulatory processes. But Ellis and Sweet applied the techniques of phonetic analysis both to the description of contemporary pronunciation and also to the whole field of historical phonological investigation. Ellis, in fact, will be chiefly remembered for his massive work *On Early English Pronunciation*, published in five volumes between 1869 and 1889. In these volumes Ellis traces the history of English pronunciation and, at the same time, contributes descriptive phonetic studies of contemporary dialects. It is not surprising that a work of such enormous scope should since have been found to be inadequate in many respects, but it cannot be denied that Ellis was a great pioneer in the application of objective techniques to the description of past and present states of the language. Although his assessment of the value of many grammarians from the sixteenth century onwards was often faulty, he initiated a study of their work which has continued unabated to this day. Henry Sweet, a greater phonologist and scholar, applied stringent phonetic techniques to all his work, so that, whether it be a question of phonetic theory or the history of English or the description of a language such as Welsh or Danish, his basic approach and the majority of his conclusions remain valid to-day. He belongs as much to the twentieth century as to the nineteenth and his influence is clearly to be seen in the work of Daniel Jones, who has dominated British English phonetics of this century.

This brief and selective outline goes some way towards revealing a line of phonetic inquiry which has been continuous in England from the sixteenth century to the present day. The techniques for describing speech and language have become progressively more objective, modern instrumental methods for physiological and physical investigation providing the latest stage in the process. A problem confronting linguists of to-day concerns the correlation of concrete data, which is being accumulated in great detail by modern instrumental analysis, with abstract linguistic realities, many of which have for centuries been implicit in the work of writers on language.

6.2   Sound Change

The language spoken in England has undergone very striking changes during the last thousand years, changes which have affected every aspect of the language, its morphology, syntax, and vocabulary as well as its pronunciation. Old English[1] is so different from present-day English from every point of view that it is unintelligible to the modern Englishman either in its written form or in a reconstructed spoken form; Chaucer's poetry presents difficulties in print and, when read in what is presumed to be the pronunciation of the fourteenth century,

---

[1] The following abbreviations will henceforward be used: OE—Old English (up to approximately A.D. 1100); ME—Middle English (approx. 1100–1450); eModE—early Modern English (approx. 1450–1600); PresE—present-day English; AN—Anglo-Norman; OF—Old French.

offers a sound pattern which it is not easy for the modern listener to interpret; even Shakespeare, though phonetically not far removed from ourselves, raises problems of syntax and meaning.

The pronunciation of a language seems to be subject to a continuous and inevitable process of change. Indeed, it would be surprising if a means of communication, handed on orally from one generation to another, showed no variation over the centuries. It is not difficult to find examples of changes which are taking place in our own times, e.g. the centralization of the first element of the diphthong in *home* appears to be a fairly recent development; the vowel in *saw* seems to be somewhat closer, with stronger lip-rounding, amongst young people in the South of England to-day than it is in the pronunciation of older people. A change of a different kind—the use of another phoneme in a class of words—is illustrated by the case of words such as *poor* and *sure*; these tend to be said by the older generation with /ʊə/, whereas the new generation much more commonly uses /ɔː/. At any given moment, therefore, we must expect several pronunciations to be current, representing at least the older, traditional, forms and the new tendencies.

To-day there are a number of reasons why we might expect these processes of change to operate less rapidly. The fact that communication throughout the whole country is easy, the spread of universal education and the resultant consciousness of the printed word, the constant impact of broadcasting with its tacit imposition of a standard speech, these are all influences which are likely to apply a brake to change in pronunciation. They are, however, factors which have operated only in comparatively recent times. In former stages of the development of English, there was no mass, nation-wide influence likely to lead to stability and levelling. Printing, it is true, has been with us for four hundred years, but the wide dissemination of books, as of education, is a modern development. Indeed, as we have seen, the spelling of English, even in printed books, was not finally standardized until the eighteenth century. With such freedom from restraint, especially before the eighteenth century, we must expect the history of spoken English to give evidence of drastic change; but the changes which took place were not all of the same kind.

6.2.1 Types of Change

(1) The most important kind of change tends to affect the realization of a phoneme in all its occurrences. Such changes, not usually being set in motion by any immediate, outside influence, are in this sense *independent*; they are often known as *isolative internal* changes. Thus, the ME realization of the phoneme in a word such as *house* had the sound [uː], which has generally become [aʊ] in modern English; similarly, the ME vowel phoneme having a value of the [aː] type, as in a word such as

name, is in most cases realized as a kind of [eɪ] in PresE. Changes of this type apply particularly to the English vowel system, which underwent a remarkable evolution of values, known as the *Great Vowel Shift*, during the centuries preceding the modern period.

(2) Another kind of change which affects the realization of a phoneme is that which is brought about by the occurrence of phonemes in particular contexts—a *dependent* change, often called *internal combinative*. Thus, the phoneme in *mice*, having now the sound [aɪ], results from an earlier [iː] by means of an isolative change; but this [iː] sound in [miːs] arose as a result of a combinative process of *vowel harmony*, or *i-mutation*, through the stages [muːsi], [myːsi] > [miːs], where the change [uː] > [yː] can be explained by the fronting of [uː] under the influence of the [iː] of the following syllable. Such a combinative change belongs to OE, but a more recent change of this type is exemplified by words such as *swan*. This word was probably pronounced [swan] or [swæn] in about 1600, but the [w] sound has rounded and retracted the vowel to give the modern form [swɒn]. The large majority of earlier [w] + [a] sequences have now given [w] + [ɒ], or [ɔː], by reason of this combinative change affecting this particular sound sequence, e.g. *want, quality, war, water*, etc.

(3) Some changes are neither independent nor dependent upon the phonetic context; they may be said to be *external* to the main line of evolution. Thus, it was fashionable in Elizabethan times to pronounce such words as *servant* and *heard* with [ær] or [ar], perhaps originally a dialect form, rather than with [ɛr], the regular form of development; these words, with some exceptions such as *clerk*, have reverted to the normal development of ME [ɛr],—[ɜː] rather than [ɑː]. It was also fashionable to pronounce the termination *-ing* as [ɪn], only now retained as a special form of affectation or of vulgar speech. Such changes, involving a change of distribution of phonemes among word and morpheme classes, do not affect the phonemic system of the language. The introduction of foreign words may, however, at least temporarily and in the speech of a restricted number of individuals, disturb the number of phonemes or their distribution as regards position in the word. Thus, if the French word *beige* is used in English with the pronunciation /beɪʒ/, we have a case of a final /ʒ/ unknown in English words; or again, if *restaurant* is pronounced with any kind of nasalized vowel in the last syllable, the possibility of a new kind of vocalic opposition is introduced into the language. However, such foreign borrowings generally tend to conform to the English system: words with a final French /ʒ/, such as *prestige, camouflage*, etc., may be realized in the English form with /dʒ/ and a word with a nasalized vowel like *restaurant* will be normalized to /ˈrestərɒŋ/, /ˈrestərɒnt/ or /ˈrestrənt/, etc.

(4) In addition to changes of quality, there have also to be taken into

account changes involving *quality* and *accentual pattern* (stress). Thus, the vowel in such words as *path*, *half*, *pass*, still short three hundred years ago, is now long in the South of England. Or again, the vowels in *good*, *book* and *breath*, *death*, once long, are now relatively short. Changes of accent are particularly striking in the case of words which have come into the language from French: in ME, such words as *village* or *necessary* retained a stress accent accompanied by length on the penultimate syllable—/vɪˈlɑːdʒə/ and /ˌnɛsɛˈsɑːrɪə/. Now, the main stress accent has shifted to an earlier syllable in the English fashion, with the qualitative changes which weak accent involves—/ˈvɪlɪdʒ/, /ˈnɛsəsrɪ/. Later borrowings, or those in less common use, often retain the French accentual pattern—thus, *hotel* or *machine*, with stress accent on the final syllable, whereas, if they had conformed to the English system, we might have had such modern forms as /ˈhəʊtl/ and /ˈmætʃɪn/ or /ˈmeɪtʃɪn/, in the same way that the thoroughly anglicized form of *garage* gives /ˈgærɪdʒ/. (See §6.3.4 on current changes.)

6.2.2 Rate and Route of Vowel Change

The English vowels have been subject to more striking changes than have the consonants. This is not surprising, for a consonantal articulation usually involves an approximation of organs which can be felt; such an articulation tends to be more stable in that it is more easily identified and transmitted more exactly from one generation to another. Changes in the consonantal system comparatively rarely involve a modification of sound (an example of such a modification would be the affrication, for combinative reasons, of the OE palatal plosives [c, ɟ] to [tʃ, dʒ] as in *church* < OE *cirice* and *bridge* < OE *brycg*). Far more common is the type of distributional change involving the conferment of phonemic status on an existing sound (e.g. [v, ð, z], allophones of /f, θ, s/ in OE, later obtain contrastive, phonemic, significance), or the disappearance of an allophone (e.g. postvocalic [x] and [ç] in such words as *brought* and *right* were largely lost in the South of England by the seventeenth century), or the insertion of an existing phoneme in a particular class of words (e.g. the initial /h/ in words of French origin such as *herb*, *homage*). Whether it is a question of consonantal change, loss, or addition, it is usually possible to explain the type of modification which has taken place and the approximate period during which it occurred.

A modification of vowel quality will, however, result from very slight changes of tongue or lip position and there may be a series of imperceptible gradations before an appreciable quality change is evident (or is capable of being expressed by means of the Latin vowel letters). It is particularly difficult to assess rate and phonetic route of change in the case of those internal independent vowel changes which affect the realization of a phoneme throughout the language. It is known, for instance, that the modern homophones *meet* and *meat* had in ME different vowel forms, approximately of the value [eː] and [ɛː]. The [eː] vowel of *meet* became [iː] by about 1500 and it might be postulated that by a process of gradual change the [ɛː] of *meat* first closed to [eː] and then, by the eighteenth century, coalesced with the [iː] in *meet*. The available evidence, however, suggests that the change [ɛː > iː] may not have been either simple or gradual, but that two pronunciations existed side by side for a long period (the conservative [ɛː] beside another form [iː] which had resulted from an early coalescence with the *meet* vowel) and that it is the [iː] form which has in most cases survived. In other vowel changes, it may be agreed that the change was gradual, but it is difficult to date precisely the stages of development. Thus, the modern /aɪ/ of *time* results from a ME [iː] value; it is clear that the change has been one of progressive, widening, diphthongization, but there may have been a period of incipient diphthongization when there was hesitation between the pure vowel [iː] and some such diphthong as [ɪi] or [əi]. It is well to remember, therefore, that at any particular time in history there are likely to be a number of different, coexistent, realizations of vowel phonemes, not only as between regions but also between generations and social groups. An example of such variety in modern English is provided by the diphthong in the word *home*, which in the South of England may be rendered as [əʊ] by the younger generation and something more like [oʊ] by the older people. The speech of any community may, therefore, be said to reflect the pronunciation of the previous century and to anticipate that of the next.

6.2.3   Sound Change and the Linguistic System

It is convenient to study sound change in terms of the development of particular phonemes or sounds, but it is misleading to ignore the relationship of the sound units to the system within which they function and which may, in fact, not be changing. In other words, although there may be considerable qualitative changes, the number and pattern of the terms within the system may show relative stability. The ME /iː/ phoneme, for instance, is now realized as [aɪ], but there is still a phonemic opposition which contrasts such words as *time*, *team*, *tame*, *term*, *tomb*, etc., and, in any case, a new phoneme /iː/ has emerged in words of the *team* type. On the other hand, the system may change because a sound, without itself changing, may receive a new, phonemic, value, e.g. the sound [ŋ] has always existed in English as a realization of /n/ followed by the velars /k/ or /g/, but when the final /g/ in a word like *sing* was no longer pronounced, /ŋ/ contrasted significantly with /n/ and /m/.

Since the system of our language consists of a framework of significant oppositions by means of which we communicate, it may be assumed that there is a tendency for the system to remain stable, the loss of an opposition involving a possibility of confusion. In fact, of course, the redundancy of English is such that some degree of neutralization of phonemes is easily tolerated: thus, to-day, few speakers in the South of England distinguish *saw* and *sore* by means of an opposition /ɔ:/-/ɔə/, yet the loss of the /ɔə/ diphthong is no impediment to communication. An example of an earlier coalescence of vowel phonemes is that illustrated by the homophony of *meet* and *meat*. On the other hand, new oppositions may emerge in the language, e.g. the phonemes /v, ð, z, ŋ/, as we have seen. Nevertheless, despite the adjustments in the number of phonemes which have taken place, the history of the English sound system displays, over the last 1,000 years, a considerable degree of stability.

Though the relationships within the system may tend to remain stable, a change of phonetic realization of any phoneme is likely to have qualitative repercussions throughout the system. Such a disturbance may be observed in modern English. The phonetic relationship of the vowel phonemes in *set* and *sat*, in one type of pronunciation, is of a front vowel between half-close and half-open to a front vowel between half-open and open. If, however, the vowel of *sat* has a closer articulation than that described, that of *set* must be raised, too. A limit of raising is imposed by the presence of *sit* and *seat*, for it is not possible to raise the vowel of *sit* to any extent without danger of confusion with that of *seat*, unless the latter vowel becomes strongly diphthongal. (It may be objected that a quantitative as well as qualitative difference distinguishes /i:/ from /ɪ/; but, in the examples given—*seat* and *sit*—the phonetic context imposes a quantity on /i:/ which is practically the same as that of /ɪ/. If /ɪ/ were too close to the region of /i:/, the opposition would be maintained only by realizing /i:/ as fully long at the expense of the shortening influence of the final /t/ or by a process such as diphthongization.) Alternatively, if the vowel phoneme of *sat* is realized as a front open vowel, as in many English regional dialects, the vocalic area in which the phoneme of *set* can be realized becomes more extensive; in fact, in those kinds of English where this occurs, the vowel in *set* tends to be half-open variety. Such considerations of the phonetic relationship of phonemes have a relevance in the historical, *diachronic*, study of English. In ME there were, for instance, four long vowels in the front region—/i:, e:, ɛ:, a:/. By 1600 /i:/ had diphthongized and the remaining vowels closed up. Such a movement may have been caused by pressure upwards from /a:/ or by the creation of an empty space brought about by the diphthongization of the pure vowel /i:/.

Although, therefore, it is often convenient in diachronic studies to investigate the development of individual phonemes in terms of the quality of their realization, it is clear that many sound changes can be

explained only by reference to a readjustment of the phonetic relationships of the phonemes of the system as a whole. Moreover, any
particular point in the development of a language's sound system is not
simply to be considered as a stage in the process of change of a number
of sound units but rather as the presentation of the functioning of a
system at a certain historical moment. The primary significance of the
sounds of modern English is their function in the system of to-day; in
the same way, the English sounds of 1600 are to be viewed in terms not
only of their past and future forms but also of their contemporary,
synchronic, relationships and functions.

Some sound changes are, indeed, the result of an influence which
applies to the system as a whole. A prosodic, or supra-segmental,
feature such as the stress-accent provides an example of this kind.
English has always possessed a strong stress-accent, certain syllables of
a word or utterance being made more prominent than their neighbours
because of, amongst other things, the greater force with which they are
said. Those drastic changes of vowel quality known as the *Great Vowel
Shift* mainly affect vowels in accented syllables. But vowels in most
unaccented syllables (especially those in word final positions) have
undergone, in the last thousand years, an equally striking, though different, type of change. Henry Sweet has called OE the period of *full*
endings, *stanas* being realized as ['stɑː nɑs]; ME, the period of *levelled*
endings, when *stones* was pronounced ['stɔː nəs]; and eModE and later
English, the period of *lost* endings, when *stones* is [stoː nz], [stəʊnz].
There is, therefore, a general tendency for all unaccented vowels to
shorten (if long) and to gravitate towards the weak centralized vowels
[ɪ] or [ə], or sometimes [ʊ], if not to disappear altogether. This fact
accounts for the high frequency of occurrence of [ɪ] and [ə] in PresE and
for the complete elision of many vowels in unaccented syllables in rapid
colloquial speech, e.g. *suppose* [sˈpəʊz], *probably* [ˈprɒbblɪ].

6.2.4   Sources of Evidence for Reconstruction

Whether our aim is to reconstruct the phonological system of English at
any particular moment in history or to estimate the nature of the
development affecting particular phonemes, it is necessary to establish
the sound values which were used in the pronunciation of the language
—relative values in the case of the system, absolute values as far as
possible in the case of sound development. An investigation of the
phonological structure of PresE would have to include direct observation of its phonetic features. For this purpose, future generations will
have the benefit of recordings of the speech of to-day. Obviously this
type of evidence cannot be used for the reconstruction of past states of
the spoken language. The further back we go into history the scantier
the evidence of spoken forms becomes. Our conclusions will, therefore,

be based on information mostly of an indirect kind; yet such is the agreement generally amongst the various types of evidence that the broad lines of sound change can be conjectured with reasonable certainty.

(1) *Theoretical paths of development.*—If, in dealing with the changing realization of a particular phoneme, we can be reasonably sure of its sound value at two points in history, we can, from our knowledge of phonetic possibilities and probabilities, infer theoretically the intervening stages of development. We can, of course, be sure of the pronunciation of PresE. If, then, the evidence suggested unequivocally that, for instance, the vowel in *home* was pronounced as [ɑː] in OE, the development to be described and accounted for would be [ɑː] > [əʊ]. It is likely that the articulation has always involved the back, rather than the front, of the tongue; the change has clearly meant a closing of the tongue position, to which at some stage there has been added a gliding (diphthongal) movement. We might, therefore, postulate such developments as [ɑː > ɑʊ > ɔʊ > oʊ > əʊ] or [ɑː > ɔː > oː > oʊ > əʊ]. The available evidence will then confirm or refute the hypothesis—in this case the second solution being more in keeping with the information. Such recognition of phonetic probabilities will always be implicit in the tracing of change. It must be considered unlikely that [ɑː] on its way to [oʊ] or [əʊ] would have passed through a stage of front articulation, without any combinative influence. Nevertheless, the possibility of a type of change which is not the most probable theoretically must never be excluded, for often the evidence points to only one conclusion. It would, therefore, be dangerous to predict, merely according to phonetic probablities, the way our present sound system will develop. The half-close back rounded ME [ʊ] has generally developed in PresE to an advanced back half-open unrounded vowel—[ʌ]; but this vowel now, in the South of England, appears to have been fronted to something nearer [a] or [ä]. Its future must be quite uncertain.

(2) *Old English.*—It is most important in an investigation of the development of English sounds over the last thousand years that the pronunciation of OE should be established with some certainty. If this can be done, we shall have a 'starting point' for the phonetic route of change to PresE. The term Old English, however, spans a period of some four hundred years from about A.D. 700 to A.D. 1100. Moreover, the invasion of the Angles, Saxons, and Jutes in the fifth and sixth centuries introduced four separate varieties of English: the Angles, in the Midlands, north-east England, and the south of Scotland, using types of English known as *Mercian* and *Northumbrian* (or, in general terms, *Anglian*); the Saxons, in the south and south-west, using the *West-Saxon* dialect; and the Jutes, settling mainly in the region of Kent and using a dialect called *Kentish*. Of the four dialects, West-Saxon, which was to become a kind of standard language, is the one about

which most is known from the extant texts. In its later form—that in use between about A.D. 900 and A.D. 1100—it is referred to as Classical OE.

The broad lines of the pronunciation of this language can be conjectured from a comparison of the development of the other members of the West Germanic group of languages to which it is related. But by far the most explicit evidence concerning its sounds is to be inferred from the *alphabet* in which it is written. The earlier Runic spelling was replaced by a form of the Latin alphabet. This alphabet was probably introduced into the country in the seventh century by Irish missionaries. It can be assumed, therefore, that the sounds of OE were represented as far as possible by the Latin letters with their Latin values, with some modifications of an Irish kind. A great deal is known about the pronunciation of Vulgar Latin, whose sound system had much in common with that of modern Italian. If an Italian, knowing no English, were today asked to write down with his own spelling the PresE pronunciation of the word *milk*, [mɪɫk], he would have no difficulty in representing the first sound, which he could spell as *m*; the vowel [ɪ] might, however, seem to him to resemble the sound he would write in Italian as *e* rather than as *i*; the 'dark' [ɫ] would appear to have a back vowel glide accompanying it, requiring a spelling such as *ol*; and, since he has no *k* letter, he would spell the final [k] as *c*. His transcription of the word might, therefore, be *meolc*, which is, in fact, a West-Saxon spelling of the word now written *milk*. This is a fortuitous example and must not be taken to suggest that OE was pronounced in the same way as PresE. But it does demonstrate that OE spellings, which may appear to be very different, are often less surprising when we keep in mind the Latin values originally attached to the letters.

Sometimes the simple forms of the Latin alphabet were evidently inadequate for representing the English sound: thus, the joined form *æ* was used to symbolize a sound between *C*[a][1] and *C*[ɛ]; the sounds [θ] and [ð] were written in the earlier manuscripts as *th* initially and *d* medially and finally in a word, and later as ð or the rune þ, regardless of the sound's position in the word or its voiced or voiceless quality; the rune þ frequently replaced the earlier *u* or *uu*. The vowel values of the OE system were particularly difficult to represent with the five Latin vowel letters. Sometimes the spelling used will hesitate between two letters: thus, the vowel of *mann*, probably of a *C*[ɑ] or [ɒ] quality, is written either with *a* or *o*, indicating a vowel between the open central unrounded value of the Latin letter *a* and the back half-open to half-close rounded value of *o*. Unaccented vowels, too, already beginning to be obscured and levelled, presented a problem to the scribes, the Latin alphabet offering no way of showing a central vowel of the [ə] type.

---

[1] Henceforth a cardinal vowel value will be referred to as *C*, followed by the appropriate symbol.

Unaccented æ, e, and i soon begin to be written as e and unaccented a, u, o later tend to be used indifferently, indicating that the vowel distinction was being lost. A diphthong such as the one written as ea must probably be interpreted as a glide to a central [ə] quality.

Quantity is often shown in the case of vowels by doubling the letter or by the use of an accent and in the case of consonants by doubling the letter. The stress-accent in a word is also sometimes shown by the use of a mark; but, in any case, it is agreed, from a comparison of the West Germanic languages, that the word accent in OE fell generally on the first syllable of words, with the exception of certain compounds.

The written form of OE provides us, therefore, with considerable information concerning the language's pronunciation; we have a working hypothesis from which to begin our investigations. The study of later forms of English will often, in fact, confirm that the OE pronunciation postulated from the spelling and the comparison of Germanic languages is the only one from which later forms can be expected to have developed.

(3) *Middle English.*—Spelling forms can also help us to deduce the pronunciation of the ME period, roughly A.D. 1100–1450. Generally speaking, it may be said that the letters still had their Latin values and that those letters which were written were meant to be sounded. Thus, the initial k in a word such as *knokke* was still pronounced and the vowel in *time* would have an [i] quality. This persistence of Latin values in spelling was no doubt due to the influence of the Church, which was still the centre of teaching and writing, and the absence of a thoroughly standardized spelling accounts for its predominantly phonetic char acter. However, English spelling was modified by French influences. Notably, the French ch spelling was introduced to represent the [tʃ] sound in a word such as *chin* (formerly spelt *cinn*), where the new spelling form indicates no change of pronunciation; in addition ou, or ow, represents the sound [u], formerly written u, e.g. *hous*, in OE *hus*. The simple u spelling was retained to express both the French sound [y] in words like *duke* and *fortune* and the OE short [u] sound, though this latter sound is often written as o, especially when juxtaposed to letters of the w, m, n type, e.g. *wonne* rather than *wunne*, to avoid confusion between the letter shapes.

Rhymes, too, have their value, especially as, in this period, they are likely to have been satisfactory to the ear as well as to the eye—in the whole of Chaucer's work, for instance, there are very few rhymes which appear to involve the pairing of different vowel sounds. Nevertheless, evidence from rhymes is valueless unless it is possible to be certain, from other sources of evidence, of the pronunciation of one member of the pair. Thus, the Chaucerian rhyme *par cas* :: *was*, because we can be sure that the French word *cas* had a vowel of the [a] quality, is evidence to confirm the view that the [w] of *was* had not yet retracted and rounded the vowel to [ɒ] and, the final *s* in the two words being still likely to represent [s], that the word was probably pronounced [was].

Again, words imported from French can give us information concerning the timing of sound changes. Thus, French words such as *age* and *couch*, which we know from French sources had [aː] and [uː] at the time of their introduction into English, fell in with the English vowel development [aː] > [eɪ] and [uː] > [aʊ] in words like *name* and *house*; we can conclude, therefore, that at the time the French words came into the language the [aː] and [uː] vowels had not begun their change.

Moreover, after the ME period, as we shall see, a great deal of direct evidence is available to us, so that our conjectures from about 1500 onwards can be made with considerable certainty. We may often, therefore, be able to deduce from our knowledge of pronunciation in the sixteenth century the stage probably reached in the ME period in the development of a sound from OE. The OE [iː] sound in *time*, for example, was beginning to be diphthongized generally very early in the sixteenth century. It is reasonable to suppose (even if other evidence to support the theory did not exist) that *time* still had a relatively pure [iː] for much of the ME period.

Finally, the metre of verse reveals the stress accent of words. It is for this reason that we know that French words, in Chaucer's verse, generally retained their original accentual pattern, e.g. *courage* [kuˈraːdʒə], and that the accent shift in these cases is a phenomenon of at least late ME.

(4) *Early Modern English.*—The same sources of evidence which we have already considered remain available for the eModE period, roughly A.D. 1450–1600. The introduction of printing brought standardization of spelling and already the spoken and written forms of the language were beginning to diverge. But individuals, especially in their private correspondence, often used spellings of a largely phonetic kind, in the same unsophisticated and logical way that children still do. If a modern child writes *He must have gone* as *He must of gone*, he is only representing the phonetic identity of the weak forms of *have* and *of* ([əv]), an identity which he will learn to ignore when he adopts the conventional spelling distinction. In the same way, if fifteenth- and sixteenth-century spellings show the word *sweet* occasionally written as *swit*, it may be assumed that this original ME [eː] was by now so close that it could be represented by *i* with its Latin value. Or again, the spelling form *sarvant* instead of *servant* reflects an open type of vowel in the first syllable which was current throughout the eModE period in such words. Moreover, the conventional adoption of an unphonetic spelling can sometimes provide us with positive evidence as to its value: thus, when words like *delight* (formerly *delite*) began to be spelt with *gh*, this spelling form *gh* clearly no longer had the consonantal fricative

value which it had formerly represented in *light*, since there never was a consonantal sound between the vowel and final [t] in *delight*. We may conclude, therefore, that *gh* no longer had its former phonetic significance in words such as *light*. Care must, of course, be taken to identify the increasing number of learned or technical spellings adopted by printers. The initial letter group *gh* in *ghost* (OE *gast*) indicates no change in pronunciation—*goose* was also sometimes spelt *ghoose* in this period. Again, spellings which aim at revealing the etymology (true or false) of a word must usually be discarded as phonetically valueless, e.g. *debt, island*. It is above all from the writings of individuals that some general indications concerning sound changes may be gathered and used to supplement evidence derived from other sources.

Rhymes, too, continue to be useful as complementary evidence. A rhyme such as *night :: white* confirms the view that postvocalic *gh* no longer had a consonantal value; or again, *can :: swan* suggests that the rounding of [a] after [w] had not yet taken place. Yet, just as in the case of ME, rhymes must be treated with caution, more particularly as eye-rhymes were doubtless beginning to become more prevalent. There is, however, in Elizabethan literature, additional evidence afforded by the frequent use of puns, which usually rely for their effect upon similarities, if not identities, of phonetic value. Shakespeare, for instance, plays on the phonetic identity of such pairs as *suitor, shooter* (both capable of being pronounced [ʃuː tər]) and *known, none* (both [noːn]); such puns suggest that the pronunciation of the two words was commonly sufficiently close to make an immediate impression upon an audience.

The most important and fruitful evidence for this period is, however, of a *direct* kind. It is provided by the published works of the contemporary grammarians, orthoepists, and schoolmasters, some of whom have been mentioned above (§6.1 *et seq.*). They are of unequal value and their statements have often to be interpreted in the light of other evidence; yet they provide us with the first direct descriptive accounts of the pronunciation of English. From the sixteenth century onwards, our conclusions rely more and more on their descriptive statements and less on clues of an indirect kind. Sometimes there appears to be a conflict between the phonetic probabilities, the statements of grammarians, and evidence from other sources. Frequently the solution must be that there existed at any time a variety of current pronunciations, resulting from differences of dialect, generation, fashion, and place in society, in the same way that a description of PresE (even that of a restricted area such as the south of England) would have to take into account a large number of variants.

The following representative systems are conjectures of one possible set of phonemes current in the period in question.

6.2.5   Classical OE Sound System

Vowels   iː, ɪ; yː, y   uː, ʊ
   eː, ɛ   oː, ɔ
   æː, æ
   ɑː, ɑ (allophone [ɒ] before nasal consonants)
   [ə] occurs in certain weakly accented syllables.

Diphthongs   ɛːə, ɛə; eːə, eə

Consonants   p, b, t, d, k, g (allophone [ɣ])
   tʃ, dʒ
   m, n (allophone [ŋ] before velar consonants)
   l, r
   f, θ, s (medial allophones [v, ð, z])
   ʃ, h (allophones [x, ç])
   j, w

Consonants may be long or short.

The spellings *hn, hl, hr, hw* may be interpreted as phoneme sequences /h/ + /n, l, r, w/; alternatively, if it is assumed that *h* is here an indication of voiceless [n̥, l̥, r̥, w̥], these four sounds may be counted as contrastive, i.e. of phonemic status.

Text (St. John, Chapter 14, verses 22, 23)

22. ˈjuːdɑs ˈkwæθ toː hɪm. næs nɑː seː ˈskarɪɔt. ˈdrɪçtən, ˈhwæt ɪs jəˈwordən θæt θuː wɪlt θeː ˈsylfnə jəˈswʊtɛlɪjən ʊs næs ˈmɪddɑnɛərdə.

23. seː ˈhæːlənd ˈɒndswarɔdə ɒnd ˈkwæθ hɪm; jɪf hwɑː meː ˈlʊvaθ heː ˈhɪlt miː nə ˈspræːtʃə ɒnd miːn ˈfædər ˈlʊvaθ hɪnə ɒnd weː ˈkʊmaθ toː hɪm ɒnd weː ˈwyrkɪaθ ˈɛərdʊŋstoː wə mɪd hɪm.

Authorized Version

22. Judas saith unto him, not Iscarioth, Lord, how is it that thou wilt manifest thyself unto us, and not unto the world?

23. Jesus answered and said unto him, If a man love me, he will keep my words; and my Father will love him, and we will come to him, and make our abode with him.

6.2.6   ME Sound System

Vowels   iː, ɪ   uː, ʊ
   eː   oː
   ɛː, ɛ   ɔː, ɔ
   aː, a   ɑː
   [ə] occurs in unaccented syllables.

Diphthongs   ɛi, (æi), ɔi, iu, (eu), ɛu, ɔu, (ɑu)

Consonants   p, b, t, d, k, g, tʃ, dʒ
   m, n (allophone [ŋ] before velar consonants)
   l, r

f, v, θ, ð, s, z, ʃ, h (allophones [x, ç])
j, w (allophone [ʍ] after /h/)
Text (from the *Prologue* to the *Canterbury Tales*)[1]
'hwan θat 'aːprɪl ˌwɪθ hɪs 'ʃuːrəs 'soːtə
θə 'drʊxt ɔf 'martʃ haθ 'pɛrsəd ˌtoː ðə 'roːtə,
and 'baːðəd 'ɛːvrɪ 'væin ɪn 'swɪtʃ lɪ'kuːr
ɔf 'hwɪtʃ vɛr'tiu ɛn'dʒɛndərd ˌɪs θə 'fluːr,
hwan ˌzɛfɪ'rʊs ɛːk ˌwɪθ hɪs 'sweːtə 'brɛːθ
ɪn'spiːrəd 'haθ ɪn 'ɛːvrɪ 'hɔlt and 'hɛːθ
θə 'tɛndər 'krɔppəs, ˌand ðə 'jʊŋə 'sʊnnə
'haθ ɪn ðə 'ram hɪs 'halvə 'kʊrs ɪ'rʊnnə,
and 'smaːlə 'fuːləs 'maːkən ˌmɛlɔ'diːə,
θat 'sleːpən 'aːl ðə 'nɪçt wɪθ 'ɔːpən 'iːə—
sɔː 'prɪkəθ 'hɛm naː'tiur ɪn 'hɪr kʊ'raːdʒəs—
θan 'lɔːŋgən 'fɔlk toː 'gɔːn ɔn ˌpɪlgrɪ'maːdʒəs.

6.2.7 Early ModE Sound System

Vowels   iː, ɪ   uː, ʊ
          eː   oː, ɤ
          ɛː, ɛ   ə
          æ   ɒː, ɒ
/eː/ was probably /iː/ or /ɛː/ in certain types of pronunciation
[a] and [aː] occur as contextual variants of /æ/ and /ɒː/.
Diphthongs əi, əu, iu (or ju), eu, ou, ɔi, ui, ɛi
Consonants p, b, t, d, k, g, tʃ, dʒ
             m, n, ŋ
             l, r
             f, v, θ, ð, s, z, ʃ, ʒ (later, in medial positions), h
             j, w (allophone [ʍ] after /h/)
Text (*Macbeth*, Act II, Scene 1)
             nəu oːər ðə wɤn haːf wɤrld
             neːtər siːmz dɛd, ənd wɪkɪd dreːmz əbjuːz
             ðə kɤrtɛind sliːp: wɪtʃkraft sɛlɪbreːits
             peːl hɛkəts ɒfərɪŋz: ənd wɪðərd mɤrdər,
             əlarəmd bəi hɪz sɛntɪnəl, ðə wʊlf,
             huːz həulz hɪz watʃ, ðɤs wɪθ hɪz stɛlθɪ peːs,
             wɪθ tarkwɪnz rævɪʃɪŋ strəidz, tuːərdz hɪz dɪzəin
             muːvz ləik ə goːst. ðəu sjuːr[2] ənd fɛrm-sɛt ɛrθ
             heːr nɒt məi stɛps, hwɪtʃ wɛi ðɛi wɒːk, fər feːr

---

[1] The type of transcription given here is slightly archaic for Chaucer's pronunciation, e.g. long consonants were probably lost in later ME and such words as *and*, *that*, would have had a weak vowel.
[2] Alternatively, [ʃ] or [ʃj] for [sj].

ðəi vɛrɪ stoːnz prɛːt əv məi hwɛːrəbəut,
ənd tɛːk ðə prɛzənt hɒrər frəm ðə təim,
hwɪtʃ nəu sjuːts[1] wɪð ɪt.

6.2.8   PresE Sound System

Vowels   iː, ɪ   ʊ, uː
          e
                  ɜː, ə   ɔː
          æ
              ʌ
                  ɑː   ɒ
Diphthongs eɪ, əʊ, aɪ, aʊ, ɔɪ, ɪə, ɛə, ʊə
Consonants p, b, t, d, k, g
             tʃ, dʒ, (tr, dr)
             m, n, ŋ
             l, r
             f, v, θ, ð, s, z, ʃ, ʒ, h
             j, w

6.2.9   Modifications in the English System[2]

1. *Distribution of phonemes.*—The similarities of the systems given above may obscure the fact that the same sound, especially as far as the vowels are concerned, may occur in different categories of words according to the period. Thus [uː], now in *food*, occurred in OE in words such as *town*; [iː], now in *team*, occurred in OE in *time*. The following summary shows some of the most striking changes affecting the vowel quality used in particular word categories:—

	OE	ME	eModE	PresE
time	iː	iː	əi	aɪ
sweet	eː	eː	iː	iː
clean	æː	ɛː	eː (or [iː])	iː
stone	ɑː	ɔː	oː	əʊ
name	ɑ	aː	ɛː	eɪ
moon	oː	oː	uː	uː
house	uː	uː	əu	aʊ
love	ʊ	ʊ	ɤ	ʌ (or [ä])

2. *Vowel changes.*—Several trends become apparent from a study of quality changes:—

[1] See footnote 2 on previous page.
[2] It should be noted that some present-day regional accents preserve distinctions or realizations manifested at earlier stages in the history of the language. See J. C. Wells, *Accents of English*, Cambridge University Press, 1982.

(*a*) OE long vowels have closed or diphthongized; on the other hand, PresE [əʊ] and [eɪ] show signs of monophthongization.

(*b*) Certain phonemic qualitative oppositions have coalesced, e.g. OE /eː/ and /æː/; the originally separate diphthongs of *day* and *way*; the diphthong of *know* with the originally pure vowel of *no*; the diphthongs of *day*, *way* with the former pure vowel of *name*; OE /yː, y/ with /iː, ɪ/ (or /ɛ/).

(*c*) Short vowels, with the notable exceptions of the OE /ɑ, æ/ (and the short diphthong /ɛə/) in open syllables and ME /ʊ/, have remained relatively stable.

(*d*) Rounded front vowels have been lost, e.g. OE /yː, y/ and earlier /øː, ø/.

(*e*) The loss of post-vocalic [r] in the eighteenth century gave rise to the PresE centring diphthongs /ɪə, ɛə, ʊə/, the pure vowel /ɜː/ and introduced /ɑː, ɔː/ into new categories of words (*cart*, *port*).

(*f*) Vowels under weak accent are increasingly obscured to [ə] or [ɪ], or are elided.

(*g*) Changes of quantity affected certain phonemes in particular contexts or sets of words, e.g. lengthening of OE /ɑ, æ, ɛə/ in open syllables and of ME /a/ + /f, θ, s/; and shortening of ME /oː/ in words like *good*, *book*, *blood*, and of ME /ɛː/ in such words as *breath*, *death*, *head*.

3. *Consonant changes.*—Changes in the consonantal system are less striking, but the following may be noted:—

(*a*) Double (or long) consonants within words were lost by late ME; certain other consonant clusters cease to be tolerated, e.g. /hl, hr, hn/ by ME and /kn, gn, wr/ in the eModE period; post-vocalic /r/ was lost in much of the south-east of England in the eighteenth century.

(*b*) Allophones of certain phonemes have been lost, e.g. the [ɣ] allophone of /g/ in late OE and the [x, ç] allophones of /h/ in eModE.

(*c*) New phonemes have emerged, e.g. /tʃ, dʒ/ in OE, /v, ð, z/ in ME, and /ŋ, ʒ/ in eModE; in addition, /h/ is used initially in words of French origin where, originally, no [h] sound was pronounced (*habit*, *herb*, *humble*, etc).

6.3 Standards of Pronunciation

The English are to-day particularly sensitive to variations in the pronunciation of their language. The 'wrong accent' may still be an impediment to social intercourse or to advancement or entry in certain professions. Such extreme sensitivity is apparently not paralleled in any other country or even in other parts of the English-speaking world. There are those who claim, from an elocution standpoint, that modern speech is becoming increasingly slovenly, full of 'mumbling and mangled vowels and missing consonants'. Alexander Gil and others made the same kind of complaint in the seventeenth century. There is, in fact, no evidence to suggest that the degree of obscuration and elision, often characteristic of a dynamic stress language such as English, is markedly greater now than it has been for four centuries. Of more significance—social as well as linguistic—is the attitude which regards a certain set of sound values as more acceptable, even more 'beautiful' than another. Judgments of this kind suggest that there is a standard for comparison; and it is clear that such a standard pronunciation does exist, although it has never been explicitly imposed by any official body. A consideration of the origins and present nature of this unofficial standard goes some way towards explaining the controversies and emotions which it arouses at the present day.

6.3.1   The Emergence of a Standard

It is clear that the controversy does not centre around the written language: the spelling of English was largely fixed in the eighteenth century; the conventions of grammatical forms and constructions as well as of the greater part of our vocabulary have for a long time been accepted and adhered to by the majority of educated English speakers. Indeed, the standardization of the written form of English may be said to have begun in the ninth and tenth centuries. But there has always existed a great diversity in the spoken realizations of our language, in terms of the sounds used in different parts of the country and by different sections of the community. On the one hand, the sounds of the language always being in process of change, there have always been at any one time disparities between the speech sounds of the younger and older generations; the advanced speech of the young is traditionally characterized by the old as slovenly and debased. On the other hand, especially in those times when communications between regions were poor, it was natural that the speech of all communities should not develop either in the same direction or at the same rate; moreover, different parts of the country might be exposed to different external influences (e.g. foreign invasion) which might influence the phonetic structure of the language in a particular area. English has, therefore, always had its *regional* pronunciations in the same way that other languages have been pronounced in a variety of ways for basically geographical reasons. Yet, at the same time, especially for the last five centuries, there has existed in this country the notion that one kind of pronunciation of English was preferable socially to others; one regional accent began to acquire *social* prestige. For reasons of politics, commerce, and the presence of the Court, it was the pronunciation of the south-east of England, and more particularly to that of the London region, that this prestige was attached. The early phonetician John Hart notes (1569) that it is in the Court and London that 'the flower of the

English tongue is used' . . . 'though some would say it were not so, reason would we should grant no less: for that unto these two places, do daily resort from all towns and countries, of the best of all professions, as well of the own landsmen, as of aliens and strangers . . .'. Puttenham's celebrated advice in the *Arte of English Poesie* (1589) recommends the 'usual speech of the Court, and that of London and the shires lying about London within 60 miles and not much above. . . . Northern men, whether they be noblemen or gentlemen, or of their best clerks, (use an English) which is not so courtly or so current as our Southern English is'. Nevertheless, many courtiers continued to use the pronunciation of their own region; we are told, for instance, that Sir Walter Raleigh kept his Devon accent. The speech of the Court, however, phonetically largely that of the London area, increasingly acquired a prestige value and, in time, lost some of the local characteristics of London speech. It may be said to have been finally fixed, as the speech of the ruling class, through the conformist influence of the public schools of the nineteenth century. Moreover, its dissemination as a class pronunciation throughout the country caused it to be recognized as characteristic not so much of a region as of a social stratum. With the spread of education, the situation arose in which an educated man might not belong to the upper classes and might retain his regional characteristics; on the other hand, those eager for social advancement felt obliged to modify their accent in the direction of the social standard. Pronunciation was, therefore, a marker of position in society.

6.3.2   The Present-day Situation

(1) Great prestige is still attached to this implicitly accepted social standard of pronunciation. Often called *Received Pronunciation* (RP), the term suggesting that it is the result of a social judgment rather than of an official decision as to what is 'correct' or 'wrong', it has become more widely known and accepted through the advent of radio. The BBC formerly recommended this form of pronunciation for its announcers mainly because it was the type which was most widely understood and which excited least prejudice of a regional kind. Indeed, attempts to use announcers who had a mild regional accent provoked protests even from the region whose accent was used. Thus, RP often became identified in the public mind with 'BBC English'. This special position occupied by RP, basically educated Southern British English, has led to its being the form of pronunciation most commonly described in books on the phonetics of British English and traditionally taught to foreigners.

(2) Nevertheless, it cannot be said that RP is any longer the exclusive property of a particular social stratum. This change is due partly to the

influence of radio in constantly bringing the accent to the ears of the whole nation, but also, in considerable measure, to the modifications which are taking place in the structure of English society. Just as the sharp divisions between classes are beginning to disappear, so the more marked characteristics of regional speech and, in the London region, the popular forms of pronunciation, are tending to be modified in the direction of RP, which is equated with the 'correct' pronunciation of English. This tendency does not, as yet, mean that regional forms of pronunciation show signs of disappearing, but it has to be recognized that those who wish, for any reason, to modify their speech have models of RP always readily available to their ears while, at the same time, the social inhibitions concerning movement between classes, which were formerly so strongly operative, no longer, in the face of the standardization of society as a whole, exert the same pressure.

Moreover, it must be remarked that some members of the present younger generation reject RP because of its association with the 'Establishment' in the same way that they question the validity of other forms of traditional authority. For them a real or assumed regional or popular accent has a greater (and less committed) prestige. It is too early to predict whether such attitudes will have any lasting effect upon the future development of the pronunciation of English. But, if this tendency were to become more widespread and permanent, the result could be that, within the next century, RP might be so diluted that it could lose its historic identity and that a new standard with a wider popular and regional base would emerge. Such a change is made more likely through the recent more permissive attitude of the BBC (and of the commercial television companies) in their choice of announcers, several of whom now have markedly non-RP or non-British accents.

(3) Certain types of regional pronunciation are, indeed, firmly established. Some, especially Scottish English speech, are universally accepted; others, particularly the popular forms of pronunciation used in large towns such as London, Liverpool, or Birmingham, are generally characterized as ugly by those (especially of the older generations) who do not use them. This rejection of certain sounds used in speech is not, of course, a matter of the sounds themselves: thus, [paɪnt] may be acceptable if it means *pint*, but 'ugly' if it means *paint*. It is rather a reflection of the social connotations of speech which, though they have lost some of their force, have by no means disappeared. Indeed, RP itself can be a handicap if used in inappropriate social situations, since it may be taken as a mark of affectation or a desire to emphasize social superiority.[1] It may be said, too, that if improved communications and radio have spread the availability of RP, these same influences have rendered other forms of pronunciation less

---

[1] For accounts of attitudes to RP, see works by Giles in the bibliography.

remote and strange. An American pronunciation of English, for instance, is now completely accepted in Britain; this was not the case at the time when the first sound films were shown in this country, an American pronunciation then being considered strange and even difficult to understand. Speakers of RP are becoming increasingly aware of the fact that their type of pronunciation is one which is used by only a very small part of the English-speaking world.

(4) A comparison of two regional or social types of pronunciation will reveal differences of several kinds (as mentioned in §5.3.6):—

(a) *realizational differences* the system, i.e. the number of distinctive (phonemic) terms operating, may be the same, but the phonetic realizations of the phonemes may be different: e.g. the RP opposition between the vowels of *bet* and *bat* may be maintained, but the realization of both vowels is much more open than in RP (see §7.9.4), so that the sound of /æ/ may come near to that of one type of RP /ʌ/ (see §7.9.5); or when, as in Cockney, an allophone [ʔ] in unaccented positions represents /t/ and often /k/ or /p/ (see §8.2.7); or when the final allophone of /l/ is [l] rather than [ɫ] (see §8.7);

(b) *systemic differences* (i.e. differences in *phoneme inventory*) The system may be different, i.e. the number of oppositions may be smaller or greater: e.g. the RP /æ/−/ɑː/ opposition may not be present in those Ulster or Scottish forms which do not distinguish *Sam* and *psalm*; or when RP /aɪ/ homophones, as in *side* and *sighed* may be differentiated qualitatively or quantitatively, as in some types of Scottish English; or when, as in some forms of RP, /ɑː/ levels with /aɪ/ and /aʊ/ before /ə/ (see §7.11); or when the presence of /g/ after [ŋ] in such a word as *sing* deprives [ŋ] of its phonemic status (see §8.6.2);

(c) *lexical differences* (i.e. differences of *lexical incidence*) The system may be the same, but the incidence of phonemes in words is different: e.g., in those Northern forms which have the RP opposition /uː/−/ʊ/, but nevertheless use /uː/ in *book, took*, etc. (see §§7.9.9− 10); or when /ɒ/ is used instead of /ʌ/ in *one, among*, etc., though the opposition /ɒ/−/ʌ/ exists (see §7.9.5); or when the choice of phoneme is associated with the habits of different generations, e.g. /ɔː/ for /ɒ/ in *off, cloth, cross*, etc. (see §7.9.7) or /eɪ/ for /ɪ/ in *Monday, holiday*, etc.

(d) *distributional differences* The system may be the same, but the phonetic context in which certain phonemes occur may be limited: e.g. in RP /r/ has a limited distribution, being restricted in its occurrence to pre-vocalic position as in *red* or *horrid*. Accents which display this limited distribution of /r/ are referred to as *non-rhotic accents*, whilst those in which /r/ has a full distribution (such as most American and Scottish accents) are termed *rhotic*. In the latter accents /r/ occurs pre-consonantally and pre-pausally as well as pre-vocalically, thus *part* and *car* will be pronounced /pɑːrt/ and /kɑːr/ whereas in non-rhotic accents the pronunciation will be /pɑːt/ and /kɑː/ respectively. See §8.8.

(5) It is possible to make some classification of the various kinds of British English pronunciation in the light of the regional and social criteria mentioned. Features of *regional* pronunciation, without any contamination from RP, will be found in highly educated and less educated speech (to be distinguished briefly as *educated regional* and *popular regional*); lack of conventional education will often, in addition, reveal itself by the use of non-standard grammatical and lexical forms. On the other hand, a regional pronunciation may be termed *modified* when it has adopted certain characteristics of RP, e.g. the adoption of the RP [ɑː] in words such as *ask, after, path* rather than [a]. In the case of the speech of the Greater London population, there are a great number of gradations to be noted amongst the popular regional forms, through educated regional to RP; such varying mixtures of regional and RP are typical of the suburban districts.

Within RP itself it is convenient to distinguish three main types: the *conservative* RP forms used by the older generation and, traditionally, by certain professions or social groups; the *general* RP[1] forms most commonly in use and typified by the pronunciation adopted by the BBC; and the *advanced* RP forms mainly used by young people of exclusive social groups—mostly of the upper classes, but also, for prestige value, in certain professional circles. In its most exaggerated variety, this last type would usually be judged 'affected' by other RP speakers, in the same way that all RP types are liable to be considered affected by those who use unmodified regional speech. Advanced pronunciations, however, whenever they are not the result of temporary fashion, may well indicate the way in which the RP system is developing and be adopted in the future as general RP, e.g. the originally advanced ('affected') diphthong in *home*, involving increased centralization and a tendency towards monophthongization, seems likely to become general in a very short time.

These various types of British English pronunciation may be summarized as follows:—

Regional	(Reg)	*Received*	(RP)
educated	(educ)	conservative	(cons)
popular	(pop)	general	(gen)
modified	(mod)	advanced	(adv)

6.3.3   Notions of Correctness

Within RP, those habits of pronunciation that are mostly firmly established tend to be regarded as 'correct' whilst innovation tends to be stig-

[1] Also called *mainstream* RP.

matized. Thus conservative forms tend to be most generally accepted, sometimes even by those who themselves use other pronunciations.

Where the stress patterns or the phonemic structure of disparate words is concerned, this attitude may result in a speaker's use of the conservative variant in a formal situation and the use by the same speaker of a less well-established variant in more casual speech, e.g. the avoidance of /ˌverɪˈfaɪəbl/ (*verifiable*) and /ˈdʒʊərɪŋ/ (*during*) in more formal speech and their replacement with the more conservative /ˈverɪfaɪəbl/ and /ˈdjʊərɪŋ/. It may be of interest that the pronunciation /ˈdʒʊərɪŋ/ with initial coalescent assimilation was acknowledged by Daniel Jones in the *English Pronouncing Dictionary* in the 1960's and noted as long ago as 1913 by Robert Bridges in his *Tract on English Pronunciation*. Nevertheless, there is still resistance to accepting coalescence word-initially in stressed syllables.

Where realizational variation (below the level of the phoneme) is affected, most speakers are unaware of their own changing speech patterns. Objections to the use of the glottal stop are often made, its use being popularly associated with Cockney speech, and yet its occurrence as a realization of preconsonantal /t/ is increasingly frequent within the speech of the middle and younger generations of RP speakers. (See §8.2.7 b.)

It is not, therefore, possible to be certain that the resistance to accepting certain innovatory pronunciations will be overcome. For that reason, it is most realistic here to sketch only the more widespread general trends.

6.3.4 Current Changes[1]

(1) *Realizational changes*

Several vowels should be mentioned here, notably /æ/ with an opener and more retracted quality than in more conservative speech, /eə/ with a monophthongal realization in some environments, a tense word-final /ɪ/ with a somewhat closer quality than is traditional, and /aɪ/ and /aʊ/ sharing the same central open starting point. (See Chapter 7 for detailed discussion of each vowel.)

As has been mentioned in §6.3.3, the realization of preconsonantal /t/ as a glottal stop is increasingly common in present-day RP. (See §8.2.7.)

(2) *Systemic changes*

The one recent systemic change that is now more or less completed is the loss of /ɔə/ from the phoneme inventory.

[1] For more detail, see Susan Ramsaran, 'RP: Fact *and* Fiction'.

(3) *Lexical changes*

There is a strong trend towards selecting /ə/ instead of unstressed /ɪ/ in weak syllables, the choice of /ə/ being particularly favoured after /l/ and, more especially, /r/, e.g. *angrily* /ˈæŋgrɪlɪ/ > /ˈæŋgrəlɪ/. For further detail and examples, see §7.9.2.

The other noticeable trend is the replacement of /ʊə/ by /ɔː/ in many common words, e.g. *poor* /pɔː/, *sure* /ʃɔː/, though /ʊə/ still retains its phonemic status, its contrastive function being illustrated in the speech of most speakers by such sets as *doer, dour, door* /ˈduːə, dʊə, dɔː/ (the first, as in *evil-doer*, serving to illustrate that [ʊə] is not merely a realization of /uː/ + /ə/).

(4) *Distributional changes*

The most noteworthy trend concerning a regular change in the occurrence of a phoneme is the loss of /j/ after alveolar consonants in such words as *allude* /əˈljuːd/ > /əˈluːd/, *luminous* /ˈljuːmɪnəs/ > /ˈluːmɪnəs/, *supersede* /ˌsjuːpəˈsiːd/ > /ˌsuːpəˈsiːd/. /j/ is most commonly dropped after /l/ and /s/ (as, indeed, it was long ago after /r/). In the case of the alveolar plosives + /j/, coalescence is now increasingly common except initially in a stressed syllable where /t/ + /j/ or /d/ + /j/ tend to be retained. Thus *educate* /ˈedjuːkeɪt/ > /ˈedʒuːkeɪt/, *statuesque* /ˌstætjuːˈesk/ > /ˌstætʃuːˈesk/.

(5) *Stress changes*

Certain patterns may be detected, especially in the change affecting adjectives in *-able/-ible* and *-ary/-ory*. In both classes of words, the stress tends now to fall later in the word, thus ˈapplicable > apˈplicable, ˈexplicable > exˈplicable, ˈjustifiable > ˌjustiˈfiable, ˈfragmentary > fragˈmentary, ˈmandatory > manˈdatory.

Similarly, the feminine suffix *-ess* increasingly attracts primary stress in words like *counˈtess, lioˈness, prioˈress, stewarˈdess*.

Other current changes do not display such regular patterns and it remains to be seen which variant pronunciations at present co-existent will persist.

6.3.5   English Worldwide

Finally, it has to be recognized that the role of British RP in the English-speaking world has changed very considerably in the last century. Over 300 million people now speak English as a *first* language, and of this number native RP speakers form only a minute proportion; the majority of English speakers use some form of American pronunciation.

However, despite the discrepancy in numbers, RP continues for historical reasons to serve as a model in many parts of the world, and, if a model is used at all, the choice is still effectively between RP and American pronunciation.

A disturbing development concerns the use of English in the Indian and African continents, where English functions as a *lingua franca* superimposed upon a large number of indigenous languages. In these regions, the interference of the indigenous phonological structures is such that the efficacy of spoken English as a means of communication is fast being lost; intelligibility tends to fall to a low level within quite restricted areas, for reasons which are primarily phonetic. Even where some reasonable degree of intelligibility is retained within any one country, there are serious deficiencies of a mainly phonological kind which become apparent when English is used as an international means of communication. It is conceivable that, if such divergencies are not restrained, communication will be easily maintained only in the written language. It is for this reason of universal importance that efforts should be made to relate these developing forms of English pronunciation to either a British or American model.

When it is a question of teaching English as a *second* language, there is clearly much greater adherence to one of the two main models. Most teaching textbooks describe either RP or American pronunciation, and allegiances to one or the other tend to be traditional or geographical: thus, for instance, European countries continue on the whole to teach RP, whereas much of Asia and South America follow the American model (see also Chapter 12).

7

The English Vowels

7.1 The Distinctive Vowels

A large number of vowel sounds (either relatively pure or clearly gliding in nature) have a distinctive syllabic function in English. Their oppositional nature may be established by the commutations possible in such series as:—

heed	feel	bead	pea
hid	fill	bid	*city, except*
head	fell	bed	
had		bad	
hard		bard	par
hod			
hoard	fall	board	paw
hood	full		
	fool	booed	
		bud	
heard	furl	bird	purr
			sitter, accept
	fail	bayed	pay
	foal	bode	
hide	file	bide	pie
	fowl	bowed	
	foil		
		beard	peer
		bared	pair
			poor

A general phonetic assessment of the qualities of syllabic vowels, in terms of the Cardinal values, may be made from the following examples, in word final and non-final positions:—

	Final.	*Non-final.*	*Quality.*	*Notation.*
I. *Short*				
	city	bid	retracted, raised [e]	ɪ
	—	bed	between [e] and [ɛ]	e

92

Final.	*Non-final.*	*Quality.*	*Notation.*
—	had	between [ɛ] and [a]	æ
—	hod	[ɒ]	ɒ
—	hood	advanced, raised [o]	ʊ
—	bud	centralized, raised [a]	ʌ
sitt*er*	*a*ccept	central	ə[1]

II. *Long* (*relatively pure*)

pea	bead	lowered [i] or [ɪi] or [ij]	iː
do	food	lowered [u] or [ʊu] or [uw]	uː
par	bard	fronted [ɑ]	ɑː
paw	board	raised [ɔ]	ɔː
purr	bird	mid central	ɜː

III. *Long* (*diphthongal glides, with prominent 1st element*)

(*a*) glide to [ɪ]

pay	paid	lowered [e] → [ɪ]	eɪ
pie	hide	[a] → [ɪ]	aɪ
coy	coin	[ɔ] → [ɪ]	ɔɪ
(—	ruin	[ʊ] → [ɪ]	ʊɪ)[2]

(*b*) glide to [ʊ]

low	load	mid [ə] → [ʊ]	əʊ
bough	bowed	between [a] and [ɑ] → [ʊ]	aʊ

(*c*) glide to half-open [ə]

peer	beard	[ɪ] → [ə]	ɪə
pair	bared	[ɛ] → [ə]	ɛə
(soar	soared	[ɔ] → [ə]	ɔə)
poor	moored	[ʊ] → [ə]	ʊə

Notes

(1) Most people will make a considerable difference of length between the vowels in *hat*, *had*, and *bad* when the words are said in isolation, the vowel in *bad* being as long as any of the 'long' vowels. Nevertheless, this length is not a constant distinctive feature of the vowel, but is rather dependent upon the context or is characteristic of the pronunciation of particular words. Since the short vowel is the more common and because the distribution of [æ] is like that of the other short vowels, the vowel is included in the table of short vowels.

(2) The so-called pure vowels of *bee* and *do* frequently contain a glide between two distinct elements, especially in a final position. Nevertheless, because the qualities of the elements are phonetically closely related and because a non-gliding vowel is not uncommon or

[1] Occuring only in unaccented syllables (see §7.9.12).
[2] [ʊɪ] may be regarded as a reduced version of /uː/ + /ɪ/ (see §7.11).

thought to be un-English, these two vowels may on phonetic grounds be included in the 'long, pure' list.

(3) Many speakers do not possess the distinction *saw/soar*, i.e. pure vowel *v.* diphthong, but use the pure vowel in both cases. For this type of pronunciation, class III (*c*) will be reduced by one item.

(4) The vowel glide [ʊɪ] exemplified by such words as *ruin, fluid, suet*, is of extremely rare occurrence within one syllable, though it may occur as a reduced form of [uː] + the suffix *-ing*, i.e. in the case of the juxtaposition of two syllables, e.g. in *doing*. The sequence [ʊ] + [ɪ] may occur across word boundaries as a result of smoothing e.g. *newest* [njʊɪst]. (See §7.11.) Since this diphthong carries such a low distinctive weight, it may be omitted from the list of contrasting vowels.

(5) Of the short vowels, it is to be noted that [ə] occurs only in unstressed syllables.

7.2 Vowel Glides with a Non-prominent 1st Element

We find that the sounds (semi-vowels) [j] and [w] regularly occur in positions preceding most of the above basic vocalic elements:—

[j + ɪ] yiddish	[w + ɪ] wit
[j + e] yet	[w + e] wet
[j + æ] yap	[w + æ] wax
[j + ɒ] yacht	[w + ɒ] watch
[j + ʊ] you (weakly stressed)	[w + ʊ] wood
[j + ʌ] young	[w + ʌ] won
[j + ə] fail*ure*	[w + ə] were (weakly stressed)
[j + iː] yeast	[w + iː] week
[j + uː] youth	[w + uː] woo
[j + ɑː] yard	[w + ɑː] waft
[j + ɔː] yawn	[w + ɔː] wall
[j + ɜː] yearn	[w + ɜː] word
[j + eɪ] yea	[w + eɪ] way
[j + aɪ]	[w + aɪ] wide
[j + ɔɪ] yoick	[w + ɔɪ] quoit
[j + əʊ] yeoman	[w + əʊ] woe
[j + aʊ] yowl	[w + aʊ] wound
[j + ɪə] year	[w + ɪə] weir
[j + ɛə] (Yare)	[w + ɛə] wear
[j + ʊə] lure	[w + ʊə]

Since [j] and [w] are often purely vocalic from a phonetic standpoint, being rapid vocalic glides from [i] and [u] positions, it is possible to consider their combination with other vowels as constituting:—

(*a*) a rising diphthong, in the case of [j] or [w] followed by a short vowel or long, relatively pure, vowel, i.e. vowel glides in which the 2nd element rather than the 1st is the more prominent;

(b) a triphthong, in the case of [j] or [w] followed by a vocalic glide, i.e. a vowel glide in which there are three vocalic elements, the central one being most prominent.

Nevertheless, since such combinations affect almost all our previously established basic vowels and glides, it would add enormously to our inventory of basic vowels if we were to include these combinations in our list. Moreover, these [j] and [w] elements function very much as if they were consonants, marginally rather than centrally in a syllable, and, indeed, in cases such as the [j] in *tune* or the [w] in *queen* tend to be voiceless and to have the friction which is phonetically characteristic of a consonant. For these reasons, it is more convenient to treat initial [j] and [w] as separate from the vocalic nucleus of the syllable and to include them in the list of consonants.

Note

It is possible, in the same way, to express the brief [ɪ] and [ʊ] elements occurring post-centrally in the diphthongal glides as consonantal /j, w/ following a simple syllabic element. Thus, if [iː] and [uː] are interpreted as glides and [ʊɪ] similarly included, the following statement may be made: [iː] = /ij/, [eɪ] = /ej/; [aɪ] = /aj/; [ɔɪ] = /ɔj/; [ʊɪ] = /ʊj/; [əʊ] = /əw/; [aʊ] = /aw/; [uː] = /uw/, with, in addition, the following possibilities of /j/ or /w/ preceding and following the central syllabic element: /jij, wij, jej, wej, waj, jɔj, wɔj, jəw, wəw, wuw, juw, wuw/. In the present treatment of RP vowels, however, such post-central [ɪ, ʊ] elements are regarded as vocalic rather than consonantal because:—

(i) they do not have a distribution after all vocalic elements as general as that which we find in the case of pre-central /j, w/;

(ii) they are in RP very weakly articulated (compared with pre-central /j, w/) and may be realized merely as a prolongation of the central syllabic vowel quality, e.g. [e̞ː] as a variant of [eɪ];

(iii) they have none of the fricative (phonetically consonantal) allophones characteristic of pre-central /j, w/ following /p, t, k/.

7.3   Glides to [ə]

Similarly, glides to [ə] are treated here as composite vocalic units, since in general RP [ə] combines with a syllabic vowel element only after [ɪ, ɛ, ʊ] and may with some RP speakers be realized merely as an extension of the preceding syllabic vowel element.

7.4   Vowel Length

There are traditional relationships between short and long vowels in English, as illustrated by the following words:—

bid and *bead*	/ɪ-iː/
good and *food*	/ʊ-uː/
cad and *card*	/æ-ɑː/
cod and *cord*	/ɒ-ɔː/
(*for*)*ward* and *word*	/ə-ɜː/

Notes

(*a*) Only in the case of /ə-ɜː/ can there be said to exist an opposition solely of length and even in this case it has to be stated that /ə/ occurs only in unaccented syllables, whereas /ɜː/ can occur in syllables carrying primary or secondary accent.

(*b*) In the other cases the opposition between the members of the pairs is a complex of quality and quantity; and of the two factors it is likely that quality carries the greater contrastive weight. Indeed, in the particular case of the *cad/card* opposition, both vowels may be equally long.

(*c*) In a transcription which sets out to show explicitly certain phonetic characteristics, it would seem advisable to indicate especially the qualitative opposition, at the same time noting quantity by means of the length mark.

(*d*) Such insistence on purely phonetic characteristics, as compared with what is phonemically relevant, is justified when variations of vowel length are taken into consideration. In *accented syllables* the so-called long vowels are fully long when they are final or in a syllable closed by a lenis consonant, but they are considerably shortened when they occur in a syllable closed by a fortis consonant.[1] Thus:—

/iː/ in *beat* is only about half as long as the /iː/ of *bee* or *bead* and may, in fact, be of approximately the same length (duration) as the /ɪ/ vowel of *bid*;

/uː/ in *boot* is only about half as long as the /uː/ of *do* or *food* and again has about the same duration as the /ʊ/ vowel in *good*.

This is also true of /ɑː, ɔː/ and /ɜː/. If the length sign [ː] is retained merely to show length, then it is possible when desirable to indicate phonetic variations thus:—

bee, bead, beat, bid	[biː, biːd, bit, bɪd]
do, food, boot, good	[duː, fuːd, but, gʊd]
car, card, cart, cat	[kɑː, kɑːd, kɑt, kæt]

---

[1] This reduction process is referred to by J. C. Wells as *pre-fortis clipping*.

caw, cord, caught, cod   [kɔː, kɔːd, kɔt, kɒd]
her, heard, hurt   [hɜː, hɜːd, hɜt]

A single length mark may be used to indicate a further intermediate duration if so desired e.g. [biˑn].

(*e*) The same considerable shortening before fortis consonants applies also to the diphthongs:—

cf. *play, played, plate*
row, road, wrote
tie, tide, tight
cow, loud, shout
boy, noise, voice
fear, fears, fierce
scare, scares, scarce

Here the variation of length might, if desirable, be shown explicitly thus: [pleːɪ, pleːɪd, pleɪt].

Since lenis /m, n, l/ do not have fortis counterparts, the variation of length in the preceding vowel does not apply when they close a syllable; /ŋ/ does not normally close a syllable containing a long vowel or diphthong.

(*f*) Many phoneticians have measured the duration of English vowels in different phonetic contexts. A recent study of this kind is that of Kalevi Wiik (1965), which shows, in summary, the following average relationships in csecs. in accented monosyllables:

	Final or + lenis C	*+ nasal C*	*+ fortis C*
Short vowels	17·2	13·3	10·3
Long vowels	31·9	23·3	16·5
Diphthongs	35·7	26·5	17·8

(i) /æ/ is not included in the category of short vowels, because of the special length often associated with it (see §7.9.4), but is classified separately as 'neutral'. The following measurements for /æ/ are given by Wiik: + lenis fricative—25·2 csecs., + lenis plosive + 21·6 csecs., + nasal—19·6 csecs., + fortis fricative—16·5 csecs., + fortis plosive— 15·0 csecs.

(ii) An example of the relationship of two vowels traditionally paired (/iː/∿/ɪ/) shows the following typical descending durations:— /iː/ + lenis fricative—36· csecs., /iː/ + lenis plosive—28·5 csecs., /iː/ final—28·0 csecs., /iː/ + nasal—19·5 csecs., /ɪ/ + lenis fricative —18·6 csecs., /ɪ/ + lenis plosive—14·7 csecs., /iː/ + fortis fricative —13·0 csecs., /iː/ + fortis plosive—12·3 csecs., /ɪ/ + nasal—11·0 csecs., /ɪ/ + fortis fricative—8·3 csecs., /ɪ/ + fortis plosive—7·3 csecs. Thus, it will be seen that /iː/ is typically shorter in a word such as *seat* (12·3 csecs.) than /ɪ/ in a word such as *hid* (14·7 csecs.).

7.5   Phonemic Interpretation of the Vowels

There are a number of ways, all equally legitimate, of allocating the English vowels to phonemic categories. Most phonemic analyses will apply to only one type of English, but some attempts[1] have been made to provide categories which are valid for all kinds of English. It is doubtful, given the tremendous variety of pronunciations of English throughout the world, whether such analyses are desirable or wholly successful. But several solutions have been proposed for RP and of these no solution can be said to be more 'correct' than another. The choice of solution will depend largely on the purpose of the analysis. Thus, one kind of analysis will be convenient when dealing with the synthesis of speech, whereas others will be appropriate when it is a question of teaching English pronunciation to a particular nationality or when a comparative study of various types of English is being made. In particular, it is not always to be assumed that the most economical analysis is the most useful.

The main variations of interpretation concern the treatment of the long vowels and diphthongs. Daniel Jones, for instance, lays emphasis upon the distinctive importance of length. His analysis of the English vowels is concerned not only with categories of quality (phonemes), but also postulates two categories of length (long and short *chronemes*). He is able in this way to distinguish the members of the pairs [iː, ɪ; ɔː, ɒ; uː, ʊ; ɜː, ə] by means of a length, or chronemic, feature, to which the qualitative contrast is subordinate. These vowels are, therefore, long and short members of four phonemes and the pairs may be written in the simplified form /iː, i; ɔː, o; uː, u; əː, ə), where the sign [ː] indicates conventionally not only length but also a related quality. It is possible on purely logical grounds to extend this analysis to include, despite the considerable qualitative separation, the pair [ɑː, æ], which might then be expressed /aː, a/. Such an analysis reduces the number of vowel phonemes by five. A transcription based on this analysis is simple for the phonetician to handle, but may have the disadvantage of being less explicit and more conventional than a beginner or student may require.

Other types of analysis begin with a basis of the short vowels. The basic vowel phonemes of English may, for instance, then be considered as /ɪ, e, æ, ɔ, ʊ, ʌ, ə/, simplified in notation to /i, e, a, o, u, ʌ, ə/. The remaining vowel sounds are then regarded either as sequences of these elements or as compounds of one of these elements + /j/ or /w/ (see §7.2). Thus:—

> [iː] is interpreted as /ɪ + i/ or /ij/
> [uː]   ″   ″   /ʊ + u/ ″ /uw/
> [eɪ]   ″   ″   /e + ɪ/ ″ /ej/

[1] See G. L. Trager and H. L. Smith, *An Outline of English Structure*, 1951.

[aɪ]	″	″	/a + ɪ/ ″	/aj/
[ɔɪ]	″	″	/o + ɪ/ ″	/oj/
[əʊ]	″	″	/ə + ʊ/ ″	/əw/
[aʊ]	″	″	/a + ʊ/ ″	/aw/

and [ɪ, e, ʊ] combine with /ə/ to give /ɪə, eə, ʊə/. There remains the difficulty of [ɑ:, ɔ:, ɜ:]. These may be treated symmetrically as glides to [ə] (e.g. /aə, oə, əə/), or as sequences of /a + a, o + o, ə + ə/, or again, as /a + r, o + r, ə + r/. This last notation would repose, as far as RP is concerned, upon the complicated convention that, in a pronunciation which regularly uses an 'intrusive' [r] when [ɑ:, ɔ:, ə] occur finally in a word followed by another word beginning with a vowel (e.g. *Shah of* . . ., *saw it, vanilla ice*), the sequences /a + r, o + r, ə + r/ are to be treated as [r]-less vowels before a pause or when a consonant follows. Thus, *far* /far/ = [fɑ:]; *saw* /sor/ = [sɔ:]; *cur* /kər/ = [kɜ:]; *palm* /parm/ = [pɑ:m]; *lawn* /lorn/ = [lɔ:n]; *colonel* /kərnl/ = [kɜ:nl]. Such words as *carry, lorry, periphery* /'kari, 'lori, pə'rifəri/ would be distinguished from *starry, story, furry* thus: /'starri, 'storri, 'fərri/. [ɑ:, ɔ:, ɜ:] may also be analysed as /a, o, ə/ + /h/,[1] /h/ being realized here in vocalic form in complementary distribution with its more usual consonantal articulation. It will be seen that, although the basic phonemic units may be reduced in number to seven, an analysis in terms of composite units is complicated and may be remote from a speaker's impression of reality and that the resultant notation will depend for interpretation on a great number of conventions.

7.6 Conclusion

The solution used in the following pages is one which does not seek ultimate economy of categories, gives a good deal of explicit information in the notation about the phonetic realization of the phonemes (especially the relation of quality and quantity), and takes some account of the RP speaker's own feelings as to the distinctive vowel counters which he uses. We will, therefore, treat twenty vocalic phonemes, made up of the following vowels or vowel glides:—

> 7 *short*: /ɪ, e, æ, ɒ, ʊ, ʌ, ə/
> 5 *long* (relatively pure): /i:, u:, ɑ:, ɔ:, ɜ:/
> 3 *long* (glides to [ɪ]): /eɪ, aɪ, ɔɪ/
> 2 *long* (glides to [ʊ]): /əʊ, aʊ/
> 3 *long* (glides to [ə]): /ɪə, ɛə, ʊə/

---

[1] See G. L. Trager and H. L. Smith, op. cit.

7.7 Description of the Vowels

In the following detailed descriptions the RP vowel phonemes will be treated in a sequence based upon their quality relationships, viz.:—

/iː, ɪ, e, æ, ʌ, ɑː, ɒ, ɔː, ʊ, uː, ɜː, ə/
/eɪ, aɪ, ɔɪ, əʊ, aʊ/
/ɪə, ɛə, ʊə/

The treatment of each vowel will include:—

(1) Illustrations of spelling forms of variations of length of long vowels and diphthongs, of vowels followed by 'dark' [ɫ], and comparative examples for practising variation of length or differentiation from neighbouring phonemes.

(2) Articulatory description and an assessment of quality in relation to the Cardinal Vowels. (In all cases, unless otherwise stated, the soft palate will be assumed to be in its raised position, the vocal folds vibrating, and the tongue tip behind the lower teeth.) Remarks on distributional features in the word and syllable.

(3) Indications of some of the chief variants—regional and social.

(4) Remarks on the principal historical sources of the vowel.

(5) Difficulties encountered by foreign learners, with appropriate advice.

7.8 Acoustic Features

The following formant regions[1] (in cps) are representative of RP relatively pure vowel values (excluding /ə/, whose quality varies greatly according to its situation and for which an average value may be taken to be equivalent to that of /ɜː/); in vowel synthesis, a combination of variable F1 and F2, with a fixed F3 in the region of 3,000 cps, gives good results.

	F1	F2	F3
/iː/	280	2,620	3,380
/ɪ/	360	2,220	2,960
/e/	600	2,060	2,840
/æ/	800	1,760	2,500
/ʌ/	760	1,320	2,500
/ɑː/	740	1,180	2,640
/ɒ/	560	920	2,560
/ɔː/	480	760	2,620
/ʊ/	380	940	2,300

[1] The formant figures given here were provided by Dr. J. C. Wells, University College, London, from an unpublished thesis on the formant structure of RP vowels.

| /u:/ | 320 | 920 | 2,200 |
| /ɜ:/ | 560 | 1,480 | 2,520 |

7.9 Short and Long (Relatively Pure) Vowels

7.9.1   /iː/

(1) *Examples.*—*ee*—tree, cheese, canteen
e—complete, be, these
ea—leaf, reason, sea
ie—piece, field, siege
ei, ey—seize, key, receive
i—machine, police, prestige, suite

(*Note*: /iː/ in 'quay, people, Beauchamp' /ˈbiːtʃəm/.)

Long [iː]—see, seed, seen; fee, feed, fees
Reduced [i]—seat, feet, piece, lease, beef, reach
Compare [iː], [i]—bead, beat; seize, cease; leave, leaf; liege, leach;
            Eden, eaten
[ɫ] *following*—feel, meal, field, eels.

(2) *Description.*—The front of the tongue is raised to a height slightly below and behind the close front position; the lips are spread; the tongue is tense, with the side rims making a firm contact with the upper molars. The quality is nearer to *C*[i] (with the glide mentioned below) than to *C*[e]. /iː/ does not normally occur in a syllable closed by /ŋ/.

(3) *Variants.*—The vowel is often noticeably diphthongized, especially in final positions. A slight glide from a position near to [ɪ] is

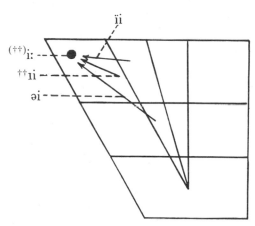

Fig. 9.—/iː/ and variants.

common amongst RP speakers, being more usual than a pure vowel. Any glide having a starting point in the central area is, however, dialectal, that is, characteristic of a regional accent; a glide of the type [ïi] is characteristic of the local pronunciation of Liverpool and Birmingham, whereas a lower central starting point may be heard in popular London English and many other dialects. The use of a pure vowel in a final position may be typical of an over-cultivated pronunciation; this is not the case, however, in Scottish English, where the vowel generally does not have the length charac-teristic of RP and is not, therefore, subject to the same tendency to diphthongization.

(4) *Chief Sources.*—(a) Many of the words now said with /iː/ have had this vowel since at least 1500; these are frequently spelt with *ee* or *ie*. Such words are those which in OE[1] had a long vowel in the region of C [e] (*cheese*, *sleeve*); or had developed C [eː] from a diphthong [eːə] (*deep*, *thief*); or from a more open vowel near C [ɛː] (*deed*, *needle*); or from [øː] (*geese*, *green*), or from a lengthening of [ɪ] in an originally open syllable (*week*) or [ɛ] before [ɫd] (*field*). In addition, a number of words from OF [ie] through AN [eː] (*siege*, *niece*, *grief*).

Foreign words with [iː], adopted after the English [iː] vowel from the above sources had become established, fell in with the usual pronuncia-tion of *ee* in English and sometimes changed their spelling from *i* to *ee* (*esteem*, *canteen*; *machine*, *routine*).

(*b*) Another group of words, frequently spelt now with *ea*, finally developed [iː] at about the end of the seventeenth century. Their chief origins are: an OE long vowel in the region of C [ɛː] (*sea*, *leave*, *teach*); an OE diphthong [ɛːə] (*leaf*, *stream*, *east*); an OE short [ɛ] lengthened in originally open syllables (*meant*, *eat*); and, in addition, a large number of words from OF [ai, ɛi] through AN [ɛː] (*please*, *eager*, *season*, *peace*).

(5) *Advice to foreign learners.*—This vowel should give little diffi-culty to foreign learners, all of whom will have in their language a vowel of approximately the same quality. Their own vowel may not have the diphthongization which is typical of RP, but they should attempt to imitate this glide only with caution, since any exaggeration will sound vulgar or dialectal. More important is the reduction of length before fortis consonants, as exemplified above, since the differentiation between two words such as *seize* and *cease* is achieved more by the variation of the vowel length than by the quality of the final consonant. The reduced form of the vowel should, however, remain relatively tense and not be confused with [ɪ].

---

[1] For meaning of abbreviations see §6.2.

7.9.2   /ɪ/

(1) *Examples.*—*i*—sit, fifth, with, rich
                    y—city, rhythm, symbol
                    e—pretty, needed, wicket, wicked, except, careless,
                        houses
                    ie—ladies, cities
                    a—village, private

(*Note*: 'build' /bɪld/, 'Sunday' /ˈsʌndɪ/ (and the other days of the
week), 'business' /ˈbɪznɪs/, 'women' /ˈwɪmɪn/, 'minute' (n.) /ˈmɪnɪt/,
'England' /ˈɪŋglənd/.)

Compare [iː], /ɪ/— feel, fill; seen, sin; bead, bid
              [i], /ɪ/—least, list; reach, rich; sheep, ship; week, wick;
                    feet, fit
              [iː], [i], /ɪ/—seed, seat, sit; league, leak, lick; seized,
                    ceased, cyst
[ɫ] *following*—will, hill, milk, built, film, kiln

(2) *Description.*—The short RP vowel /ɪ/ is pronounced with a part
of the tongue nearer to centre than to front raised just above the half-
close position; the lips are loosely spread; the tongue is lax (compared
with the tension for /iː/), with the side rims making a light contact with
the upper molars. The quality is that of a centralized C[e] = [ë]. /ɪ/
may occur in all positions in the word.
    (3) *Variants.*—The degree of closeness and centralization varies
according to the accentual force falling upon the vowel and its position
in the word (cf. the realizations of /ɪ/ in the word *visibility*, those of
syllables 1 and 3 being near to the sound described above, those of
syllables 2 and 4 being somewhat more centralized, and that of the last
syllable sometimes having a tongue position lower than half-close[1]). A
trend towards /ə/ in unaccented syllables, traditionally with /ɪ/, is
becoming increasingly noticeable among RP speakers of the middle and
younger generations.
    (a) In some terminations, /ə/ is now more common than /ɪ/, e.g.
-ity: /-ətɪ/ rather than /-ɪtɪ/ as in *sincerity, quality*, etc.
-itive: /-ətɪv/ rather than /-ɪtɪv/ as in *positive, fugitive*, etc.
-ily: /-əlɪ/ rather than /-ɪlɪ/ (especially after /r/) as in *merrily, pri-
        marily* and also *easily, happily*, etc.
-ate: often /-ət/ rather than /-ɪt/ as in *fortunate, chocolate*, etc.
        (Words such as *magistrate, candidate* sometimes have /-eɪt/; cer-
        tain words such as *climate, private* still show /-ɪt/ as dominant.)
-ible: /-əbl/ (as for *-able*) rather than /-ɪbl/ as in *possible, visible*, etc.

---

[1]Note that /ɪ/ is not opposed to /e/ in final, open syllables, where such lowering is
particularly apt to occur in conservative speech.

-em: /-əm/ rather than /-ɪm/ or /-em/ (conservative RP) as in *problem*, *system*, *item*, etc.

(b) In the case of other weak syllables, both /ɪ/ and /ə/ are heard from RP speakers, e.g.

-ess: /-ɪs/ or /-əs/ as in *useless*, *goodness* (/-əs/ being preferred by the younger generation); in cases where *-ess* is strongly felt as a feminine suffix and may be accented by some speakers, /-es/ may be used whether the syllable is strong or weak.

-ace: /-ɪs/ or /-əs/ as in *necklace*, *palace*, *preface*, with an increasing tendency to /-əs/.

(c) In other cases, /ɪ/ remains dominant, e.g.

-age: predominantly /-ɪdʒ/ in *manage*, *village*, etc. (Recent French borrowings such as *barrage*, *camouflage*, etc., tend to have /-ɑː(d)ʒ/.)

-et: predominantly /-ɪt/ especially following /k, g, tʃ, dʒ/ as in *pocket*, *target*, *hatchet*, *budget*, etc. However, the endings *-let*, *-ret* often have /-ət/, as in *bracelet*, *scarlet*, *claret*, *garret*, etc.

be-: /ɪ/ is more common than /ə/, as in *begin*, *between*, *become* (though in *believe*, *belong*, *behave*, etc., /ə/ is often heard).

(*Note*: Although *se-*, as in *sedition*, *select*, may sometimes have /sə-/ rather than the more usual /sɪ-/, *de-*, as in *deposit*, *deny*, *desire*, etc., is almost invariably with /dɪ-/.)

In the preceding cases, no significant oppositions between /ɪ/ and /ə/ were involved. Where an opposition exists, it might be expected that there would be some pressure to retain the /ɪ/ ∿ /ə/ distinction, as in the inflected forms *offices* /-ɪz/ v. *officers* /-əz/ or *chatted* /-ɪd/ v. *chattered* /-əd/. The neutralization of this opposition is typical of several non-RP forms of English, but the opposition is still strongly maintained by RP speakers. On the other hand, potential oppositions between /ɪ/ and /ə/ in such pairs as *effect*, *affect* and *except*, *accept* are commonly lost in favour of /ə/.

In final, unaccented positions, as in *city*, *Mary*, *lady*, etc., /ɪ/ is increasingly replaced in the speech of the younger generations by a short variety of /iː/. In popular London speech, this final /iː/ will usually be realized as a glide [əi]. On the other hand, in most kinds of English, /ɪ/ may replace /iː/ in the unaccented (weak) forms of such words as *he*, *she*, *been*, etc.

Some RP speakers—especially those using the type of speech which has the [ë] variety in unaccented syllables—will diphthongize /ɪ/ towards [ə] particularly in accented monosyllables, e.g. in *big*, *did*, *thin*, *wish*, etc.

(4) *Chief sources.*—As in the case with many of the PresE short vowels, /ɪ/ has shown considerable stability since OE. The OE forms of such words as *ship*, *quick*, *give*, *drink*, *this*, *smith*, etc., probably had vowels similar in quality to that of RP /ɪ/. PresE /ɪ/ also derives from

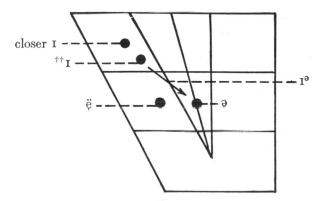

FIG. 10.—/ɪ/ and variants.

OE [iː] (*wisdom, bliss*); from OE [y] (*king, kiss, bridge*); from OF [i] (*rich, simple, mirror, prison*). In addition, OE or OF [e] + nasal consonant has often given PresE /ɪ/ (*England, string, ink, chimney*).

In unaccented syllables many new cases of /ɪ/ have arisen, notably from [ɛ] or [ə] in such suffixes as *-es, -ed, -ness, -less, -est* (*horses, waited, kindness, hopeless, biggest*); from formerly accented syllables with [ɐ] or [aː] (*hostess, prophet, village, Highgate, orange*); in prefixes and medial vowels spelt with *e* (*describe, enquire, despite, before, declare, expect, elegant, benefit*); from earlier diphthongs (*forfeit, sovereign, fountain, journey*); and many cases of PresE final /ɪ/ from earlier [iː > əi] with a secondary accent (*charity, majesty, memory, heavenly*).

(5) *Advice to foreign learners.*—It is of the utmost importance that a proper qualitative relationship should be maintained between /iː/ and /ɪ/. Many languages have a short variety of [i], e.g. French, Italian, etc., but one which is likely to be too tense and close for the English /ɪ/; others, e.g. Polish or Russian, have a centralized type of [ɪ] which has too much of an [ə] quality for English; others, e.g. German, have a type of [ɪ] near to the English variety but yet often too tense. Speakers of those languages which possess a vowel of the *C*[e] type (which is approximately on the same level as the English /ɪ/) should modify this sound in the direction of [ə]; alternatively, a [y] sound, as in French *but*, said with relaxed spread lips, will come near to the English /ɪ/ as in *bit*.

Of equal importance is the quantitative relationship of /iː/ and /ɪ/. Once the correct quality of /ɪ/ has been acquired, most learners can distinguish *bead* [biːd] from *bid* [bɪd], where the distinction is a complex of quality and quantity. But an opposition of the sort *beat* [bit] —*bit* /bɪt/, where the difference of vowel length is insignificant, is more difficult. Three types of vowel should, therefore, be practised:

close, tense, long [iː] (*bead*); close, tense, short [i] (*beat*); and the half-close, lax, short [ɪ] (*bit, bid*), as in the comparative examples given in (1) above.

The fact that /ɪ/ occurs very frequently in unaccented syllables should also be noted, since an unreduced vowel in the weak syllables of such words as *village, waited, fountain, describe,* may seriously deform the accentual pattern for the native listener.

7.9.3　　　　　　　　　　/e/

(1) *Examples.*—*e*—set, bed, went
　　　　　　　ea—dead, head, breath
　　　　　　　a—many, Thames

(*Note*: the following words with /e/—'says, said, bury, Geoffrey' /ˈdʒefrɪ/, 'Leicester' /ˈlestə/, 'friend, ate, again' /əˈgen/ or /əˈgeɪn/.)

Compare.—/ɪ/, /e/—sit, set; tin, ten; will, well; disk, desk
　　　　　　/iː/, /ɪ/, /e/—neat, knit, net; reach, rich, wretch; reed,
　　　　　　　　　　　　　rid, red; feel, fill, fell
[ɬ] *following*—well, sell, else, health, elm, held

(2) *Description.*—For the short RP /e/, the front of the tongue is raised between the half-open and half-close positions; the lips are loosely spread and are slightly wider apart than for /ɪ/; the tongue may have more tension than in the case of /ɪ/, the side rims making a light contact with the upper molars. The quality lies between that of *C*[e] and that of *C*[ɛ] = [ḙ] or [ɛ̞]. /e/ does not occur in final, open syllables.

(3) *Variants.*—The general RP variety of /e/ tends to be closer to *C*[e] rather than to *C*[ɛ]. This may be due to the fact that /æ/ in this type of pronunciation is only a very little more open than half-open; /e/

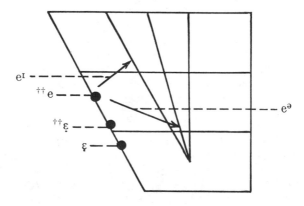

FIG. 11.—/e/ and variants.

is, therefore, considerably closed in order to maintain the qualitative distinction. An /e/ which is very near to *C* [e] is typical of over-refined RP and may often be associated with the closer type of /æ/. If /e/ has a quality nearer to the half-open type, as in some kinds of RP and many regional dialects, /æ/ in turn is more open.

An advanced RP form of /e/ is diphthongized in the direction of [ə], e.g. *men, said, get* [meᵊn, seᵊd, geᵊt]. Such diphthongization is often characterized as 'affected'. Another diphthongal glide, in this case in the direction of [ɪ], is heard in popular London speech, particularly in monosyllables closed by a lenis consonant, e.g. *bed, leg* [beᶦd, leᶦg].

(4) *Chief sources.*—The majority of PresE /e/ forms can be traced to: OE [ɛ] (*bed, neck, edge, best*); shortened OE [eː] (*fed, met*); OE [eːə] (*theft, friend*); OE [æ] (*let, ever, flesh*); eModE shortening of ME [ɛː] (*bread, death, deaf*); OE [y] (*bury, merry*)—the Kentish [ɛ] form having been adopted; OF [ɛ] (*debt, press, accept, second, member*). Some modern /e/ forms previously vacillated between /e/ and /æ/ (*then, when, any, many*); others derive from a former [ɛi] (*Leicester, said, says*).

(5) *Advice to foreign learners.*—This vowel may present difficulties to those foreign learners whose native language possesses two types of *e* usually of *C* [e] and *C* [ɛ] qualities. Very often such a learner equates the English /e/ with his own half-open variety, thereby using a vowel of too open a quality which might be confused by RP listeners with /æ/. He should therefore modify his vowel in the direction of his own, closer, *C* [e] sound.

7.9.4   /æ/

(1) *Examples.*—*a*—sat, hand, lamp, rash, marry
           ai—plait, plaid
Compare.—/e/, /æ/—pet, pat; peck, pack; said, sad; ten, tan;
           lend, land; merry, marry
    /ɪ/, /e/, /æ/—bid, bed, bad; big, bed, bag; tin, ten,
           tan; miss, mess, mass
    [æː] (before /b, d, g, dʒ/) and [æ]—cab, cap; bad, bat;
           bag, hack; badge, batch
[ɫ] *following*—alphabet, shall (accented form), Pall Mall, balcony,
           scalp

(2) *Description.*—The mouth is slightly more open than for /e/; the front of the tongue is raised just below the half-open position, with the side rims making a very slight contact with the back upper molars; the lips are neutrally open. In the south of England /æ/ is often produced with considerable constriction in the pharynx, the tongue itself having rather more tension than is the case for /e/. The quality is nearer to *C* [ɛ] than to *C* [a] = [ɛ̞].

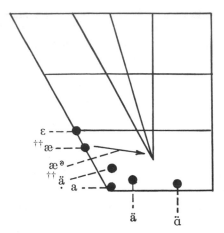

FIG. 12.—/æ/ and variants.

This traditionally short vowel appears to be lengthened in RP especially before the lenis consonants /b, d, g, dʒ, m, n/ (*cab, bad, bag,
badge, jam, man*). Though vowels are regularly longer before syllable-
final lenis consonants than before fortis consonants, the lengthened [æ]
is equivalent in quantity to the longest varieties of /iː, ɑː, ɔː, ɜː/. In
terms of the system, this may be due to the increasing qualitative pro-
ximity in RP of /e/ and /æ/, the extra length serving as an additional
distinctive feature; the qualitative-quantitative relationship of /æ/-/e/
tends, therefore, to become of the same type as /iː/-/ɪ/, i.e.
[æː]-[æ]-[e] (*bad, bat, bet*), cf. [iː]-[i]-[ɪ]. /æ/ does not occur in final,
open syllables.

(3) *Variants.*—/æ/, the most open of the RP true front vowels, is
closer than fully open. This compression of the front phonemes is a
characteristic of RP, but regional dialects often show a greater qualitative separation of these phonemes. Thus, where RP /e/ and /æ/ have
the values described, other types of English will have values *C*[ɛ] and
C[a], or [ä] or even [ɑ̈]. (A more relaxed /æ/—in the region of *C*[a]—is
also heard amongst children in the south of England who otherwise
have an RP system and who, later in life, adopt the tenser and closer
variety of /æ/. Such a lowered /æ/ is maintained by many young
women, although /ʌ/ continues to be realized as the low front variety
described in §7.9.5. The result can be a confusion of /æ/ and /ʌ/, the
meaning being resolved by the context.)

On the other hand, that type of refined RP (and also popular
London) which realizes /e/ in the *C*[e] region also raises /æ/ to
approximately *C*[ɛ]. In this case, the /e/-/æ/ opposition is reinforced
either by the lengthening of /æ/ already mentioned, or by a diph-

thongization of /æ/ towards [ə], e.g. *bad, cat* [bæ³d, kæ³t] (cf. similar diphthongization of /ɪ/ and /e/).

(4) *Chief sources.*—PresE /æ/ derives regularly from: OE [ɑ] (*man, cat*); OE [æ] (*sad, back, apple*); OE [ɛːə] (*shadow, shank*); shortened OE [ɑː] (*hallow*) or OE [æː] (*ladder, mad*)—this shortening being earlier than that of the *death* type where ME [ɛː] > eModE [ɛ]; Scandinavian [ɑ] (*flat, anger*). Also regularly from OF [a] (*lamp, manner, passage*) and occasionally from OF [au] (*salmon, savage*). Most earlier sequences of the type [wa-] have given [wɒ-] or [wɔː-] (*watch, quality, water*); /æ/ is, however, retained in some cases, especially when a velar consonant follows (*wag, wax, twang*).

(5) *Advice to foreign learners.*—The main difficulty for all those whose own languages have a less complex vowel system lies in the establishment of the qualitative oppositions /ɪ/-/e/-/æ/, while at the same time using a type of /æ/ which is not too open. Foreign learners often find it helpful to make a conscious constriction of the pharynx for /æ/. The opposition /e/-/æ/ may be emphasized by making use of the length component now a feature of RP /æ/ in certain contexts, e.g. in *men, man*; *bed, bad*. Where length may not be so distinctive, e.g. in *net, gnat*, the quality separation should not be such that /æ/ comes near to C[a]; if this does occur, there is the danger, in the south of England, of confusion with the /ʌ/ of *nut*.

7.9.5   /ʌ/

(1) *Examples.*—*u*—sun, cut, dull
  o—son, come, among, one, done, month, colour, monkey, mother, nothing, Monday, onion, London, oven
  ou—country, southern, couple, enough, young
  oo—blood, flood
  oe—does

(*Note:* many earlier *u* spellings have been changed to *o*, especially in the vicinity of *u, m, n, w, v*, e.g. in 'love, some, won', etc.)

Compare /æ/, /ʌ/—cat, cut; lamp, lump; match, much
  /ɑː/, /ʌ/—cart, cut; barn, bun; march, much
  /ɒ/, /ʌ/—cot, cut; fond, fund; wander, wonder
  /ɜː/, /ʌ/—curt, cut; fern, fun; turf, tough
[ɫ] *following*—dull, result, pulse, bulge, bulb

(2) *Description.*—The short RP /ʌ/ is articulated with a considerable separation of the jaws and with the lips neutrally open; the centre of the tongue (or a part slightly in advance of centre) is raised just above the fully open position, no contact being made between the

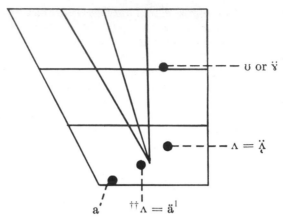

FIG. 13.—/ʌ/ and variants.

tongue and the upper molars. The quality is that of a centralized and slightly raised *C*[a] = [ä]. /ʌ/ does not occur in final, open syllables.

(3) *Variants.*—The variety of /ʌ/ described above is that of general RP as used by younger people, especially in the London region. Conservative RP speakers will often use a more retracted vowel, i.e. an unrounded and centralized type of *C*[ɔ]. Regional speech of the London area has for /ʌ/ an open front vowel very close to *C*[a]. In northern regional speech, a half-close back vowel is used, with or without lip-rounding, i.e. [ʊ] or [ɤ̈]. In the same type of English, some words, spelt with *o* and with /ʌ/ in RP, may have /ɒ/, e.g. *one, among, nothing.* In RP both /ʌ/ and /ɒ/ may be heard (for an earlier /ʌ/) especially in words where the spelling form *o* is followed by a nasal consonant in an accented syllable, e.g. *Montgomery, Bromley, accomplish, combat, Tonbridge, comrade, conduit, constable.*

(4) *Chief Sources.*—PresE /ʌ/ is the regular development of the ME fronted back, half-close lip-rounded [ʊ]. This in turn derives from OE and OF sources: OE [ʊ] (*sun, love, nut, ugly*); shortened OE [uː] (*us, husband, utter, enough, scum*); OE [y] (*blush, much, such*); OF [u] (*cousin, touch, dozen, colour, cover*) and OF [u] or [o] before a nasal consonant (*number, sum, front, uncle, comfort, money*); OF [y] (*just, judge, public, study*). The ME [ʊ] sound has, in those words where we now have /ʌ/, i.e. [ä], been lowered and has lost its lip-rounding. The unrounded stage appears to have been reached by or during the seventeenth century in the London region, though at that time the lowering may not have been very considerable, i.e. a centralized variety of *C*[ɤ].

[1] This maybe transcribed as [ɐ]. See I.P.A. chart on pp. 340–1.

A half-open stage (probably somewhat fronted from true back) may be postulated for the eighteenth century, with the quality C[ʌ̈] typical of the nineteenth century, the tongue position being by the end of the century rather below half-open. Thus, PresE /ʌ/ is the result of qualitative changes greater than those which have affected any other short vowel. Further progress into the front region is likely to be inhibited by the presence of the /æ/-/ɑ:/ opposition, unless the lengthening of /æ/ becomes general, in which case /ʌ/ may fulfil the function of a short open front vowel opposed to both /æ:/ and /ɑ:/.

It is to be noted that some PresE /ʌ/ forms have developed from a ME [oː] (*flood, blood, done, month, glove, mother*). ME [oː] must have shortened in time for it to develop, as ME [ʊ] ([o] being similar in quality to [ʊ]), to PresE /ʌ/. The words *one, none*, should regularly give PresE */ɔun, nɔun/, this being the normal development of ME [ɔː]; this regular sound change is attested into the seventeenth century and is retained in the PresE form of the compound *alone*. The modern RP form with unrounded /ʌ/ derives from a shortened, raised ME vowel, preceded in the case of *one* by a glide [w], originally considered a vulgarism; the vowel of *none* results from an analogy with that of *one*.

(5) *Advice to foreign learners.*—Most languages possess a vowel of the [a] or [ä] type. The English /ʌ/ should be related to this quality and, indeed, good results can often be obtained in teaching by transcribing the English vowel as /a/ rather than with the traditional /ʌ/ symbol. In this way prejudice induced by the frequent orthographic spelling with *u* or *o* is avoided; if the quality thus obtained is too fronted, it may be modified in the direction of /ɑ:/. A proper qualitative distinction should be maintained between the vowels in such words as *match, much, march; ban, bun, barn; hat, hut, heart*. Above all, there should be no lip-rounding such as might produce a type of front open-rounded [œ].

7.9.6   /ɑ:/

(1) *Examples.*—*a*—pass, after, bath, tomato, father, branch, camouflage
ar—part, car, march
ear—heart, hearth
er—clerk, Derby, sergeant
al—calm, palm, half
au—aunt, laugh

(*Note*: /ɑ:/ in 'vase', and in recent borrowings from French in which the French -*oir* [waːr] is realized in English as /wɑ:/, e.g. 'reservoir'.)

Long—bar, far, farm, large, hard
Reduced—part, last, raft, lark, arch

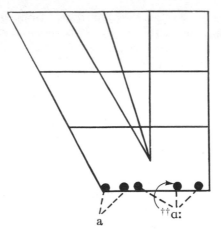

FIG. 14.—/ɑː/ and variants.

Compare [ɑː], [ɑ]—card, cart; parse, pass; carve, calf; large, larch
/ɑː/, /ʌ/—cart, cut; harm, hum; march, much; lark,
luck; dance, dunce
[ɫ] *following*—snarl, gnarled, Charles

(2) *Description*.—This normally long vowel is articulated with a considerable separation of the jaws and the lips neutrally open; a part of the tongue between the centre and back is in the fully open position, no contact being made between the rims of the tongue and the upper molars. The quality is somewhat nearer to C[ɑ] than to C[a]. Although there is a difference of length according to whether it occurs in a syllable closed by a fortis or lenis consonant, the shortening effect of a closing fortis consonant is not as marked as for other long vowels; thus, whereas the reduced [i] of *beat* may be of similar length to the /ɪ/ of *bit* the reduced [ɑ] of *cart* is somewhat longer than the short /ʌ/ of *cut*. /ɑː/ does not normally occur before /ŋ/.

(3) *Variants*.—A variety of /ɑː/ retracted near to the quality of C[ɒ] is typical of some advanced (refined) RP speakers; a variety of /ɑː/ fronted towards C[a] is also heard among some RP speakers and in many regional types of English, e.g. in Australian English.

Many regional forms of English do not make the RP distinction between /æ/ and /ɑː/, using for both a vowel in the region of C[a]. These forms of English not having developed historically in the same way as RP (see following section), two main word groups show a variance from RP system: firstly, those cases of /ɑː/ in RP in a syllable closed by /f, θ, s/ or by /m, n/ + consonant (*craft, laugh, bath, pass, sample, branch*); secondly, those words, originally with vowel + /r/, now with /ɑː/ in RP (*cart, hard, large, heart, sergeant*). In the first group a short front vowel is typical of many regional types of English, though some dialects will use a lengthened front vowel; in the second group, either [a] or [æ] + [r] is used or a lengthened [aː] or [æː]. Thus the distinction *cat-cart* may be [kat]-[kart] or [kat]-[kaːt], etc.

In RP, too, there are many cases of indecision between /æ/ and /ɑː/ in words where the vowel is followed by /f, θ, ð, s/ or by nasal consonant + consonant. Thus, *lather, transfer, elastic, plastic*, are words in which /æ/ or /ɑː/ may be heard. Sometimes the use of /ɑː/ as against the more usual general RP /æ/, e.g. in *gymnastic, Atlantic*, denotes either a special, conservative RP or a form of regional speech over-normalized towards RP. One of the main vocalic features which, in the popular mind, distinguishes RP from much regional speech is the presence in the former of the /æ/-/ɑː/ opposition, especially in the category of words containing vowel + /f, θ, s/ or nasal consonant + consonant. There are, however, in RP many cases where /æ/ rather than /ɑː/ occurs in these phonetic contexts: e.g. /ɑː/ in *pass, glass, can't, grant, chance, dance, demand, slander, caster, aghast*, but /æ/ in *passage, ass, cant, rant, finance, romance, expand, random, aster, gas*.

(4) *Chief sources.*—Of the many sources of RP /ɑː/, the following are the most important: (*a*) through loss of post-vocalic /r/ in the eighteenth century, short [a] or [æ] > /ɑː/ (*charm, march*); the [a] or [æ] in question may often result from ME [ɛ] (*far, star, heart*) as well as from an earlier French [ɛ] (*farm, clerk, sergeant*); (*b*) lengthening of [a] or [æ] > /ɑː/, due to the following fricative (especially /f, θ, s/), incipient at the end of the seventeenth century (*staff, after; path, bath; pass, ask, cast; father, rather*); (*c*) reduction of OF [ɑ̃] > ME [aun] > [ɒː] > /ɑː/ (*aunt, branch, command, chant*); (*d*) reduction of ME [au] and late ME loss of [ɫ] > /ɑː/ (*half, calf, palm, balm*); (*e*) approximations of foreign values in more recent borrowings—mainly from French and Italian (*charade, moustache, memoir, sonata, tomato, drama, saga*).

It should also be noted that a new /ɑː/ is appearing in PresE, resulting from the levelling of the sequences [aɪə] and [aʊə] (*fire, tower*)—see §7.11.

(5) *Advice to foreign learners.*—Many languages do not have a qualitative opposition, in the relatively open region, of the English /æ/-/ɑː/ type. The retracted nature of RP /ɑː/ should be insisted upon, especially in those words of the *after, path, pass, chance* categories. This retraction may be achieved by modifying /ɑː/ in the direction of /ɒ/ (see §7.9.7) and comparing such pairs as *cart, cot; calf, cough; lark, lock; large, lodge*.

In addition, in the case of words in which /ɑː/ is shown in the spelling by vowel letter + *r*, the temptation to pronounce any kind of [r] should be overcome (except when word final *r* may link to a following word beginning with a vowel). It is helpful to consider such post-vocalic *r* letters simply as a mark of length for the preceding vowel. French learners should be careful not to use undue nasalization in words of French origin which suggest modern French forms, e.g. *branch, plant,* etc.

7.9.7 /ɒ/

(1) *Examples.*—*o*—dock, dog, holiday, sorry, gone

a—was, what, swan, want, watch, quality

ou, ow—cough, trough, Gloucester, knowledge

au—because, sausage, laurel, Austria, Australia, cauliflower

(*Note*: /ɒ/ in 'yacht' /jɒt/.)

Compare /ɒ/, /ɑː/—lodge, large; cot, cart; cough, calf; impossible, impassable

/ɒ/, /ɔː/—cod, cord; don, dawn; stock, stalk

[ł] *following*—doll, involve, revolver, solve

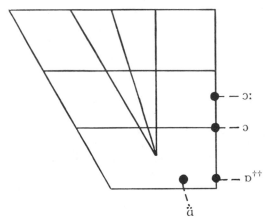

FIG. 15.—/ɒ/ and variants.

(2) *Description.*—This short vowel is articulated with wide open jaws and slight, open lip-rounding; the back of the tongue is in the fully open position, no contact being made between the tongue and the upper molars. The quality is that of an open lip-rounded *C*[ɑ], i.e. secondary *C*[ɒ], /ɒ/ does not occur in a final, open syllable.

(3) *Variants.*—The type of /ɒ/ described above has a very slight degree of lip-rounding. Some varieties of /ɒ/ (notably those of south-

west England and American English) have no lip-rounding and a tongue raising often somewhat advanced from true back. There is, therefore, considerable qualitative similarity between this kind of /ɒ/ and RP /ɑː/. The phonemes are kept distinct either through a complex of length and quality, e.g. *cough, calf* being distinguished by the length and fronted nature of /ɑː/, or through the pronunciation of post-vocalic *r* (vowel + *r* being the most common spelling of RP /ɑː/), e.g. in *dock, dark* or *lodge, large*.

Many words containing /ɒ/ + /f, θ, s/ have an alternative pro-nunciation with /ɔː/, e.g. *off, cloth, cross*. Such a variant is typical of conservative RP and had a social prestige value in southern England, but is generally now replaced by /ɒ/. This shift away from the tradi-tional /ɔː/ in such contexts may be due to the fact that /ɔː/ is also typical of popular London speech (Cockney), which uses /ɔː/ in these situations and also in such words as *dog, gone*, etc. There is some varia-tion, too, in certain words spelt with *au* or *a*, both /ɒ/ and /ɔː/ being heard, e.g. in *Australia, Austria, fault, salt*—the first two being more commonly with /ɒ/, the last two more commonly with /ɔː/.

It is noticeable that in sequences /ɒl/ + /C/ the pronunciation /əʊl/ + /C/ is becoming more common, especially when /v/ is the final con-sonant, e.g. in *involve, evolve*, etc. This is partly due to pressure exerted by the fact that /əʊl/ sequences (*roll, bowl, soul, mole*, etc.) are con-siderably more frequent than /ɒl/ (*doll, loll, col*), and that /ɒl/ + /C/ sequences are themselves rare, e.g. *lolled, dolls, golf, solve; salt, fault* are more often said with /ɔː/ than with /ɒ/, *volt* more commonly with /əʊ/ than with /ɒ/. In addition, the replacement of traditional /ɒ/ by /əʊ/ before /lC/ may be due in the London region to an analogous hypercorrection of the popular allophone [ɒʊ] for /əʊ/ before [ɫ] (see §7.10.4).

In Scottish English the /ɒ/-/ɔː/ distinction is often not made, *cot* and *caught* both having a vowel in the region of C[ɔ] and *cord* being kept separate from *cod* by the additional distinction provided by the pronunciation of post-vocalic *r*.

(4) *Chief sources.*—PresE /ɒ/ derives regularly from OE [o] (*dog, cock, song, long*) and OF [ɔ] (*offer, lodge, jolly*), and occasionally from shortened OE [oː] (*blossom, soft*). It is likely that the short [ɔ] of OE and ME was somewhat closer than PresE [ɒ], the more open type of articulation having been reached at the end of the eModE period. Between the sixteenth and eighteenth centuries, many words, having [ɔ] in ME, were pronounced with [a] or [æ], e.g. in *God, strop, stop, plot*. This pronunciation, typical during those centuries of both fashionable and vulgar London speech, is now retained only in the forms *strap* and *Gad* (exclamation).

ME short [a] preceded by [w] is often rounded to [ɒ] (*what, watch, was, want, quality*), a change which appears to have become established during the seventeenth century. The rounding has not taken place when a velar consonant follows, e.g. in *wag, wax, swagger, twang*, nor, in some pronunciations, when /f/ follows, e.g. *quaff, waft* (/kwɑːf, wɑːft/), nor in the word *swam*.

Shortening of ME [ɔː] has taken place in such words as *gone, shone* (though the regular development with [oː] was still used in the seventeenth century); monophthongization and shortening has affected the ME forms of *knowledge, sausage*, etc. The lengthened form of ME [ɔ] before /f, θ, s/ appears in the second half of the seventeenth century and has existed beside the short /ɒ/ ever since, though it seems to be losing ground to-day. /ɒ/ + nasal consonant occasionally represents [ã] in recent French borrowings, e.g. *restaurant, fiancé* /'restrɒnt, fɪ'ɒnseɪ/.

(5) *Advice to foreign learners.*—Short back open vowels occurring in other languages often differ from the English /ɒ/ in that either they are somewhat closer or more centralized, or are pronounced with stronger lip-rounding. The extremely open nature of the English vowel can be emphasized by relating it to /ɑː/. Words such as *part, large, calf*, should be said as far back in the mouth as possible, with the jaws wide apart and only the very slightest lip-rounding. In this way, a quality near to the /ɒ/ of *pot, lodge, cough*, may be obtained.

7.9.8   /ɔː/

(1) *Examples.*—*or*—cord, horse, sword, born
        aw—saw, lawn, jaw, yawn
        ou, au—bought, ought, daughter, fault, cause
        a—all, talk, salt, water, war, quart
        ore, oor, oar, our—before, more, door, floor, oar,
                               board, court, four

(*Note*: /ɔː/ in 'broad, sure'—or with /ʊə/ in the second word.)

Long [ɔː]—saw, war, born, board, dawn
Reduced [ɔ]—sort, ought, horse, chalk, quart
Compare [ɔː], [ɔ]—saw, sort; war, wart; board, bought; saws, sauce
         /ɒ/, /ɔː/—cod, cord; don, dawn; stock, stork
         /ʊ/, /ɔː/—put, port; could, cord; bull, ball
         /əʊ/, /ɔː/—code, cord; cold, called; bone, born
[ɬ] *following*—all, ball, bald, walled, halt, false

(2) *Description.*—This relatively long RP vowel is articulated with medium lip-rounding; the back of the tongue is raised between the half-open and half-close positions, no contact being made between the tongue and the upper molars. The quality lies between C[ɔ] and C[o], i.e. [ɔ̞] or [o̞]. /ɔː/ does not normally occur before /ŋ/.

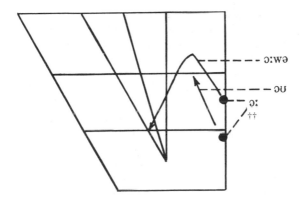

FIG. 16.—/ɔː/ and variants.

(3) *Variants.*—The traditional relationship between /ɔː/ and /ɒ/, i.e. one in which the opposition is mainly a matter of quantity (as in *offal—awful, cot—caught*), appears to be lost in PresE general RP. The quality of /ɔː/ is now closer, so that, in advanced RP, it often approaches *C*[o]. Thus, if the word *cord* were to be said in this style of speech with an unusually short /ɔː/, it would resemble *could*. Moreover, /ɔː/ increasingly replaces earlier [ɔə] forms in the words spelt with *ore, oor, oar, our* (*before, door, soar, four*), though [ɔə] is retained both in conservative RP and in many regional dialects. Alternatively, those words containing *r* may have in regional types of speech [ɔ] or [o] + /r/. Even when the pronunciation of *r* has been reduced to [ə], this distinction of the preceding vowel may persist, e.g. *horse* /hɔrs/ or /hɔəs/, *hoarse,* /hors/ or /hoəs/; *born* /bɔrn/ or /bɔən/, *borne* /born/ or /boən/. In RP some [ɔə] forms < /ʊə/ have a form with /ɔː/, e.g. *sure, your* (also often *you're*), *poor.*

In popular London speech /ɔː/ is often realized in open syllables as [ɔːwə], both in cases deriving from original vowel + /r/ (*door, four*) and also in those where no [r] has previously existed (*saw, law*); a diphthong of the type [ɒʊ] or [ɔʊ] is often used before a consonant, not only before [ɫ] (*fall, ball*) but also in such words as *caught, daughter, born, horse, talk, board,* etc.

(4) *Chief sources.*—The tendency of PresE RP /ɔː/ to become closer is a continuation of a historical closing process. Many instances of modern /ɔː/ result from a ME diphthong [ɑu], which is likely to have had a variant [ɑː]. This diphthong or open vowel derives in turn from: OE open vowel + velar or labial consonant sequences, e.g. [ɑ] + [w] (*thaw*), [ɑ] + [ɣ] (*law*), [æː] + [x] (*taught*), [ɑ] + [v] (*hawk < hafoc*); an earlier OE [ɑ] with [ʊ] glide before [ɫ] (*all, call, fall*) and with later (approximately seventeenth-century) loss of [ɫ] (*talk, walk*); OF

[ã] or OF [ɑ] + [u] or [o] sequences (*cause, autumn, sauce, haunt, lawn*) or sometimes as a reduction of [ɑ] + [v] (*saunter, laundry*). ME diphthong [ɔu] is also often realized in PresE /ɔː/; this ME form derives from OE [ɔ] + [x] (*bought, wrought*), from OE [oː] + [x] (*thought, brought, daughter*) and from OE [ɑː] + [x] (*ought*).

In addition, in the same way that ME [a] preceded by [w] generally gives modern /ɒ/, [w] has also rounded ME [a] or [aː] to /ɔː/ during the seventeenth century (*water, quart, warn, warm*). Finally, a large number of instances of RP /ɔː/ result from the loss of post-vocalic /r/ in the eighteenth century (*horse, lord, source, forth*) via such stages as [ɔə] or [oə]. This change has levelled several ME vowel distinctions, e.g. ME [ɔ] + /r/ (*short, horse*), ME [ɔː] + /r/ (*force, board*), and ME [oː] or [uː] + /r/ (*sword, fourth, floor, mourn, pour*); such lowering and monophthongization of earlier [uə] is also extended by some speakers to such words as *sure, poor*. Vowel distinctions preceding retained /r/ or its replacement are still kept in regional dialects (see (3) above).

(5) *Advice to foreign learners.*—In many countries a type of /ɔː/ is taught which is rather more open than the general RP variety described above and which can no longer be said to be typical of RP. The slightly higher tongue position should be accompanied by closer lip-rounding. Many languages have a vowel in the region of C[o]; this latter sound may serve as a starting point for acquiring RP /ɔː/, the tongue and lip positions being relaxed until the correct quality is reached.

The spelling forms of /ɔː/ often cause difficulty. No *r* should be pronounced where it occurs in the spelling of such words as *port, sort, lord, more*, except when, in a word final position, it is used as a link with a following word beginning with a vowel, e.g. *pour out* /ˈpɔːr ˈaʊt/. Words having /ɔː/ and spelt with *au, aw, ou*, e.g. *taught, saw, ought*, are often wrongly given a [ɔu] or [ou] type of diphthong. The monophthongal nature of /ɔː/ should be insisted upon, especial care being taken to keep a proper distinction between /ɔː/ and /əʊ/ in such pairs as *caught, coat*; *saw, so*.

7.9.9   /ʊ/

(1) *Examples.*—*u*—put, full, sugar, cushion, butcher
        o—wolf, woman, bosom
       oo—good, book, wood, wool
      ou—could, should, would, courier

    (*Note*: 'Worcester' /ˈwʊstə/, 'worsted' (cloth) /ˈwʊstɪd/.)

Compare /ʊ/, /uː/—full, fool; wood, wooed
          /ʊ/, /ɔː/—could, cord; wood, ward
[ɫ] *following*—full, pull, wool, wolf

(2) *Description.*—The short RP vowel /ʊ/ is pronounced with a part of the tongue nearer to centre than to back raised just above the half-close position; it has, therefore, a symmetrical back relationship with the front vowel /ɪ/; the tongue is laxly held (compared with the tenser /uː/), no firm contact being made between the tongue and the upper molars. The lips are closely but loosely rounded. The quality is that of a centralized *C*[o] = [ö]. This vowel occurs in both accented and unaccented syllables, being present in the accented syllable of a relatively small number of words, though some of these are of common occurrence, e.g. *put, good, look, would*, etc. /ʊ/ does not occur in word initial positions nor before final /ŋ/ and finally only in the unaccented form of *to* /tʊ/.

(3) *Variants.*—Little striking variety is found in RP realizations of /ʊ/. Some speakers use less lip-rounding and a lower tongue position than that described above, notably in the common word *good* [gö̞d] or [gɤd], and also in *should, could* and, to a lesser extent, *would*. (The unaccented forms of these last three words very often have /ə/ rather than /ʊ/.) In some words there is a variation between /ʊ/ and /uː/, e.g. *room, groom, broom, tooth*, the commoner phoneme being /uː/. A form of [ɤ] represents /ʊ/ in some northern regional speech, e.g. *butcher* [ˈbɤtʃə]; and again, in northern speech, many words spelt with *oo* have /uː/, e.g. *cookery book*. In Scotland the opposition /ʊ/-/uː/ may be neutralized, a centralized [ü] being used for both, so that *pull* and *pool* have a similar vowel quality.

(4) *Chief sources.*—As we have seen ME short [ʊ] has a regular development to PresE /ʌ/. A number of cases of ME [ʊ], however, whether from OE sources (*full, bull, wolf, wool, wood*) or from OF sources (*push, butcher, pulley*), have retained their [ʊ] quality; the presence of a preceding labial consonant may be said to account for the retention of a lip-rounded vowel, but there are several cases where /ʌ/ has developed despite a labial consonant (*butter, bud, pulse*). In another group of words, PresE /ʊ/ derives from a ME [oː] which regularly gives PresE /uː/ (*food, moon*); such words are *good, foot, stood, book, look*, for which alternative pronunciations with /uː/ or /ʊ/ existed into the seventeenth century. The northern pronunciation with /uː/ in many such words (mentioned above) retains the closer form, abandoned in the London region.

(5) *Advice to foreign learners.*—The difficulty of /ʊ/ is similar to that of /ɪ/, i.e. just as the vowels /iː/, /ɪ/, presented three oppositions involving complexes of quality and quantity, [iː]-[i]-[ɪ], so /ʊ/ has to be distinguished from /uː/ sometimes by quality alone (*foot-boot*), sometimes by quality and quantity (*good-food*). The quality of /ʊ/ must be kept quite distinct from that of the reduced form of /uː/; if a vowel of the quality of *C*[o] occurs in the learner's own language, this may be used as a starting point for learning English /ʊ/—essentially a

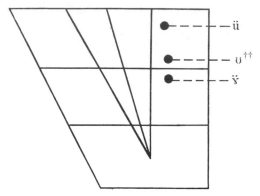

FIG. 17.—/ʊ/ and variants.

centralized [o]. Thus, in the case of French learners, for instance, the vowel in *foot* may be usefully related to the French vowel in *faute* and the English vowel acquired by relaxing the whole articulation. Relating /ʊ/ and C[o] in this way underlines the fact that /ʊ/ is not a kind of [u] sound. If the centralization of /ʊ/ is not sufficient, the starting point may be a central [ə] modified in the direction of [o]. The opposition between /ʊ/ and fully long /uː/ is less difficult once the distinction /ʊ/-reduced /uː/ is established (see following section for comparative exercises).

7.9.10   /uː/

(1) *Examples.*—*oo*—food, soon, moon, spoon
　　　　　　　o—do, who, move, lose
　　　　　　　ou—group, soup, wound (n.), through
　　　　　　　u—rude, June, Susan
　　　　　　　ew, ue, ui, oe—chew, blue, juice, shoe

(*Note*: in many cases of the spelling *u, eu, ew, ue, ui,* /uː/ is preceded by /j/, e.g. 'music, duke, neuter, new, few, hue, argue, nuisance, beauty'; in some words, both /uː/ and /juː/ are heard, e.g. 'suit, enthusiasm'.)

Long [uː]—two, blue, food, move
Reduced [u]—boot, fruit, hoof, group, douche, hoop
Compare [uː], [u]—shoe, shoot; rude, root; lose, loose; use (v.),
　　　　　　　　　　use (n.); nude, newt; Jews, juice
　　　　　　[uː], /ʊ/—food, good; pool, pull
　　　　　　[u], /ʊ/—boot, foot; loop, look
[ɬ] *following*—cool, rule, schools, fooled

(2) *Description.*—RP long /uː/ is a back close vowel, but the tongue

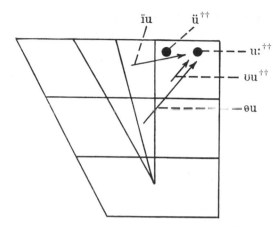

FIG. 18.—/uː/ and variants.

raising is relaxed from the closest position and is somewhat advanced from true back; its relationship with /ʊ/ is similar to that between /iː/ and /ɪ/, the articulation of /uː/ being tense compared with that of /ʊ/, though no firm contact is made between the tongue and the upper molars. The lips tend to be closely rounded. The quality is that of a relaxed, slightly lowered and centralized *C*[u]. /uː/ does not normally occur before /ŋ/.

(3) *Variants.*—The absence in English of any opposition between /uː/ and a vowel of the front, close rounded type, [y], is an important reason for the relaxation and fronting of this phoneme from a true back position. Considerable centralization, [ü], appears increasingly to be a feature of certain types of RP, especially in the London region. In this latter area, centralization is a characteristic of the regional dialect, both popular and modified. Extreme centralization amongst RP speakers is, therefore, inhibited to a certain extent for social reasons. In those cases where /uː/ is preceded by /j/ (*new, beauty*), the palatal nature of /j/ normally entails considerable centralization of /uː/. A type of [ü] is also to be heard in many forms of Scottish English as a realization of RP /uː/ (and /ʊ/).

Just as RP /iː/ is rarely pure, so RP /uː/ is usually diphthongized, [ʊu] or [uw], especially in final positions (*do, shoe, who*). Any exaggeration of the diphthong, e.g. [əü] or [ïü], with total loss of liprounding on the first element (or, occasionally, on both elements) is typical of popular (Cockney) London speech. On the other hand, a quality of /uː/ which is too near to a pure *C*[u], with strong liprounding, is characterized as affected or over-cultivated.

(4) *Chief sources.*—PresE /uː/ derives regularly via ME [oː] from OE [oː] (*doom, soon, to, tool, goose*). Scandinavian [oː] (*root, boon*)

and OE [ɑː] preceded by [w] (*womb, whom, two*); also from OF [oː] (*fool, prove, proof*). *o* and *oo* are, therefore, the typical spelling forms of the regular development to [uː], which was reached by about 1500. Certain French words with [uː] (*ou* spelling), introduced after the change [uː] > [aʊ] had begun, i.e. after about 1400, retained their [uː] quality (*route, routine, group, soup*). In many cases, too, especially in those words where the French stress-accent on the last syllable has been kept, French *-on* (= probably [õ]) has given English /uː/ with a spelling change to *oo* (*platoon, balloon, saloon, typhoon*).

PresE /juː/ derives from many sources. The chief of these are: (*a*) ME [iu], [eu] or [yː] < OE [i] + [w] (*Tuesday, hue*), < OE [eːə] + [w] (*you, knew*), < OF [iu] (*adieu, lieu*), < OF [eu] (*due, view*), < OF [y] (*duke, accuse, deluge*), < OF [ui] (*suit, pew, nuisance*). It is likely that in these cases a ME falling diphthong [iu] changed the relative prominence of its elements to give [juː] in the sixteenth century (a variant with [yː] perhaps remaining in some kinds of English). (*b*) ME [ɛu] < OE [ɛːə] or [æː] + [w] (*few, dew, hew*); and < later French (post-1400) [ɛu] (*feud, neuter*). This ME diphthong closed to [eu] by eModE (still being kept separate from [juː]) and finally coalesces with [juː] in the late seventeenth century.

(5) *Advice to foreign learners.*—The quality of this vowel should cause no difficulty to most learners, many of whom will have a close back rounded vowel in their own language. A pure vowel of this kind will usually be suitable in English, though too energetic lip-rounding should be avoided. The typical RP centralization or diphthongization should be imitated only with caution, since any exaggeration of the movement will produce an effect which is judged vulgar or dialectal. The centralization of /uː/ following /j/ need not be consciously aimed at. Those learners, such as Norwegians, who have a centralized [ü] in their own languages, should avoid using this sound in English because of its dialectal connotations; and those whose own close back vowel is unrounded, as in Japanese, should add fairly close lip-rounding.

More difficult is the relationship of fully long [uː], reduced [u] and short [ʊ] as in *food, boot*, and *foot*. It should be noted, for instance, that *use* (v.) [juːᶎ] differs from *use* (n.) [jus] more by the length of the vowel than by the quality of the final consonant, and that the difference between the vowels of *boot* ([u]) and of *foot* ([ʊ]) lies more in their quality than in their length.

7.9.11　　　　　　　　/ɜː/

(1) *Examples.*—*ir, yr*—bird, first, girl, myrtle
　　　　　　　er, err, ear—her, serve, err, earth, heard
　　　　　　　ur, urr—turn, church, nurse, purr

w + or—word, world, work, worse
our—journey, courtesy, scourge

(*Note.* /ɜ:/ in 'colonel' /ˈkɜ:nl/.)

Long [ɜ:]—fur, burn, bird, urge
Reduced [ɜ]—first, earth, worse, church
Compare [ɔ:], [ɜ]—cur, curt; heard, hurt; surge, search; purrs,
                    purse; Thursday, thirsty; serve, surf
[ɫ] *following*—earl, curl, world, girls

(2) *Description.*—RP /ɜ:/ is articulated with the centre of the
tongue raised between half-close and half-open, no firm contact being
made between the tongue and upper molars; the lips are neutrally
spread. The quality is, therefore, remote from all peripheral Cardinal
vowel values.

The quality of /ɜ:/ often coincides with that of unaccented /ə/, both
being central vowels. It is possible to treat /ə/ as an unaccented allophone of /ɜ:/, since it may be claimed that no true opposition between
the vowels exists. Thus, in the pair *foreword* /ˈfɔ:wɜ:d/, *forward*
/ˈfɔ:wəd/, the second syllable of *foreword* may be said to carry a
secondary accent. In any case, there is a difference of quantity between
/ɜ:/ (not carrying a primary accent) and unaccented /ə/, the /ɜ:/ of
foreword being longer than the /ə/ of *forward*; or again, the relatively
unaccented, reduced /ɜ:/ of *commerce* is longer than the /ə/ of
commas—[ˈkɒmɜs] v. /ˈkɒməz/. It is to be noted that /ɜ:/ frequently is
reduced to /ə/ when it is associated with no kind of stress-accent, e.g.
were /ˈwɜ:/, but /wə/; *amateur* /ˈæmə‚tɜ:/, but /ˈæmətə/; *pennyworth*
/ˈpenɪ‚wɜ:θ/ = [ˈpenɪ‚wɜθ], but /ˈpenɪwəθ/, where the reduced form of

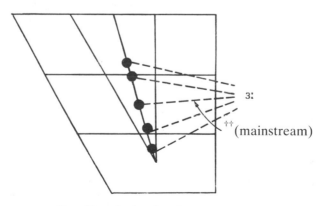

FIG. 19.—/ɜ:/ and variants.

/ɜː/ is still longer than unaccented /ə/. /ɜː/ does not normally occur before /ŋ/.

(3) *Variants.*—/ɜː/ being the only RP accented vowel in the central area, great latitude of degree of tongue raising is permissible, varying from a sound in the half-close region or slightly above to one in the half-open region or slightly below. Both variants may be heard in RP, especially in the conservative type. The closer variety is also typical of certain regional speech, e.g. that of Birmingham and Liverpool and, to a lesser extent, in some Australian English. A very open kind of /ɜː/, i.e. one below the half-open central region, entails repercussions in the phonetic realization of the opposition /ɜː/-/ɑː/, if a qualitative distinction is to be maintained between two words such as *heard, hard*. Those using the very open variety of /ɜː/ usually achieve such a distinction by pronouncing the most retracted form of /ɑː/ (see §7.9.6(2)).

In most cases PresE /ɜː/ has derived from a vowel + /r/, as the spellings suggest. A pronunciation with vowel (usually [ɪ, e, ʌ] or [ʊ]) + /r/ is retained in many types of English where post-vocalic /r/ is still pronounced, e.g. Scottish English and some kinds of northern English; such forms of speech do not possess /ɜː/ as a distinctive sound. Other kinds of English, e.g. south-west British and American, retain a post-vocalic (usually retroflexed) /r/ but obscure the preceding vowel to [ə], e.g. *bird* [bərd], or pronounce an [ə] sound with tongue retroflexion (*r-coloured* vowel), e.g. [bɚd] or [bɹd]. (The same impression of retroflex quality can, in fact, be given without actual retroflexion of the tip of the tongue but with contraction of the body of the tongue.)

The RP, non-retroflexed, /ɜː/, being essentially central in relation to the remainder of the vowel system, can be regarded as having a neutral quality in comparison with the other English vowels. It is the indeterminate sound often used for hesitation in English; if it is substituted in an utterance for all other vowel phonemes, a high degree of intelligibility is retained, provided that the appropriate variations of quantity remain.

(4) *Chief sources.*—The great majority of cases of PresE /ɜː/ derive from: ME [ɛ] + /r/ (*virtue = vertue, earth, heard, fern*) or ME [ɪ] + /r/ (*shirt, birth, myrrh*); or ME [ʊ] + /r/ (*word, journey, spur*). ME [ɛ], [ɪ], and [ʊ] (> [ʌ] with loss of lip-rounding) all centralized before final /r/ or /r/ + consonant, so that the pronunciation [ər] for all three was incipient in the London region in the sixteenth century and general in the late seventeenth century, though contemporary grammarians still often insisted upon the earlier vowel quality especially in the case of ME [ɛ] and [ʊ] words. With the loss of /r/ in post-vocalic positions in the eighteenth century, the PresE central long /ɜː/ was reached. Some attempts to reproduce the French [œːr] in final accented syllables have also resulted in /ɜː/, e.g. *connoisseur* /ˌkɒnəˈsɜː/; liqueur /lɪˈkɜː/ (also

/lɪˈkjʊə/); *amateur* /ˌæməˈtɜː/ (also /ˈæmətə, ˈæmətjə, ˈæmətʃə, ˈæməˌtjʊə/); *chauffeur* /ʃəʊˈfɜː/ (also /ˈʃəʊfə/).

(5) *Advice to foreign learners.*—It is comparatively rare to find a long central vowel such as /ɜː/ in other languages. Many languages, however, possess somewhat centralized front rounded vowels of the [ø] and [œ] types. These are quite unacceptable in English because of the lip-rounding. An articulation with spread lips should, therefore, be insisted upon, keeping if necessary approximately the same lip position for such words as *fur, bird, learn,* as for *fee, bead, lean.* Lip-spreading is particularly important after /w/, e.g. in *word, world, work,* etc. In addition, the quality must be of a central rather than fronted kind, though some latitude may be allowed as far as the degree of raising of the tongue is concerned.

Since nearly all cases of /ɜː/ occur in words having an *r* in the spelling, care must also be taken to avoid post-vocalic /r/ (except as a liaison form as in *stir up* /ˈstɜːr ˈʌp/) or any retroflexion of the tongue such as would produce *r*-colouring.

7.9.12 /ə/

(1) *Examples.*—/ə/ may be spelt with most vowel letters and their combinations, e.g. *i* (poss*i*ble), *e* (gentlem*e*n), *a* (wom*a*n), *o* (*o*blige), *u* (s*u*ppose), *ar* (particul*ar*), *er* (moth*er*), *or* (doct*or*), *ou* (fam*ou*s), *our* (col*our*), *ure* (fig*ure*), etc. It is most frequently in opposition either with zero vowel, e.g. *about, bout; waiter, wait,* or with unaccented /ɪ/, e.g. *affect, effect; accept, except; razors, raises; grocers, grosses; mitre, mighty; waiter, weighty; sitter, city; battered, batted.*

In addition, it should be noted that /ə/ is normal in common unaccented (weak) forms of such words as *a, an, the, to, for, but, and,* etc. (see §10.4).

(2) *Description.*—/ə/ has a very high frequency of occurrence in unaccented syllables. Its quality is that of a central vowel with neutral lip position, having in non-final positions a tongue-raising between half-open and half-close, e.g. in 'alone, fatigue, decorative, afterwards', etc.; in the vicinity of the velar consonants /k, g/ and /ŋ/, however, the tongue may be slightly more raised and retracted, e.g. 'long ago' /ˈlɒŋ əˈgəʊ/. But in final positions, e.g. in 'mother, doctor, over, picture, China', the vowel may be articulated either in the half-open central position or in the most open region of the central area. The acoustic formants of /ə/ are, therefore, likely to be similar to those for /ɜː/ or /ʌ/ according to the situation.

(3) *Variants.*—As is the case for /ɜː/, /ə/ has no qualitative opposition within the central area of vowel articulation, so that considerable variation is possible within this region. In particular, as has been stated,

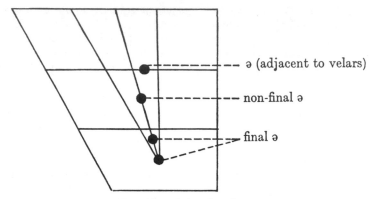

ə (adjacent to velars)

non-final ə

final ə

FIG. 20.—/ə/ and variants.

the quality of final /ə/ tends to be of a more open kind. In certain types of RP, both conservative and advanced, this variety reaches an articulatory area similar to that associated with /ʌ/ (i.e. a slightly raised, centralized front open vowel), but may have the same degree of opening as /ɑː/ (i.e. fully open), e.g. the final vowel of *mother* /ˈmʌðə/ may be more open than the first; or again, the two vowels of *father* /ˈfɑːðə/ may be of similar quality, cases of final /ɑː/ which might contrast with /ə/ being rare. The opening of final /ə/ to this extent is, however, commonly felt to be an exaggeration characteristic of affected speech.

In those kinds of English where post-vocalic /r/ is still pronounced, the cases of RP /ə/ represented in the spelling by vowel + *r* are realized as retracted [ɪ] or [ʌ] + /r/, e.g. in Scottish English, or as [ə] + [ɹ] or as syllabic [ɹ], e.g. some kinds of American and south-west British English. Because of the presence of an articulation corresponding to the *r* spelling in these types of English, words such as *finer* and *China* (rhymes in RP) are phonetically different in their final syllable.

(4) *Chief sources.*—As the great variety of spellings indicates, /ə/ may represent the reduced (obscured, 'schwa') form of any vowel or diphthong in an unaccented position. This reduction of unaccented vowels, typical of a stress-accent language such as English, has been a feature of the English sound system for over a thousand years. Since our spelling of vowels is based on the Latin vowel letters, our written language has always concealed these obscurations of quality. But it is evident from confusions in the use of vowel letters that such reductions were taking place in unaccented syllables even in OE. Thus, OE letters *æ*, *e*, *i*, in unaccented syllable are very often confused, probably indicating a sound [ë]; *o* and *u*, too, are often interchanged, though remaining separate from *a* representing [ɑ]. By the eleventh century all these major distinctions of weak [ɛ], [ʊ], and [ɑ] tend to be confused,

especially in unaccented final syllables, no doubt with an obscuration in the direction of [ə]. This tendency continued in the ME period, so that it has been suggested[1] that by the middle of the fifteenth century the vowels of unaccented syllables showed much the same kind of obscuration (towards [ə] or [ɪ]) as in PresE. Thus, fifteenth-century spellings such as *disabey, Bishap, tenne a clocke, sapose,* seem to indicate a vowel of the [ə] type.

Accentual patterns in ME, however, especially in respect of French words, were not always the same as now. A word such as *adversary* would, in ME, have a double accent [ˌadverˈsaːri(ə)], with a full vowel [aː] in the penultimate syllable, which now, being unaccented, has [ə] or no vowel at all. Moreover, a secondary accent (following the main accent) was kept in many words into the seventeenth century (cf. modern American English), thus inhibiting obscuration towards [ə], e.g. *temporary* (eModE [ˈtɛmpəˌreːrɪ], Pres American [ˈtempoˌrerɪ]), *emperor* (eModE [ˈɛmpəˌruːr]). But, generally speaking, Shakespeare's English can be taken as having [ə] where PresE has it, e.g. in such words as *second, among, palate, father, colour, vulgar, measure* (in these last cases [ə] + [ɹ]), and even in the last syllable of *follow* (cf. *fellow* with a modern variant /ˈfelə/), where to-day the diphthong is kept in educated speech. Sometimes, however, eModE has [ɪ] where in PresE /ə/ is more general, e.g. *pigeon, stomach, reason, squirrel.*

(5) *Advice to foreign learners.*—The quality of this vowel, including the two main allophones described in (2) above, does not usually present difficulties to the foreign learner, provided that he remembers that English /ə/ has no lip-rounding and is extremely short. Moreover, when /ə/ is spelt with vowel + *r*, the learner should avoid pronouncing any kind of [r] sound, except when in final positions an /r/ is pronounced as a link to a following word beginning with a vowel, e.g. *father and mother* /ˈfɑːðər ən ˈmʌðə/.

In particular, the learner should note those syllables of a word containing /ə/, remembering that /ə/ is a sound which occurs very frequently in English and that correct obscuration of the unaccented syllables of a word is as much a part of the word's accentual pattern as the stress expended on the accented syllables. In this connection, the learner may gain greater familiarity with the occurrence of /ə/ by reading English texts transcribed phonetically and by himself making a phonetic transcription of connected English.

7.10 Diphthongal Vowel Glides

The sequences of vocalic elements included under the term 'diphthong' are those which form a glide within one syllable. They may be said to

[1] H. C. Wyld, *History of Modern Colloquial English*, p. 258.

have a 1st element (the starting point) and a 2nd element (the point in the direction of which the glide is made). The RP diphthongs have as their 1st element sounds in the general region of [ɪ, e, a, ə, ʊ] and for their 2nd element [ɪ, ʊ, ə]; these elements may be treated as separate phonemic entities (see §7.2, *et seq.*). The following generalizations refer to all the RP diphthongs:—

(1) Most of the length and stress associated with the glide is concentrated on the 1st element, the 2nd element being only lightly sounded (see §§7.12.1, 7.12.3, for the exceptional cases of /ɪə, ʊə/); diphthongs of this type are said to be 'falling'.

(2) They are equivalent in length to the long (pure) vowels and are subject to the same variations of quantity, e.g. *plays* [pleːɪz], *place* [pleɪs]. The reduced forms show a considerable shortening of the 1st element.

(3) They are particularly susceptible to variation in different regional and social types of speech. Even within the RP varieties, considerable variation is possible in both elements. For this reason, and because these diphthongs consist largely of articulatory movement, 'typical' formants are not given, though the glides may be identified acoustically in terms of the formant structure of the 1st element (with a relatively steady state) and that of the 2nd element.

(4) No diphthong occurs before /ŋ/, except where word final /n/ is assimilated to /ŋ/ in connected speech (see §11.3.4).

(5) With the exception of /ɔɪ/, the RP diphthongs often derive from earlier pure vowels.

7.10.1   /eɪ/

(1) *Examples.—a*—ape, late, make, lady, waste, base
        ai, ay—day, may, waist, rail, aim, rain
        ei, ey— eight, veil, weigh, rein, they, whey
        ea—great, steak, break

   (*Note*: 'halfpenny' /'heɪpnɪ/, 'gauge' /geɪdʒ/, 'gaol' /dʒeɪl/.)

Long [eːɪ]—day, made, game, gaze
Reduced [eɪ]—eight, late, face, safe, ache
Compare [eːɪ], [eɪ]—played, plate; ray, race; way, waist; save, safe
        /e/, /eɪ/—bet, bate; fell, fail; chess, chase; west, waist
[ɫ] *following*—male, pail, failed, sails

(2) *Description.*—The glide begins from slightly below the half-close front position and moves in the direction of RP /ɪ/, there being a slight closing movement of the lower jaw; the lips are spread. The starting point is, therefore, *C*[ẹ] (somewhat closer than RP /e/ of *bet*). Before [ɫ], the [ɪ] element is often absorbed into the [ə] or [ʊ] glide on to [ɫ], e.g. *sail* [se ᵊɫ].

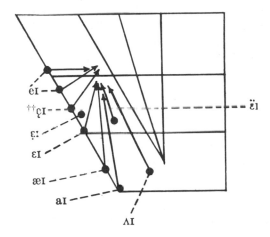

FIG. 21.—/eɪ/ and variants.

(3) *Variants.*—In RP the only diphthong in the front region (other than the diphthongized version of /iː/-[ɪi]) with which /eɪ/ is in contrast is /aɪ/. The 1st element has, therefore, considerable latitude of articulation (especially between the half-close and half-open positions) before it risks confusion with the fully open 1st element of /aɪ/. In general RP starting points of the type *C* [e, ẹ, ɛ, ɛ] and a centralized [ë] are all found. In some regional speech, however, especially in popular London dialect, the 1st element may be as open as [æ] or *C* [a] or a sound similar to that used for RP /ʌ/. In such cases, since confusion with RP /aɪ/ would be likely, the realization of /aɪ/ has a more retracted 1st element (*C* [ɑ] or [ɒ]), so that *fate* [faɪt] is kept distinct from *fight* [fɑɪt], [fɒɪt]. The use of such a 'wide' diphthong as [aɪ] or [æɪ] for RP /eɪ/ is considered unacceptable for social reasons. Many RP speakers react against the popular 'wide' realization by using the closest and 'narrowest' variety of /eɪ/. In advanced RP, however, there may be little or no vocalic glide in the realization of this phoneme, especially in the fully long allophone, e.g *day, game, made*, with [ɛː] or [ẹː]; this monophthongized form may also be heard in cases where, for rhythmic reasons, the quantity is somewhat reduced, e.g. *lady, nature, relation*, with [ẹ].

A long monophthong of a type varying between *C* [eː] and [ɛː] is also to be heard in many British regional dialects as a form corresponding to the diphthongal RP /eɪ/.

(4) *Chief sources.*—The main sources of PresE /eɪ/ are ME [aː] and [æɪ] or [ɛɪ]. Of these, ME [aː] develops from: OE [æ] or [ɑ] lengthened in an open syllable (*name, ape, raven, ale*) or from Scandinavian words with a similar vowel (*gate, take*); OF [aː] (*male, nature, cave, state*);

earlier OF [au] (*chamber, change, strange, safe*). This ME [aː] was closed in the eModE period to [ɛː] and, perhaps, in some pronunciations, to [eː]. (Note the pronunciation of such words as *great, steak, break*—with ME [ɛː]—which have /eɪ/ in PresE instead of the more usual /iː/ deriving from this ME vowel.)

ME [æi] or [ɛi] develops from: OE [æ] + [j] (*day, again*); OE [æː] + [j] (*grey, clay*); OF [ai] (*pay, chain*); OE [ɛ] + [j] (*way, play*); Scandinavian [ei] (*they, swain*); OF [ei] (*faith, obey*). It will be seen that the ME diphthong of the type [ɛi] results from a coalescence of two earlier distinct diphthongs of the types [æi], [ai] and [ɛi], [ei], from both English and French sources. In many cases the modern spelling reflects the origins, e.g. *vain* as against *vein*, but often the spelling has been changed, e.g. *way* < [ɛi], *grey* < [æi]. The coalescence of the two earlier diphthongs took place at the end of the ME period, producing a glide of the [ɛi] or [æi] type. The evidence suggests that this glide was monophthongized in the eModE period, though the diphthongal pronunciation continued to be recommended by the earlier grammarians. The new monophthong was of the [ɛː] type, thus coalescing with [ɛː] < ME [aː].

In the seventeenth century, therefore, a pure vowel [ɛː] was probably used in both classes of words, though careful speakers might still use a diphthong in the second group. The general diphthongization of this [ɛː] is likely to have begun in the eighteenth century, developing towards a glide of the present type.

In addition, a number of words of more recent importation to-day have /eɪ/ in imitation of the French [e] or [ɛ], e.g. *fiancé, soirée, ballet, bouquet, beige, crêpe*.

(5) *Advice to foreign learners.*—Foreign learners should give sufficient length to the first element of this diphthong, making the correct reduction of quantity in the appropriate contexts. Care should also be taken that the quality remains within the permitted RP limits, i.e. preferably slightly more open than *C*[e] and not as open as *C*[ɛ]. The second part of the diphthong should be only lightly touched on and should never reach the region of fully close [i]. Those who do not have a diphthong in this area in their own language should avoid substituting for it either [eː] or [ɛː]; the lower jaw should make an appreciable closing movement.

7.10.2   /aɪ/

(1) *Examples.*—*i, y*—time, write, bite, climb, cry, dry, by
             igh, eigh—high, light, fight, might, height
             ie, ye—die, lie, pie, tried, dye
             ei, ai—either, eider, aisle

             (*Note*: /aɪ/ in 'eye, buy'.)

Long [aːɪ]—fly, die, mine, hide, eyes
Reduced [aɪ]—fight, like, ice, ripe
Compare [aːɪ], [aɪ]—tie, tight; tidal, title; eyes, ice; riding, writing
[ł] *following*—mile, aisle, piles, mild

(2) *Description.*—The glide of RP /aɪ/ begins at a point slightly behind the front open position, i.e. *C*[ä], and moves in the direction of the position associated with RP /ɪ/, although the tongue is not usually raised to a level closer than *C*[ë]; the glide is much more extensive than that of /eɪ/, the closing movement of the lower jaw being obvious. The starting point may be similar to the articulation used in RP /ʌ/ (see §7.9.5). The lips change from a neutral to a loosely spread position. Before [ł] the [ɪ] element is often absorbed into the [ə] or [ʊ] glide on to the [ł], e.g. *pile* [paːˀł].

(3) *Variants.*—Variants commonly used in the realization of this diphthong consist mainly in differences of starting point of the glide. Since RP /eɪ/ is realized between the limits [eɪ] and [ɛɪ], /aɪ/ cannot, while remaining contrastive, have a first element closer than *C*[ɛ]. Those RP speakers who use the closest form of /eɪ/ will probably have a type of [æɪ] glide for /aɪ/, while those whose /eɪ/ is nearer to [ɛɪ] may realize /aɪ/ with a more retracted type of [a] or fronted [ɑ]. In those types of pronunciation, e.g. popular London speech, where /eɪ/ is realized as [æɪ] or [aɪ], /aɪ/ must have a very much more retracted 1st element, i.e. [ɑ] or [ɒ]. Again, as for /eɪ/ in advanced RP speech, there is a variety of /aɪ/ with an extra-long 1st element and very little glide, usually long fronted [ɑː] (or the equivalent of long /ʌ/) with perhaps a slight movement to [ë]; such a realization is most commonly heard in

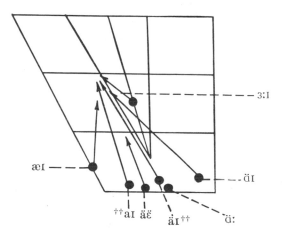

FIG. 22.—/aɪ/ and variants.

those situations where the phoneme is fully long, e.g. *die*, *try*, *fine*, or where there is, for rhythmic reasons, a slight reduction of quantity, e.g. *Friday*, *libel*, *climber*.

In some regional speech a considerably centralized 1st element may be heard, i.e. [ɜːɪ]; in Scottish English, /aɪ/ may be distinguished from a glide starting from a retracted, short [ʌ] as 1st element, used especially in uninflected word forms, e.g. *side* with [ʌɪ] as against *sighed* with /aɪ/ = [ae].

(4) *Chief sources.*—PresE /aɪ/ derives regularly from ME [iː], whose main sources are: OE [iː] (*ice*, *like*, *time*, *life*); OE lengthened [ɪ] (*child*, *find*, *wild*); OE or Scandinavian [yː] (*hide*, *mice*, *kind*, *sky*); OE [eː] or [ɛː] + [j] (*fly*, *lie*, *dye*, *eye*); OE [eː] + [ç] (*light*, *night*); OF [iː] (*fine*, *arrive*, *licence*, *price*). The pure vowel [iː] probably diphthongized by the beginning of the sixteenth century, the 1st element following a central route with increasing opening: [ɪi] in the late ME (cf. PresE diphthongization of /iː/), [əi] in the sixteenth and early seventeenth centuries, [ʌi] (where [ʌ] has a half-open back to central value) in the late seventeenth and eighteenth centuries, and a variety of [aɪ] from the late eighteenth century. In the speech of some speakers even to-day, especially among those using a conservative type of RP, a more centralized and retracted 1st element of /aɪ/ may still be heard.

In the case of the words *either* and *neither*, /aɪ/ exists to-day beside a variant with /iː/ deriving from an earlier [eː].

(5) *Advice to foreign learners.*—Apart from observing the proper reductions of quantity in syllables closed by a fortis consonant, foreign learners should avoid over-retraction of the quality of the 1st element, so as to remain within the limits of the RP vowel; a front open starting point is to be recommended. Care should also be taken not to glide to too close a position, i.e. to the C[i] area, such as is reached in diphthongs of this type in many languages.

7.10.3   /ɔɪ/

(1) *Examples,*—*oi*, *oy*—boy, toy, noise, voice, boil, point

(*Note*: 'buoy' /bɔɪ/.)

Long [ɔːɪ]—boy, noise, void, coin
Reduced [ɔɪ]—voice, joist, joint, choice
Compare [ɔːɪ], [ɔɪ]—noise, voice; joys, joist
[ɫ] *following*—soil, coiled, boils

(2) *Description.*—For RP /ɔɪ/ the tongue glide begins at a point between the back half-open and open positions and moves in the direction of /ɪ/, generally not reaching a level closer than [ɛ̈]. The tongue movement extends from back to centralized front, but the range of

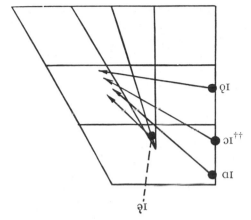

FIG. 23.—/ɔɪ/ and variants.

closing in the glide is not as great as for /aɪ/; the jaw movement, though considerable, may not, therefore, be as marked as in the case of /aɪ/. The lips are open rounded for the 1st element, changing to neutral for the 2nd. Before [ɫ] the [ɪ] element is often absorbed into the [ə] or [ʊ] glide on to the [ɫ], e.g. *oil* [ɔːˀɫ].

It will be noted that this is the third diphthongal glide towards an [ɪ] sound; it is, however, the only glide of this type with a back starting point (if the case of [ʊɪ], as in *ruin*, is discounted). To this extent, /ɔɪ/ may be considered asymmetrical in the RP diphthongal system.

(3) *Variants.* The variants of this diphthong are less striking than those affecting the diphthongs so far treated. The starting point may vary between *C*[ɑ] (only rarely for some conservative RP speakers) and *C*[ɒ] (popular London). The latter variant is to be related to the London realization of /aɪ/ as [ɑɪ]; the 1st element of the diphthong in a word such as *boy* must be closer than in RP in order to maintain the contrast with the glide in *buy* [bɑɪ]. In some conservative RP (now rare), especially in the traditional pronunciation of the clergy, a considerably centralized and unrounded 1st element [ɵɪ] is used. In all varieties of /ɔɪ/ the quality of the final element rarely reaches the position associated with /ɪ/, a sound of the [ë̞] type being more usual, while [ë] is not uncommon among RP speakers. It will be seen that, when the latter final element is preceded by [ə], the gliding movement of the tongue is very limited.

(4) *Chief sources.*—PresE /ɔɪ/ derives mainly from OF sources with [ɔɪ] (*choices, noise*), [oɪ] or [ʊɪ] (*boil, point*). In ME some words, now with /ɔɪ/, were pronounced with [ʊɪ]; a regular development of this latter diphthong's 1st element would result in eModE [ʏɪ] or [əɪ]. Confusion was, therefore, possible between words containing this glide

and those containing [əɪ] < ME [iː], now with /aɪ/. We find, in fact, that some PresE /ɔɪ/ words have [ʊɪ] in eModE (*boil, coin, point, join*) and that, in some cases, there is confusion with PresE /aɪ/ words, e.g. *boil* rhyming with *bile*. Such pronunciations were current in educated English until late in the eighteenth century and since then have occurred in popular regional forms of speech.

(5) *Advice to foreign learners.*—This diphthong does not present very great difficulties to foreign learners, provided that, in addition to the appropriate variations of quantity, the quality of the 1st element lies between the sounds of RP /ɔː/ and /ɒ/ and that the glide does not extend beyond the half-close front level, i.e. [ë].

7.10.4　　　　　　　　　　　/əʊ/

(1) *Examples.*—*o*—so, old, home, both, folk
　　　　　　oa—oak, road, foal, toast, soap
　　　　　　oe—toe, doe, sloe, foe, hoe
　　　　　　ou, ow—soul, though, shoulder, know, blow

(*Note*: /əʊ/ in 'mauve, brooch, beau, sew, shew'—variant spelling of 'show'—'don't, won't')

Long [əːʊ]—go, toe, home, road, pose
Reduced [əʊ]—goat, rope, oak, post, both
Compare [əːʊ], [əʊ]—robe, rope; toes, toast; grows, gross; road, wrote; cold, colt
　　　　　/əʊ/, /ɜː/—foe, fur; own, earn; goal, girl; oath, earth; coat, curt; foam, firm
　　　　　/əʊ/, /ɔː/—so, saw; pose, pause; bold, bald; load, lord; boat, bought; choke, chalk
　　　　　/əʊ/, /ɜː/, /ɔː/—foe, fur, four; bone, burn, born; woke, work, walk; coat, curt, caught; coal, curl, call
[ɫ] *following*—hole, roll, old, moult, bolt, poles

(2) *Description.*—The glide of RP /əʊ/ begins at a central position, between half-close and half-open, and moves in the direction of RP /ʊ/, there being a slight closing movement of the lower jaw; the lips are neutral for the 1st element, but have a tendency to round on the 2nd element. The starting point may have a tongue position similar to that described for /ɜː/.

(3) *Variants.*—A number of variants of this narrow diphthong are to be found within RP. The type described above is that which has in recent years become general. A more conservative diphthong, however, has its starting point in a more retracted region, [ö] or [ö̞] and the whole glide is accompanied by increasing lip-rounding. Another variety (of an advanced kind and usually characterized as an affectation) has a start-

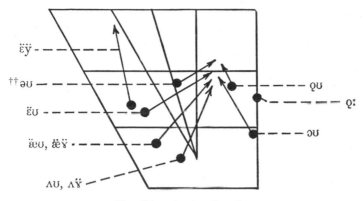

FIG. 24.—/əʊ/ and variants.

ing point more forward than the central area, i.e. [ę] or [ë̞]. It is also to be noted that, in the speech of many speakers of general RP, the 1st (central) element is so long that there may arise for a listener a confusion between /əʊ/ and /ɜː/, especially when [ɫ] follows, e.g. *goal*, *girl* (the [ʊ] element of /əʊ/ being confused with the glide on to [ɫ]). Though this may be a source of possible confusion for a listener, the speaker will often retain a qualitative distinction between /əʊ/ and /ɜː/, the latter being realized with a very open type of central vowel.

In popular London speech the diphthong has a more extensive glide, the starting point being equivalent to that of a fronted [ʌ] or [æ] (the latter having a degree of pharyngeal constriction which distinguishes it from the starting point of the affected version [ë̞ʊ] mentioned above). The glide finishes in a fronted back position between half-close and close, usually without lip-rounding, i.e. [ü] or [ÿ]. In this type of speech, widening of the diphthongal glide is necessary, since a narrow diphthong of the [əʊ] type is used as a realization of RP /uː/, [səʊp] being dialectal *soup* and RP *soap*. In modified London region speech, though the starting point may be closer and more central than that of the popular form, lip-rounding is again often absent, so that the 2nd element resembles [ü]; or lip-rounding may accompany a more fronted vowel, i.e. [əü] or [əy]. In London, too, a more open 1st element is often heard before [ɫ], e.g. in *dole, roll, cold* (see §8.7).

In other parts of Britain there occur for RP /əʊ/ diphthongs of the types [ɔʊ] and [oʊ], where the glide begins with a back vowel, or of the type [ë̞ÿ] where the 2nd element is a fronted, rounded close vowel; or again, many regional types of speech have a pure long vowel varying between *C* [oː] and *C* [ɔː].

The resemblance between /əʊ/ and a central vowel is further revealed by the behaviour of /əʊ/ in unaccented syllables, e.g. /fə'netɪks,

ˌdɪsə'beɪ/ for the more careful forms with /əʊ/ or [ou] or [o]; also the familiar pronunciation of *fellow* as /'felə/ and the vulgarism /'wɪndə/ for *window*. The reduction of /əʊ/ to /ə/ may produce in colloquial speech homophones which are distinct in a more formal style, e.g. *ferment, foment*—both /fə'ment/, *hypertension, hypotension*—both /ˌhaɪpə'tenʃn/.

(4) *Chief sources.*—PresE /əʊ/ derives chiefly from ME [ɔː] or ME [ou]. Of these, ME [ɔː] has the following main sources: OE [ɑː] (*no, go, home, loaf, ghost*); OE [ɛə] or [æ] + [ld] (*old, told, cold*); OE [ɔ] in open syllables (*over, open, nose, hope*); OF accented [ɔ] (*robe, rose, coat, toast, gross*). This pure vowel had probably reached a quality near *C*[oː] in the sixteenth and seventeenth centuries.

ME [ou] derives mainly from: OE [ɑː] or [ɔ] + [w] or [ɣ] (*know, blow, soul, snow, own, dough*); OE [oː] + [w] (*glow, flow, row*). This diphthong probably reached the stage [ou] by the seventeenth century, with an alternative pronunciation [oː]. The coalescence with [oː] < ME [ɔː] took place in the seventeenth century and the new [oː] was diphthongized to [ou] in the eighteenth and nineteenth centuries, to give PresE /əʊ/.

/əʊ/ is also used in PresE in imitation of French [o] or [ɔ] in more recent importations such as *beau, vaudeville, hotel, bureau*.

(5) *Advice to foreign learners.*—In some current books dealing with the pronunciation of British English, this diphthong is transcribed as 'ou'. Since the 1st element is now clearly of a central type, such a transcription may be misleading. Foreign learners should avoid starting the glide with a truly back vowel, but any kind of front rounded vowel, e.g. [ø] or [œ] is also wrong. It is advisable to learn /ɜː/ first and to modify /ɜː/ by adding lip-rounding to the end of the vowel. Thus, *fur* may be modified to *foe, girl* to *goal, burn* to *bone*, etc. In this way, the diphthong will be kept distinct from /ɔː/ (see comparative examples in (1) above). In addition, proper prominence must be given to the 1st element and reduction of the total length of the glide made in the appropriate contexts.

7.10.5　　　　　　　　/aʊ/

(1) *Examples.*—*ou, ow*—house, sound, out, cow, town, allow

(*Note*: 'Macleod' /mə'klaʊd/.)

Long [aːʊ]—how, loud, town, cows
Reduced [aʊ]—shout, about, mouse, mouth
Compare [aːʊ], [aʊ]—allows, a louse; found, fount; mouth (v.), mouth (n.); loud, lout
[ɫ] *following*—cowl, foul, owls

(2) *Description.*—The glide of RP /aʊ/ begins at a point between the back and front open positions, slightly more fronted than the position for RP /ɑː/, i.e. C[ä], and moves in the direction of RP /ʊ/, though the tongue may not be raised higher than the half-close level, i.e. [ö]. The glide is much more extensive than that used for /əʊ/ and is symmetrically opposed to the front glide of /aɪ/. The lips change from a neutrally open to a weakly rounded position.

(3) *Variants.*—The RP diphthong /aʊ/ is in opposition in the back region with /əʊ/; if the latter has a starting point in the central area below half-close, the starting point of /aʊ/ cannot be raised to any extent without the possible loss of contrast between such words as *tone* and *town*. RP variants, therefore, involve particularly the fronting or retraction of the starting point rather than its raising. Considerable latitude is permitted between the values C[ä] and C[ɑ]; for many speakers, the 1st element of /aɪ/ and /aʊ/ may in fact be identical. Since, however, several popular regional forms of speech (especially a modified popular variety of the London region) have typically a 1st element in the C[a] or [æ] areas, reaction amongst careful speakers causes the diphthong to have a more retracted starting point, sometimes reaching C[ɑ]. In some kinds of RP, usually of an advanced type, the [ɑ] element is extra long, especially in those contexts in which the diphthong has its fully long form, with a weak glide involving comparatively little raising of the tongue and little, if any, lip rounding; *loud* and *lard* may, therefore, be distinguished only by a slight movement at the end of the vowel. In London speech, both in the popular and modified forms, the 1st element may be of the [ɛ] or [æ] varieties. It would appear

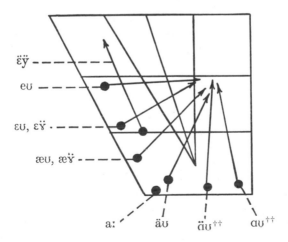

Fig. 25.—/aʊ/ and variants.

that with such a glide there would be risk of confusion with the popular London realization of /əʊ/ as [æ̈ʊ] or [ä̈ɤ̈], as between such words as *now* and *no*; in fact, the starting point used for /əʊ/ may be more open than that of /aʊ/, e.g. *no* [nä̈ɤ̈], *now* [në̈ʊ]. Even if the two starting points are on the same level, however, the diphthongs are kept phonetically separate by the greater centralization of the 1st element of /əʊ/ and also, in some cases, by the closer end point reached in /əʊ/ as compared with that of /aʊ/: [æ̈ɤ̈], [ä̈ɤ̈], [ä̈ʊ] or [æ̈ɯ] for /əʊ/ as against [æɔ̈] or [ɛɔ̈] for /aʊ/. In addition, in popular London speech, /aʊ/ may be realized as a long, relatively pure vowel of the [a] type, e.g. *town* [taːn].

In those kinds of English, e.g. Scottish and some Northern, which use [oː] or [oʊ] for RP /əʊ/, a more central type of starting point is often used for /aʊ/, i.e. [əʊ] or [ä̈ʊ]. In the regions surrounding London a closer, front starting point may be heard, i.e. [eʊ], often with unrounding of the 2nd element, [eɤ̈]; in the West Country the 2nd element may be rounded but fronted, [ë̈ÿ] or [ä̈ÿ].

(4) *Chief sources.*—RP /aʊ/ has origins and development in the back vowel area similar to those of RP /aɪ/ in the front. PresE /aʊ/ derives regularly from ME [uː], whose main sources are: OE [uː] (*cow, house, mouth*); lengthened OE [ʊ] (*ground, found*); OE [ʊ] or [oː] + [w] or [ɣ] (*fowl, bow, bough*); OF or Anglo-Norman [uː] (*allow, powder, couch, count, mountain*). Diphthongization of the pure vowel begins in the fifteenth century ([ʊʊ]) and the 1st element is progressively lowered by a central route ([əʊ] or [ä̈ʊ]) during the sixteenth and seventeenth centuries, there being no confusion with the development ME [ɔː] or [ɔu] > [oː] or [ou] > PresE /əʊ/. The more open 1st element of /aʊ/ must have become established during the eighteenth and nineteenth centuries.

In types of Northern and Scottish English the diphthongization did not take place, the original [uː] being retained, e.g. *house* [hu(ː)s]. The pure vowel [uː] is also sometimes retained in RP in the vicinity of bilabial consonants, e.g. in *wound* ('to injure'), *droop, stoop*; in other case, ME [uː] was shortened and gives PresE /ʌ/ (*plum, crumb, thumb*).

The present spelling forms *ou, ow*, for /aʊ/ result from the French influence on the language. OE /uː/ was spelt with *u*, but this letter had a different value in French, [y]; by ME, therefore, the French spelling *ou* or *ow* for the sound [uː] was generally used.

(5) *Advice to foreign learners.*—Just as for /aɪ/, foreign learners should be careful to use a correct 1st element, i.e. a variety which is not so fronted or raised as to be dialectal; a starting point too near to *C*[ɑ] is also to be avoided. The 1st element should be the most prominent and the 2nd element only lightly touched on, the tongue closing to a position not higher than half-close, i.e. [ö].

7.11 Diphthongs + [ə]

All the preceding diphthongal glides /eɪ, aɪ, ɔɪ, əʊ, aʊ/ are *falling* (i.e. with length and stress on the 1st element) and *closing* (i.e. gliding from a more open to a closer position); three of them, /aɪ, ɔɪ, aʊ/, require an extensive movement of the tongue. All may be followed by [ə] within the word, either as an inseparable part of the word, e.g. *Noah, fire, choir, iron, hire, society, our, sour, tower* /nəʊə, faɪə, kwaɪə, aɪən, haɪə, sə'saɪətɪ, aʊə, saʊə, taʊə/ or as a suffix (morpheme) appended to the root, e.g. *greyer, player, slower, mower, higher, drier, employer* /greɪə, pleɪə, sləʊə, məʊə, haɪə, draɪə, ɪm'plɔɪə/ or, sometimes, as a separable element internal in a composite form, e.g. *nowadays* /'naʊədeɪz/. In such cases, a third vocalic element [ə] may, in slow speech, be added to the two elements of the diphthongal glide; but there is a tendency in rapid and advanced RP to omit the 2nd ([ɪ] or [ʊ]) element, especially when [ə] is not felt as a separable morpheme. This process is sometimes known as *smoothing*.

(1) [aɪə] > [aːə] in general RP, e.g. in *fire, tyre, choir, society, hire, shire, byre, lyre, liable,* and also in cases where [ə] may be considered as a separable suffix, e.g. *higher, shyer, buyer, liar.*

(2) [aʊə] > [ɑːə] in general RP, e.g. in *our, shower, flower, coward, nowadays.*

It will be seen that the reduction of the phonetic sequences [aɪə, aʊə] to [aːə, ɑːə] results in a phonemic opposition relying on a distinction between [aː] and [ɑː]. It is natural that such a tenuous qualitative difference should be levelled out, with the result that both original [aɪə] and [aʊə] are frequently reduced to a diphthongal glide whose 1st

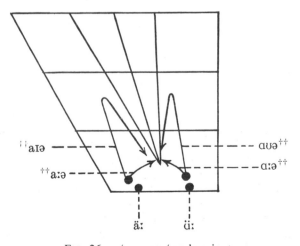

FIG. 26.—/aɪə, aʊə/ and variants.

element is a central open vowel. Several new homophones are produced in this way, e.g. *tyre, tower*; *shire, shower*; *sire, sour*.

In addition, in advanced RP the diphthongal pronunciations thus produced are often further reduced to a long monophthong, i.e. [aːə] > [aː] and [ɑːə] > [ɑː]. If [aː] and [ɑː] are kept distinct, there is nevertheless confusion between [ɑː] < [aʊə] and /ɑː/, resulting in such homophones as *shower, Shah*; *tower, tar*. A more extensive levelling (criticized as an affectation and also as a Cockney vulgarism, but widely heard amongst educated RP speakers) reduces both [aːə] and [ɑːə] to [ɑː], so that homophones of the type *shire, shower, Shah*; *tyre, tower, tar*; *byre* (or *buyer*), *bower, bar*, are produced, all with /ɑː/. This monophthongization of /aɪə/ and /aʊə/ and their coalescence with /ɑː/ is likely to be one of the most striking sound changes affecting Southern British English in the twentieth century.

(3) [eɪə] > [eːə] in general RP, e.g., in *player, greyer, conveyor, layer*. In these examples, in which it is a question of /eɪ/ + an /ə/ suffix, the resultant diphthong is frequently levelled with the /ɛə/ of *there, rare*, etc. Thus, such homophones as *prayer, pray-er*; *lair, layer*, are produced (see §7.12.2 for reduction /ɛə/ to [ɛː]).

(4) [əʊə] > [əː] = /ɜː/ in general RP, levelling frequently occurring between *mower, slower*, and *myrrh, slur* (with /ɜː/).

(5) [ɔɪə] > [ɔːə] in general RP, as in *employer, enjoyable, buoyant, joyous*. In these cases the [ɔː] element of the diphthong is qualitatively distinct from the value associated with /ɔː/, since it has a tongue position not higher than half-open. Thus, *drawer* ('one who draws') with /ɔː/ + /ə/ may have a closer initial vowel element than the starting point of the glide in the reduced form of *coir*, with [ʔːə].

Some speakers distinguish between sequences of diphthong + /əl/, usually in the case of terminations spelt *-el, -al*, e.g. *trial, towel, royal*, and sequences of diphthong + /l/, e.g. *tile, owl, toil*. However, the first sequence, containing three vocalic elements, may be reduced to a centring diphthong; and, in the case of the second type of sequence, an [ə] (or [ʊ]) glide is present before [ł], so that a similar triphthongal glide reducible to a centring diphthong is produced. Thus, /eɪ, aɪ, aʊ, ɔɪ/ followed by either /l/ or /əl/ tend to be realized as [eːə, aːə, aːə *or* aːʊ, ɔːə], the examples given above being perfect rhymes. In the case of /əʊ/ + [ł], the [ʊ] element of the diphthong may be retained, both because it is reinforced by the glide on to [ł] and also in order to maintain the distinction /əʊ/-/ɜː/ as in *pole, pearl*.

The reduction of diphthong + [ə] to a centring diphthong takes place not only within words but also between a word final diphthong followed by word initial /ə/, e.g. *they are* [ðeːə] or [ðɛːə], rhyming with *there*; *go away* [ˈgəːəˈweɪ] = /ˈgɜːəˈweɪ/; *buy a house* [ˈbaːəˈhaʊs]; *now and then* [ˈnaːənˈðen]; *boy and girl* [ˈbɔːənˈgɜːl].

The weakness of the final elements of diphthongs is also demonstrated by their instability before vowels other than [ə]. Thus, in the case of /eɪ, aɪ, ɔɪ/, when /iː/ or /ɪ/ follow (i.e. a vowel articulation at or closer than the end point of the diphthongal glide, the [ɪ] 2nd element of the diphthong may be lost, e.g. in *playing, way in, they eat it, highest, hyaena, buy it, try each, annoying, the boy easily . . .*; the [ɪ] element may also be absorbed before other vowels, e.g. in *way up, by all means, they understand, toy engine*, though some glide in the direction of [ɪ] is likely to be made when the following vowel has a quality near to that of the 1st element of the diphthong (especially of the wide diphthongs /aɪ, ɔɪ/), e.g. in *may end, my uncle, the boy often. . . .* In the case of /əʊ, aʊ/, absorption of the [ʊ] element before /ʊ/ or /uː/ rarely arises, since a following /ʊ/ or /uː/ is unusual. Again, absorption of the [ʊ] element of the narrow diphthong /əʊ/ frequently occurs before other vowels, e.g. in *go easy, glowing, no end, go off, know all, show up*, though when /ɜː/ follows some movement towards [ʊ] and lip-rounding normally takes place, e.g. in *so early*. Loss of the [ʊ] element of /əʊ/ does not, in pre-vocalic positions, lead to confusion with /ɜː/, since /ɜː/ in such a position will normally be realized with a linking /r/, cf. *slow it* /ˈsləʊ ɪt/ or /ˈslɜː ɪt/ and *slur it* /ˈslɜːr ɪt/. In the case of /aʊ/, loss of the [ʊ] element may also occur before vowels other than [ə], e.g. in *allow each, vowing, how else, now or never*, but when the following vowel has an open quality similar to that of the 1st element of /aʊ/ some tongue movement towards [ʊ] and lip-rounding normally takes place, e.g. in *how are they, plough up, how odd*. This tendency to absorb the 2nd element of diphthongs before other vowels is a feature which is more marked in advanced RP than in either the general or the conservative forms of this kind of English.

A similar weakening of the monophthongs /uː/ and /iː/ sometimes occurs across syllable boundaries. /uː/ may be replaced by /ʊ/ and /iː/ by /ɪ/ before vowels in such phrases as *two in the morning* /ˈtʊ ɪn ðə ˈmɔːnɪŋ/ and *three o'clock* /ˈθrɪ əˈklɒk/. It is possible in a word such as *ruin* to regard the pronunciation /ˈrʊɪn/ as a version of /ˈruːɪn/ exhibiting smoothing.

Foreign learners should be aware of this tendency to reduction of vowel sequences, in order that they may understand colloquial English. They will observe that such reduced forms are normal among many educated speakers. Nevertheless, like most changes of pronunciation, these reductions are often condemned as vulgarisms—frequently by those who use them and are not aware of the fact. Foreign learners should, therefore, avoid the extreme forms of reduction, e.g. [aː] and [ɑː] for [aɪə] and [aʊə], and [ɜː] for [əʊə]. But the levelling to [aːə], [ɑːə], [eːə], and [ɔːə], described above, may be taken to be current and permissible. Certainly such pronunciations are preferable to sequences containing an exaggerated [ɪ] or [ʊ] element, i.e. [j] or [w], giving [ajə], [awə], [əwə], [ejə], [ɔjə], etc.

7.12　Centring Diphthongs /ɪə, ɛə, ʊə/

7.12.1　　　　　　　　　　/ɪə/

(1) *Examples.*—*eer, ear, ere*—deer, dear, tear (drop of liquid), here
　　　　　　eir, ier, ir—weird, fierce, fakir
　　　　　　ea, ia, eu, eo—idea, Ian, museum, theological

(*Note:* 'hero' /ˈhɪərəʊ/, 'year' /jɪə/ or /jɜː/.)

Long [ɪːə]—dear, here, cheer, beard
Reduced [ɪə]—pierce, fierce
Compare [ɪːə], [ɪə]—fears, fierce
[ɬ] *following*[1]—real

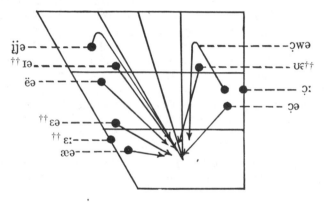

FIG. 27.—Final /ɪɔ, ɛə, ʊə/ and variants.

(2) *Description.*—The glide of RP /ɪə/ begins with a tongue position approximately that used for /ɪ/, i.e. centralized front half-close, and moves in the direction of the more open variety of /ə/ when /ɪə/ is final in the word; in non-final positions, e.g. in *beard, fierce*, the glide may not be so extensive, the quality of the [ə] element being of a mid type. The lips are neutral throughout, with a slight movement from spread to open.

It has been pointed out by Daniel Jones[2] that the sequence [ɪ] + [ə] may not always constitute the falling diphthong described, i.e with pro-

---

[1] This solitary example of /ɪə/ + [ɬ] may be taken as a variant of /iː/ + [ɬ] (cf. also *ideal*). It is possible to pronounce *real* with /iː/ in the same way as *meal, feel*, etc.; /ɪə/, however, seems to be more common in this particular word, cf. *reel* /riːl/, *rill* /rɪl/.

[2] See Daniel Jones, 'Falling and Rising Diphthongs,' Miscellanea Phonetica, II (International Phonetic Association, 1954).

minence on the 1st element. In unaccented syllables the [ɪ] element may be the weaker of the two, being equivalent to [j], cf. the two [ɪ] + [ə] sequences in both syllables of *period, serious* ['pɪərĭəd] or ['pɪərjəd] and ['sɪərĭəs] or ['sɪərjəs]. The glide of the rising type [ĭə] is often used when the [ə] represents a termination with morpheme status, e.g. *easier, carrier*, in which case [ɪ] and [ə] are conveniently treated as a hiatus of vowels in two syllables[1] with a variant monosyllabic pronunciation [jə]. Such a solution may also be applied to those cases where it is not a question of a morpheme boundary, e.g. *hideous, genius, idiom, billiard, morphia*, etc. In some cases the choice between a falling or a rising diphthong may depend upon the accentual pattern placed upon the word, e.g. *theological* [ˌθɪə'lɒdʒɪkl] (falling diphthong on the first syllable which carries secondary accent) or [θĭə'lɒdʒɪkl] (rising diphthong when the first syllable is unaccented). It may, therefore, be said that the falling diphthong in the last syllable of *reindeer* depends upon a degree of accent on that syllable, cf. the rising diphthong in the unaccented last syllable of *windier*.[2]

(3) *Variants.*—In some kinds of advanced and conservative RP, and especially when /ɪə/ is final, the prominence and length shift to the 2nd element of the accented diphthong, this final quality often being the most open type of /ɜː/ or /ʌ/ or even /ɑː/. Thus, *here, dear*, may be realized as /hjɜː, djɜː/ or /hjɑː = [ça:], djɑː/. The form with /ɑː/ is usually characterized as an affectation. In popular London speech a glide from a relatively close to an almost open position may be heard— [i̞] → [ä], sometimes with an intervening [j]. In those kinds of English where post-vocalic /r/ is pronounced, RP /ɪə/ is realized as /iː/ + /r/ in those words which have an r in the spelling of the RP diphthong, e.g. *here* /hiːr/.

(4) *Chief sources.*—PresE /ɪə/ results generally from ME [eː] + [r] (*here, hear, dear, weary, appear, clear*) and from early ME [ɛː] + [r] (*ear, shear, fear, beard*). In the sixteenth and seventeenth centuries some variation existed between [iːɹ] and [eːɹ], but by the seventeenth century [iːɹ] was predominant; [ɹ] was lost and replaced by [ə] in the eighteenth century. In those cases where no r occurs in the spelling, e.g. *idea, Ian, museum*, the [ə] element derives as usual in English from the obscuration of the weak vowel.

(5) *Advice to foreign learners.*—Foreign learners should avoid using a 1st element which is too close, i.e. /ɪ/ should be used rather than /iː/. Although the r, which occurs frequently in the spelling of this

---

[1] Increasingly a closer vowel is to be heard in such words, as [i̞ːzɪə], ['kærɪə] which may be interpreted as /i̞ːziː ə/ and /'kæriː ə/, an interpretation which supports the view that there is vowel hiatus.

[2] See B. S. Andrésen, '-*dier* and -*deer*; an experiment,' *Le Maître Phonétique*, No. 108, 1957.

diphthong, should not be pronounced finally or before a consonant, it should be remembered than an [r] link is regularly made before a following vowel, either initial in the next word of the group, e.g. *here and there* /ˈhɪər ən ˈðɛə/, or occurring in the following syllable of the same word, cf. *hear* /hɪə/ and *hearing* /ˈhɪərɪŋ/.

7.12.2   /ɛə/
                         (See Fig. 27)

(1) *Examples.—are*—care, rare, share, mare
                  air—air, fair, pair, chair
                  ear—bear, pear, wear, tear (v.)

(*Note*: with /ɛə/, 'heir, there, their, Mary, Sarah, scarce, aorist'.)

Long [ɛːə]—pair, there, chairs, cared
Reduced [ɛə]—scarce
Compare [ɛːə], [ɛə]—scares, scarce

                  (No cases of /ɛə/ + [ɫ].)

(2) *Description.*—The glide of RP /ɛə/ begins in the half-open front position, i.e. approximately C[ɛ],[1] and moves in the direction of the more open variety of /ə/, especially when the diphthong is final; where /ɛə/ occurs in a syllable closed by a consonant, the [ə] element tends to be of a mid [ə] type. The lips are neutrally open throughout. (See §7.11(3) for the reduction of /eɪ/ + /ə/ to /ɛə/.)

(3) *Variants.*—RP /ɛə/ has variants mainly in respect of the degree of openness of its 1st element. The presence of the opposition /ɪə/-/ɛə/, e.g. *fear-fair*, would appear to inhibit too great a raising of the starting point of /ɛə/. Nevertheless, in popular London speech, where the starting point of /ɪə/ may be closer (see §7.12(3)), /ɛə/ tends to start at a point slightly lower than C[e], i.e. slightly below half-close. A feature of conservative and advanced RP is an even greater opening of the 1st element of /ɛə/, i.e. [ɣə] or [æə], the glide being very slight. Another form of advanced RP uses a long pure vowel [ɛː], often somewhat centralized, especially in a non-final syllable, e.g. *careful, scarcely* [ˈkɛːfɫ], [ˈskɛːslɪ]. A centralized pure vowel is also a feature of certain Midland and Northern speech, notably that of Birmingham and Liverpool. In those types of regional English where post-vocalic *r* is pronounced, RP /ɛə/ is replaced by /eːr/ or /ɛːr/, e.g. *fair* /feːr/.

(4) *Chief sources.*—PresE /ɛə/ derives from three ME sources: ME [aː] + [r] (*care, hare, mare*); ME [ɛi] or [æi] + [r] (*their, air, hair, fair*); ME [ɛː] + [r] (*bear, there, where, swear*). We have seen (§7.10.1(4))

---

[1] It is to underline the half-open beginning of /ɛə/ that the diphthong is transcribed here with [ɛ] rather than [e]. A simplified transcription using [e] would, however, lead to no ambiguity in the representation of the RP vowel system.

that ME [aː] and [æi] tended to coalesce into [ɛː] in eModE and they in turn are confused by the seventeenth century with the descendent of ME [ɛː] when followed by [r]. It is likely that all words with PresE /ɛə/ were pronounced with [ɛːɹ] (or perhaps [eiɹ]) in the seventeenth century. The diphthongal glide to [ə] results from the loss of post-vocalic [ɹ] in the eighteenth century.

(5) *Advice to foreign learners.*—The post-vocalic *r* of the spelling forms should not be pronounced, except as a linking form when a following word begins with a vowel, e.g. *pair of shoes* /ˈpɛər əv ˈʃuːz/, or when a vowel occurs in the following syllable of the same word, e.g. *care* /kɛə/, but *caring* /ˈkɛərɪŋ/. Attention should also be paid to the half-open articulation of the 1st element of /ɛə/; in order to emphasize this point, it is often helpful to begin the glide from the quality of RP /æ/, cf. *cat* and *care*.

7.12.3	/ʊə/
	(See Fig. 27)

(1) *Examples.*—*oor*—poor, moor
　　　　　　ure—pure, endure, cure, sure
　　　　　　ur—curious, spurious, during, security
　　　　　　ewer—sewer
　　　　　　our—tour, dour, gourd

(*Note*: /ʊɔ/ usually occurs in 'jewel, fluent, truant'.)

(2) *Description.*—RP /ʊə/ glides from a tongue position similar to that used for /ʊ/ towards the more open type of /ə/ which forms the end-point of all three centring diphthongs with, again, a somewhat closer variety of [ə] when the diphthong occurs in a closed syllable. The lips are weakly rounded at the beginning of the glide, becoming neutrally spread as the glide progresses.

In the same way that the sequence [ɪ] + [ə] may constitute a rising diphthong, the sequence [ʊ] + [ə] may also, in unaccented syllables, have the prominence on the 2nd element,[1] e.g. in *influence, valuable, vacuum, jaguar*, etc., the 1st element often weakening to [w]. In many cases of such sequences, [ʊ̆ə] represents a realization of a final unaccented /uː/ + morpheme /ə/, e.g. *rescuer*, /ˈreskjuː/ + /ə/ > [ˈreskjŭə].[2]

(3) *Variants.*—/ɔə/ having coalesced with /ɔː/ for most RP speakers, the pattern of centring diphthongs is rendered asymmetrical, there being only one back glide of this type opposed to the two front glides. As a result, the 1st element of /ʊə/ can be lowered considerably

---

[1] See Daniel Jones, op. cit.
[2] As with /ɪə/ (see §7.12(2)) this unaccented /uː/ may be realized as a closer short vowel, thus [ˈreskjuə].

without risk of confusion. Thus several words with /ʊə/, which have a pronunciation [ʊə] for some RP speakers, are given by others a glide [ɔə], e.g. in *poor, sure*. This glide [ɔə] may in turn be levelled with the realization of /ɔː/. Thus, *Shaw, sure, shore*, still pronounced by some /ʃɔː, ʃʊə, ʃɔə/, are levelled by many others to /ʃɔː/ for all three words; or again, *you're* (most frequently with /ʊə/) may be realized as /jɔː/, i.e. identical with *your*. It is to be noted, however, that such lowering or monophthongization of /ʊə/ is rarer in the case of less commonly used monosyllabic words such as *dour, gourd*.

Where /j/ precedes /ʊə/, e.g. in *cure, curious, puerile, secure, endure, bureau*, the glide from close front [j] through back rounded [ʊ] to central half-open [ə] may be reduced not only to /jɔː/, as described above, but also to a glide from [j] to a long central vowel, i.e. [jə̞ː] or [jʌ̈ː]. This latter pronunciation is a characteristic of upper-class RP. In popular London speech, /ʊə/ levelled with /ɔː/ in such words as *poor, sure*, may be realized as [ɔːwə] (see also §7.9.8(3)). In those kinds of English in which post-vocalic *r* is pronounced, RP /ʊə/ is realized as /u(ː)/ + /r/ in those words which have an *r* in the spelling, e.g. *poor* /puːr/.

(4) *Chief Sources.*—PresE /ʊə/ derives generally from an earlier vowel or diphthong + [r], e.g. < ME [oː] or [ɔː] + [r] (*moor, poor, boor*); < ME [uː] + [r] (*mourn*, for those RP speakers who use /ʊə/ rather than /ɔː/)—it is to be noted that most cases of pure vowel + [r] have been lowered to /ɔː/, e.g. *fourth, floor, court* (see §7.9.8(4)); and < ME [iu] or [ɛu] + [r] or morpheme [ər] (*sure, pure, fewer*). In these cases the [ə] element developed with the loss of [ɹ] in the eighteenth century. Sometimes, however, /ʊə/ arises from the juxtaposition of /uː/ or /ʊ/ and another vowel which has weakened to [ə] (*influence, truant, virtuous, jewel*).

(5) *Advice to foreign learners.*—Care should be taken to use a 1st element of a half-close kind rather than a quality resembling that of /uː/. In addition, the spelling *r* should not be pronounced, except when a [r] link is made before a following vowel, either occurring initially in the next word, e.g. *poor old man* /ˈpʊər ˈəʊld ˈmæn/, or in the following syllable of the same word, e.g. *tour* /tʊə/ but *touring* /ˈtʊərɪŋ/.

7.13   Vowels in Relatively Weakly Accented Syllables

Except in the case of /ə/, which occurs normally only in unaccented syllables, we have so far dealt mainly with vowels in syllables carrying a strong accent (see Chapter 9 for the nature of accent in words).[1] In each polysyllabic word one syllable is said with more stress than the others

---

[1] For a detailed analysis of the relation of vowel qualities and word accentual positions, see G. F. Arnold, *Stress in English Words* (North-Holland Publishing Co., 1957).

and has a special prominence, e.g. the second syllable in *endeavour* or the penultimate syllable in *examination*. This is the *tonic* or *primarily accented* syllable (marked here with [ˈ]). The remaining syllable or syllables may be unaccented, or may carry a *secondary* accent associated with a rhythmic beat or particular vowel qualities (marked here with [ˌ]). The following table illustrates the occurrence of vowels in a selection of non-tonic situations—in words containing from two to five syllables. The first column, *Remote Preceding*, shows vowels in a place more than one syllable removed from the tonic; the second, *Adjacent Preceding*, vowels immediately preceding the tonic; the third, *Adjacent Following*, vowels immediately following the tonic; and the fourth, *Remote Following*, vowels in a place more than one syllable after the tonic.

	Remote Preceding	*Adjacent Preceding*	*Adjacent Following*	*Remote Following*
(a) /ɪ/	ina'bility	e'ffect	'sorry	'apathy
/ʊ/	superi'ority[1]	silhou'ette	'ambulance	'neighbourhood
/ə/	conside'ration	a'llow	'mother	'character
(b) Short				
/e/	refe'ree	Sep'tember	'prefect	'architect
/æ/	maga'zine	can'teen	'syntax	'caravan
/ʌ/	subjec'tivity	sul'phuric	'product	'aqueduct
/ɒ/	poli'tician	Oc'tober	'diphthong	'catalogue
Long				
/iː/	precon'ceive	aes'thetic	'phoneme	'obsolete
/ɑː/	arti'san[1]	sar'castic	'placard	'reservoir
/ɔː/	audi'bility	au'gust (adj.)	'record	'corridor
/uː/	super'sede	Ju'ly	'nephew	'residue
/ɜː/	perpen'dicular	ur'bane	'expert	'universe
Diphthongs				
/eɪ/	phrase'ology	a'orta	'detail	'magistrate
/aɪ/	bio'logical	mi'nute (adj.)	'missile	'civilize
/ɔɪ/		employ'ee	'convoy	'celluloid
/əʊ/	photo'graphic	No'vember	'window	'episode
/aʊ/	counter'act[1]	out'rageous	'compound	'eiderdown
/ɪə/	superi'ority	theo'logical	'frontier	'overseer
/ɛə/	varia'bility	where'by	'fanfare	'underwear
/ʊə/	neuro'logical	cu'rator	'contour	'manicure

It will be seen that totally unaccented syllables are associated particularly with vowels of a central or centralized quality (or a syllabic consonant), i.e. /ə/, /ɪ/, and /ʊ/ (though /ʊ/ in a weak situation is normally replaceable by /ə/ or may be reduced to /w/ before a

[1] In the speech of some people.

following vowel). The other vowel phonemes of RP may also, however, occur in syllables not carrying the primary accent, but the examples in (b) above illustrate tendencies of correlation between degree of accentuation and vowel quality:—

(1) The relevant syllables of the examples of Remote Preceding and Adjacent Preceding occurrences tend to carry a secondary accent, e.g. *referee* /ˌrefəˈriː/, *canteen* /ˌkænˈtiːn/. Alternatively, all the examples of Adjacent Preceding occurrences, with the exception of those containing /æ/, /aɪ/, /ɔɪ/ and /aʊ/, may be heard pronounced in a totally unaccented form with /ə/, /ɪ/, or /ʊ/, or, in the case of *theological* with /jə/.

(2) The relevant syllables of the examples of Remote Following occurrences may also carry a secondary accent, of a rhythmical kind, especially when the syllable contains a long vowel or diphthong, e.g. *reservoir* /ˈrezəˌvwaː/, *civilize* /ˈsɪvəˌlaɪz/.

(3) A rhythmic secondary accent may also be associated with the final syllable of Adjacent Following words under (b), again especially if it is a question in RP of a long vowel or diphthong, e.g *record* /ˈreˌkɔːd/, *detail* /ˈdiːˌteɪl/; if this secondary accent is lacking, as in other educated and popular forms of English, the vowel may be elided or reduced to /ə/ or /ɪ/, e.g. *product, placard, record, nephew, missile, window*, as /ˈprɒdəkt, ˈplækəd, ˈrekəd, ˈnevɪ, ˈmɪsl, ˈwɪndə/.

(4) With the possible exception of *subjectivity* (/ˌsʌbdʒekˈtɪvətɪ/ or /ˌsʌbdʒɪkˈtɪvətɪ/), all intervening unaccented vowels in the Remote Preceding and Remote Following examples in (b) above are /ə/ or /ɪ/.

It may be concluded, therefore, that, especially in the case of words in common use, the maintenance of a vowel quality other than /ə/, /ɪ/, or /ʊ/ in syllables not carrying the tonic accent will often depend upon the presence of a secondary degree of accent on the syllable in question. Alternatively, it may be said that our feeling for such secondary accents derives largely from the quality of the vowels contained in the syllables.

The present relationship of vowel quality and degree of accentuation arises from the various conflicting phonological influences to which English has been exposed over the last 1,000 years. As a general rule, weak accent in OE led to the obscuration of short vowels and the shortening of long vowels. By ME, however, new long vowels or diphthongs under relatively weak accent emerged as a result of vocalization of earlier consonantal articulations, e.g. [iː] < OE [ɪ] + [g] or [j] (*holy*), [ou] deriving from an intrusive [o] or [ɔ] before [ɣ] or [w] (*follow*). Moreover, words of French origin such as *empire, increase* (n.), while shifting their main accent back to the first syllable, kept the full vowel quality in the final syllable or, in the case of polysyllables such as *justify, temporary*, retained a secondary accent on a syllable following the primary accent. (In words of the *temporary, secretary* type, American English, for instance, keeps this secondary accent on the penultimate syllable with a full [e] vowel, as was the case in English up to the eighteenth century, whereas in present RP the secondary accent has been lost and the former [e] or [ɛ:] reduced to [ə] or elided.) As a result of influences of this kind, full vowels and usually secondary accent are found in eModE in a number of situations where to-day greater accentual and qualitative weakening is once again the rule,[1] e.g. *certain, bargain*, with [eɪ] in the final syllable in eModE, *history, majesty, tragedy* (and also an English word such as *merrily*) with [əi] finally, and *emperor, saviour*, with [əur] finally in eModE.

7.14 The Frequency of Occurrence of RP Vowels

According to an investigation by D. B. Fry[2] of the frequency of vowels in colloquial RP, /ə/ (10.74 per cent) and /ɪ/ (8.33 per cent) clearly emerge as the vowels having the highest count. This is to be expected, since /ə/ is the most common vowel in unaccented syllables in a language which has a high proportion of unaccented syllables, and /ɪ/ has a high frequency of occurrence in both accented and unaccented syllables. The following is the order of the remaining RP vowels:—

%	%
/e/—2·97	/u:/—1·13
/aɪ/—1·83	/ʊ/ 0·86
/ʌ/ 1·75	/ɑ:/—0·79
/eɪ/—1·71	/aʊ/—0·61
/i:/—1·65	/ɜ:/—0·52
/əʊ/—1·51	/eə/—0·34
/æ/—1·45	/ɪə/—0·21
/ɒ/—1·37	/ɔɪ/—0·14
/ɔ:/—1·24	/ʊə/—0·06

Total all vowels: 39·21%

[1] For an account of vowels in unaccented syllables in eModE see E. J. Dobson, *English Pronunciation 1500–1700*, vol. II, pp. 827–926 (Oxford, 1957).
[2] D. B. Fry, 'The Frequency of Occurrence of Speech Sounds in Southern English,' *Archives Néerlandaises de Phonétique Expérimentale*, XX (1947), pp. 103–6.

8

The English Consonants

8.1 The Distinctive Consonants

It is possible to abstract from a continuous utterance of English by means of a process of commutation (see §5.3) twenty-four distinctive units which are consonantal both in terms of their function (i.e. they tend to be non-central or marginal in the syllable—see §5.5) and also, in the majority of cases, in terms of their phonetic nature (i.e. they have, at least in some of their realizations, articulations involving the obstructions or narrowings which produce, acoustically, a noise component —see §4.2).

These twenty-four consonantal phonemes are classified in the table below in two general categories:—

A. Those articulations in which there is a total closure or a stricture causing friction, both groups being typically associated with a noise component (obstruents); in this class there is a distinctive opposition between fortis and lenis types. (For the reasons given in §4.3.6—i.e. that the distinctive voicing feature is not always operative in the pairs /p, b; t, d; k, g; tʃ, dʒ; f, v; θ, ð; s, z; ʃ, ʒ/—it seems preferable to use the more generally valid labels *fortis* and *lenis* to categorize the two sets rather than 'voiceless' and 'voiced').

B. Those articulations in which there is only a partial closure or an unimpeded oral or nasal escape of air; such articulations, typically voiced and frequently frictionless (sonorants, without a noise component) may share many phonetic characteristics with vowels.

		Bilabial.	Labio-Dental.	Dental.	Alveolar.	Post-Alveolar.	Palato-Alveolar.	Palatal.	Velar.	Glottal.
A.	*Plosive*	p, b			t, d				k, g	
	Affricate					(tr, dr)	tʃ, dʒ			
	Fricative	(ʍ)	f, v	θ, ð	s, z		ʃ, ʒ			h
B.	*Nasal*	m			n				ŋ	
	Lateral				l					
	Approximant[1]	w				r		j		

[1] or frictionless continuant or glide (semi-vowel).

150

Note

(1) In some types of RP it may be necessary to include the labial-velar fortis voiceless fricative [ʍ] as a phoneme.

(2) In practical teaching it may also be convenient to treat /tr/ and /dr/ as distinctive affricates as well as /tʃ/ and /dʒ/ (see §8.3).

(3) The glottal stop [ʔ] has been excluded, since it is not phonemically distinctive in RP; its use as a reinforcement for vowels and its allophonic association with /p, t, k/ will be treated in §8.2.7.

It will be seen from the arrangement above that:—

(*a*) the plosive and nasal phonemes fall into three contrastive groups as far as the place of articulation is concerned, i.e. bilabial, alveolar, and velar;

(*b*) the affricate, lateral, and /r/ phonemes have an alveolar basis;

(*c*) the fricatives have five areas of articulation, i.e. labio-dental, dental, alveolar, palato-alveolar, and glottal.

These basic areas of articulation, convenient for labelling the phoneme, may be extended in the various allophonic realizations of the phoneme, but for any particular situation in a context the number of oppositions involving the place of articulation will remain unchanged; thus, the allophones of /t/ may be dental or post-alveolar, or the allophones of /k/ palatal, without constituting additional distinctive areas of articulation, since such variants are conditioned by the context.

Class A
Consonants Involving Closure or Stricture (Obstruents)

8.2 Plosives

The complete articulation of a pulmonic egressive plosive, or stop, consonant consists of three stages:—

(1) the *approach* or *closing* stage, during which the articulating organs move together in order to form the obstruction; in this stage, there is often an *on-glide* or *transition* audible in a preceding sound segment and visible in an acoustic analysis as a characteristic curve of the formants of the preceding sound:

(2) the *hold* or *compression* stage, during which lung action compresses the air behind the closure; this stage may or may not be accompanied by voice, i.e. vibration of the vocal folds;

(3) the *release* or *explosion* stage, during which the organs forming the obstruction part rapidly, allowing the compressed air to escape abruptly; if stage (2) is voiced, the vocal fold vibration may continue in

stage (3); if stage (2) is voiceless, stage (3) may also be voiceless (aspiration) before silence or before the onset of voice (as for a following vowel), or stage (3) may coincide with the onset of vocal fold vibration, as when a voiceless plosive is followed without intervening aspiration by a vowel; again, an *off-glide* or transition associates the plosive with a following sound.

Since a condition of plosive articulation is that the whole of the speech tract behind the primary closure should form a chamber sealed to the escape of air, and since the primary closures for the English plosives are normally made in the oral cavity, the soft palate must be held in its raised position for at least the first two stages of these articulations.[1]

8.2.1   The Significant Phonetic Features of English Plosives

The RP plosive phonemes comprise three pairs: /p, b/; /t, d/; /k, g/. The following words illustrate oppositions in word initial, medial, and final positions:—

	/p/	/b/	/t/	/d/	/k/	/g/
Initial	pole	bowl	toll	dole	coal	goal
Medial	riper	—	writer	rider	—	—
	—	—	bitter	bidder	bicker	bigger
	caper	caber	cater	—	—	—
	—	rubber	—	rudder	—	rugger
	lopping	lobbing	—	—	locking	logging
Final	rip	rib	writ	rid	rick	rig

These oppositions may be realized by means of one or several of the following phonetic features:—

(1) *Place of articulation.*[2]—/p, b/, bilabial; /t, d/, alveolar; /k, g/, velar.

(2) *Force of articulation.*—/p, t, k/ tend to be pronounced with more muscular energy and a stronger breath effort than /b, d, g/; the former are known as relatively strong or *fortis*, the latter as relatively weak or *lenis*. (See §8.5 for *fortis/lenis* as phonological categories.)

(3) *Aspiration.*—The fortis series /p, t, k/, when initial in an accented syllable, are usually accompanied by aspiration, i.e. there is a voiceless interval consisting of strongly expelled breath between the

---

[1] When a nasal consonant precedes a plosive, the soft palate is raised in the first stage of the plosive. i.e. there is a nasal approach.

[2] i.e. the allophones of these phonemes are usually bilabial, alveolar and velar respectively.

release of the plosive and the onset of a following vowel, e.g. *pin, tin, kin* ['pʰɪn, 'tʰɪn, 'kʰɪn]. (The feature of aspiration is commonly regarded from an acoustic point of view as the voiceless interval occurring between the release burst of the stop and the onset of the voicing of the following sound, the time measured, which may be of the order of 40–70 msecs., being referred to as the voice onset time—VOT: see, for instance, Abramson, 1977.) When /l, r, w, j/ follow /p, t, k/ in such positions, the aspiration is manifested in the devoicing of /l, r, w, j/, e.g. in *please, pray, try, clean, twice, quick, pew, tune, queue*; some devoicing may also occur in relatively unaccented situations, e.g. *apricot, atlas, applicant, heckler, buckram, vacuum*, etc. In other positions, i.e. preceding a vowel in an unaccented syllable and finally, such aspiration as may occur is relatively weak, e.g. /p/ in *polite, lip*. When /s/ precedes /p, t, k/ initially in a syllable, there is practically no aspiration, even when the syllable carries a strong accent, cf. *pin* ['pʰɪn] and *spin* ['spɪn] (see §5.3.5).[1] In final positions, i.e. preceding silence, /p, t, k/ may have no audible release (see §8.2.3(1)). The lenis series /b, d, g/ is not normally aspirated (see, however, the next section).

(4) *Voicing.*—The lenis series /b, d, g/ may have full voice during their second stage when they occur in positions between voiced sounds, e.g. in *labour, leader, eager, rub out, read it, egg and . . ., to be, to do, to go*. In initial and especially in final positions, i.e. following or preceding silence, /b, d, g/, while remaining lenis, may be only partially voiced or completely voiceless, e.g. in *hill, done, game, cub, lid, bag*, /b, d, g/ may be realized, initially, with vocal fold vibration beginning only in the last portion of the second stage and, finally, as [b̥, d̥, g̊]. It is, therefore, unusual in normal speech for the release stage of /b, d, g/ in final positions to be accompanied by a voiced off-glide [ə]; with complete devoicing, any audible release will be accompanied by weak aspiration. The fortis series /p, t, k/ is not voiced.

The parametric diagrams (below) provide a schematic representation of the timing of vocal fold vibration in different phonetic contexts.

(5) *Length of preceding sounds.*—When the RP plosives occur finally in a syllable, their value is determined largely (since the voicing factor is not strongly operative) by the length of the syllable which they close. It is a feature of RP that syllables closed by fortis consonants are considerably shorter than those which are open, or closed by a lenis

---

[1] Accented /p, t, k/ also show some loss of aspiration as a result of a preceding /s/ which may be regarded as not in the same syllable, e.g. /k/ in *discussed* is only very weakly aspirated compared with the /k/ of *custard*, so that *discussed* may be distinguished from *disgust* only by the fortis nature of /k/. Other pre-stop consonants (especially fortis fricatives) appear to exert a certain absorption-effect upon the aspiration of initial /p, t, k/ in a following syllable or word—compare the degree of aspiration of the accented fortis plosives in *half-past, push past*, and *go past; brief talk, finish talking*, and *no talking; rough coat, fresh coat*, and *two coats*.

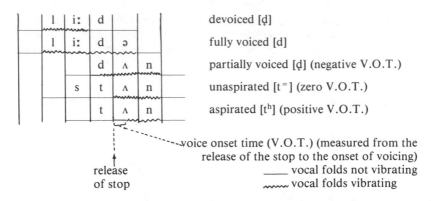

l	iː	d				devoiced [d̥]
l	iː	d	ə			fully voiced [d]
		d	ʌ	n		partially voiced [d̥] (negative V.O.T.)
	s	t	ʌ	n		unaspirated [t꞊] (zero V.O.T.)
		t	ʌ	n		aspirated [tʰ] (positive V.O.T.)

release
of stop

voice onset time (V.O.T.) (measured from the release of the stop to the onset of voicing)
_____ vocal folds not vibrating
〜〜〜 vocal folds vibrating

consonant. We have seen in the chapter on vowels that this variation of length is particularly noticeable when the syllable contains a 'long' vowel or diphthong, cf. the fully long vowels or diphthongs in *robe*, *heard*, *league* (closed by lenis /b, d, g/) with the reduced values in *rope*, *hurt*, *leak* (closed by fortis /p, t, k/). Preceding consonants, notably /l, n, m/, are also shortened by a following /p, t/ or /k/, especially when the consonants are themselves preceded by a short vowel, e.g. compare the relatively long /l/ in *killed*, *Elbe*, /n/ in *wand*, and /m/ in *symbol* with the reduced varieties in *kilt*, *help*, *want*, *simple*. A phonemic transcription of *rope*, *robe*, as /rəʊp, rəʊb/ is, therefore, to be interpreted as indicating that the words are distinguished not only or even primarily by a difference of the final consonant, but rather by a complex of quantitative and qualitative contrasts extending over the greater part of the word. The same effect of reduction also operates when /p, t, k/ occur medially in a word, cf. the length of /aɪ/ in *rider*, *writer*, although in this situation a more strongly contrastive voicing feature is likely to be present in /b, d, g/. This reduction in the length of a vowel or a sonorant consonant before fortis consonants is sometimes known as *pre-fortis clipping*.

Summary.—The RP plosives may, therefore, be said to be distinguished:—

(*a*) by means of a three-term series in respect of place of articulation—bilabial v. alveolar v. velar;

(*b*) at each point of articulation by the following phonetic features according to the situation (taking the bilabial oppositions as examples which are valid for the other two places of articulation):—

Initial in accented syllable—/p/ voiceless fortis aspirated v. /b/ partially voiced or voiceless lenis unaspirated, e.g. *pole* v. *bowl*.

Medial, following accented syllable—/p/ voiceless fortis weakly aspirated v. /b/ voiced lenis unaspirated, e.g. *rapid* v. *rabid*.

Finally—/p/ voiceless fortis weakly aspirated, if released, reducing length of preceding sounds v. /b/ voiceless (or voiced only at the beginning of the compression stage) lenis weakly aspirated, if released, preceding sounds retaining relatively full length, e.g. *rope* v. *robe*.

It is clear that, initially in accented syllables, /p, t, k/ and /b, d, g/ are distinguished by the listener mainly through the presence or absence of aspiration, rather than through the presence or absence of voice.

Foreign learners are, therefore, advised to pay particular attention to the aspiration of /p, t, k/ when these phonemes occur initially in an accented syllable. If a word such as *pin* is pronounced [pɪn], instead of [pʰɪn], there is the danger that the English listener may understand *bin*, since he interprets lack of aspiration as a mark of the lenis /b/. The danger is particularly great for speakers of those languages, e.g. many in the Romance and Slav groups, where the opposition between lenis and fortis stops relies purely upon presence or absence of voice. (The aspiration distinction between /p, t, k/ and /b, d, g/ should also be retained, when /p, t, k/ are followed by /l, r, j, w/, by the devoicing of these latter, e.g. compare *plight, try, crate, tune, twelve*, with *blight, dry, great, dune, dwell*.) Such speakers should also avoid excessive voicing of the lenis series /b, d, g/, especially in final positions. On the other hand, speakers of some languages, e.g. of the Germanic type, tend to neutralize the /p/ /b/ kind of opposition in final positions, using a fortis plosive for both. It must be remembered that /b, d, g/ finally, though they may not be voiced, remain weak as compared with /p, t, k/, the preceding sounds retaining full length.

8.2.2 Acoustic Features of English Plosives

Perceptual cues, capable of being expressed in acoustic terms, may be provided by all three stages of plosive articulations, so that it is possible to distinguish: (1) plosives from other consonants, (2) /p, t, k/ from /b, d, g/, (3) the bilabial, alveolar, and velar types.

(1) Plosives differ from other consonants mainly in the stage corresponding to the articulatory 'hold'. This part of the consonant is generally characterized acoustically by a perceptible period of silence throughout the whole spectrum or, in the voiced /b, d, g/, an absence of energy except at a low frequency.

(2) /b, d, g/ may be distinguished from /p, t, k/ by means of a low frequency component present in the former, i.e. voice. Moreover, there is likely to be a marked rising bend of F1 of the adjacent vowel in the case of /b, d, g/, which is not as marked in the case of /p, t, k/. However, as we have seen, /b, d, g/ may often be voiceless, in which case they are distinguished from /p, t, k/—initially, by the comparatively weak burst of noise associated with the release stage and by the absence

of the gap (aspiration) characterizing /p, t, k/; finally, by their influence on the duration of the preceding sounds; medially, by the longer closure period (absence of energy) required for /p, t, k/.[1]

(3) Cues to distinction as between the bilabial, alveolar, and velar plosives are provided, in some measure, by the noise burst related to their release stage. (Effective recognition is stimulated if the noise has a frequency span of some 480 cps and a duration of 15 msecs.) The actual situation of the burst of noise for each plosive category may, however, depend on the nature of the following sound. Thus, though the alveolars have a typical noise burst in the range of 3,000 to 4,000 cps, the bilabials may be characterized by a noise burst in the region of 360 cps in the vicinity of all vowels, but considerably higher frequency bursts (e.g. in the region of 2,000 cps) may produce an impression of a bilabial plosive when in the vicinity of the closer front and back vowels. Again, the situation of the release burst recognized as velar will depend very much upon the nature of the following vowel. It has been found that, before /uː/, velar recognition is achieved with a burst in the region of 700 cps; the frequency of the characteristic burst seems to rise throughout the series /uː/-/ɑː/-/iː/, following the rising frequency of F2 of the vowels, and reaches about 3,000 cps for a vowel of the type *C*[e], although in the case of the front vowels there is a second burst stimulus possible at considerably lower frequencies (matching to some extent the varying F1 of the vowels). The burst cues for velar plosives tend to be the inverse of those for bilabials in the range 300–2,000 cps.

A particular curvature (or transition) of F2 of the adjacent vowel also provides a primary cue for the distinction between the three types of English plosive articulation. Thus, in the case of the bilabials, F2 of a following vowel will typically curve upwards to its steady state and that of a preceding vowel downwards from its steady state (a *minus* transition); the alveolars exhibit small minus transitions in F2 of an adjacent /iː/ vowel and large plus transitions in F2 with an adjacent /uː/; the characteristic transitions associated with the velars seem to be largely the inverse of those for the alveolars, F2 having plus transitions but the greatest plus transition being related to an open vowel of the /ɑː/ type. Such considerable variation in cues for velar plosives, both in the release burst and in the transitions, would appear to reflect the extensive articulatory variation associated with the English velar plosives (see §8.2.6).

Any plosive + vowel or vowel + plosive sequence is, therefore, characterized by the curving of F2 of the vowel in a typical direction, as

---

[1] See Leigh Lisker, 'Closure Duration and the Intervocalic Voice-Voiceless Distinction in English,' *Language*, vol. 33, no. 1, 1957, in which it is shown that intervocalic /b/ has an average duration of 75 msecs compared with an average of 120 msecs for an intervocalic /p/.

though from, or to, a fixed point in the spectrum known as the 'locus'. This point is defined experimentally when several vowels are employed. The transition does not, however, extend from the steady state to the locus, but merely points in the direction of the latter. It would appear from experiments with synthesized speech that the best recognition is achieved if the first half of the transition from plosive to vowel consists of silence; if the curve is extended too far, glides of the type /j, w/ may be perceived. Research suggests that the transition of F2 and of F3 adjacent to the vowel is related to the *place* of articulation, whereas the nature of F1 is related to the *manner* of articulation.[1]

8.2.3 The Release Stage of English Plosives

It is not always the case that plosives in English have a third stage[2] consisting of a sudden oral release of air, either in the form of aspiration or as an immediately following vowel. The main variants are:—

(1) *No audible release in final positions.*—In final positions, as in *map, mat, mack,* or *robe, road, rogue,* the closure stage may be maintained, the air compression becoming weak and the release being achieved by a gentle, delayed, and relatively inaudible opening of the oral closure; or the compressed air may be released nasally and relatively inaudibly by lowering the soft palate and delaying the separation of the organs forming the oral closure. When an audible third stage is missing, the plosive is sometimes termed 'incomplete'. The absence of an audible release stage entails the loss of the release noise burst as a cue to the identification of the plosive. Unreleased final bilabial, alveolar, and velar plosives will, therefore, be distinguished mainly by the transitional features of the preceding sound. The sensitivity of English listeners to such cues is proved by the high percentage of correct discrimination between such pairs as *mat, mack,* or *road, rogue,* presented without a context, even when the final plosive is not released. The fortis series /p, t, k/ will, of course, be distinguished in final positions from the lenis series /b, d, g/ either by the reduction of length of the sounds preceding /p, t, k/ or by the presence of some voicing in /b, d, g/, or by a combination of both factors. The non-release of final plosives is a feature of colloquial RP. Careful speakers, however, tend to release such plosives audibly and those who, in ordinary

---

[1] For details of research in this field see publications listed in the Bibliography under the names of: Delattre, Libermann, Copper, Lisker, and Harris; Joos; Potter, Kopp, and Green; Halle, Hughes and Radley; Fry and Denes; Borden and Harris.

[2] Some writers (notably G. F. Arnold in 'Concerning the theory of plosives,' *Le Maître Phonétique,* no. 125, 1966) argue that this stage should be separated into a 'release' (an articulatory feature which is the converse of the 'closure') and a 'plosion' (an auditory feature). Such an additional distinction can be of value in describing the special cases considered in paragraphs (1)–(5) of this section.

conversational style, use the unexploded variety will often use an audible release in more formal circumstances. (See §11.6 on stylistic variation.)

(2) *No audible release in stop clusters.*—It is also a feature of most kinds of English that in a cluster of two stops (plosives or plosive + affricate) either within a word or at word boundaries, the first plosive has no audible release, e.g. in *dropped* (/p/ + /t/), *rubbed* (/b/ + /d/), *white post* (/t/ + /p/), *good boy* (/d/ + /b/), *locked* (/k/ + /t/), *big boy* (/g/ + /b/), *object* (/b/ + /dʒ/), *great joke* (/t/ + /dʒ/), *big chin* (/g/ + /tʃ/). In those languages where plosives in such situations are released audibly, the result is an intervening [h] in the case of voiceless plosives and an obscure vowel of the [ə] type in the case of voiced plosives. In English the closure for the second stop is made before the release of the first, forming a further obstacle to the airstream if the second closure is at a more advanced point, e.g. /t/ + /p/ in *white post*, or checking the air pressure if the second closure is at a more retracted point, e.g. /t/ + /k/ in *white cat*. Release of the first plosive is also delayed in cases of gemination, e.g. *top people* (/p/ + /p/), *good dog* (/d/ + /d/), *big girl* (/g/ + /g/), the second (hold) stage, consisting of silence or voice, being prolonged. The same delay in the release occurs when plosives, which are homorganic but different in fortis-lenis terms, are in sequence, e.g. *top boy* (/p/ + /b/), *white dog* (/t/ + /d/), *big car* (/g/ + /k/); in these cases, cues to recognition may be provided by the onset or cessation of voice, by the aspiration characteristic of the fortis series in syllable initial positions, and by the influence on the duration of preceding sounds of syllable final lenis plosives. It should also be noted that, in addition to the omission of an audible third stage of the first plosive in clusters, the first stage (onglide, transition) of the following stop is also inaudible. Thus, in sequences of three plosives,[1] e.g. *wept bitterly* (/p/ + /t/ + /b/), *locked door* (/k/ + /t/ + /d/), *jogged by* (/g/ + /d/ + /b/), the central plosive has no audible first or third stage; when this position is occupied by /p, t, k/, the plosive is manifested only by a silence of a certain duration, i.e. the length of its second stage. It will be seen that the past tense termination /t/, following /k/ or /p/ and not released in a final position, as in *worked, slipped*, may provide no audible clue as to the tense; to a lesser extent, this is also true of /d/ following /b/ or /g/, as in *robbed, tugged*. In such cases, the verbal tense is supplied by the context.

(3) *Glottal reinforcement*[2] *of final* /p, t, k/. It is increasingly typical of many types of British English that final /p, t, k/, in such words as

---

[1] i.e. when the alveolar plosive is articulated in such sequences. (See §11.3.6.)

[2] The term 'reinforcement' is used by J. D. O'Connor in 'RP and the reinforcing glottal stop', *English Studies*, xxxiii, 1952.

shop, shot, shock, have the oral closure reinforced by a glottal closure [ʔ]. In some cases this glottal coincides in time with the oral closure, inhibiting much of the air-pressure behind the oral closure, whether or not this latter is released audibly; in others the glottal closure may slightly anticipate the articulation of the oral obstruction; in other, rarer, cases there may be some compression of the air between the glottal and oral closures by means of the raising of the larynx and a constriction of the pharyngeal cavity, resulting in a potential ejective release. In such a case the plosive is no longer glottally reinforced or glottalized but is instead produced using the egressive glottalic (or pharyngeal) airstream mechanism. In certain cases, too, [ʔ] may replace /p, t, k/, see §8.2.7.

(4) *Nasal release.* —When a plosive is followed by the homorganic nasal consonant, either syllabic or initial in a following syllable, the release of air is normally effected not by a removal of the oral closure, which is retained, but by the escape of the compressed air through the nasal passage, opened by the lowering of the soft palate for the nasal consonant, e.g. /p/ + /m/ *topmost*, /p/ + [m] sometimes in *happen* [ˈhæpm̩], /b/ + /m/ *submerge*, /b/ + [m̩] sometimes in *ribbon* [ˈrɪbm̩], /t/ + /n/ *chutney*, /t/ + [n̩] *cotton*, /d/ + /n/ *madness*, /d/ + [n̩] *sudden*; and, more rarely, /k/ + /ŋ/ *thicken* [ˈθɪkŋ̩], /g/ + [ŋ̩] *organ* [ˈɔːgŋ̩]. The same release takes place when the plosive and homorganic nasal occur at word boundaries, e.g. *cheap meat, robe mistress, not now, red nose*, etc. (Since /ŋ/ does not occur initially in syllables, this last generalization does not apply to /k/ and /g/.)

A different kind of nasal release occurs when the nasal consonant following a plosive is not homorganic, e.g. in *cheap nuts, rub now, nutmeg, bad man, black magic, big nose, big man*, etc. In these cases the plosive closure is not normally released until the articulatory movements for the nasal consonant, i.e. the second oral closure and the lowering of the soft palate, have been accomplished.

(5) *Lateral release.* —The most frequent tongue contact for English /l/ being alveolar, the sequences /t/ or /d/ + /l/ are homorganic (i.e. made at the same place of articulation). /t/ and /d/ in such situations are normally released laterally, i.e. one or both sides of the tongue are lowered to allow the air to escape, the tongue-tip contact remaining. Such a release occurs whether the following /l/ is syllabic, e.g. in *cattle, medal*, or if it is initial in the next syllable or word, e.g. in *atlas, at last, regardless, bad light*. Such homorganic lateral release is to be distinguished from sequences of /p, b, k, g/ + /l/, e.g. in *apple, up late, bubble, blow, rub lightly, tackle, clean, blackleg, glow, eagle, big lad*. In these cases, the partial alveolar contact for /l/ is made before or at the time of the release of the plosive and, in this sense, the escape of air is lateral; but since /p, b/ and /k, g/ may be released in a truly lateral way, i.e. by the removal of one or both sides of the bilabial or velar

closure, the term 'lateral release' is best reserved in English for the homorganic alveolar + /l/ sequences. Such true lateral releases must be taken as typical of English usage, there being no intervening removal of the tongue contact on the alveolar ridge, such as would result in aspiration or an obscure vowel. Pronunciations of the type ['lɪtʰɫ], ['mɪdᵊɫ] for *little, middle*, are frequently to be heard in the speech of children.

(6) *Affrication of plosives.*—If the release of plosive closures is not made rapidly, a fricative sound, articulated in the same area of articulation as the plosive, will be heard; plosives made with this slow, fricative release are said to be *affricated*. Common realizations of the English plosives /p, b, t, d, k, g/ might, therefore, be followed by brief fricatives of the types [ɸ, β, s, z, x, ɣ]. In some varieties of English the alveolars /t, d/ may frequently be heard in affricated form [tˢ, dᶻ]: in strongly accented positions, e.g. in *time, day*; in relatively weakly accented positions, e.g. in *waiting, riding*; and in final positions, e.g. in *hat, bed*. (Note that, in these last two examples, the forms [tˢ] and [dᶻ] differ from the realization of the plural terminations /t/ + /s/ and /d/ + /z/ mainly in the brevity of the friction associated with the affricated plosives.) Affrication is also occasionally heard with the velar plosives, i.e. [kˣ] and [gʸ], e.g. in hesitant or emphatic speech in accented situations in such words as *come, good*, or, more commonly with /k/, in weakly accented or final positions, e.g. in *talker, talk*. /p/ and /b/ are rarely affricated. Affrication of plosives, especially of the alveolars, is particularly characteristic of popular London speech.

It should also be noted that in rapid, familiar speech, where easy intelligibility rather than articulatory precision is the aim, the closure, of plosives is often so weak that the corresponding fricative sound, without a preceding stop, is produced, especially in weakly accented intervocalic positions. The following examples have been noted among educated speakers; *imported* [ɪmˈpɔːsɪd], *invaded* [ɪnˈveɪzɪd], *baker* ['beɪxə], *dagger* ['dæɣə] (this latter, on the stage, in the *Macbeth* 'dagger' soliloquy), and even *pepper* ['peɸə], *rubber* ['rʌβə].

(7) *Advice to foreign learners.*—All the foregoing variants of the hold and release stages of English plosives may be heard from RP speakers. A foreign speaker of English may be generally intelligible without adopting any of these features, such is the redundancy of information carried in the English utterance. But the foreign learner who aims at a near approximation to the speech of English natives should adopt the following features at least:—

(*a*) Inaudible release of plosives preceding other plosives or affricates.

(*b*) Nasal release of plosives followed by a homorganic nasal, especially /t, d/ + /n/.

(*c*) Lateral release of /t, d/ + /l/.

(*d*) Affrication of /p, t, k/ as a stage in learning aspiration of these plosives in strongly accented positions.

8.2.4 Bilabial Plosives

/p, b/

(1) *Examples*

/p/—*fortis* (regularly spelt with *p*; note 'hiccough' /'hɪkʌp/, and silent *p* in 'pneumonia, psalm, ptarmigan, receipt, cupboard', etc.)

    accented, aspirated—pin, pill, pain, appear, impatient; play, pray, pew

    accented after /s/, *unaspirated*—spin, spill, Spain, spear; splay, spray, spew

    weakly accented, relatively unaspirated—upper, capable, opportunity, gospel; simply, apricot, champion

    syllable final—cheap, lip, lap, shape, lisp, pulp, pump; upright, chaplain, upward

    with no audible release—captain, topcoat, wiped, hop picker, top boy, top girl, top dog, ripe cheese

    followed by nasal consonant—topmost, halfpenny, happen, cheap meat

    followed by lateral consonant—apple, couple, please, up late

/b/—*lenis* (regularly spelt with *b*; note silent *b* in 'limb, thumb, comb', etc., and 'debt, subtle, doubt')

    initial, partially devoiced—big, boast, banana, begin, blow, brain, beauty

    intervocalic,[1] *voiced*—rubber, labour, harbour, husband, symbol

    final, voiceless—rib, ebb, sob, robe, bulb

    with no audible release—obtain, rubbed, subconscious, sob bitterly, sub-prefect, Bob goes, object

    followed by nasal consonant—submerge, robe mistress, ribbon

    followed by lateral consonant—bubble, blow, rub lightly

Compare /p/, /b/—post, boast; peach, beach; rapid, rabid; dapple, dabble; sopping, sobbing; simple, symbol; cup, cub; rope, robe; plead, bleed; pray, bray; puke, rebuke; mopped, mobbed.

(2) *Description.*—The soft palate being raised and the nasal resonator shut off, the primary obstacle to the air stream is provided by the closure of the lips. Lung air is compressed behind this closure, during which stage the vocal folds are held wide apart for /p/, but may vibrate for all or part of the compression stage for /b/ according to its situation in the utterance. The air escapes with force when the lip closure is

---

[1] i.e. in the sense of 'between voiced sounds'.

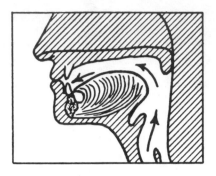

FIG. 28.—/p, b/.

released, unless the air-stream has been blocked by a second closure at a point behind the lips (as for /t/) or has been diverted through the nose by the lowering of the soft palate (as for /m/); when a lateral sound follows, the air-stream will have a lateral escape round the point of alveolar closure. In those cases where a bilabial plosive precedes a labio-dental sound (/f, v/), as in *cup-full*, *obvious*, the stop is often made by a labio-dental rather than a bilabial closure, in anticipation of the following fricative articulation, thus [kʌp̚fʊl], [ɒb̪vɪəs]. Tongue movements involved in vowels or consonants adjacent to the bilabial stop are made independently of the lip closure, e.g. the /ɔ:/ tongue position is maintained through the /b/ closure in *four balls* and the /l/ alveolar contact through the /p/ closure in *helpless*.

(3) *Variants.*—No important variants of /b/ occur, except in respect of the amount of voicing in initial and final positions, full voicing in either position being rare. On the other hand, many speakers tend to devoice in intervocalic positions, retaining the lenis nature of the consonant. In the same way, the amount of aspiration given to /p/ varies between speakers, though the accented form will always tend to be more strongly aspirated than the unaccented form (see §§8.2.1, 8.2.3).

(4) *Chief Sources.*—PresE /p/ and /b/ develop regularly from the same OE phonemes (single and geminated) and from French /p/ and /b/. In some cases /b/ derives from earlier /p/, e.g. *lobster*, *pebble*, and /p/ from earlier /b/, e.g. *pudding*, *purse*, *gossip*.

(5) *Advice to foreign learners.*—See general remarks in §§8.2.1, 8.2.3, and examples for practice in (1) of this section.

8.2.5   Alveolar Plosives

/t, d/

(1) *Examples*

/t/—*fortis* (regularly spelt *t*, *tt*; sometimes with *th*, e.g. 'Thames, Thomas'; also *-ed* in verbal past tenses and participles after fortis consonants other than /t/, e.g. 'jumped, looked, laughed, guessed, pushed'; *t* silent in 'castle, Christmas', etc.)

   accented, aspirated—take, tall, tone, attend, obtain; try, between, tune

   accented after /s/, *unaspirated*—steak, stall, stone

   weakly accented, relatively unaspirated—butter, letter, after, taxation, phonetic; entry, antler, outward

   syllable final—beat, boat, late, past, sent, halt, tuft, rushed, act, fetched

   with no audible release—outpost, hatpin, football, catgut, white tie, that dog, white chalk, great joke

   with homorganic nasal release—cotton, button, eaten, not now

   followed by /m/—nutmeg, utmost, that man[1]

   with homorganic lateral release—little, cattle, atlas, at least

/d/—*lenis* (regularly spelt *d, dd*)

   initial, partially devoiced—do, dog, double, date; dry, dwindle, duke

   intervocalic, voiced—leader, order, adorn, hiding, London, elder, under, middle, sundry, fiddler, endways

   final, voiceless—bid, mad, road, rubbed, bend, old, loved, bathed, raised, judged

   with no audible release—head boy, head girl, bad pain, red car, good dog, bed time, good judge, good cheese

   with homorganic nasal release—sudden, madness, red nose

   followed by /m/—admit, road map

   with homorganic lateral release—middle, padlock, headless, badly, good luck

Compare /t/, /d/—town, down; latter, ladder; water, warder; written, ridden; metal, medal; fated, faded; sat, sad; wrote, road; kilt, killed; bent, bend; train, drain; twin, dwindle; tune, dune

   /t/, /θ/—tin, thin; taught, thought; eater, ether; fort, fourth; tent, tenth; welt, wealth

   /d/, /ð/—dough, though; day, they; den, then; udder, other; loading, loathing; breed, breathe; side, scythe

(2) *Description.*—The soft palate being raised and the nasal reso-

---

[1] If the alveolar plosive is articulated as such. See §§8.2.7(2)(b)(3), 11.3.5.

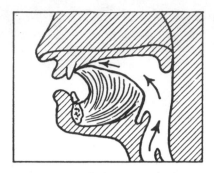

FIG. 29.—/t, d/.

nator shut off, the primary obstacle to the air-stream is formed by a closure made between the tip and rims of the tongue and the upper alveolar ridge and side teeth. Lung air is compressed behind this closure, during which stage the vocal folds are wide apart for /t/, but may vibrate for all or part of the compression stage for /d/ according to its situation in the utterance. The lip position for /t/ and /d/ will be conditioned by that of the adjacent sounds, especially that of a following vowel or semi-vowel, e.g. spread lips for /t/ in *teeth*, anticipatory lip rounding for /t/ in *tooth, twice*. The air escapes with force upon the sudden separation of the alveolar closure, unless the airstream has been blocked by a second closure either behind the alveolars (as for /k/) or forward of the alveolars (as for /p/), or unless it has been diverted through the nose by the lowering of the soft palate (as for /n/); if the release is lateral, only part of the alveolar obstruction is removed, the tongue-tip contact remaining.

 The alveolar stop contact is particularly sensitive to the influence of the place of articulation of a following consonant. Thus, followed by /r/ as in *try, dry*, the contact will be post-alveolar [t̠, d̠]; followed by /θ, ð/ as in *eighth, not that*, dental [t̪, d̪]; followed by /ʃ/ as in *cheap, reach*, accompanied by a considerable anticipatory raising of the front of the tongue. In addition, word final /t, d/ assimilate readily to /p, k/ and /b, g/, when followed by word initial bilabial and velar consonants (see §11.3.4).

(3) *Variants*.—In addition to the general plosive variations commented on in §§8.2.1, 8.2.3, it should be noted that /t, d/ are especially liable to affrication (particularly in the south of England) and even replacement by the equivalent fricative in weakly accented situations, e.g. *time* [tˢaɪm], *important* [ɪmˈpɔːtˢənt]. In Irish English, /t, d/ may be strongly dentalized and affricated before /r/. For some speakers, and generally in American English, /t/ is realized in weakly accented intervocalic positions as a lenis, rapid tap resembling a /d/ or one tap [ɾ], e.g. *butter, latter, put it over there*. Increasingly, /t/ in syllable final

positions is reinforced or replaced by a glottal closure unless a vowel or syllabic /n/ or /l/ follows, e.g. *late, want, cricket, outright, chutney*. Some RP speakers will also use [ʔ] to replace /t/ when [n̩] follows, e.g. *cotton, certain*; but the use of [ʔ] for /t/ preceding [l̩], and more particularly in unaccented intervocalic positions, is typical of regional varieties of English (e.g. those of popular London and Glasgow), as in *kettle, butter, later, a lot of* (see §8.2.7 for [ʔ]).

The instability of alveolar articulations is further demonstrated by the ease with which /t/ or /d/ may be elided in consonantal clusters (see §9.6 for examples within words and §11.3.6 for examples at word boundaries).

(4) *Chief sources.*—PresE /t/ and /d/ derive from the same phonemes of OE (single and geminated) and from French introductions with /t/ and /d/. Some words, now spelt with *th* and pronounced with /θ/, had /t/ until eModE, e.g. *throne, orthography, diphthong, authority*. There are, in addition, many cases in PresE of established elision of an earlier /t/ or /d/, e.g. in *castle, hasten, Christmas, often, fasten, Hertfordshire, Wednesday, handsome*, in which words the /t/ or /d/ was probably sounded up to the seventeenth century. In other cases /t, d/ have been added to earlier French stems ending in /n/, e.g. *peasant, parchment, sound, astound*, and to certain English and French words after a fortis fricative, e.g. *against, amongst*; *graft*. It should also be noted that the past tense and participle termination *-ed* (earlier [əd]) of weak verbs assimilated to /t/ following fortis consonants—other than /t/—on the loss of the intervening weak vowel, e.g. *wrapped, missed, annexed, pierced, blessed*, etc.

(5) *Advice to foreign learners.*—In addition to the general remarks in §§8.2.1, 8.2.3, and the examples for practice given in (1) of this section, it is to be emphasized for foreign learners that the general articulation of /t, d/ is an alveolar one, made with the tongue-tip raised. The corresponding phonemes of many other languages have a dental rather than an alveolar point of contact. Those learners who carry over from their own language a dental articulation should practise the slightly affricated forms of /t, d/, i.e. [tˢ], [dᶻ], in words such as *time, day*. If the closure point remains dental, the affrication produced will be clearly of the [tᶿ], [dᵟ] type. Those learners who, in their own language, have two varieties of stop closure made with the tongue-tip, e.g. speakers of Indian languages having dental and post-alveolar or retroflex varieties, should avoid using their retroflexed plosives in English, since these sound over-retracted to the English ear; they should also avoid using their dental /t, d/ for English /θ, ð/.

8.2.6   Velar Plosives

/k, g/

(1) *Examples*

/k/—*fortis* (spelt *k*; *c*, *cc* + *a*, *o*, *u*; *qu*; *ch*, e.g. 'kind, cake, accord, conquer, stomach, chemist, bouquet'; *qu* = /kw/ in 'quiet, quart', etc.; silent *c* or *k* in 'muscle, knew, knit', etc.)

accented, aspirated—come, car, kin, incur, according; cry, clean, quick, queue

accented after /s/, *unaspirated*—scum, scar, skin

weakly accented, relatively unaspirated—income, baker, talking, biscuit, anchor; secret, duckling, equal, dockyard

syllable final—leak, duck, rock, choke, bank, bulk, desk

with no audible release—Blackpool, locked, blackboard, thick dust, black cat, dark grey, deckchair, lock-jaw

followed by nasal consonant—acknowledge, dark night, thicken (sometimes /'θɪkŋ/), black magic

followed by lateral consonant—buckle, clean, close, blackleg

/g/—*lenis* (regularly spelt, *g*, *gg*; sometimes *gh*, *gu*, e.g. 'ghost, guard'; *g* silent in 'gnaw, gnat, diaphragm, sign, reign', etc.)

initial, partially devoiced—go, geese, guess, girl; glass, grass, Gwen

intervocalic, voiced—eager, hunger, figure, ago, begin, eagle; juggling, angry, anguish, argue

final, voiceless—dog, leg, rogue, vague

with no audible release—rugby, begged, bagpipes, wagtail, big game, eggcup, big jaw, big chin

followed by nasal consonant—dogma, ignore, quagmire, big man, drag-net, organ-grinder

followed by lateral consonant—bugle, struggle, glow, wriggling, dog lead

Compare /k/, /g/—cap, gap; coat, goat; clue, glue; decree, degree;

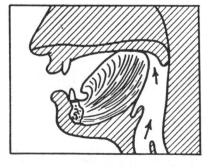   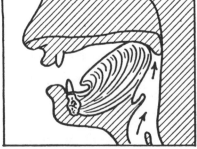

FIG. 30.—/k, g/ + /iː/.   FIG. 31.—/k, g/ + /ɒ/.

bicker, bigger; stacker, stagger; lacked, lagged; ankle, angle; hackle, haggle; pick, pig; back, bag; duck, dug; crate, great

(2) *Description.*—The soft palate being raised and the nasal resonator shut off, the primary obstacle to the air-stream is formed by a closure made between the back of the tongue and the soft palate. Lung air is compressed behind this closure, during which stage the vocal folds are wide apart for /k/, but may vibrate for all or part of the compression stage for /g/ according to its situation in the utterance. The lip position will be conditioned by that of adjacent sounds, especially following vowels or semi-vowels, e.g. spread lips for the plosives in *keen, geese,* and somewhat rounded lips for the plosives in *cool, goose, quick.* The air escapes with force upon the sudden separation of the linguo-velar closure, unless the air-stream has been blocked by a second closure forward of the velum (as for /p/ or /t/), or has been diverted through the nose by the lowering of the soft palate (as for /ŋ/); when a lateral sound follows, the air-stream will have a lateral escape round the point of alveolar closure.

The velar stop contact is particularly sensitive to the nature of an adjacent vowel (especially a following vowel). Thus, when a front vowel follows, e.g. /iː/ in *key, geese,* the contact will be made on the most forward part of the soft palate and may even overlap on to the hard palate; when a back vowel follows, /ɒ/ in *cot, gone,* the contact on the soft palate will be correspondingly retracted; a contact in the central region of the soft palate is made when a vowel of a central type follows, e.g. /ʌ/ or /ɜː/ as in *come, gun, girl* (see Figs. 30, 31).

(3) *Variants.* The actual extent of advancement or retraction of the velar closure will depend upon the nature of the extreme vowels /iː/ and /ɒ/ used by an individual; if /iː/ has a very front and tense articulation, the /k, g/ closures will in turn be near palatal, i.e. [c, ɟ] (noted by John Wallis in the seventeenth century as *ky, gy*), whereas, if /ɒ/ is of the most back and open variety, the velar closure will be of the most retracted kind. (For other variations affecting all plosives, see §§8.2.1, 8.2.3.) Since the initial clusters /kl, gl/ as in *clean, glean,* are not in opposition with /tl, dl/ which do not occur initially, a substitution of /tl, dl/ for /kl, gl/ in such positions may occasionally be heard both in RP and in other forms of English.

(4) *Chief sources.*—PresE /k, g/ derive from the same phonemes in OE (in single and geminated forms) and in French introductions. Some English forms with /k/ (spelt with *c* or *ck*) as in *pocket, carpenter,* derive not from the affricates usual in Central French (*pochette, charpentier*) but from the plosive equivalents of Northern French dialects. Again, some early French borrowings with *qu* retain the original /kw/ pronunciation, e.g. *quit, squadron,* where modern French has lost the /w/ element (cf. the later borrowing *bouquet*). Occasionally, a learned *c* spelling has been introduced with a resultant /k/ pronunciation, e.g. *perfect, subject* (note that in *victuals,* despite

the introduction of a *c* in the spelling, no /k/ is pronounced). The phoneme /g/ is sometimes spelt *gu* before *e, i*, in words of English origin, e.g. *guest, guilt*, by analogy with words of Central French origin such as *guide, guerdon*. /k, g/ initially before /n/ (*know, gnaw*) were finally lost late in the seventeenth century; /g/ following /n/ was lost in the south of England, e.g. in *sing, rung*, etc., in the seventeenth century, though it is kept intervocalically in certain words, e.g. *finger, longer, single*, and in all positions in many Midland and Northern dialects (see §8.6.3 for the origins of /ŋ/).

(5) *Advice to foreign learners.*—Note the general remarks in §§8.2.1, 8.2.3, and the examples for practice given in (1) of this section. French learners should be particularly careful not to over-palatalize /k, g/ both before and after front vowels; Spanish learners should avoid reducing intervocalic /g/ to a fricative [ɣ] or pronouncing initial /g/ (especially before a back vowel) as [gw] or [w].

8.2.7   Glottal Plosive

[ʔ]

(1) *Description.*—In the case of the glottal plosive (stop), the obstruction to the air-stream is formed by the closure of the vocal folds, thereby interrupting the passage of air into the supra-glottal organs. The air pressure below the glottis is released by the sudden separation of the vocal folds. The compression stage of its articulation consists of silence, its presence being perceived auditorily by the sudden cessation of the preceding sound or by the sudden onset (often with an accompanying strong breath effort) of the following sound. The plosive is voiceless and must be assigned to the *fortis* category both because of the strong air compression involved and also because, when substituted for or reinforcing a fortis plosive in final positions, e.g. in *shape, feet, back*, it has the same effect of reducing the length of the preceding sounds as a fortis consonant. The articulation of [ʔ] must be distinguished from that type of glottalization or laryngealization which involves tension in the laryngeal region and either an excessively slow rate of vibration of the vocal folds ('creaky voice') or a vibration of the false vocal folds situated just above the true vocal folds. In the production of these latter sounds, often heard in the lowest pitches of intonation and associated with weak intensity (though sometimes with muscular tension, e.g. at the lower level of the fall-rise tune) or on almost any pitch level in certain affected voice qualities, there is no total closure of the vocal folds.

It is clear from the description given above that there is no acoustic manifestation of the glottal plosive other than the abrupt cessation or onset of the adjacent sounds.

(2) *Usage.*—The glottal plosive, though frequently used by RP speakers, is not a significant sound in the RP system. Moreover, a distinction must be made between its regular occurrence in RP, certain tendencies for its more extended use in RP, and special cases which are found exclusively in regional speech.

(*a*) *General RP usage.* [1]—[ʔ] serves regularly for many RP speakers as a syllable boundary marker, when the initial sound of the second syllable is a vowel. Thus, a hiatus of vowels belonging to different syllables (especially when the second vowel is accented), may in careful speech be separated by [ʔ] instead of being joined by a vocalic glide, e.g. *co-operate, geometry, reaction* [kəʊˈʔɒpəreɪt, dʒɪˈʔɒmətrɪ, rɪˈʔækʃn], and even when the second vowel is weakly accented, e.g. *day after day* [ˈdeɪ ɑː ftəˈdeɪ]. This usage of [ʔ] is extended amongst careful speakers to those cases where there is a danger of an intrusive /r/ (see §11.3.7) at a point of vowel hiatus, e.g. in *Shah of Iran, law and order, drama and music*; the glottal marker is in turn applied by some speakers in cases where a regular linking /r/ is permissible, e.g. in *later on, far off, four aces*, but where some inhibition is imposed by the fact that the final vowel in the first word is /ə, ɑː/ or /ɔː/, i.e. those associated with intrusive /r/ sounds. In these latter cases, and in those cases of true hiatus where the second vowel is weakly accented, the glottal action may be one of unusual stricture rather than of total closure.

Finally, any initial accented vowel may be reinforced by a preceding glottal stop when particular emphasis is placed on the word, whatever the preceding sound, e.g. in *It's* [ʔ] *empty, I haven't seen* [ʔ] *anybody, She's* [ʔ] *awfully good*; or again, any vowel, initial in an accented syllable, may receive this glottal reinforcement, e.g. *It's un* [ʔ] *eatable, such dis*[ʔ]*order*.

(*b*) *Extended usage in RP.*—(i) *Reinforcement of final fortis plosives.*—As was pointed out in §8.2.3(3), word final /p, t, k/ and also /tʃ/ may be reinforced by a glottal closure which may coincide with the mouth closure or slightly precede it, especially when the word is final in the utterance, or, medially in the utterance, when the following word begins with a consonant. The release of such a glottal closure takes place at the same time as, or slightly preceding, that of the mouth closure (if the mouth closure is audibly released), so that the final release is not normally ejective. This appears to be true whatever the vowel or continuant consonant preceding the fortis stop, as the following examples of possible reinforced stops illustrate:—

[1] See also: P. Christophersen, 'Glottal Stop in English,' *English Studies*, xxxiii, 1952; J. D. O'Connor, 'RP and the reinforcing Glottal Stop,' *English Studies*, xxxiii, 1952; B. S. Andrésen, 'The Glottal Stop in the Received Pronunciation of English,' *Universitetet i Bergen, Arbok*, 1958; *Preglottalisation in English Standard Pronunciation*, Oslo, 1968.

	+ /p/	+ /t/	+ /k/	+ /tʃ/
/iː/	leap	feet	leak	reach
/ɪ/	rip	bit	lick	rich
/ɑː/	sharp	cart	lark	arch
/ʌ/	cup	cut	luck	much
/əu/	rope	boat	joke	coach
nasal	limp	went	bank	branch
/l/	help	belt	bulk	mulch
/s/	lisp	list	risk	—
/f/	—	lift	—	—

Note

(1) The glottal closure is perceived most abruptly when it is a question of cutting off a preceding short vowel.

(2) In the case of the stop being preceded by a fortis fricative (/f, θ, s, ʃ/), the glottal reinforcement appears usually to be simultaneous with the oral closure rather than anticipating it.

(3) In the case of word or morpheme final fortis clusters, e.g. /ps, pt, ts, ks, kt, tʃt/ in *corpse, apt, writes, axe, act, reached*, the glottal reinforcement is applied to the first element of the cluster and may continue into the second, if this is also a plosive.

Such reinforcement is also sometimes heard in utterance-medial positions. This is the case when the word medial or final stop is made by /tʃ/ or one of the clusters mentioned above and is followed by a vowel, e.g. *creature, reach it, watch it, drops it, dropped it, liked it, likes it, fits it*. It is very rare for reinforcement to be heard in association with word final /p, t, k/ + vowel.

In those final positions where reinforced /p, t, k/ are not released, the type of plosive is identifiable by means of the preceding vowel transition; when [ʔ] precedes the plosive, thereby cutting off much of the vowel transition, the plosive is frequently released.

(ii) *Replacement of* /p, t, k/ *by* [ʔ].—Some RP speakers replace word or morpheme final /p, t, k/ by [ʔ] when a consonant follows, no oral closure being made. Such a glottal closure often replaces /t/ when the following consonant is homorganic, i.e. /t/, /d/, /tʃ/, or /dʒ/ as in *that table, get down, that chair, great joke*, or /n/ as in *witness, not now*, or (less frequently) /l/ as in *Scotland, at least*; but [ʔ] is also heard for /t/ before other plosives, e.g. in *football, gatepost, cat-call, catgut*, and somewhat less commonly before nasals, e.g. *not time, nutmeg*, fricatives, e.g. *Catford, not for me, not very, what thing, out there, outset, great zeal, nutshell*, and /r, w, j/, e.g. *outright, cart-wheel, not yet*. Indeed, pure [ʔ] is to be heard for /t/ before all non-syllabic consonants except /h/. It is more common before a stressed syllable e.g. *at last* [əʔˈlɑːst] is more common than *Scotland* [ˈskɒʔlənd] and *outran* [auʔˈræn] more common than *outright* [ˈauʔraɪt]. Before /h/,

[ʔ] for /t/ is comparatively rare, e.g. *not here, boathouse*. In the case of following syllabic /l/, i.e. where /l/ has a vowel function, e.g. in *little*, the use of [ʔ] for the preceding /t/ is not generally accepted in RP, although it is sometimes to be heard for /t/ before syllabic /n/ as in *cotton, Eton*.

The replacement of final /p, k/ by [ʔ] is much less frequent among RP speakers, except when the following consonant is homorganic, e.g. *soappowder, cap-badge, back-garden, bookcase*. The use of [ʔ] for /p, k/ in such cases as *cup-full, reptile, capture, upset, lecture, back-door, breakfast*, is not generally acceptable as RP.

RP speakers may occasionally be heard to use [ʔ] for the [t] element of final /tʃ/, e.g. in *coach, much, catch, couch*.

(c) *Usage of regional speech.*—The replacement of /t, k/, and more rarely of /p/, in final positions by [ʔ], without any mouth closure, is typical of several kinds of regional speech, e.g. popular London, as in *Mind your feet* ['mɑ̃ɪ dɔʒə 'fəɪʔ], *Have a look* ['æv ə'lʊʔ], *get up* [ˌged 'ʌʔ]. Such replacements result in the neutralization of oppositions otherwise signalled by vowel transitions or release bursts, e.g. between *type, tight, tike*, the loss of this information being made good by other cues supplied by the context.

Very commonly, in this kind of regional speech, an unaccented /t/ is replaced by [ʔ] between vowel or /n, l/ and vowel, and between vowel and syllabic /n, l/, e.g. in *daughter, butter, Saturday, Waterloo, writing, potato* [pə'tæɪʔə], *salty, wanted, mutton, little*, or within the phrase as in *not in* [nɒʔ 'ɪn], *but what he ought to do* [bəʔ 'wɒʔ iː ɔːʔ ə 'dəʊ]. In rapid speech, however, especially when a number of articulations come in quick succession, the glottal closure is likely to be very weak.

Glottal replacements of /p, k/ also occur in similar situations, e.g. in *supper, paper, cup of tea* ['kʌʔ ə 'tˢəɪ], *lucky, joker, he doesn't like it* [əɪ 'dʒʊʔ 'lɑɪʔ ɪʔ], but there appears to be a greater tendency to retain a bilabial or velar closure. In cases of /-mpl, -ntl, -ŋkl/, as in *simple, mental, uncle*, if the nasal consonant is articulated, the [ʔ] used for /p, t, k/ is likely to be accompanied by the already formed bilabial, alveolar, or velar closure; if, however, as often happens in London speech, /-ɪm, -en, -ʌŋ/ are realized as [ĩ, ẽ, ʌ̃], the following stop may be only glottal.

In London speech, [ʔ] also replaces the fricative /f/, especially in the phrase *half a*, e.g. *half a minute* ['ɑːʔ ə 'mɪnɪʔ]. It should also be noted that, initial /h/ often being elided, vowels thus rendered initial may have glottal emphatic reinforcement applied to them, especially in hiatus with a preceding vowel, e.g. *I hate him* [ɑɪ 'ʔæɪʔ ɪm], *we haven't* [wi 'ʔævnʔ].

(3) *History.*—Since it would appear that [ʔ] has never been a significant sound in English, it is not to be expected that its stylistic use should

have been described in detail by the early grammarians. It is, however, mentioned in the seventeenth century[1] as a feature of the onset of initial vowels and, in works dealing with singing technique, has traditionally been described as the 'hard attack'. But the substitution of [ʔ] for a fortis plosive in regional speech is not explicitly mentioned until the nineteenth century and it is only in recent years that the phenomenon of reinforcement has been explicitly noted. Lack of descriptive evidence concerning this non-significant sound is not, however, a reason for assuming that [ʔ] is a feature of recent occurrence in English speech; we have little information concerning intonation patterns before the second half of the eighteenth century, but it is unlikely that the language has not made use of pitch distinctions in the utterance from the earliest times.

8.3   Affricates

1. *Definition.*—The term 'affricate' denotes a concept which is primarily of phonetic importance. Any plosive whose release stage is performed in such a way that considerable friction occurs approximately at the point where the plosive stop is made, may be called 'affricative'. It should be noted that the plosive and homorganic fricative will have the same voicing. The friction present in an affricate is of shorter duration than that which characterizes the fricatives proper. In English, apart from the exceptional affrication mentioned in §8.2.3(6), only /t, d/ may have this type of release, namely in /tʃ, dʒ, tr, dr, ts, dz, tθ, dð/.

2. *Phonemic status.*—From a functional or distributional point of view these compound sounds may be considered either as single phonemic entities or as sequences of two phonemes. As always, the choice of phonemic solution will depend upon the purpose of the analysis, but the following factors may be taken into account:—

(1) *The distribution of the sound complex*, especially in the following situations:—

(a) syllable initial
(b) syllable final, within the same syllable or morpheme
(c) word medial, with close-knit stop and fricative elements
(d) word medial or final, with stop final and fricative initial in adjacent syllables or morphemes.

A sound complex which has a general distribution and shows an opposition between *close-knit* medial realizations and *disjunct* (i.e.

---

[1] See D. Abercrombie, 'Forgotten Phoneticians', *Transactions of the Philological Society*, 1948.

with the elements in separate syllables or morphemes) realizations may
be treated as a complex phonemic entity.

	(a)	(b)	(c)	(d)
/tʃ/	chap	patch	butcher	lightship
/dʒ/	jam	badge	aged	—
/tr/	tram	—	mattress	footrest
/dɹ/	dram	—	tawdry	handrail
/ts/	—	quartz	curtsey(?)	cats, outset
/dz/	—	adze	Pudsey(?)	roads
/tθ/	—	—	—	eighth
/dð/	—	—	—	(width)

The table above shows that /tʃ, dʒ/ best fulfil these conditions,
behaving in an intervocalic position very much as a simple consonant,
i.e. without separation of the elements between the syllables (cf.
pitches, pities; aged, aided). /tr, dr/ lack occurrences in final positions,
but have a high degree of close-knit distinctiveness as a complex. /ts,
dz/ do not occur initially[1] (except in rare foreign words) and only
doubtfully in close-knit medial situations. /tθ, dð/ have an occurrence
restricted to the final position in very few words. Thus, /tʃ, dʒ/, and to
a lesser extent /tr, dr/, may be treated as single, complex, phonemes,
such an interpretation being particularly valuable in the teaching of RP
to most nationalities.

If /tʃ, dʒ, tr, dɹ/ are treated as sequences of two phonemes, the
realization of the second element will differ according to whether it
occurs in the same syllable or morpheme as the stop (i.e. shorter friction
in the case of /tʃ, dʒ/ and fricative /r/ in the case of /tr, dr/) or whether
a syllable or morpheme boundary occurs between the elements (i.e.
longer friction in the case of /t/ + /ʃ/ and a less fricative /r/ in the case
of /t, d/ + /r/—no boundary being possible between /d/ and /ʒ/,
since /ʒ/ does not occur in syllable or morpheme initial position).

(2) *Possibilities of commutation of the elements.*—(a) The elements
of /tʃ/ may be commutated within the same syllable: word initially, in
the stop, with zero only, cf. *chip, ship*; in the fricative, with /r, w/ and
zero, cf. *chip, trip, tip, chin, twin*[2]; word medially, in the stop, with
zero only (a syllable boundary being possible between /l/ and /ʃ/ in
such a case as *welshing*, and the medial sequence /-nʃ/ being an alternative form of /-ntʃ/ as in *pinching*), cf. *matches, mashes*; in the

---

[1] The different length of friction as between the fricative element of an affricate and a
fricative following a plosive is shown by a comparison of the affricated /t/ in *cat* [kætˢ]
and the longer friction of the plural form cats /kæts/. Dialectal affrication of /t/, d/ is,
however, more common initially (where /t, d/ + /s, z/ is unusual) than finally, being
inhibited in final positions by the risk of confusion with the inflected forms.

[2] There is a tendency for initial /tj/ to become /tʃ/ as it does medially; oppositions
between initial /tj/ and /tʃ/ are rare, but cf. the first syllable of *Tuesday* with *choose*.

fricative, with /r/ or zero (a syllable boundary occurring between /t/ and /w/, /l/, /n/, etc., as in *outward, atlas, chutney*), cf. *enchants, entrance* (v.), *marcher, martyr*; word finally, in the stop, with /l/ or zero (final /-nʃ/ as in *French* being an alternative for /-ntʃ/), cf. *watch, Walsh, wash*, and in the fricative, with /s/ or zero, cf. *catch, cats, cat*.

The elements of /dʒ/ have a more restricted possibility of commutation owing to the rarity of syllable initial /ʒ/. Thus, the elements commutate within the same syllable: word initially, in the fricative only, with /r, j, w/ and zero, cf. *jest, dressed, June, dune* (with a tendency for /dj/ to become /dʒ/), *dwell, jell, jam, dam*; medially, in the stop, with zero, cf. *ledger, leisure*, and in the fricative, with /r/ and zero in the same syllable, cf. *orgy, Audrey, larger, larder;* word finally, in the fricative only, with /z/ or zero, cf. *hedge, heads, head* (final /ʒ/ being a variant of /dʒ/).

Thus the possibilities of commutation are restricted in the case of the elements of /tʃ/ to zero (and occasionally /l/) for the stop, and to zero, /r, w/ and /s/, according to the situation, for the fricative. The commutability of the elements of /dʒ/ is also restricted, i.e. with zero in the case of the stop (medially), and with zero, /r, j, w/ or /z/, according to the situation, in the fricative. Moreover, /tʃ/ is in opposition to /dʒ/ as a complex in all positions (see §8.3.1 for examples).

(*b*) /tr, dr/, on the other hand, have considerable possibilities of commutation especially in the first element: in the case of /tr/, cf. *try, cry, pry, fry, rye; true, shrew, drew, grew, threw, brew; tree, three, tea; trill, chill, twill; Troon, tune; train, chain*; in the case of /dr/, cf. *drew, true, crew, grew, brew, threw, shrew, rue, do, due, Jew; dry, fry, pry*, etc.

On the basis of commutability, therefore, /tr, dr/ are more reasonably to be considered as consisting of separable elements than /tʃ, dʒ/.

(3) *Native speakers' reaction.*—It seems that the native speaker does not regard /tʃ, dʒ/ as composite sounds, i.e. composed of distinctive elements. He is likely, for instance, to consider that *chip, catch*, consist of three parts in the same way as *tip, ship*, or *cat, cash*; or again, *jam, badge*, as structures equivalent to *dam, bad*. (It is, of course, true that PresE /tʃ, dʒ/ derive in many cases from earlier (OE or OF) plosives [c] or [ɟ], as well as from a coalescence of /t/ or /d/ + /j/—see §8.3.1— but this is irrelevant in any consideration of the present structure of the language.) On the other hand, /tr, dr/ are not normally regarded as anything but sequences of /t, d/ + /r/ and, in many dialects where the /r/ has a tap or trill realization, there is no question of affrication.

(4) *Conclusion.*—In view of the considerations stated above, /tʃ, dʒ/ will here be treated as complex phonetic but single phonemic entities. /tr/ and /dr/ will also be considered as units, but mainly on account of the phonetic relationship of the elements, i.e. the retracted nature of the [t̠] and the friction associated with the [ɹ] in general RP,

and because, in teaching non-English learners, the treatment of RP /tr, dr/ as single articulations is an effective pedagogic procedure.

3. *Acoustic features.*—The acoustic features of affricates are those appropriate to stops (see §8.2.2) and fricatives (see §8.4). Since, however, the release stage is fricative, the most essential perceptual cues will be provided by the transition between the preceding vowel and the stop and by the explosive onset of the friction. Nevertheless, in the case of /tʃ, dʒ, tr, dr/, the transition will not be that which is typical of the alveolar plosives, since the stops of /tʃ, dʒ/ will be of a palatalized type and those of /tr, dr/ of a post-alveolar kind; there may be also, in the case of /tʃ, dʒ/, a brief intervening friction of the alveolar /s, z/ type before the [ʃ, ʒ] elements proper.[1]

8.3.1 Palato-alveolar Affricates

/tʃ, dʒ/

(1) *Examples*

/tʃ/—*fortis* (spelt *ch, tch, t* + *ure, eous,* and *t* + *ion* when *t* is preceded by *s,* e.g. 'chain, watch, nature, righteous, question')
  word initial—cheese, chain, charge, charm, choke, cheer
  word medial (intervocalic)—feature, richer, wretched, orchard, butcher, nature, merchant
    (*consonant preceding*)—gesture, posture, mischief, juncture, capture, lecture, pilchard, culture, adventure
  word final—wretch, catch, larch, porch, much, coach
    (*consonant preceding*)—inch, conch, bench, branch, filch, mulch
/dʒ/—*lenis* (spelt *j, g, dg,* sometimes *gg, dj, de, di, ch,* e.g. 'jam, gem, midget, suggest, adjacent, grandeur, soldier, Norwich')
  word initial—gin, jest, jar, jaunt, Jew, jerk, joke, joist, jeer
  word medial (intervocalic)—midget, ledger, margin, fragile, urgent, orgy, adjacent, agenda, major
    (*consonant preceding*)—avenger, danger, stringent, soldier, Belgian, bulges, object
  word final—ridge, edge, large, dodge, judge, huge, age, doge, gouge
    (*consonant preceding*)—bilge, bulge, hinge, sponge, change
Compare /tʃ/, /dʒ/—chin, gin; chest, jest; choose, Jews; choke, joke; cheer, jeer; catches, cadges; nature, major; a venture, avenger; riches, ridges; leech, liege; larch, large; perch, purge; lunch, lunge; cinch, singe; beseech, besiege

---

[1] See P. Strevens, 'Spectra of Fricative Noise in Human Speech,' *Language and Speech*, vol. 3, 1, 1960.

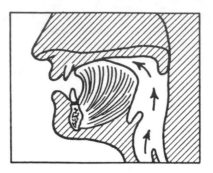

FIG. 32.—Stop phase of /tʃ, dʒ/.

(2) *Description.*—The soft palate being raised and the nasal resonator shut off, the obstacle to the air-stream is formed by a closure
made between the tip, blade, and rims of the tongue and the upper
alveolar ridge and side teeth. At the same time, the front of the tongue is
raised towards the hard palate in readiness for the fricative release. The
closure is released slowly, the air escaping in a diffuse manner over the
whole of the central surface of the tongue with friction occurring
between the blade/front region of the tongue and the alveolar/front
palatal section of the roof of the mouth. During both stop and fricative
stages, the vocal folds are wide apart for /tʃ/, but may be vibrating for
all or part of /dʒ/ according to the situation in the utterance. (/dʒ/
shares the features of devoicing in initial and final positions exhibited
by plosives, see §8.2.1(4), and fricatives, see §8.4(3).) /tʃ, dʒ/ differ
from plosives in that they never lose their fricative release stage. The lip
position will be conditioned by that of adjacent sounds, especially that
of a following vowel (cf. the greater lip-rounding of /tʃ/ in *choose* in
relation to that of *cheese*), though with some speakers a certain amount
of lip-protrusion is always present.

In addition, it should be noted that the fortis /tʃ/, when final in a
syllable, occasions pre-fortis clipping, having the same effect of
reducing the length of preceding sounds as was noted for /p, t, k/ (see
§8.2.1(5)); comparatively full length of preceding sounds is retained
before /dʒ/. This effect must be taken as a primary distinctive feature
of the /tʃ/-/dʒ/ opposition in final positions.

Since there is no opposition between /tʃ, dʒ/ and /tr, dr/ in syllable
final positions, the palatalization of /tʃ, dʒ/ is not significant in such
situations; the articulation of post-alveolar affricates in such cases as
touch, *large*, will generally be perceived as /tʃ, dʒ/.

(3) *Variants.*—No important variants of /tʃ, dʒ/ occur, except in the
matter of the degree of lip-rounding used. Some very careful speakers,
however, use /t/ and /d/ + /j/ in words which frequently have /tʃ/ or

/dʒ/ e.g. *gesture, culture, virtue, statue, righteous, fortune, literature, question, posture, Christian, soldier, grandeur*. Little confusion arises from the retention of /tj/ and /dj/ forms, since oppositions between medial /tʃ, dʒ/ and /tj, dj/ are rare, e.g. a potential case is *verdure* with /dj/ and *verger* with /dʒ/. In the case of /t, d/ + *u*, both the palato-alveolar affricate and /t/ or /d/ + /j/ may be heard, e.g. in *actual, punctual, mutual, obituary, individual, gradual, educate*. Some speakers omit the stop element in the clusters /ntʃ, ndʒ/ in word final positions as in *pinch, French, lunch, branch, paunch, hinge, revenge, challenge, strange, scrounge*, etc., and also medially as in *pinching, luncheon, avenger, danger*, etc.

(4) *Chief sources.*—PresE /tʃ, dʒ/ derive from: early OE [c] and [ɟ] (*child, chin, kitchen, teach, church, edge, bridge*), this change being accomplished by the late OE period; OF [tʃ, dʒ] (*chief, chair, chamber, choice, merchant, branch, judge, major, age, village, change*); a coales-cence of medial /tj/ or /dj/ (*nature, virtue, question, creature, grandeur, soldier*)—this latter change was not general until the early eighteenth century; a number of eighteenth-century coalesced forms have now reverted to a stop + /j/ or /ɪ/ sequence, e.g. *piteous, bestial, tedious, odious*.

(5) *Advice to foreign learners.*—Some learners (especially Scandina-vians) are apt to articulate /tʃ, dʒ/ with too much lip-spreading and over-palatalization, producing sounds resembling /tç, djʲ]. Particular attention should also be paid to the shortening of sounds preceding syllable final /tʃ/, the examples in (1) of this section providing practice for this feature. Moreover, sequences of affricates should be practised, care being taken to pronounce the fricative elements of both affricates, e.g. *which chair; Dutch cheese; large jar; Judge Jeffreys*.

8.3.2 Post-alveolar Affricates

/tr, dr/

(1) *Examples*

/tr/—*fortis* (spelt *tr*; *note* 'naturally' often /ˈnætrəlɪ/, and /trɪ/ < /tərɪ/, e.g. 'history, territory', etc.)
    word initial—tree, trick, trend, trod, true, truck, tripe
    word medial (*initial in syllable*)—attract, poetry, petrol, sultry, mattress, poultry, pastry, country, entrance (n.) /ˈentrəns/, entrance (v.) /ɪnˈtrɑːns/
/dr/—*lenis* (spelt *dr*; *note* /drɪ/ < /dərɪ/, e.g. 'boundary', etc.)
    word initial—dream, drip, dram, drop, drawl, drum, draft, drove, drought, dreary, Drury
    word medial (*initial in syllable*)—address, adroit, hydrangea, tawdry, sundry, hindrance, Andrew

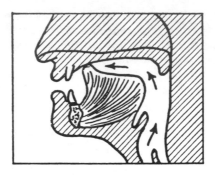

FIG. 33.—Stop phase of /tr, dr/.

Compare /tr/, /dr/—trip, drip; trench, drench; tram, dram; trunk, drunk; troop, droop; try, dry

/tr/, /tʃ/—trees, cheese; trip, chip; trap, chap; true, chew; train, chain

/dr/, /dʒ/—drill, gill; dressed, jest; draw, jaw; drew, Jew; dram, jam; drear, jeer; Drury, jury

(2) *Description.*—In the pronunciation of RP /tr, dr/, the soft palate being raised and the nasal passage shut off, the obstacle to the airstream is formed by a closure made between the tip and rims of the tongue and the rear edge of the upper alveolar ridge and the upper side teeth. The centre of the tongue is hollowed in readiness for the [ɹ] type friction, which results from the slow release of the stop (see §8.8 for the articulation of /r/). During the stop and fricative stages, the vocal folds are wide apart for /tr/; in the case of /dr/, voice is present throughout the affricate when medial, but may be associated only with the fricative element when initial. /tr, dr/ do not occur in syllable final position. The lip position is conditioned mainly by that of the following vowel, though some speakers will always use a certain amount of lip protrusion typical for /r/. A feature of the close-knit complexes /tr, dr/ is the fricative nature (voiced or voiceless) of the [ɹ] element, which in this respect differs from the usual realization of RP /r/.

(3) *Variants.*—In those regional types of English where the normal /r/ is realized as a lingual or uvular tap or trill, the post-alveolar type of stop + fricative complex described above may not be used, but rather a clear sequence of stop + trill or tap (see §8.8 for varieties of /r/).

(4) *Chief sources.*—Except in the case of elision of intermediate /ə/ (see §9.6), /tr, dr/ derive from similar earlier complexes.

(5) *Advice to foreign learners.*—For those foreign learners whose own *r* sound is either a lingual trill or a uvular trill or fricative, it is often helpful to approach the English RP /r/ through the affricate complexes /tr, dr/, thus establishing the correct place of articulation. Learners

should start from /ʧ, dʒ/ and retract and hollow the tongue until suitable /tr, dr/ affricates are achieved; the comparative examples given in (1) of this section will serve as practice material for this exercise.

8.4 Fricatives

In the articulation of a fricative consonant, two organs are brought and held sufficiently close together for the escaping air-stream to produce local air turbulence; fricatives are, therefore, like plosives and affricates, characterized by a noise component. This turbulence may or may not be accompanied by voice. There is an on- or off-glide in respect of an adjacent sound, most appreciable if the adjacent sound is a vowel.

The RP fricative phonemes comprise four pairs /f, v; θ, ð; s, z; ʃ, ʒ/ and /h/. [x], a voiceless (fortis) velar fricative, occurs exceptionally in some speakers' pronunciation of Scottish words such as *loch*; for [ɸ, β, s, z, x, ɣ] occurring as the fricative element of affricated plosives, see §8.2.3(6), and for the fricative allophones of /r, j, w/, see §§8.8–8.9.2.

The following words illustrate oppositions, especially between members of the fricative pairs, in word initial, medial, and final positions:—

	Initial.	*Medial.*	*Final.*
/f/	feel	proofing	leaf
/v/	veal	proving	leave
/θ/	thigh	earthy, ether	wreath
/ð/	thy	worthy, either[1]	wreathe
/s/	seal	racer	peace
/z/	zeal	razor	peas
/ʃ/	sheet	fission, Confucian	ruche
/ʒ/	gigolo	vision, confusion	rouge
/h/	heat	behave	—

These oppositions may be realized by means of one or several of the following phonetic features:—

(1) *Place of articulation.*—/f, v/—labio-dental; /θ, ð/—dental; /s, z/—alveolar; /ʃ, ʒ/—palato-alveolar; /h/—glottal. Such a series must be considered to be relatively complex. The existence, in particular, of place-oppositions between the dental, alveolar, and palato-alveolar areas of articulation necessitates a precision of articulation in English which is not required in languages lacking, for instance, either the dental or the palato-alveolar pairs. Thus, the lack of palato-alveolar fricative phonemes in Spanish permits the retraction of articulations in the alveolar region, e.g. /s/; whereas the absence in French and many

---

[1] If pronounced as /ˈiːðə/—rarer than /ˈaɪðə/.

other languages of dental fricative phonemes allows a dentalized quality in the alveolar articulations, which is liable in English to cause confusion with /θ, ð/ or to produce a 'lisping' fricative which is considered socially undesirable.

(2) *Force of articulation.*—Within the four pairs, /f, θ, s, ʃ/ tend to be pronounced with relatively more muscular energy and stronger breath force than /v, ð, z, ʒ/; the former are *fortis,* the latter *lenis.*[1] /h/ is normally fortis in character, but may have a lenis allophone (see §8.4.6).

(3) *Voicing.*—Like the lenis plosives and affricates, /v, ð, z, ʒ/ tend to be fully voiced only when they occur between voiced sounds, e.g. in *cover, other, easy, leisure, a van, all that, by the zoo.* In initial and (especially) in final positions, the lenis fricatives may be only partially voiced or completely voiceless, e.g. initially in *van, that, zoo* (i.e. with silence preceding) only the latter part of the friction is likely to be voiced, and finally in *leave, breathe, peas, rouge* /ruːʒ/ (i.e. with silence following) the friction is typically voiceless, though the consonant remains lenis—[v̥, ð̥, z̥, ʒ̥]. The fortis series is voiceless in all positions. /h/, however, ŏccurring only in word initial and medial situations, though voiceless in an initial position, may have some voicing medially between voiced sounds, e.g. *anyhow.*

(4) *Length of preceding sounds.*—When /f, θ, s, ʃ, v, ð, z, ʒ/ occur finally, their value is determined largely (since the voicing factor is not strongly operative) by the length of the syllables which they close.[2] Like all fortis consonants, /f, θ, s, ʃ/ have the effect of reducing the length of the preceding vowel (particularly a long vowel or diphthong) and of /l, m, n/ interposed between the vowel and the fricative, cf. *fife, loath, place, leash, self, pence,* with *five, loathe, plays, (liege), selves, pens,* etc. The same pre-fortis clipping is operative when the fortis fricatives occur in a medial position, although here a contrastive voicing feature is likely to be present in /v, ð, z, ʒ/, cf. *proofing, proving; earthy, worthy; racer, razor; fission, vision.*

Summary.—The RP fricatives may, therefore, be said to be distinguished:—

(*a*) by means of a five-term series in respect of place of articulation—labio-dental v. dental v. alveolar v. palato-alveolar v. glottal, and

(*b*) at each of the first four points of articulation, by an opposition between fortis and lenis in all contextual situations; by the possibility of some voicing in the lenis members in initial positions; by an opposition of presence and absence of voice in medial positions; by an opposition of the length of preceding sounds.

---

[1] But see §8.5 concerning 'fortis' and 'lenis' as phonological categories.
[2] P. Denes, 'Effect of Duration on the Perception of Voicing,' *Journal of the Acoustical Society of America,* 27, 261 (1955).

Foreign learners, quite apart from using the correct mouth articulations, should pay particular attention to the degree of voicing in the lenis series and to the influence which the fortis series has on the length of preceding sounds.

8.4.1 Acoustic Features of English Fricatives

In acoustic terms,[1] our perception of the various types of fricative (whose characteristic feature is a continuous noise component) appears to depend upon the following factors:—

(1) *Extent and position of noise component.*—Continuous noise in the spectrum is appropriate to articulatory friction regions:—

alveolars—	a noise range from about			3,600–8,000 cps
palato-alveolars—	"	"	"	2,000–7,000 cps
labio-dentals—	"	"	"	1,500–7,000 cps
dentals—	"	"	"	1,400–8,000 cps
glottal—	"	"	"	500–6,500 cps

(2) *Intensity of noise component.*—/s, ʃ/ have relatively high intensity; /f, θ, h/ relatively low intensity. The lenis series has an overall lower intensity than that of the fortis series.

(3) *Low frequency component.*—The lenis series may have a periodic low frequency component (voicing) which is absent in the fortis series (see §3.1.4 and P. Denes, op. cit.)

(4) *Formant transitions.*—Especially in the case of the low intensity labio-dentals and dentals, most information comes from the nature of the adjacent vocalic glide. In the case of /h/ (often an anticipatory voiceless version of the following vowel), the spectral pattern is likely to mirror the formant structure of the following vowel.

(5) *Duration of fricative noise.*—The friction of the lenis series is shorter than that of the fortis series.

8.4.2 Labio-dental Fricatives

(1) *Examples*

/f/—*fortis* (spelt *f, ff, ph, gh*, e.g. 'fork, off, physics, enough')
 word initial—feet, fit, fat, father, fool, fail, photo

---

[1] See K. S. Harris, 'Cues for the Identification of the Fricatives of American English', *J.A.S.A.*, 26, 952, 1954, also 'Cues for the Discrimination of American English Fricatives in Spoken Syllables', *Language and Speech*, vol. 1, 1, 1958; D. B. Fry and P. Denes, 'The Solution of some Fundamental Problems in Mechanical Speech Recognition,' *L. and S.*, vol. 1, 1, 1958; P. Strevens, 'Spectra of Fricative Noise in Human Speech,' *L. and S.*, vol. 3, 1, 1960; G. W. Hughes and M. Halle, 'Spectral Properties of Fricative Consonants,' *J.A.S.A.*, 28, 303, 1956.

word medial—affair, defend, offer, tougher, loafer, suffer, selfish, comfort

word final—leaf, laugh, cough, stuff, roof, loaf, strife

in word initial clusters—fry, fly, few, sphere

in word final clusters—/fθ(s)/ fifth(s), /ft(s)/ raft(s), /mf(s)/ triumph(s),[1] /lf(s)/ wolf('s), /lft/ engulfed, /lfθ(s)/ twelfth(s), /fn(z, d)/ soften (s, ed), /fl(z, d)/ baffle(s, ed), /fs/ coughs.

/v/—*lenis* (spelt, *v*, *f*, *ph*, e.g. 'vine, of, nephew')

word initial—veal, vex, vat, vast, vain, vice, voice

word medial—ever, nephew, over, silver, cover, event, canvas

word final—leave, give, have, of, move, dove, grove

in word initial clusters—/vj/ view

in word final clusters—/vz/ loaves, /vd/ loved, /vn(z)/ oven(s), /lv(z, d)/ solve(s, d), /vl(z, d)/ grovel(s, ed), etc.

Compare /f/, /v/—fine, vine; fat, vat; few, view; offer, hover; surface, service; laugher, larva; camphor, canvas; leaf, leave; proof, prove; safes, saves

(2) *Description.*—The soft palate being raised and the nasal resonator shut off, the inner surface of the lower lip makes a light contact with the edge of the upper teeth, so that the escaping air produces friction. The actual point of contact will vary somewhat according to the adjacent sound, e.g. in the case of a back strongly rounded vowel or of a bilabial plosive (*fool*, *roof*, *obvious*), the contact on the lower lip tends to be more retracted than in the case of a front spread vowel (*feel*, *leaf*). For /f/, the friction is voiceless, whereas there may be some vocal fold vibration accompanying /v/, according to its situation (see §8.4(3)). The tongue position of an adjacent vowel will persist or be anticipated during the labio-dental friction; in the case of intervocalic /f, v/, the tongue will articulate independently for the vowels or, if the vowels are similar, e.g. in *stiffest*, *giving*, will retain its position during the labio-dental friction.

(3) *Variants.*—No important articulatory variants for /f, v/ occur among RP speakers, although word final /v/ may assimilate to /f/ before a fortis consonant initial in the following word, e.g. regularly in *have to* and more rarely in such sequences as *love to*, *have some* (see §11.3.3) or may, in familiar speech, be elided in the case of the unaccented form of *of*, *have*, e.g. in *a lot of money*, *I could have bought it* /ə 'lɒt ə 'mʌnɪ, aɪ kəd ə 'bɔːt ɪt/, where /ə/ is phonetically equivalent to the unaccented form of *are*, *a* (see §11.1).[2] In West Country speech, the fortis /f/ is often replaced by a weaker articulation approaching that of /v/.

---

[1] An epenthetic /p/ may be inserted, thus /ˈtraɪʌmpfs/ see §8.4.4(3).

[2] Note the accepted forms of *man-of-war*, *tug-of-war*, *o'clock*, *will-o'-the-wisp*, with /ə/ rather than /əv/ for *of*.

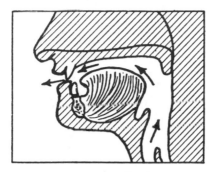

FIG. 34.—/f, v/.

(4) *Chief sources.*—PresE /f/ derives from OE initial and final [f] (*foot, fowl, free, thief, leaf, wife*) and from OF [f] (*fine, fruit, profit, chief*). The spelling *ph* next to *th* (as in *diphthong*) was pronounced with /p/ rather than /f/ in eModE, and often spelt with *p*; such a pronunciation with a bilabial plosive is still widely heard. An earlier final [x] following a rounded vowel gave [f] by late ME (*dwarf, laugh, rough, cough*); in words such as *plough, dough, bough*, the PresE pronunciation derives from the inflected form in which [x] has been lost, as also in the final [xt] sequence (*ought, thought*). An irregular change [u] > [v] > [f] has taken place in the word *lieutenant*, though the regular development /l(j)uːˈtenənt/ is used in the Navy and in American English. The increasing use of /f/ in *nephew* is a spelling pronunciation, instead of the earlier, regular /v/.

PresE /v/ derives from OE /f/ = [v] between voiced sounds (*love, devil, wolves, wives, driven*), from SW dialect initial OE [v] for [f] (*vat, vixen, vane*) and from OF [v] (*vain, very, cover, serve*).

(5) *Advice to foreign learners.*—Some learners (particularly Indians) use too weak a contact for /v/, so that the friction is lost, giving the labio-dental frictionless continuant [ʋ]; others (particularly Germans and Hungarians) use bilabial friction [β] instead of the labio-dental sound. In both of these cases, there is a tendency to use the same sound for both /v/ and /w/. Care should, therefore, be taken to distinguish such pairs as *vain, wane; verse, worse; vest, west*, etc., using strong friction between the lower lip and upper teeth for /v/. In addition, attention should be paid to the degree of voicing in /v/ according to its situation and to the length of sounds preceding /f/ (see §8.4(3), (4), and examples in (1) of this section).

8.4.3   Dental Fricatives

/θ, ð/

(1) *Examples*

/θ/—*fortis* (spelt always *th*)
   word initial—thief, thick, thatch, thong, thought, thumb
   word medial—ether, ethics, lethal, method, author, anthem, lengthy,
     atheist, athletic, deathly, worthless
   word final—heath, smith, breath, path, cloth, earth, fourth, oath
   in word initial clusters—three, throw, thew, thwart
   in word final clusters—/θt/ earthed, /θs/ mouth's, /pθ(s)/ depth(s),
     /tθ(s)/ eighth(s), /fθ(s)/ fifth(s), /ksθ(s)/ sixth(s), /mθ/ warmth,[1]
     /nθ(s) month(s), /lfθ(s)/ twelfth(s), /ŋkθ(s)/ length(s), /lθ(s)/
     health('s), /θl(z)/ Ethel('s), /θn/ earthen
/ð/—*lenis* (spelt always *th*)
   word initial—there, this, then, the, though, thy, they
   word medial—breathing, leather, gather, father, mother, northerly,
     southern, worthy, either, although
   word final—seethe, with, soothe, lathe, clothe, writhe, mouth (v.)
   in word final[2] *clusters*—/ðm(z)/ rhythm(s), /ðn(z)/ southern('s),
     /ðl(z)/ betrothal(s), /ðz/ clothes, /ðd/ writhed, /dð/ width (if
     pronounced /wɪdð/)
Compare /θ/, /ð/—thigh, thy; ether, breather; earthy, worthy;
   wreath, wreathe; mouth, mouth (v.); oath, clothe; truth's, truths
     /θ/, /s/—thick, sick; thought, sort; thumb, sum; mouth,
   mouse; worth, worse
     /θ/, /t/—thick, tick; thought, taught; three, tree; heath, heat;
   both, boat; fourth, fort
     /ð/, /z/—seethe, seas; lathe, laze; clothe, close (v.); breathe,
   breeze
     /ð/, /d/—then, den; though, dough; there, dare; other, udder;
   worthy, wordy; seethe, seed; writhe, ride

(2) *Description.*—The soft palate being raised and the nasal resonator shut off, the tip and rims of the tongue make a light contact with the
edge and inner surface of the upper incisors and a firmer contact with
the upper side teeth, so that the air escaping between the forward
surface of the tongue and the incisors causes friction. With some
speakers, the tongue-tip may protrude between the teeth. For /θ/ the
friction is voiceless, whereas for /ð/ there may be some vocal fold
vibration according to its situation (see §8.4(3)). The lip position will

---

[1] An epenthetic /p/ may be inserted, thus /wɔ:mpθ/. See §8.4.4(3).
[2] /ð/ does not occur in a word initial cluster.

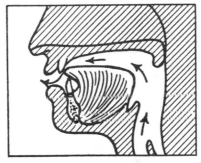

FIG. 35.—/θ, ð/.

depend upon the adjacent vowel, e.g. being spread for *thief, heath, these*, etc., and somewhat rounded for *thought, truth, soothe*, etc.

(3) *Variants.*—No important RP variants of /θ, ð/ occur, but since /θ, ð/ offer difficulties of articulation when followed by /s, z/, they are sometimes elided, e.g. *clothes* /kləʊz/, *months* /mʌns/, or /mʌnts/. In sequences of the type /s, z/ followed by unaccented /ð/ as in *Is there any?, What's the time?*, the preceding alveolar articulation may influence the dental fricative in rapid speech—/ˈɪz zər ˈenɪ, ˈwɒts zə ˈtaɪm/. Again, in popular London speech, the difficulties of the dental articulation may lead to their replacement by labio-dental fricatives, e.g. *throw it, Smith* /ˈfrəʊ ɪt, smɪf/, *mother, breathe in* /ˈmʌvə, ˈbriːv ˈɪn/. In this kind of speech, too, other alveolar articulations may be heard for the weak /ð/, e.g. *all the way* /ˈɔːl də ˈweɪ/, *in the morning* /ɪn nə ˈmɔːnɪn/.

(4) *Chief sources.*—PresE /θ/ derives from initial and final (including morpheme final) OE [θ] (*think, throat, bath, tooth, earthly, worthless*), from OF [ð] (*faith*), from learned Greek forms (*theory, thesis*) and others which until ModE commonly had /t/ (*catholic, authority, theatre*).

PresE /ð/ derives from OE /θ/ = [ð] between voiced sounds (*other, feather, breathes*). Note that of the English words where there is initial /ð/ rather than /θ/ (which is to be expected from the OE forms), e.g. *the, this, then, that, than, they*, etc., most are words which are frequently medial and unaccented in an utterance.

(5) *Advice to foreign learners.*—Foreign learners should avoid using /t/ or /s/ for /θ/, and /d/ or /z/ for /ð/. In particular, those words with /ð/ which are normally unaccented, e.g. *the, than, they*, etc. should not be pronounced with /d/. The difficulty of /θ, ð/ lies not so much in their articulation, which most learners can perform correctly in isolation, as in their combination with other fricatives, especially /s/ and /z/. Learners should, therefore, practise with drills containing such combinations involving rapid tongue glides, e.g. /s + θ/ *this*

thing, sixth, /z + θ/ *his thumb,* /s + ð/ *pass the salt,* /z + ð/ *is this it?*, /θ + s/ *fifths,* /θ + s + ð/ *Smith's there,* /ð + z + ð/ *soothes them,* etc., /s, z/ preceding /θ, ð/ should never be allowed to assimilate to /θ, ð/ (see §11.5).

8.4.4   Alveolar Fricatives

/s, z/

(1) *Examples*

/s/—*fortis* (spelt *s, ss, c, sc, x* (= /ks/), e.g. 'so, pass, niece, science, axe')

> *word initial*—cease, sat, sample, soon, soap, sign, soil
> *word medial*—pieces, losses, essay, axes, concert, escape, pencil, whisper, wrestler, excite, useless
> *word final*—niece, farce, pass, puss, goose, famous, dose, ice, mouse, fierce, scarce
> *in word initial clusters*—/sp/ spare, /st/ stain, /sk/ scarce, /sm/ smoke, /sn/ snake, /sl/ slow, /sf/ sphere, /sw/ swear, /sj/ sue, /spl/ splice, /spr/ spray, /spj/ spume, /str/ stray, /stj/ stew, /skr/ scream, /skj/ skewer, /skw/ square
> *in word final clusters*—/sp(s, t)/, gasp(s, ed), /st(s)/ rest(s), /sk(s, t)/ ask(s, ed), /sm/ lissom, /sn(z)/ listen(s), /sns/ licence, /sl(z)/ muscle(s), /ns(t)/ mince(d), /nsl(z)/ pencil(s), /lst/ whilst, /snt/ decent, /ps(t)/ lapse(d), /mps(t)/ glimpse(d), /lps/ helps, /ts/ cats, /kts/ acts, /pts/ opts, /lts/ faults, /nts/ tents, /ls/ pulse, /fts/ drafts, /ks(t)/ tax(ed), /ŋks/ thanks, /lks/ milks, /mfs/ nymphs, /fs/ laughs, /θs/ fourths, /fθs/ fifths, /lfθs/ twelfths, /nθs/ months, /ksθ(s)/ sixth(s), /tθs/ eighths, /dst/ midst, /mpts/ prompts, /stl(z)/ pistol(s), /tns/ pittance, /dns/ riddance, /vns/ grievance, /ʃns/ patience, etc.

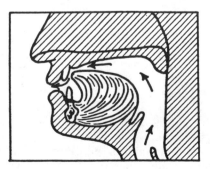

FIG. 36.—/s, z/.

/z/—lenis (spelt *s*, *ss*, *z*, *zz*, *x* (= /gz/), e.g. 'roses, scissors, zoo, dizzy, exact')

word initial—zeal, zest, zinc, zoo, zone, zero

word medial—easy, hesitate, bazaar, bosom, hawser, lazy, thousand, palsy, pansy, husband

word final—fees, is, says, as, was, ooze, does, butchers, gaze, rose, cows, noise, ears, airs, tours

in word final clusters [1]—/bz/ ribs, /dz/ heads, /gz/ legs, /mz/ limbs, /nz(d)/ cleanse(d), /ndz/ hands, /ŋz/ rings, /lz/ holes, /vs/ caves, /ldz/ holds, /lvz/ valves, /lbz/ bulbs, /lmz/ films, /lnz/ kilns /ðz/ clothes, /zm(z)/ prism(s), /zn(z, d)/ emprison(s, ed), /zl(z, d)/ puzzle(s, d), /zd/ raised, /zml/ dismal, /plz/ apples, /blz/ bubbles /tlz/ battles, /dlz/ saddles, /klz/ buckles, /glz/ eagles, /tʃlz/ Rachel's, /dʒlz/ cudgels, /mlz/ camels, /nlz/ channels, /θlz/ Ethel's, /slz/ thistles, /vlz/ evils, /flz/ ruffles, /ʃlz/ officials, /tnz/ kittens, /dnz/ saddens, /fnz/ orphans, /vnz/ ovens, /snz/ hastens, /ʃnz/ oceans, /ʒnz/ visions, /ðnz/ heathens, /znt/ present, /mplz/ samples, /mblz/ symbols, /zndz/ thousands, /ndlz/ sandals, /ntlz/ lentils, /ŋklz/ uncles, /ŋglz/ angles, /stlz/ pastels, /mzlz/ damsels, etc.

Compare /s/, /z/—seal, zeal; sink, zinc; decease, disease; passing, parsing; fussy, fuzzy; racer, razor; peace, peas; loose, lose; use (n.), use (v.); gross, grows; place, plays; ice, eyes; house (n.), house (v.); scarce, scares: pence, pens; false, falls

(?) *Description.*—The soft palate being raised and the nasal resonator shut off, the tip and blade of the tongue make a light contact with the upper alveolar ridge, and the side rims of the tongue a close contact with the upper side teeth. The air-stream escapes by means of a narrow groove in the centre of the tongue and causes friction between the tongue and the alveolar ridge. There is very little opening between the teeth. With some speakers, the tongue-tip is in contact with the lower teeth, so that friction is produced between the blade of the tongue and the alveolar ridge. For /s/ the friction is voiceless, whereas for /z/ there may be some vocal fold vibration, according to its situation (see §8.4(3)). The lip position will depend upon the adjacent vowel, e.g. spread for *see*, *zeal*, *piece*, *bees*, etc., and somewhat rounded for *soon*, *zoo*, *loose*, *lose*, etc. Some speakers make a light additional contact between the lower lip and the upper teeth, thus giving the sounds a secondary labio-dental quality. A lisp, i.e. a substitution of /θ, ð/ for /s, z/ or a strongly dentalized version of /s, z/, is a common speech defect or habit, despite the loss of phonemic opposition involved, which might be expected to exert pressure towards the maintenance of the dental/alveolar fricative distinction.

[1] /z/ does not occur in an initial cluster apart from /zj/ in *zeugma* and *Zeus*.

(3) *Variants.*—Apart from the articulatory variants mentioned above, which are individual rather than social or regional, the fortis /s/ is often replaced in West Country speech by a weaker articulation approaching that of /z/. Before /r/, the approximation of the tongue to the alveolar ridge may be more retracted, e.g. in *horse-riding, newsreel*. Word final /s, z/ exhibit a readiness to assimilate before /ʃ, j/ (see §§11.3.2, 11.3.5).

Few RP speakers regularly maintain the distinction between /ns/ and /nts/ which is widespread in regional speech: e.g. distinguishing the final clusters in *mince—mints, tense—tents, assistance—assistants, dance—plants,* /nts/ tending to be used in all cases. This *plosive epenthesis*, the insertion of /t/ between /n/ and /s/, results from the raising of the soft palate before the oral closure for /n/ is relaxed for the fricative /s/. Similarly, when /m/ or /ŋ/ precedes the /s/, an epenthetic plosive homorganic with the nasal may occur, e.g. *Samson* /sæmsən/ > /sæmpsən/, *Kingston* /kɪŋstən/ > /kɪŋkstən/, such variation being reflected in the spellings of proper names such as *Sam(p)son* and *Sim(p)son*.[1] On the other hand, /nz/ and /ndz/ are kept distinct by most RP speakers, e.g. in *wins—winds, tens—tends, fines—finds*, except in the most rapid speech when it is /d/ which may be elided.

(4) *Chief sources.*—PresE /s/ derives from OE [s, ss] (*soon, sun, kiss, mice, wasp*) and from OF [s] (*sudden, strange, lesson, beast, pace, false*).

PresE /z/ derives from OE /s/ = [z] between voiced sounds (*rise, wise, thousand, wisdom*) and from OF [z] (*zeal, easy, dozen, cause*). In addition, the weak termination [əs] gives [z], on the loss of [ə] by eModE, when following a voiced sound (*loves, dogs, lands, stones*); where the vowel is retained—as /ɪ/ in PresE—(e.g. after /s, ·z, ʃ, tʃ, dʒ/), the [z] fricative form is also used in the weak ending (*passes, roses, rushes, touches, pages*). In the same way, words like *is, as, was, has, his*, which occur most commonly in weakly accented positions, were pronounced with final [z] by eModE. In French words, an earlier [s] occurring medially between weakly accented and strongly accented syllables often > [z] (*resemble, possess, observe, disease, exact*); but many exceptions occur, perhaps for reasons of analogy of the spelling pronunciation or because the [s] is felt to belong to a separable prefix or to be initial in a common word preceded by a separable prefix (e.g. *assist, excite, dishonest, research*). In words where the medial fricative, especially final in the prefix *dis-*, precedes a voiced consonant, both /s/ and /z/ are heard, e.g. in *disdain, disgust*.

(5) *Advice for foreign learners.*—In many languages, especially

---

[1] Similar epenthesis may take place in sequences of nasals + other voiceless fricatives. The epenthetic plosive is always homorganic with the nasal.

those where no dental fricatives exist, /s, z/ are articulated nearer to the teeth than the English varieties. Such a dentalized articulation is to be avoided in English because of the danger of confusion with /θ, ð/ (both in terms of the phonemic opposition involved and of the difficulties of alveolar/dental clusters). The more retracted articulation for /s, z/ should be practised in opposition with /θ, ð/ in such pairs as: *sing, thing; sort, thought; close* (v.), *clothe; sees, seethe; mouse, mouth; use* (n.), *youth.* On the other hand, those whose /s, z/ are often too retracted for English, e.g. Spaniards and Greeks, should practise oppositions between /s, z/ and /ʃ, ʒ/: *sin, shin; sort, short; lasses, lashes; Caesar, seizure; leased, leashed; mess, mesh.* In addition, because /s, z/ occur so frequently in final positions, particular attention should be paid to the degree of voicing in /z/ (which should never be allowed to become a fortis consonant) and to the length of sounds preceding /s/ (see §8.4(3) and the examples in (l) of this section).

8.4.5 Palato-alveolar Fricatives

/ʃ, ʒ/

(1) *Examples*

/ʃ/—*fortis* (spelt *sh, ch, sch, s* or *ss* before *u, -ti-, -si-, -sci-, -ci-, -ce-,* e.g. 'shoe, machine, schedule, sure, assure, nation, mansion, mission, conscience, special, ocean'; *note: x* in 'luxury' – /kʃ/)
   word initial—sheet, shed, shop, sugar, charade, shout
   word medial—Asia, bishop, ashore, mission, luscious, bushel, cushion, rashly, machine
   word final—dish, cash, wash, push, douche, rush, finish, ruche
   in word initial clusters[1]—/ʃr/ shrink
   in word final clusters—/lʃ(t)/ welsh(ed), /ʃn(z, d)/, fashion(s, ed), /ʃnt(s)/ patient(s), /nʃn(z, d)/[2] mention(s, ed), /ʃt/ pushed, /ʃl(z, d)/ marshal(s, led); where /n/ precedes final /tʃ/, e.g. in *bench, lunch,* some speakers use a final cluster /nʃ/, without the [t] stop.
/ʒ/—*lenis* (spelt *-si-, s, z* before *u* and, in French loan words, final *-ge,* e.g. 'vision, measure, seizure, beige')
   word initial—(in French loan words) gigolo, gigue, jabot, genre
   word medial—pleasure, leisure, usual, confusion, decision
   word final (only in French loan words; an alternative pronunciation with /dʒ/ is possible)—prestige, barrage, rouge, beige

---

[1] /tʃ/, /dʒ/, having been treated as single complex phonemic entities, are not considered here as initial or final clusters.
[2] An epenthetic /t/ may be inserted, thus /ˈmentʃn(z, d)/. See §8.4.4(3).

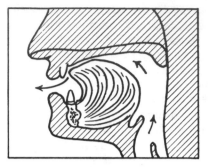

FIG. 37.—/ʃ, ʒ/.

in word initial clusters[1]—does not occur

in word final clusters—/ʒn(z)/ vision(s); in French words, when said with final /ʒ/, the cluster /ʒd/ is possible, e.g. in *camouflaged.* Moreover, for those who use final /ʒ/, rather than /dʒ/, after /n/, e.g. in *arrange(d)*, the clusters /nʒ(d)/ may occur.

Compare /ʃ/, /tʃ/—sheep, cheap; shore, chore; shoes, choose; leash, leech; dish, ditch; wash, watch

  /ʒ/, /dʒ/—leisure, ledger; vision, pigeon

  /ʃ/, /ʒ/—Aleutian (when pronounced /əˈljuːʃn/), allusion; Confucian (when pronounced /kənˈfjuːʃn/, confusion

(2) *Description.*—The soft palate being raised and the nasal resonator shut off, the tip and blade of the tongue make a light contact with the alveolar ridge, the front of the tongue being raised at the same time in the direction of the hard palate and the side rims of the tongue being in contact with the upper side teeth. The escape of air is diffuse (compared with that of /s, z/), the friction occurring between a more extensive area of the tongue and the roof of the mouth. The articulation is also laxer than that of /s, z/. The palatalization effect (i.e. the [i]-ness caused by the raising of the front of the tongue) is less marked than in sounds of the [ʃ, ʒ] type in some other languages, indicating either that the front raising is less close or that the tongue as a whole is slightly more retracted. In the case of /ʃ/, the friction is voiceless, whereas for /ʒ/ there may be some vocal fold vibration according to its situation (see §8.4(3)). Some speakers use slight lip-rounding for /ʃ, ʒ/ in all positions, for others, lip-rounding is an effect of the adjacent vowel, e.g /ʃ/ of *shoe* tends to be lip-rounded whereas /ʃ/ of *she* has neutral or spread lips.

(3) *Variants.*—Apart from the degree of palatalization or lip-

---

[1] See footnote on previous page.

rounding used, no important articulatory variants occur. Medially in certain words, however, /ʃ, ʒ/ are not used by all speakers: (a) especially before /uː/ or /ʊ/, there is often variation between /ʃ, ʒ/ and /s, z/ + /j/, e.g. in *issue, sexual, tissue, inertia, seizure, casual, usual, azure* (cf. *assume* with /sj/ and *assure* with /ʃ/); (b) a similar variation between /ʃ/ or /s/ + /ɪ/ + vowel, e.g. *ratio, appreciate, negotiate*; (c) the sequence /s, z/ + /ɪ/ (or /j/) + vowel is regularly kept in such words as *hosier, axiom, gymnasium, Parisian* (note American English /pə'rɪʒn/) and especially before the /ə/ comparative adjectival inflexion, e.g. *easier, lazier*; (d) the lack of words distinguishable by /ʃ/ and /ʒ/ results in possible alternations between /ʃ/ and /ʒ/, e.g. in *Asia, Persia, transition, version*. In word final position, where /ʒ/ exists only in comparatively recent French loan-words, e.g. *beige, rouge, prestige, garage*, etc., a variant with /dʒ/ is always possible and is felt to be the fully anglicized form. It will be seen that /ʒ/, rare initially in a word, replaceable by /dʒ/ finally and some-times varying with /ʃ/ medially, has a particularly weak 'functional load' in English.

(4) *Chief sources.*—PresE /ʃ/ derives from OE [ʃ] < earlier OE [s] + [k] or [c] (*ship, shadow, bishop, fish, English*); from OF pala-talized [s] (*cushion, cash, radish, finish*); from a coalescence of /s/ + /j/ or /ɪ/ finalized in the seventeenth century (*sure, sugar, ambition, ocean, special, patient*)—note that in the seventeenth and eighteenth centuries, several words at present with /sjuː/ were pronounced with /ʃ/ (*suit, supreme, assume*); from French /ʃ/ in words adopted after earlier French /tʃ/ had given /ʃ/ (*chemise, chic, machine, charlatan, moustache*).

PresE /ʒ/ derives from a coalescence of /z/ + /j/ or /ɪ/ finalized in the seventeenth century (*occasion, measure, treasure, usual*), /ʒ/ being considered for a long time as a foreign sound; from French /ʒ/ in words adopted after earlier French /dʒ/ had given /ʒ/ (*prestige, rouge, beige, bijou*)—many of these words still retaining a foreign flavour.

(5) *Advice to foreign learners.*—Many languages do not possess palato-alveolar fricatives and others have fricatives in this region but of a more strongly palatalized kind. In these cases, learners should avoid using sound sequences which will strike the English ear as /s/ or /z/ + /j/; a slight retraction of the tongue will often suitably 'darken' the quality of the friction. Attention should also be paid to the maintenance of the lenis character of /ʒ/ (with voicing where appropriate), despite the fact that oppositions between /ʃ/ and /ʒ/ are rare, except in the affricate complexes /tʃ/ and /dʒ/.

8.4.6 Glottal Fricative

/h/

(1) *Examples*

/h/—*fortis* (spelt *h*, *wh*, e.g. 'how, hat, who, whom')
   word initial—heat, hen, ham, hot, horse, who, hate, hoe, high, how, here, hair, hallo
   word medial—ahead, behave, perhaps, behind, spearhead, anyhow, manhood, abhor, adhere
Compare /h/ + vowel, initial vowel—heat, eat; hill, ill; hedge, edge; harbour, arbor; haul, all; hate, eight; hold, old; hear, ear

(*Note*: *h* is not pronounced initially in *hour, honest, honour, heir, heiress*; medially in such words as *exhaust, exhilarate, exhibit, vehicle, vehement*; and in some final suffixes, e.g. *shepherd, Durham, Clapham*, etc.)

(2) *Description.*—Since English /h/ occurs only in syllable initial, pre-vocalic positions, it may be regarded as a strong, voiceless onset of the vowel in question. The air is expelled from the lungs with considerable pressure, causing some friction throughout the vocal tract, the upper part of which is shaped in readiness for the articulation of the following vowel (i.e. as regards the position of the tongue, lips, soft palate, and the configuration of the pharynx). Thus differing types of friction (patterns of resonance) will be heard for /h/ in the sequences /hiː/, /hɑː/, /huː/. The friction being, therefore, largely of the mouth cavity type associated with the nature of the following vowel, this syllable-marginal sound is considered by many writers to share notable characteristics with vowel (vocoid) articulations and is interpreted phonemically as being in complementary distribution with the second element of the long vowels /ɑː, ɔː, ɜː/ and the diphthongs /ɪə, ɛə, ʊə/. Since, however, the common feature of all types of pre-vocalic /h/ is the passage of a strong, voiceless air-stream through the open glottis, the sound is here referred to as a fortis, voiceless, glottal fricative. With the onset of the vocal fold vibration of the vowel, the air-pressure is reduced. There is no distinctive fortis/lenis opposition such as characterizes the other English fricatives.

(3) *Variants.*—Although /h/ functions in English essentially as a voiceless syllable-initial margin (in the same way that /ŋ/ occurs only in post-syllabic positions), a few speakers use a voiced (or slightly voiced) allophone medially between voiced sounds, e.g. in such words as *anyhow, perhaps, behind*. In such pronunciations, the strong air-stream of /h/ is accompanied by vocal fold vibration, the result being a kind of breathy vowel or voiced glottal fricative [ɦ].

In many types of popular regional speech, /h/ is lost, so that no distinction is made between such RP minimal pairs as *hill, ill; high, eye*;

hair, air. Usually in such speech, the /h/ words will behave as if they had an initial vowel, e.g. *a hill* /ən ˈɪl/, *the house* /ðɪ ˈaʊs/, but sometimes a trace of the boundary marking function of /h/ will be shown in the use of [ʔ], or at least a weak glottal constriction, e.g. *a hill* [ə ˈʔɪl], *the hospital* [ðə ˈʔɒspɪtl]. On the other hand, the usual linking forms between article and word with initial vowel may be replaced by a glottal constriction or weak [h], e.g. *an egg* [əˈʔeg] ɔr [ɔ ˈʰeg], *the end* [ðə ˈʔend] or [ðə ˈʰend].

Such loss of /h/ is usually considered characteristic of uneducated speech, but certain form words (especially *have, has, had,* pronouns and pronominal adjectives) frequently lose /h/ in RP in unaccented, non-initial, situations in connected speech (see §10.4), e.g. *he pushed him on his back* /hiː ˈpʊʃt ɪm ɒn ɪz ˈbæk/, *I could have hit her* /aɪ kəd əv ˈhɪt ə/.

Some RP speakers treat an unaccented *h*-syllable, as in *historical,* as if it belonged to the special group *hour, honest,* etc., i.e. without an initial /h/, e.g. *an historical novel.* Such pronunciations, and also that of *humour* as /juːmə/, are nowadays used only by a minority of speakers. In the case of *hotel,* however, an /h/-less form is fairly widely spread, e.g. *an hotel,* though the pronunciation with initial /h/ is commoner. (For /h/ + /j, w/, see §8.9.)

(4) *Chief sources.*—OE had /h/ (= [h], [x], or [ç]), not only initially in a syllable before a vowel, but also in initial clusters, e.g. /hn/ (*hnutu*), /hl/ (*hláf*), /hr/ (*hréosan*), /hw/ (*hwéol*), where the realizations may have been [n̥, l̥, r̥, w̥] or [xn, xl, xr, xw]; also in medial and post-vocalic positions, with palatal or velar fricative realizations, e.g. *hliehhan, áhte, héah.* Of these occurrences, PresE retains only initial /h/ before a vowel (see §8.9.2 for /hw/), e.g. *home, high, help, horse,* etc. In addition, a new initial /h/ was introduced into English in some French words of Germanic origin, e.g. *hardy, haste, herald,* and also in a large number of French words of Latin origin, e.g. *herb, horror, habit, harass, heretic, hospital, host, humour,* etc. In the case of this latter group, spelling with *h* both in OF and ME was erratic, probably representing an /h/-less pronunciation. In certain words (*hour, heir, heiress, honour, honest*), the /h/-less pronunciation has been kept despite the general adoption of the spelling *h*. In most other cases, the letter *h* began to be pronounced in late ME in these words of Latin (via French) origin, though in some the spelling *h* was not sounded as late as the eighteenth and nineteenth centuries, e.g. *herb, hospital, humble, humour.*

The general elision of /h/ in weak pronouns and auxiliary verbs probably dates at least from eModE, whereas the loss of /h/ in accented words, as in modern popular London speech, has existed for at least two centuries and has always been considered a vulgarism.

(5) *Advice to foreign learners.*—Many languages do not possess a

phoneme of the /h/ type. Speakers of these languages should, in learning English, practise the examples given in (1) above, making a correct distinction between words with initial /h/ + vowel and those with initial vowel, e.g. *hill, ill*, etc.; they should also learn to elide the /h/ of *he, him, his, her, have, had, has*, when these words occur in weakly accented, non-initial positions in the utterance.

Those learners who in their own language have no [h] but [x] or who have an [h] said with some velar friction, e.g. in some Slav and Chinese languages, should avoid using any velar friction in English, but should practise the English /h/ as a voiceless onset to the following vowel.

8.5   Fortis and Lenis as Phonological Categories

It will be seen from the preceding sections that in various ways the members of the class /p, t, k, f, θ, s, ʃ, tʃ/ behave similarly to each other and differently from their counterparts in the class /b, d, g, v, ð, z, ʒ, dʒ/. It is not primarily in the matter of relative 'strength' of articulation but in their behaviour that the members of each pair differ. Thus, to summarize, (i) members of the fortis series are voiceless inter-vocalically whilst those of the lenis series are voiced in the same environment; (ii) the fortis plosives /p, t, k/ are aspirated (and voiceless) when initial in a stressed syllable, whilst their lenis counterparts /b, d, g/ are unaspirated (and considerably devoiced if initial in an utterance or if following a voiceless consonant); (iii) all the fortis consonants cause pre-fortis clipping whilst the vowels, nasals and laterals preceding members of the lenis series display no such reduction in duration. For this reason it is generally regarded as most useful to treat the fortis/lenis distinction as primarily a phonological classification which accounts for a complex of realizational features.

Class B
Voiced Non-fricative or Glide Consonants
(Sonorants)

Although voiceless fricative allophones of the following consonants occur, their most common realizations are voiced and non-fricative.

8.6   Nasals

(1) *Articulatory features.*—Nasal consonants resemble oral plosives in that a total closure is made within the mouth; they differ from such plosives in that the soft palate is in its lowered position, allowing an escape of air into the nasal cavity and giving the sound the special resonance provided by the naso-pharyngeal cavity. Since the air-stream

may escape freely through the nose, nasal consonants are *continuants*; they differ, however, from continuants such as fricatives in that no audible friction is produced and from the fact that they are usually voiced, without significant fortis/lenis or voiced/voiceless oppositions. In many respects, therefore, being normally *frictionless continuants*, they resemble vowel-type sounds.

(2) *Acoustic features.*—The usual voiced nasal consonant has no noise component such as results from the burst of plosives or the friction of fricatives, nor the silence gap associated with plosives; they present, on the contrary, like vowels, a regular periodic wave pattern during their steady state with a characteristic formant structure and the periodic component producing voice. The soft walls of the added nasal cavity entail very considerable damping (especially in the 1,000–2,300 cps band) and broadening of the resonance band-widths. The best responses for the various nasal consonants have been achieved synthetically[1] with the following formant structures: /m/, F1 200 cps, F2 1,100 cps, F3 2,500 cps; /n/, F1 200 cps, F2 1,700 cps, F3 2,500 cps; /ŋ/, F1 200 cps, F2 2,300 cps, F3 2,500 cps, the situation of F2 being the variable characteristic. This formant may, however, be severely mutilated in the nasals of actual speech, so that strong cues for distinction among types of nasal appear to be provided[2] by characteristic curves (transitions) of F2 of the adjacent vowel—comparable with those characterizing equivalent plosive articulations, e.g. a bilabial nasal [m] shows, like [b], extensive minus transitions; an alveolar nasal [n], like [d], plus or minus transitions; and a velar nasal [ŋ], like [g], plus transitions.

(3) *The English nasal consonants.*—(*a*) Three nasal phonemes correspond to the three oral plosive areas of articulation: *bilabial* /m/-/p, b/; *alveolar* /n/-/t, d/; *velar* /ŋ/-/k, g/. If, in the articulation of a nasal consonant, the nasal passage is blocked as, for instance, often happens during a cold, /m, n, ŋ/ will be realized as /b, d, g/, e.g. *morning* /'bɔːdɪg/, *some nice lemons* /səb 'daɪs 'lebədz/. Oppositions amongst the nasals may be illustrated as follows:—

	Bilabial /m/	Alveolar /n/	Velar /ŋ/
Initial	might	night	—
Medial	simmer	sinner	singer
Final	sum	sun	sung

It will be seen that, since /ŋ/ does not occur initially in a word or

[1] See Kazuro Nakata, 'Synthesis and perception of nasal consonants,' *J.A.S.A.*, 31, 6, 1959.

[2] See Liberman, Delattre, Cooper, Gerstman, 'The rôle of consonant-vowel transitions in the perception of the stop and nasal consonants, *Psychological Monograph* 379, 1954; also A. Malécot, 'Acoustic cues for nasal consonants,' *Language*, vol. 32, 2, 1956.

morpheme, a complete series of oppositions is found only where the nasals occur in post-vocalic positions in the same syllable or morpheme.

(*b*) The *vocalic nature* of the nasals is underlined by the fact that they readily perform the *syllabic* function of vowels: most often /n/, e.g. *mutton* [ˈmʌtn̩]; less commonly /m/ e.g. *rhythm* [ˈrɪðm̩]; occasionally, with some speakers, /ŋ/, e.g. *bacon* [ˈbeɪkŋ̍].

(*c*) Although no opposition occurs between voiced and voiceless nasals in English, a somewhat devoiced allophone of /m/ and /n/ may be heard when a voiceless consonant precedes, e.g. *smoke, smart, topmost; snake, sneeze, chutney*. The distribution of /ŋ/ being restricted, it is only rarely—in a syllabic situation as in *bacon*—that a voiceless consonant precedes, with the consequent partial devoicing.

8.6.1   Bilabial Nasal

/m/

(1) *Examples*

>   (regularly spelt with *m,·mm*, e.g. 'meat, summer'; sometimes *mb, mn*, e.g. 'comb, autumn')
>   *word initial*—meal, mat, march, move, mirth, make, mouse
>   *following word initial* /s/—smack, smock, smite, smoke, smear
>   *word medial*—demon, glimmer, lemon, salmon, Thomas, among, gloomy, summer, sermon, commit, omen; jumper, timber, empty, comfort, hamlet, simple, symbol, dismal, camel, dimly, asthma
>   *word final*—seem, lamb, harm, warm, tomb, game; (in final clusters) worms, harmed, film(s), warmth, glimpse, prompt(s), nymph(s); (syllabic) rhythm(s), prism(s), lissom.

(2) *Description.*—The lips form a closure as for /p, b/; the soft palate is lowered, adding the resonance of the nasal cavity to those of the pharynx and the mouth chamber closed by the lips; the tongue will

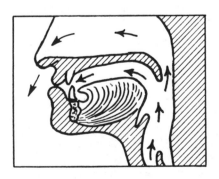

FIG. 38.—/m/.

generally anticipate or retain the position of the adjacent vowel or /l/. Except when partially devoiced by a preceding voiceless consonant, e.g. initially—*smoke*, medially—*topmost*, finally—*happen*, /m/ is voiced. (Normal expiration through the nose with the lips closed may be described as a weak [m̥]; where, because of some organic defect such as cleft palate, the nasal cavity cannot be shut off, /p/ may be realized as [m̥] and /b/ as [m].) When followed by a labio-dental sound /f, v/, the front closure may be labio-dental [ɱ] rather than bilabial, e.g. in *nymph, comfort, triumph, come first, circumvent, warm vest* (see also [ɱ] for /n/, 8.6.2(2)).

/m/ frequently results in context from a final /n/ of the isolate word form before a following bilabial, e.g. *one mile* /ˈwʌm ˈmaɪl/, *more and more* /ˈmɔːr əm ˈmɔː/, *ten pairs* /ˈtem ˈpɛəz/, *gone back* /ˈgɒm ˈbæk/; sometimes /m/ is a realization of word final /ən/ or /n/ following /p/ or /b/, e.g. *happen* /ˈhæpm/, *ribbon* /ˈrɪbm/, or, in context, *cap and gown* /ˈkæp m ˈgaʊn/ (see §11.3.5).

(3) *Variants.*—There are no important regional or social variants of /m/ articulations.

(4) *Chief sources.*—PresE /m/ derives from OE [m], [mm] (*man, hammer, swim, home*)—note [b] of [mb] was lost in word final positions in ME in such words as *climb, lamb*, though kept medially as in *timber*, or inserted as in *thimble, slumber, bramble*, before /l/ and earlier /r/; from OF |m| (*master, family, solemn, sum*).

(5) *Advice to foreign learners.*—This phoneme should present no difficulty.

8.6.2 Alveolar Nasal

/n/

(1) *Examples*

> (regularly spelt with *n, nn*, e.g. 'now, noon, funny'; or *kn, gn, pn*, e.g. 'know, gnaw, sign, pneumonia'; also /ɒn/ as a realization of French /ã/, e.g. 'rendez-vous')
>
> *word initial*—neat, knit, net, gnat, knot, gnaw, none, nurse, name, know, near
>
> *following word initial* /s/—sneeze, snatch, snore, snug, snake, snow, sneer
>
> *word medial*—dinner, many, hornet, monitor, annoy; wonder, hunter, unless, unrest, answer, pansy, infant, invoice; chutney, madness, amnesty, walnut, fastener, evening
>
> *word final*—mean, pen, gone, soon, learn, melon, down, coin; pint(s), pond(s), inch, hinge, final(s), pence, pens, month(s), kiln(s), rental(s), bundle(s), pencil(s), against
>
> *syllabic* /n/—*open, *ribbon, *sicken, *organ (*more commonly

with /-ən/), cotton, sudden, often, oven, earthen, southern, listen, dozen, mission, vision; maddening (or with non-syllabic /n/), reasonable (or with non-syllabic /n/ or /ən/), ordinary (or with non-syllabic /n/ or /ən/ or /ɪn/), southerner (or with /ən/)

(2) *Description.*—The tongue forms a closure with the teeth ridge and upper side teeth as for /t, d/; the soft palate is lowered, adding the resonance of the nasal cavity to those of the pharynx and of that part of the mouth chamber behind the alveolar closure; the lip position will depend upon that of adjacent vowels, e.g. spread lips in *neat, keen*; neutrally open lips in *snarl, barn*; somewhat rounded lips in *noon, soon*. Except when partially devoiced by a preceding voiceless consonant, e.g. initially—*snug*, medially—*chutney*, finally—*cotton*, /n/ is voiced. (Where, because of an organic defect such as cleft palate, the nasal cavity cannot be shut off, /t/ may be realized as [n̥] and /d/ as [n].) The articulation of /n/ is particularly liable to be influenced by that of the following consonant, e.g. when followed by a labio-dental sound /f, v/, as in *infant, invoice, on fire, in vain*, /n/ may be realized as [ɱ]—thus overlapping with realizations of the /m/ phoneme (see 8.6.1); /n/ before dental sounds /θ, ð/ is realized with a lingua-dental closure [n̪], as in *tenth, when they*—and sometimes when following /θ, ð/ (*earthen, southern*); before /r/, /n/ may have a post-alveolar contact, as in *unrest, Henry*; in addition, in context, word final /n/ frequently assimilates to a following word initial bilabial or velar consonant, being realized as /m/ or /ŋ/, e.g. *ten people, ten boys, ten men*, where the final /n/ of *ten* may assimilate to /m/, and *ten cups, ten girls*, where the final /n/ of *ten* may assimilate to /ŋ/ (see §11.3.4).

(3) *Variants.*—There are no important regional or social variants of /n/ articulations.

(4) *Chief sources.*—PresE /n/ derives from OE [n, nn] (*name, many, man, spin*); from OE [hn], [xn] or [n̥] (*nut*)—by the twelfth century; from OE [kn, gn] (*know, knit, gnaw, gnat*)—by the late seven-

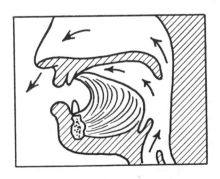

FIG. 39.—/n/.

teenth century; from OF [n] (*noble, dinner, plain*); from OF palatal [ɲ] (*sign, reign, line, mountain, onion*). Note that sometimes earlier [n] > [nt, nd] (*pheasant, tyrant, ancient, sound, pound*); and that sometimes [n] of the indefinite article has become affixed to a noun beginning with a vowel (*newt, nickname*), or initial [n] of a noun has been lost through transference to the preceding indefinite article form (*adder, apron, umpire*).

(5) *Advice to foreign learners.*—Care should be taken that /n/, like /t, d/, is normally given an alveolar rather than a dental articulation (see practice examples in (1) above).

8.6.3 Velar Nasal

$$/ŋ/$$

(1) *Examples*

(regularly spelt *ng*—or *n* followed by a letter indicating a velar consonant—e.g. 'sing, tongue, sink, anxious, uncle'; also /ɒŋ/ as a realization of French /ã/, e.g. 'restaurant'; /ŋ/ occurs usually after the short vowels /ɪ, æ, ɒ, ʌ/; rarely after /e/)

word medial—singer, hanger, longing, anxiety

word medial + /g/—finger, anger, angry, hunger, strongest, language, single, angle, England, bungle, nightingale

word medial + /k/—tinker, anchor, banquet, monkey, donkey, conquer, wrinkle, ankle, uncle, anxious

word final—sing(s), hang(s, ed), wrong(s, ed), tongue(s, ed), among

word final + /k/—sink(s), rank(s, ed), conch(sometimes/kɒŋk/), chunk(s), monk(s), distinct, amongst (or with /ŋst/), strength (with /ŋkθ/, /ŋθ/, or sometimes /nθ/)

word final syllable—(occasionally) bacon, taken, thicken, blacken, organ

/ŋ/, or less commonly /n/, in such words as—income, conclude, encourage, concrete, bronchitis, engage, enquiry

Compare /ŋ/, /n/—sing, sin; rang, ran; hanged, hand; sung, sun; mounting, mountain; gong, gone; robbing, robin

/ŋ/, /ŋk/—thing, think; rang, rank; sung, sunk; singing, sinking; hanger, hanker

(2) *Description.*—A closure is formed in the mouth between the back of the tongue and the velum as for /k, g/ (the point of closure will depend on the type of vowel preceding, the contact being more advanced in *sing* than in *song*); the soft palate is lowered, adding the resonance of the nasal cavity to that of the pharynx and that small part of the mouth chamber behind the velar closure; the lip position will depend upon that of the preceding vowel, being somewhat spread in

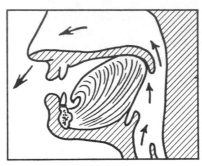

FIG. 40.—/ŋ/.

sing and relatively open in *song*. /ŋ/ is normally voiced, except for partial devoicing in the possible, though less common, case of syllabic /ŋ/ in such words as *bacon, thicken*. (Where, because of an organic defect such as cleft palate, the nasal cavity cannot be shut off, /k/ may be realized as /ŋ̊/] and /g/ as [ŋ].) Word final /ŋ/ may result in context from the isolate word final form /n/, e.g. *ten cups* (see §§8.6.2(2), 11.3.4).

(3) *Variants.*—Earlier [ŋg] forms are retained, instead of RP /ŋ/, in many regional types of speech, notably in the Midlands and north of England, e.g. *singing* [ˈsɪŋgɪŋg] for RP /ˈsɪŋɪŋ/. If /g/ is always pronounced in such situations, [ŋ] must be counted an allophone of /n/ rather than of a separate phoneme.

In some forms of regional speech, and also of some conservative RP, where /ŋ/ is a phoneme (*sin, sing*, being distinguished merely by the type of final nasal), the termination *-ing* is pronounced /ɪn/, as in *meeting, nothing*, thus producing homophones of the type *robbing, robin*.

In popular London speech, in which /ŋ/ is phonemic (cf. *sin, sing*), the word *-thing* in compounds is often pronounced /-fɪŋk/, e.g. in *something, anything, nothing*; the verbal termination *-ing* may be /-ɪŋ/ or /-ɪn/ without /k/.

(4) *Chief sources.*—PresE /ŋ/ occurs in words of OE origin (*sing, hunger, thank, tongue*) or of OF origin (*frank, rank, conquer, language*), following a short vowel. So long as [ŋ] occurred only before /k, g/, the nasal was an allophone of /n/. But with the loss of /g/ in the sequence [ŋg], /ŋ/ gained a phonemic significance, based on oppositions of the *sing, sin* type. Although loss of /g/ in [ŋg] may have occurred in popular dialects in late ME, it seems that the plosive (and allophonic nature of [ŋ]) was retained in educated speech until the end of the sixteenth century. At first, in the late sixteenth and seventeenth centuries, /g/ was elided only before consonants, the loss of /g/ in final

[ŋg] before a vowel or a pause becoming general during the seventeenth century.

The pronunciation /-ɪn/ for the termination -*ing*, common in the sixteenth and seventeenth centuries, became a general feature of fashionable speech in the eighteenth century and has been retained to-day as a characteristic of an archaic form of RP (e.g. in *huntin', shootin', and fishin'*). It is to be noted that the sequence [ŋk] has not lost the plosive element and [ŋ] in such a situation could still be treated as an allophone of /n/, were it not for the emergence of /ŋ/ as a phoneme as a result of the reduction of [ŋg] > /ŋ/. The very restricted distribution of /ŋ/ in PresE is, therefore, imposed by the circumstances of its development.

(5) *Advice to foreign learners.*—Care should be taken to articulate a velar sound (i.e. one related to /g/) rather than a palatal nasal of the [ɲ] type.

Those learners whose own language has [ŋ] only as an allophone of /n/ before /k, g/ should avoid using /g/ (or more rarely [k]) in those cases where /ŋ/ occurs in English without a following plosive, especially in sequences where final /ŋ/ is followed by a vowel, e.g. in *singing, reading out, a long essay*. In practising, the nasal /ŋ/ should be given exaggerated length and sequences such as /ŋiː, ŋɑː/ repeated in order to obtain a succession of nasal + vowel without a plosive.

8.7 Laterals

(1) *Articulatory features.*—A lateral consonant is articulated by means of a partial closure, on one or both sides of which the air-stream is able to escape through the mouth. In English, the tip of the tongue articulates normally with the centre of the upper teeth ridge; if the air escape is unilateral, an occlusion will also be made on one side between the rim of the tongue and the upper side teeth. English lateral sounds are usually voiced and frictionless, falling into the same category of voiced continuants (sonorants) as the nasals and /r/ and, to a lesser extent, /j, w/ (see following sections). They are, therefore, in many respects vowel-like, and often perform as vowels, i.e. have a central syllabic function. Most commonly, however, they behave as consonants, i.e. have a non-central situation in the syllable and, in the case of the voiceless fricative allophone [l̥], are consonantal from a purely phonetic standpoint.

(2) *Acoustic features.*[1]—The more usual types of English voiced lateral continuant have in their steady state a three-formant structure

---

[1] See O'Connor, Gerstman, Liberman, Delattre, and Cooper, 'Acoustic cues for the perception of initial /w, j, r, l/ in English,' *Word*, vol. 13, no. 1, 1957; Leigh Lisker, 'Minimal cues for separating /w, j, r, l/ in intervocalic positions,' *Word*, vol. 13, no. 2, 1957.

together with a fundamental voice component comparable with that of vowels. A steady state of from 50 to 60 msecs duration is needed if the continuant nature of the consonant is to be perceived, whereas a longer duration produces an effect of syllabicity. In cases of adjacent lateral and vowel, however, transitional cues are important in distinguishing [l] sounds from other continuants or glides such as /r, w, j/. F1 of /l/ is situated at or below F1 of the adjacent vowel, but not lower than 360 cps; F2 is within the range 960–1,800 cps before vowels of the [i, e, ɛ] type, within 840–1,800 cps for [a], and within 840–1,680 cps for such vowels as [ɔ, o, u] (in all cases depending on the F2 of the vowel); F3, crucial for distinguishing /l/ from /r/, is close to that of the vowel F3 before [i, e, ɛ] and as low as 1,920 cps before [ɔ, o, u]. Impressions of 'clear' and 'dark' qualities in the English lateral sounds are determined by the frequency of F2, the lower the frequency the 'darker' the [l] sound. The actual duration of the transition is also important—too short a transition risking confusion with nasals and stops, whereas a long transition will suggest a vowel glide. For [l] sounds, F2 and F3 have the best transition-durations at about 60–70 msecs; F1 transitions have to be much more rapid—of the order of 10 msecs.

8.7.1   *The English lateral phoneme* /l/.—Only one alveolar, lateral phoneme occurs in English, there being no opposition between fortis and lenis, voiced and voiceless, or fricative and non-fricative. Within the /l/ phoneme three main allophones occur:—

(*a*) *Clear* [l], with a relatively front vowel resonance, before vowels and /j/;

(*b*) *Voiceless* [l̥], following accented (aspirated) /p, k/ (less considerable devoicing occurs after /s, f, θ, ʃ/ or weakly accented /p, t, k/ —marked with * in the examples below); the tongue position is as for dark [ɫ] when syllabic but otherwise as for clear [l];

(*c*) *Dark* [ɫ], with a relatively back vowel resonance, finally (in a pre-junctural position) after a vowel, before a consonant, and as a syllabic sound following a consonant.

Note that the rule for the distribution of clear and dark /l/ works across boundaries e.g. the /l/ in *feel it* is a clear [l] before the initial vowel of *it*.

(1) *Examples*

(regularly spelt *l*, *ll* e.g. 'light, fill'; *l*, in pre-consonantal position is, however, frequently silent, e.g. 'talk, should, half, calm, salmon, folk, Holborn')

(*a*) *Clear* [l]

word initial—leave, let, lock, look, late, loud, leer, lewd

in word initial clusters—blow, glad, splice, *fly, *slow

word medial—silly, yellow, alloy, collar, caller, pulley, foolish, sullen, sailor, island, oily, million, failure, allow, select; medley, ugly, nobly, gimlet, inlay, bachelor, specially (with [l] or [əl]), *afflict, *asleep, *pamphlet

word final, intervocalic in context—feel it, fall out, all over, will you
  (*b*) *Voiceless* [l̥]—play, clean; (less devoicing after a weakly accented fortis plosive) *aptly, *butler, *hopeless, *sprinkler, *couplet, *antler, *simplest, *ghastly

(*c*) *Dark* [ɫ]

word final, after vowel—feel, fill, fell, canal, snarl, doll, call, bull, pool, dull, pearl, pale, pole, pile, owl, oil, royal, real, cruel

after vowel, before consonant—help, bulb, salt, cold, milk, filch, bilge, film, kiln, self, solve, health, else, bills; alpine, elbow, halter, elder, alchemy, almost, illness, alphabet, silver, wealthy, although, ulcer, palsy, Welsh, always

syllabic [ɫ]—*apple, table, *little, middle, *buckle, eagle, *satchel, cudgel, camel, final, quarrel (or with [əɫ]), *awful, oval, *Ethel, *parcel, easel, *special, usual, spaniel (or with [-jəɫ]), Oswald (or with [-wəɫd]), equal, *simple, tumble, *mantle, fondle, *uncle, angle, *sinful, *pistol; doubled, tables, measles, finally (or with [-əl-]; cf. 'finely' with [l])

variations in inflected forms of verbs having [ɫ] *in the uninflected form*—[ɫ], or [əl] (more rarely [l])—pommelling, tunnelling, cudgeling [l] (more rarely [ɫ] or [əl])—fondling, doubling, *circling, wriggling, *settling, *coupling, *whistling, puzzling, *scuffling, shovelling

It may be noted that some speakers distinguish between participles and verbal nouns, using clear [l] for the latter and dark [ɫ] or [əl] for the former; thus *coupling* [ˈkʌplɪŋ] (connecting device) and [ˈkʌpɫɪŋ] (joining). See §9.6.

(2) *Description.*—The soft palate being in its raised position, shutting off the nasal resonator, the tip of the tongue is in contact with

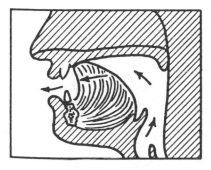
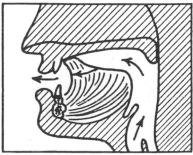
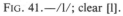

FIG. 41.—/l/; clear [l].   FIG. 42.—/l/; dark [ɫ].

the upper teeth ridge, allowing the air to escape on both sides or, in the case of a unilateral tongue-rim closure on the upper side teeth, on one side. For clear [l], the front of the tongue is raised in the direction of the hard palate at the same time as the tip contact is made, thus giving a front vowel resonance to the consonant; this resonance is often of the [ë] type, but may be closer or more open according to the following vowel, cf. *leap, loop.* For dark [ɫ], the tip contact is again made on the teeth ridge, the front of the tongue being somewhat depressed and the back raised in the direction of the soft palate, giving a back vowel (or velarized) resonance; this resonance is often of the type [ö] or [ɤ]. The lips' position is influenced by the nature of the adjacent vowel, cf. *leap, feel* (with spread lips), *loop, pool* (with somewhat rounded lips); in the case of [ɫ], and especially [ɫ], there is, with some speakers, always a tendency to lip-rounding.

Both [l] and [ɫ] are voiced, though partial devoicing may take place when a preceding consonant is fortis, as in those plosive (especially) and fricative examples marked with * in (1) (*a*), (*c*) above; after syllable initial, accented /p, k/, the devoicing is frequently complete.

The actual point of contact of the tongue for [ɫ] is conditioned by the place of articulation of the following consonant; thus, in *health, will they,* the [ɫ] has a dental contact (to a lesser extent, a preceding /θ, ð/ may cause a dental articulation [l̪], e.g. in *a month late, with love*); or, in *already, ultra, all dry,* the contact for [ɫ] is likely to be post-alveolar. [ɫ] may also be strongly nasalized by a following nasal consonant, e.g. *elm, kiln.*

The velarization of [ɫ] often has the effect of retracting and lowering slightly the articulation of a preceding front vowel, e.g. *feel, fill, fell, canal*; in the case of /iː/ + [ɫ], a central glide between the vowel and [ɫ] is often noticeable, and the [ɪ] element of /eɪ, aɪ, ɔɪ/ tends to be obscured, e.g. in *pail, pile, oil.*

(3) *Variants.*—The RP distribution of [l] and [ɫ] may be said to be: [l] when a vowel or /j/ follows; [ɫ] in all other positions, including some cases where syllabic [ɫ] occurs before a vowel. Variations in the quality of the back vowel resonance associated with [ɫ] are, however, to be found among RP speakers, with a range extending from [ö], [ʊ], or [ɤ] to [ɜ] or [ʌ]; lip positions, too, vary from neutral to loose rounding. In some speech, notably that of Cockney,[1] the tongue-tip contact for [ɫ] is omitted, this allophone of /l/ being realized as a vowel (vocoid) in the region of [ö] with weak lip-rounding or as [ɤ] with neutral or weakly spread lips, thus *sell* [seö] or [seɤ], *fall* [fɔö] or [fɔɤ], *table* ['tæɪbö] or ['tæɪbɤ]. In such speech, the lowering of /iː/ and /uː/ before [ö] is so marked that *meal, mill,* and *pool, pull,* may become homophonous or

---

[1] For a full phonetic and phonemic treatment of Cockney [ɫ], see Eva Sivertsen, *Cockney Phonology,* Oslo, 1960.

distinguished merely by the length of central syllabic vowel element, i.e. [mɪˈö] *v.* [mɪö], [pʊˈö] *v.* [pʊö]; other confusions are likely, e.g. *rail* (RP [reɪɫ], Cockney [ræö]) and *row* (RP [rɑʊ], Cockney [ræö]), *dole* (RP [dəʊɫ], Cockney [dɒö]) and *doll* (RP [dɒɫ], Cockney [dɒö]). Realizations of syllabic [ɫ] as a vowel are not, however, confined to Cockney; many RP speakers will use [ö] for [ɫ] in words such as *beautiful, careful, people, table,* etc., i.e. especially when a consonant involving a labial articulation precedes; they will, moreover, not recognize such a vocalic allophone as unusual when they hear it. The use of a vocalic allophone seems somewhat less usual when other consonants precede, e.g. in *uncle, Ethel, parcel, special, spaniel,* and is particularly avoided, as a childish pronunciation, after alveolar plosives, e.g. *little, middle,* where the consonants are regularly released laterally. On the other hand, in an artificial or somewhat precious style of speaking, [l] may be used for [ɫ].

It has been seen (in (1) (*a*) above) that word final non-syllabic [ɫ] becomes [l] when a following word begins with a vowel or /j/. In the same way, syllabic [ɫ] may tend to become clearer when a vowel follows, e.g. *finally* (when pronounced [ˈfaɪnlɪ]), *acetylene* (when [əˈsetliːn]), *special edition, parcel of books, little or nothing, middle of the road,* etc. The use of the clearer or the darker quality [l] may, however, be related to the rhythmic and sense structure of the utterance, e.g. *feel it* may have a clear [l] as in *feeling,* but the [l] of *feel* in *feel ill,* which it is possible to treat as two rhythmic groups, may be of a darker kind (see Abercrombie, 1965).

In other varieties of English the RP distribution of [l] and [l] may not obtain. Thus, in some kinds of Scottish and American English, /l/ before vowels and /j/ is realized with a back vowel resonance, whereas in Irish English a relatively clear [l] is used in those situations where RP would have [ɫ]. Note, too, that American English has syllabic [ɫ] in words such as *fertile, futile, missile, reptile,* etc., where RP retains a prominent preceding vowel [-aɪ̯l]; a reduction of the vowel, similar to the present American form, occurred in seventeenth-century British English.

(4) *Chief sources.*—PresE /l/ derives from OE [l, ll] (*land, climb, all, tell, apple*), from OE [hl], [xl] or [l̥] (*loaf, ladder*)—since OE front vowels tended to be diphthongized before /l/, it seems likely that /l/ in such a position was velarized in OE as it is to-day; from OF [l] (*lamp, close, colour, veal, able*). In many cases pre-consonantal [ɫ], especially after back or open vowels, was vocalized to [ʊ] (*walk, talk, half, folk*) in the early fifteenth century, such a pronunciation being commonly shown by the seventeenth-century grammarians; but in some cases (*halt, salt, malt*), it has been retained; in others, an /l/ has been reintroduced in spelling and pronunciation (*fault, falcon, emerald, soldier, realm*) or merely in the spelling (*calm, palm, balm*). The loss of /l/ in *could, should, would,* occurred in eModE.

(5) *Advice to foreign learners.*—Few foreign learners will possess in their own language [l] and [ɫ] sounds with the RP distribution. It is true that, since there is no phonemic opposition between [l] and [ɫ] in English, learners will be perfectly intelligible if they use only [l]. But those who wish to avoid a foreign accent and whose English otherwise conforms to an RP pattern should learn to make the dark [ɫ]. In the articulation of [ɫ] there should be no 'curling back' of the tongue, as is so often advised in books on English. To overcome such a habit already acquired, the tongue-tip may be gripped between the teeth during practice. The essential feature of [ɫ] may be said to be the accompanying weakly rounded [o] or [ɔ] quality; learners should, therefore, begin by pronouncing a vowel of the [o] type for the syllabic [ɫ] in words such as *bubble, people, awful,* i.e. where a labial consonant precedes [ɫ], thus—['bʌbo], ['piːpo], ['ɔːfo]. A pure vowel of this kind is likely to occur in their own language. Such a pronunciation will come near to that used by many English speakers (see (3) above). The same sound sequence should then be attempted with the tongue-tip touching the upper teeth ridge, thus producing a lateral sound with the correct velarized quality. The relationship of [ɫ] and [o] can further be established by practising the alternation of [o]-[ɫ]-[o]-[ɫ], only the tongue-tip moving and the [o] resonance continuing. The [ɫ] thus achieved should then be used in the examples of [ɫ] given in (1) above, first the syllabic cases and then the non-syllabic.

Care should also be taken to use a sufficiently devoiced [l̥] after accented (aspirated) /p, k/. Accented /p, k/ are distinguished from /b, g/ mainly by their aspiration; it is important that this aspiration-cue should be made clear in the sequences /pl, kl/ by the voicelessness of the /l/. If this is not done, such a word as *plot,* pronounced with a fully voiced /l/, may be understood as *blot.* Pairs for practice, relying largely for the opposition on voiceless *v.* voiced [l], are: *plot, blot; plead, bleed; plight, blight; clad, glad; class, glass; clean, glean; clue, glue.*

Some learners, especially Jugoslavs and some others speaking Slav languages, should avoid using a lateral in pre-vocalic positions which is over-velarized for RP.

8.8   Post-alveolar Approximant (Frictionless Continuant)

/r/

(1) *Examples*

> (regularly spelt *r, rr* e.g. 'red, carry'; also *wr, rh,* e.g. 'write, rhythm')
> *word initial*—reed, rag, raw, rude, rut, road, royal, rear
> *word medial, intervocalic*—mirror, very, arrow, sorry, hurry, furry, arrive, diary, dowry, dairy, eery, fury

word final (/r/-link with following word beginning with a vowel)—
far away, poor old man, once for all, here at last, there are two
in consonantal clusters

(following fortis accented plosive = [ɹ̥])—price, proud, tree, try,
cream, crow; expression, surprise, attract, extremely, decree

(following fortis fricative, unaccented fortis plosive, or accented
fortis plosive preceded by /s/ in the same syllable — somewhat
devoiced [ɹ])—fry, afraid, throw, thrive, shrink, shrug; apron,
nitrate, buckram, cockroach[1]; sprint, sprat, street, strain, scream,
scrape

(following lenis consonant = [ɹ]—fricative after /d/)—brief,
bright, dress, dry, grey, grow; umbrella, address, agree, hungry;
comrade, sovereign, general, miserable

words containing more than one /r/—brewery, library, arrowroot,
retrograde, rarer, treasury, gregarious, procrastinate

Compare—/r/, /l/—raft, laughed; rush, lush; red, led; right, light;
pirate, pilot; sherry, Shelley; two rocks, two locks; crash, clash;
pray, play; fry, fly; grew, glue; bright, blight

(2) *Description*

(*a*) *Articulatory and distributional features.*—The most common
allophone of RP /r/ is a voiced post-alveolar frictionless continuant (or
approximant) [ɹ]. The soft palate being raised and the nasal resonator
shut off, the tip of the tongue is held in a position near to, but not
touching, the rear part of the upper teeth ridge; the back rims of the
tongue are touching the upper molars; the central part of the tongue is
lowered, with a general contraction of the tongue, so that the effect of
the tongue position is one of hollowing and slight retroflexion of the
tip. The air-stream is thus allowed to escape freely, without friction,

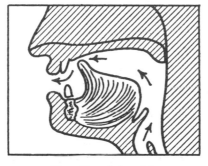

FIG. 43.—/r/ = [ɹ].

---

[1] In the case of /tr/, [r] is likely to be completely voiceless unless a junctural boundary
occurs between /t/ and /r/.

over the centre part of the tongue. The lip position is determined largely by that of the following vowel, e.g. *reach* with neutral to spread lips, *root* with rounded lips. This allophone of the RP phoneme is, therefore, phonetically vowel-like, but, having a non-central situation in the syllable, it functions as a consonant.

RP /r/ occurs only before a vowel, the above description being applicable to the realizations: initially before a vowel; following a lenis consonant (except /d/), either in a syllable initial cluster or at word or syllable boundaries; word final /r/ linking with an initial vowel in the following word. (See §11.3.7.) This limited distribution applies also to other non-rhotic accents. (See §6.3.2(4)(d).)

When /d/ precedes /r/,[1] the allophone of /r/ is fricative, the /d/ closure being post-alveolar and its release slow enough to produce friction, e.g. in *drive, tawdry* and, in rapid speech, at syllable or word boundaries, e.g. *headrest, bedroom, wide road.*

A completely devoiced fricative [ɹ̥] may be heard following accented /p, t, k/, e.g. *price, try, cream, oppress, attract, across.*[1] A partially devoiced variety of /r/ occurs: when /r/ follows an unaccented fortis plosive initial in a syllable and, in rapid speech, at syllable or word boundaries, e.g. *upright, apron, paltry,*[1] *nitrate, beetroot, cockroach, acrobat*; in the syllable initial sequences /spr-, str-, skr-/, e.g. *spring, string, scream*; after other accented fortis consonants, e.g. *fry, thrive, shrink.* Slight devoicing may also occur, in rapid speech, following these latter fortis fricatives, when they are unaccented and final in the preceding syllable or word, e.g. *belfry, saffron, necessary* /ˈnesəsrɪ/, *surfriding, birthright, horse-race, mushroom.*

(*b*) *Acoustic features.*[2]—In addition to a low frequency (voice) component, the voiced frictionless continuant type of /r/ has a three-formant structure comparable with that of vowels, with a steady state which appears to have a necessary duration of 50–60 msecs. Typical formant frequencies are: F1, between 120 and 600 cps, the lower the frequency, the greater the perceived impression of lip-rounding; F2, generally higher than that for /l/, showing a rising transition from a steady state of from 840 to 1,560 cps before [i, e, ɛ], 840 to 1,200 cps before [ɔ], and 600 to 1,200 cps before vowels of the [o, u] type, strong labialization being again associated with the lower frequencies; F3, which provides an essential cue to recognition, with a rising transition from a steady state near to that of F2, i.e. 840—1,920 before [i, e, ɛ] and not higher than 1,680 cps before [ɔ, o, u]. The duration of the transition of F2 and F3 must be greater than 50 msecs (below which the [r] is heard as a flap) and may still be heard as [ɹ] with a duration of up to 300

---

[1] /tr/ and /dr/ sequences may be treated phonetically as affricates when close-knit (see §8.3.2).

[2] See O'Connor, *et al.*, op. cit.

msecs; F1 transitions, on the other hand, may be very short (even as short as the 10 msecs characteristic of /l/) without losing the [ɹ] value.

(3) *Variants.*—There are more phonetic variants of the /r/ phoneme than of any other English consonant. Within RP, the frictionless continuant variety [ɹ] may be replaced by an *alveolar tap* [ɾ] in intervocalic positions, e.g. *very, sorry, marry, Mary, for ever,* following /θ, ð/, e.g. *three, forthright, with respect,* and also, with some speakers, after other consonants, especially /b, g/, e.g. *bright, grow.* In the case of intervocalic [ɾ], a single tap is made by the tip of the tongue on the alveolar ridge, the side rims usually making a light contact with the upper molars. The articulation of [ɾ] differs from that of /d/ in that the contact for [ɾ] is of shorter duration and less complete than that of /d/, the central hollowing of the tongue typical of [ɾ] being retained; *carry* with [ɾ] and *caddy* with /d/ are, therefore, phonetically distinct. In the case of [ɾ] following /θ, ð/, a tap is made by the tongue-tip on the teeth ridge as the tongue is withdrawn from its dental position; again, the contact is of very brief duration and some tongue hollowing is retained.

In RP, too, the degree of *labialization* varies considerably. Although for perhaps the majority of RP speakers the lip position of /r/ is determined by that of the following vowel, some speakers labialize /r/ whatever the following vowel. In some extreme cases, lip-rounding is accompanied by no articulation of the forward part of the tongue, so that /r/ is replaced by /w/ and homophones of the type *wed, red,* are produced. Such a pronunciation, once a fashionable affectation (e.g. in the late eighteenth and early nineteenth centuries) is now heard only amongst children who have not yet acquired [ɹ], or as a defective substitution for [ɹ]. (The labio-dental frictionless continuant [ʋ] is also commonly substituted for [ɹ] in defective speech.)

A *lingual trill* (or *roll*) [r] may also be heard amongst RP speakers, but usually only in highly stylized speech, e.g. in declamatory verse-speaking. This trill, i.e. a rapid succession of taps by the tip of the tongue on the alveolar ridge, is often considered typical of some Scottish types of English, though a single tap is more common in the colloquial forms of both Scottish English and some Northern speech.

A *uvular* articulation, either a trill [ʀ] or a fricative [ʁ], may be heard in the extreme north-east of England and also among some Scottish speakers and as a defective substitution for [ɹ].

Finally, the degree of *retroflexion* of the tongue for [ɹ] may be greater than in RP—[ɻ], e.g. in the speech of the south-west of England and some American English. The retroflexion of the tongue may anticipate the consonant and colour the vowel articulation; such 'r-coloured' vowels may occur in this type of speech in such words as *bird, farm, lord.*

/r/ differs in various types of English not only in its phonetic realization but also in its distribution. Most regional forms of speech, remote from the London area or unaffected by the social influence of RP, retain the earlier post-vocalic (both pre-consonantal and pre-pausal) usage of /r/, distinguishing between such RP homophones as *pour, paw*; *court, caught*. (Some older RP speakers still retain a vocalic element representing the former /r/, keeping *pour* /pɔə/ distinct from *paw* /pɔ:/.) The post-vocalic [r] used will correspond to the types given above according to the region. A retroflexed continuant, of somewhat greater duration than the pre- or post-vocalic form, may also have syllabic function, e.g. in *water, father, ladder, paper*, etc. For the use of word-final, post-vocalic /r/ as a linking form in RP, see §11.3.7.

A sequence of unaccented /r/s, separated by /ə/, is frequently reduced in rapid speech by the reduction of /rə/ to syllabic /r/ or by its total elision (see §9.6).

(4) *Chief sources.*—PresE /r/ derives from OE [r, rr] (*rise, rope, green, nearer*)—with later loss in post-vocalic positions (*horse, four*); OE [hr], [xr] or [r̥] (*ring, roof*)—[h] or the voiceless nature of [r] being lost by early ME; OE [wr] (*wrap, write, wrest, wretch*)—[w] being commonly omitted in the sixteenth century and generally by the late seventeenth, producing homophones with *rap, rite, rest, retch*; from OF [r] (*rule, remain, fruit, very*)—with later loss in post-vocalic positions (*arm, poor*). It is likely that the quality of /r/ in OE and ME was that of a linguo-alveolar trill or tap as described in (3) above. Its vibratory nature is described by writers of the sixteenth and seventeenth centuries, but /r/ had for some time exerted an influence on the preceding vowel and an [ə] resonance is identified in the sixteenth century. By the seventeenth century it is probable that the trill or tap was used only before vowels and that the approximant [ɹ] occurred, with or without friction, finally and before consonants. The change from a fricative to a non-fricative [ɹ], then to [ə], and finally to disappearance or merging with a preceding vowel in post-vocalic positions is a natural sequence. Its loss in post-vocalic positions in educated speech of the south-east of England is likely to have taken place by the end of the eighteenth century—considerably earlier in unaccented syllables and generally in popular speech. As has been stated above, total loss of earlier post-vocalic /r/ is restricted socially and regionally even to-day.

(5) *Advice to foreign learners.*—RP /r/ has a quality which is rarely encountered in other languages, the usual frictionless continuant variety having much in common with a vowel. Any strongly rolled [r] sound, whether lingual or uvular, is not acceptable in RP, although it is not a question of loss of intelligibility through phonemic confusion. A weak lingual trill is the least objectionable substitution for RP [ɹ]; but a uvular sound, trill or fricative, as so often used by French or German learners, is generally taken as a characteristic of a marked foreign

accent, despite the fact that a uvular sound is not unknown in English regional speech.

A foreign learner should, therefore, try to abandon his own prejudices as to what an [r] sound should be and approach the RP [ɹ] as if it were a vowel. The correct retraction of the tongue may be achieved by placing the tip on the rear part of the upper alveolar ridge, then slightly lowering the tip, at the same time keeping the side rims in contact with the upper molars. Once the feeling of slight curling-back of the tip and hollowing of the centre of the tongue has been achieved, the student should hold this position and pronounce the vowel /ɜː/ of *bird*. This sound, with exaggerated length and weak breath effort, may then be used initially in a word such as *red*. It is important that [ɹ] should be made unusually long in this position until the tongue articulation is established.

Alternatively, practice may start from /ʒ/, in the articulation of which the tongue has a position somewhat similar to that of [ɹ], although the sound is fricative, the narrowing between tongue and roof of the mouth made too far forward, and the tongue hollowing and lateral contraction missing. From the /ʒ/ position, the tongue should be retracted, hollowed, and slightly lowered, so that the friction is lost. With both methods, it is often helpful to hold the jaws widely separated and the lips somewhat rounded. It is particularly important that those whose own *r*-sound is of the uvular type should not make a double articulation—uvular and post-alveolar at the same time. The post-alveolar affricates /tɹ, dɹ/ may also be related to /tʃ, dʒ/, applying the same principles of retraction as just described (see also §8.3.2).

Examples for practice should be chosen according to the degree of difficulty and the phonetic nature of the /r/ allophone used. Thus, the fricative variety of the second element of the affricates /tr, dr/ may be the first to practise (to establish the post-alveolar position), but the sequence /str-/ will give greater difficulty; intervocalic [ɹ] usually presents relatively little difficulty, especially as a one-tap [r] is always permissible; the frictionless continuant, characteristic of initial positions, may be the most troublesome articulation of all.

Learners should not be misled by the spelling into pronouncing post-vocalic letter *r*. In words such as *car, arm, horse, hurt*, etc., the *r*-letter may be taken as a sign indicating length of the preceding vowel, and in *fear, there, tour*, etc., as a sign of the [ə] element of the diphthong. Nevertheless, in connected speech, the final linking /r/ form should normally be used; no special attempt to use an 'intrusive' /r/ need be made. (See examples for practice in (1) above.)

As in the case of /l/, it should be remembered that in the sequences /pr-, br-, tr-, dr-, kr-, gr-/ the oppositions between fortis and lenis plosives are indicated mainly by the degree of voicing in the following /r/. Thus, /pr-, tr-, kr-/ should have [ɹ̥], especially when accented, if they are not to be confused with /br-, dr-, gr-/; cf. such pairs as *pray*, *bray*; *try*, *dry*; *crow*, *grow*.

Some learners, such as the Japanese and other Asians, whose own language does not have an opposition of the /l/-/r/ type, should practise words distinguishing /l/ from /r/ (see (1) above).

8.9   Semi-vowels

(1) *Articulatory and distributional features.*—A semi-vowel is a rapid vocalic glide on to a syllabic sound of greater steady duration. In English the semi-vowels /j/ and /w/ glide from positions of approximately /iː/ (with spread or neutral lips) and /uː/ (with rounded lips) respectively, e.g. in *year*, *west*, *Oswald* [ˈɒzwɪd], *spaniel* [ˈspænjɪ̩]. The actual point at which the essential vocalic glide begins depends on the nature of the following sound, e.g. the glide of /j/ to /iː/ in *yeast* has a closer beginning than that of /j/ to /ɒ/ in *yacht*, and the starting point of /w/ before /uː/ in *woo* is closer than that before /ɒ/ in *what*. When /j/ is followed by a back close vowel as in *you*, or /w/ by a front close vowel as in *we*, the starting points need not be as close as in *yeast* and *woo*, since in the first cases the glide is essentially of a front to back (or vice versa) direction, rather than a movement of close to more open, as in the latter cases. In English, however, it is never necessary for the starting point of /j/ + /iː/ or /w/ + /uː/ to be so close that it falls within the fricative region beyond the vowel area, since English /iː/ and /uː/ are both sufficiently relaxed for a perceptible non-fricative glide to be made from a closer position within the vowel area.

Despite the fact that semi-vowels are, in phonetic terms, generally vocalic, they are treated within the consonant class, mainly because their *function* is consonantal rather than vowel-like, i.e. they have a marginal rather than a central situation in the syllable. /j/ and /w/ occur initially or in an initial cluster preceding a syllabic sound (see §7.2 for the treatment of final [ɪ] and [ʊ] elements of English diphthongs as an integral part of the diphthongal glide rather than as separable—consonantal—/j/ and /w/). Their consonantal function is emphasized by the fact that the articles have their preconsonantal form when followed by /j/ and /w/, i.e. *the yard*, *a yacht*, *the west*, *a wasp*, with /ðə/ or /ə/ rather than with /ðɪ/ or /ən/.

In addition, the allophones of /j/ and /w/, when following a fortis consonant, are voiceless and fricative, as in *cue*, *quick* [kjuː], [kw̥ɪk], i.e. they fall within a phonetic definition of a consonant.

(2) *Acoustic features.*[1]—Since /j/ and /w/ are vocalic glides (except in the case of the fricative allophones mentioned above), they may be

---

[1] See O'Connor, *et al.*, op. cit.

expected to have acoustic features similar to those of vowels, i.e. a characteristic two or three formant structure similar to that of /iː/ or /uː/. In fact, as for vowels, two formants are sufficient for good recognition. Compared with /r, l/, the steady state of the semi-vowels is very short, e.g. of the order of 30 msecs. F1 starting point of the glide is that of /iː/ or /uː/, i.e. about 240 cps; F2 has a starting point within the range 2,280–3,600 cps for /j/, depending on the following vowel, and within the range 360–840 cps for /w/, depending on the following vowel. The transition duration of F2 is of the order of 50–100 msecs for both /j/ and /w/, with that of F1 of the same or shorter duration.

8.9.1 Unrounded Palatal Semi-vowel

/j/

(1) *Examples*

(spelt *y, i,* e.g. 'yes, spaniel'; also /ju /, spelt *u, ew, eu, eau, ui,* e.g. 'muse, new, feud, beauty, suit')
word initial = [j]—yield, yes, yard, yacht, yawn, union, young, yearn, yokel, year, Europe
following accented /p, t, k, h/ (*only before* /uː, ʊə/) = [ç]—pew, tune, queue, cure, pure, huge; accuse, secure, peculiar, attuned
following /sp, st, sk/, *fortis fricatives or unaccented* /p, t, k/ = *slightly devoiced* [j̊]—spurious, stew, askew; enthusiasm, pursue, refuse; opulent, spatula, oculist; help you, quick yield
following lenis consonant = [j]—beauty, duty, music, new, value, view; abuse, endure, argue, manure, onion, failure, familiar, residue, senior, behaviour

(2) *Description.*—The vocalic allophones of RP /j/ are articulated by the tongue assuming the position for a front half-close to close vowel (depending on the degree of openness of the following sound) and moving away immediately to the position of the following sound; the lips are generally neutral or spread, but many anticipate the lip-rounding of the following vowel in such cases as *you, yawn,* etc. When /j/ follows a fortis consonant, devoicing takes place; especially when /j/ follows accented /p, t, k, h/, the devoicing is complete, with the result that a fortis voiceless palatal fricative [ç] is produced. (In these latter cases, it is the friction rather than the glide which identifies the phoneme.)

When /j/ is the final element of accented clusters, only /uː/, /ʊə/ or sometimes /ɔː/ may follow /j/ (*pew, cure*); in unaccented clusters, /j/ may be followed by /uː, ʊ, ʊə/ or /ə/ (*argue, opulent, tenure, senior*). The sequence /h/ + /j/ as in *hue* /hjuː/ [hçuː] may coalesce into [ç] ([çuː]). Such a realization entails oppositions between /j/, /h/, and [ç],

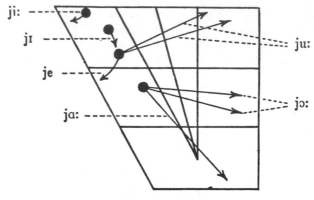

FIG. 44.—/j/.

raising the possibility of phonemic status for [ç]—*you, who, hue*. The number of words offering the sequence /h/ + /j/ > [ç] is, however, restricted (*Hugh, hew, hue, human, humour*, etc.), and alternative pronunciations with /h/ + /j/ or /h/ + [ç] (on the pattern of /p, t, k/ + /j/) are possible. [ç] is, therefore, more conveniently treated as a realization of /h/ + /j/.

(3) *Variants.*—In many cases of RP /j/ + /uː/, an alternative pronunciation without /j/ exists[1] (and is extended further in American English). Earlier /juː/ or /ɪu/ sequences (see §7.9.9) have regularly been reduced to /uː/ in PresE after /tʃ, dʒ, r/ and /l/ preceded by a consonant; /juː/ is retained after plosives, nasals, /f/, /v/, and /h/ (*pew, beauty, queue, argue, tune, dune, few, view, nephew, huge*), and when /l/ is preceded by an accented vowel (*value, curlew*); but in other cases, more variation is possible, both /uː/ and /juː/ being heard, e.g. in *absolute(ly), lute, salute, revolution, enthusiasm, pursuit, assume, suit, suet, suitable, superstition, supermarket, consume, presume*, etc, though /uː/ grows increasingly common in such words being the more common after /l/ and /s/ in a stressed syllable whilst /juː/ remains predominant after /θ, z/.

Unaccented sequences of /tj, dj, sj, zj/ coalesced in an earlier state of the language into /tʃ, dʒ, ʃ, ʒ/ (see §§8.3.1, 8.4.5). In some cases, e.g. *statue, residue, issue, seizure, Christian, immediate, educate, gratitude, usual, visual, Jesuit*, both forms may now be heard, the pronunciation with /tj, dj, sj, zj/ being characteristic of careful speech; on the other hand, the occasionally heard coalesced forms with /ʃ/ in *assume* and /ʒ/ in *presume* are regarded as old-fashioned. Such coalescences

---

[1] See Daniel Jones, *Outline of English Phonetics*, §8.17.

also occur in rapid, familiar, speech, as unaccented word boundaries, e.g. in *not yet, would you, this year, sees you* (§11.3.4).

In unaccented syllables there is often variation between /jə/ and /ɪ-ə/, e.g. in *immediate, India, audience, tedious, idiot, hideous*. In the cases involving a preceding alveolar plosive where the /jə/ form may be regarded as the primary one, this form may occasionally be further reduced to /tʃ, dʒ/ in rapid speech, e.g. /ɪˈmiːdjət, ɪˈmiːdʒəl, ɪˈmiːdɪət/. In such cases as *Romania, Bohemia, Australia, morphia*, /ɪə/ tends to be retained in careful speech, as well as in those suffixes where /ə/ has a separable morphemic value, e.g. in *easier, heavier*.

A [j] glide is sometimes heard at a point of front vowel hiatus, where the first vowel is /iː/ or a diphthong ending in [ɪ] (especially /aɪ, ɔɪ/), e.g. *seeing, saying, sighing, fire, enjoy it* [ˈsijɪŋ, ˈsejɪŋ, ˈsajɪŋ, fajə, ɪnˈdʒɔj ɪt], as well as in the regional realizations of /ɪə, ɛə/ as /ɪjə, ejə/ in such words as *dear, there* [dɪjə, ðejə]. Such a perceptible [j] results from the relatively close quality given to /iː/ and [ɪ] and the rapid glide to the following, more open, vowel; vowel sequences containing /iː/ or [ɪ] are, however, generally so relaxed that such a glide is not heard (see also §7.12).

(4) *Chief sources.*—PresE /j/ derives from OE [j] (itself deriving from a palatalized form of [g]) (*yard, year, yield, yoke, young*). PresE /j/ (+ /uː/) also derives from ME [ɪu, eu] (see §7.9.9) and from loss of syllabic value of [ɪ] before another vowel in unaccented situations, e.g. in such words of French origin as *opinion, familiar, onion, William, pavilion*, where the *i*-spelling had at an earlier stage represented the palatal nature of French /ɲ, ʎ/.

(5) *Advice to foreign learners.*—RP /j/ presents little difficulty, provided that the starting point of the glide is not so close as to produce friction in those situations where /j/ should be purely vocalic; such incorrect friction is most likely to be used before relatively close front vowels, e.g. in *yeast, yes*. Spanish learners, in particular, should avoid using a palatal plosive [ɟ] when /j/ is strongly accented, e.g. in *yes, young* [ɟes, ɟʌŋ]. /j/ should be correctly devoiced after accented /p, t, k/, e.g. in *pew, tune, queue*.

8.9.2 Labial-velar Semi-vowel

/w/

(1) *Examples*

(spelt *w, wh*; or *u* after *q, g*—west, which, quick, language; note 'one, once, choir, suite' with /w/)
word initial = [w]—weed, wet, wag, wasp, wood, womb, one, word, wave, woke, wire, weird, wear

following accented /t, k/ = [w̥]—twig, twelve, twin, twice, queen, quell, quick, quite, quaint, acquaint

following /sk/, *accented fortis fricative or unaccented* /p, t, k/ = slightly devoiced [w]—square, squash, squirrel; thwart, swim, swear, swoon; upward, outward, equal; pump water, that word, take one

intervocalic, or following lenis consonant = [w]—away, aware, inward, always, language; dwindle, dwarf, Gwen

possible /hw/ or /ʍ/—wheat, whether, which, what, white

possible oppositions /w/, /hw/, ʍ/—witch, which; weather, whether; wine, whine; Wales, whales; wear, where

Compare /w/, /v/—west, vest; wine, vine; worse, verse; wail, veil; weir, veer

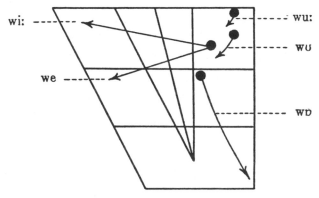

FIG. 45.—/w/.

(2) *Description.*—The vocalic allophones of RP /w/ are articulated by the tongue assuming the position for a back half-close to close vowel (depending upon the degree of openness of the following sound) and moving away immediately to the position of the following sound; the lips are rounded[1] (more closely when followed by /uː, ʊ/ or /ɔː/ than when preceding a more open or front vowel—cf. *woo, wood, war,* with *what, west, we;* in those cases where /w/ precedes /uː/, the lip-rounding for /w/ is closer and more energetic than that associated with /uː/, permitting a distinction between such a pair as *ooze, woos*). The soft palate is raised and the vocal folds vibrate; but when /w/ follows a fortis consonant, some devoicing takes place: when /w/ follows

---

[1] This is an example of double articulation, the approximation of the articulators at the bilabial and velar places of articulation constituting two strictures of equal rank.

accented /t, k/, the devoicing is complete = [w̥] or [ʍ] (a fortis voice-less labial-velar fricative—the friction being bilabial). In this latter case, it is the bilabial friction rather than the glide which identifies the phoneme; such words as *swoop, swoon,* are distinguished from *soup, soon,* not only by the stronger lip action associated with /w/ but also by its partially devoiced friction.

Consonants preceding /w/, especially initially in an accented syllable, will be lip-rounded in anticipation of /w/, e.g. in *twist, queen, swing, language, conquest,* and to a lesser extent at syllable or word boundaries, e.g. in *onward, bindweed, front wheel, this one.*

(3) *Variants.*—The main variant, both in RP and in other types of British English, concerns the pronunciation of the spelling form *wh.* Amongst careful conservative RP speakers and regularly in several regional types of speech, e.g. in Scottish English, words such as *when* are pronounced with /hw/, or, more usually, the fortis voiceless labial-velar fricative [ʍ]. In such speech, which contains oppositions of the kind *wine, whine,* shown in (1) above, /ʍ/ has phonemic status. Among RP speakers, however—especially males—the use of /ʍ/ as a phoneme has declined rapidly (though it is often taught as the correct form in verse-speaking). Even if /ʍ/ does occur distinctively in any idiolect, it may nevertheless be interpreted phonemically as /h/ + /w/ (cf. the treatment of [ç] in §8.9.1(2)). However, the fact that the stock of words in which /ʍ/ may be opposed to /w/ (e.g. in *whale, what, wheel, when, where, whet, which, whig, whin, whine, whirr, whist, whit, why*) is greater than those in which [ç] is opposed to /j/, provides some argument in favour of a monophonemic rather than a biphonemic solution for /ʍ/.

A [w] glide is sometimes heard at a point of vowel hiatus where the first vowel is /uː/ or a diphthong ending in [ʊ] (especially /aʊ/), e.g. *doing, following, our, allow it* [ˈduwɪŋ, ˈfɒləwɪŋ, awə, əˈlaw ɪt], as well as in the regional realizations of /ɔə/ (= RP /ɔː/) as [ɔwə] in such words as *door* [ˈdɔwə]. Such a perceptible [w] results from the relatively close quality given to /uː/ or [ʊ] or [ɔ] and the rapid glide to the follow-ing vowel; vowel sequences containing /uː/, [ʊ] or [ɔ] are, however, usually sufficiently relaxed for such a glide not to be heard (see also §7.9.9).

Some RP speakers omit /w/ in the context /k-ɔː/, e.g. in *quart* (= *caught*) and *quarter.*

(4) *Chief sources.*—PresE /w/ derives from OE [w] (*way, wolf, wash, widow, twin, dwarf*); from OF [w]—a northern French form, where Mod French has /g/ (*wage, ward, warrant, war*); from an earlier French [u] preceded by a velar plosive and followed by another vowel (*squire, squirrel, squadron*). In many cases an earlier [w] has been lost (*so, such, thong, two, sword, answer*) during the ME or eModE periods, and in the unaccented terminations of such place-names as

Chiswick, Dulwich, Greenwich, Woolwich; [w] in the cluster [wr] (*write, wreck, wrist*) was finally lost in the late seventeenth century.

PresE /ʍ/ derives from OE [hw], [xw] or [w̥] (spelt *hw* in OE) (*whale, wheel, where, when, which, whistle*). [hw] or [ʍ] finally merges with /w/ in educated southern speech in the late eighteenth century, although still deplored by normative elocutionists; /w/ occurs for [hw] much earlier—probably in ME—however, in popular speech. The reduction of [hw] to /w/ is parallel to that of [hr, hn, hl] to /r, n, l/; the relatively smaller number of French words entering the language with /w/ (compared with the numerous examples with initial /r, n, l/) may be a reason for the longer persistence of a /hw/-/w/ opposition, the imbalance between the voiceless and voiced varieties being not so marked as in the case of /hr, hn, hl/ *v.* /r, n, l/.

In the case of *who, whom, whose*, it is the [w] element which has been lost (probably by the eModE period), due to a merging of the [w] with the following, similar, /uː/. The addition of initial /w/ in *one, once* (cf. *alone*), occurred from late ME onwards in popular speech, existed alongside [oːn, oːns] forms in eModE, and was finally adopted as regular by the end of the seventeenth century.

(5) *Advice to foreign learners.*—/ʍ/ being of restricted usage in a relatively small number of words, there is no need for the foreign learner of RP to adopt this sound for *wh-* words. It is, however, important that the vocalic allophone of /w/ should not be replaced by a consonantal sound, i.e. either [β], a voiced bilabial fricative, or [v], a voiced labio-dental fricative, in which the lower lip articulates with the upper teeth, or [ʋ], a labio-dental approximant, in which there is again a loose approximation (without friction) between the lower lip and the upper teeth. All such substitutions will be interpreted by the English ear as /v/. The learner should protrude and round his lips, ensuring that the teeth play no part in the articulation; if necessary, in practice, an energetically rounded full [uː] vowel should be used, e.g. *wine* being pronounced as [uːaɪn], and a clear distinction being made between this word and *vine* (see examples in (1) above). The same protruded and rounded lip action (and absence of lower teeth contact) applies to the voiceless allophone [w̥], as in *quite, twin*, etc. As in the case of the voiceless allophones of /l, r, j/, it is important that /w/ should be devoiced especially after accented /t, k/, despite the fact that there are no exact pairs depending on the opposition [dw, gw]-[tw̥, kw̥], cf. *dwell, twelve*; *distinguish, relinquish*; *dwindle, twin*; *Gwen, quench*.

8.10   The Frequency of Occurrence of RP Consonants[1]

As a class, the alveolar phonemes emerge as those which occur most frequently in English, this being a generalization which appears to be

[1] See D. B. Fry, op. cit. In this investigation /tr/ and /dr/ were treated as a sequence of

applicable to many languages. The following order of frequency of occurrence has been established by D. B. Fry[1]:—

%		%	
/n/	7·58	/b/	1·97
/t/	6·42	/f/	1·79
/d/	5·14	/p/	1·78
/s/	4·81	/h/	1·46
/l/	3·66	/ŋ/	1·15
/ð/	3·56	/g/	1·05
/r/	3·51	/ʃ/	0·96
/m/	3·22	/j/	0·88
/k/	3·09	/dʒ/	0·60
/w/	2·81	/tʃ/	0·41
/z/	2·46	/θ/	0·37
/v/	2·00	/ʒ/	0·10

Total all consonants: 60·78%

It is interesting to note the discrepancies of occurrence between the fortis and lenis members of homorganic pairs of phonemes: thus, /s, ð, k/ occur considerably more frequently than their counterparts. This general discrepancy of frequency of occurrence is, however, less important, as far as oppositional significance is concerned, than the frequency of opposition in any particular position in a context. Moreover, in any general frequency count such as this, the order obtained will reflect the occurrence of such 'common' words as *the, that, which* etc., giving preponderance to /ð, w/, for example, as against /θ, j/. As is to be expected from its historical origins and its restricted contextual distribution, /ʒ/ occupies the lowest position.

/t/ or /d/ and /r/; the frequency of occurrence of these three phonemes would be slightly lower if /tr/ and /dr/ were taken as composite (monophonemic) entities.

[1] In the original article, an error arose in the figures for /t/, /d/, and /r/, resulting in a total discrepancy of 1·19%. These figures have been corrected by Mr. G. Perren (formerly of British Council, London), and the total discrepancy reduced to 0·01%. The listed quoted above includes the revised percentages for /t/, /d/, and /r/.

Part III
The Word and Connected Speech

Introduction

We have seen that speech, a manifestation of language, may most readily be investigated at the physiological and physical levels. Such investigations show, however, that it is by no means easy to analyse the data obtained for any speech event into discrete, successive units within either the articulatory or the acoustic patterns. Speech must, therefore, be considered from the phonetic point of view as an ever-changing continuum of qualities, quantities, pitch, and intensities. If, for practical purposes, e.g. in a phonetic/phonemic transcription of the spoken language, we treat speech as a succession of articulatory or auditory separable units, it is largely because we impose, upon the gross material of speech, entities which we have derived (consciously or unconsciously) from a knowledge of the *linguistically significant* oppositions operating for any particular language-system, i.e. the phonemic categories. In other words, a useful phonetic/phonemic account of speech describes those articulatory or acoustic features which are significant in distinguishing the phonemes (or the important allophones within a phoneme) of a language. It should not, however, be forgotten that such a linear presentation is an abstraction from the concrete material of speech rather than a statement of the gross phonetic material composing the continuum. In this respect, the sophisticated written form of English differs from the spoken manifestation of the language, for our writing explicitly represents a succession of discrete linguistic units—phonemes (nowadays imperfectly) and words.

If, however, for convenience, our analysis is based on discrete phonemic units, it is necessary to take into account the way in which such units combine in speech—both in the word and in longer utterances; thus, the aim of the following sections is to interpret features of the continuum in terms of the combinatory influence of qualitative and quantitative units and of the pitch and intensity relationship of such units.

9

The Word

9.1 Accent

The word, composed of one or more phonemes, has a separate linguistic identity, in that it is a commutable entity, higher than the phoneme, which may either constitute a complete utterance or may be substituted in a longer utterance for other words of its same class. It may be thought of as a shape or pattern, constituted from the qualitative and quantitative elements of its phonemes, these phonemic elements being also capable of distinctive commutation, e.g. the /t/, /d/, and vowel length commutation in *write, ride,* or *writer, rider.* In addition, in polysyllabic words, the word shape has an identity determined by the relationship of its parts. Thus, *writer, rider,* may be said to have a pattern consisting of a 'strong' syllable followed by a 'weak' syllable: ● .. This pattern obtains also for *written* /'rɪtn/; but, in the case of *return* /rɪ'tɜːn/ or *again* /ə'gen/, the pattern is . ●. It may be said, therefore, that the identity of *return, again,* depends not only on the different qualitative and quantitative elements which distinguish these words from, for example, *written,* but also on the different patterns of the total word-forms which derive from the varying *prominence* of the parts. The syllable or syllables of a word which stand out from the remainder are said to be accented, to receive the *accent.*

The accentual pattern of English words is *fixed,* in the sense that the main accent always falls on a particular syllable of any given word,[1] but *free,* in the sense that the main accent is not tied to any particular situation in the chain of syllables constituting a word, as it is in some languages, e.g. to the penultimate syllable in Polish, to the first in Czech, and to the last in French. Thus, the main accent falls regularly on the first syllable in such words as *finish, answer, afterwards;* on the second syllable in *behind, result, together, impossible;* on the third syllable in *understand, education;* or later in *articulation, palatalization,* etc.

---

[1] With certain exceptions, determined by the larger rhythmic pattern of the total context (see §11.2).

The accentual shape of a word, in terms of the degree of prominence associated with its parts, is a reality for both the speaker and the listener; but the speaker's impression of the factors which produce such a pattern of varying prominences may differ from the actual auditory cues by which the listener perceives the prominence pattern. It is, therefore, necessary to examine the factors which in English are significant for the speaker and for the listener in producing the communicated effect of prominence.

9.2 Prominence

Any or all of four factors—stress, pitch, quality, quantity—may render a syllable more prominent than its neighbours. Not all have equal validity for speaker and listener alike; they are not all equally efficient as markers of the accented syllable.

(1) *Stress.*—A sound or syllable which is stressed is one upon which there is expended in the articulation relatively great breath effort and muscular energy; in voiced sounds, greater amplitude of vibration of the vocal folds, together with the reinforcing resonation of the supra-glottal cavities, results in physical terms in relatively great intensity of the sound or syllable, such intensity being perceived by the listener as greater loudness associated with the sound or syllable. Thus, the greater energy which the speaker feels is concentrated on the first syllable of *answer* may be manifested for the listener as greater loudness. The speaker may feel several degrees of articulatory energy in producing a polysyllabic word, e.g. in the word *examination*, the syllables may be articulated with the following descending order of energy /neɪ/, /zæ/, /ɪg/, /mɪ/, /ʃn/. Nevertheless, the English speaker will normally distinguish readily only stressed and unstressed (strong and weak) syllables, to which will correspond the listener's impression of loud and weak syllables.

(2) *Pitch change.*—Stress/loudness is not, however, by itself an efficient device for signalling the situation of the accent. Thus, when they are said on a monotone and with unexaggerated quantities, it is difficult to distinguish by stress alone *insult* (n.), *import* (n.), *billow*, from *insult* (v.), *import* (v.), *below*, in which the different accentual pattern is not associated with marked qualitative changes. The accentual cue becomes clear, however, when stress is associated with pitch prominence; the verb and noun forms of *insult*, for example, are easily distinguished by pitch patterns, e.g. with a falling intonation, . ◖ against ◗ . , or, with a rising intonation, . ◞ against ◦ ˙

Pitch changes will also manifest more than one stressed syllable in a word; thus, *examination* with . ● ˙ ◖ . or . ● ˙ ● . or, within a phrase such as *the first examination was over*

. ● ˙ ● ˙ ● ˙ ˙ ● ˙ , where the stressed syllables show a change of pitch in relation to the preceding syllables. Nevertheless, among stressed syllables, some are more likely than others to be associated with pitch change; thus, when *examination* is pronounced with the pitch pattern . ● . ● . , the syllable /zæ/ (noted above as the syllable felt to be articulated with the second highest degree of energy) may have no pitch prominence in relation to its neighbours. Such accentual prominence as it has for the listener is, therefore, achieved to a large extent by stress alone; this type of accentuation may be called *secondary*, *rhythmic*, or *non-tonic*. The syllable /neɪ/, on the other hand, will always be associated with a pitch change when the word is said in isolation; this type of accentuation may be called *primary*, *nuclear*, or *tonic*. The pitch prominence of word primary accent may be lost in connected speech, e.g.:—

. . ● . ● . . ● . ● .

The examination was almost over

but the syllable of primary accent is always that on which there is a *potential* change of pitch. Such a change of pitch direction may also be associated, but less typically, with those syllables which more characteristically have secondary accentuation, e.g. *examination*, said in an indignant, emphatic manner, might well have the pitch pattern . ● . ● . , in which case /zæ/ and /neɪ/ are equal in both stress and pitch prominence. (Abnormal pitch prominence may often be given to a weakly stressed syllable, when, with a falling-rising pitch pattern, the fall may take place on the primarily accented syllable and the rise on a following, normally unstressed and unaccented, syllable, e.g. *under* ● ⌡ , *officer* ● . ⌡ .)

The most common relationship of pitch and stress in word accentuation may be summarized as follows:—

Primary accentuation—associated with a potential change of pitch direction.

Secondary accentuation—not normally associated with a change of pitch direction, but may be

(a) *prominent*, i.e. signalled by a potential change of pitch *level*, or

(b) *rhythmic*, i.e. having no pitch prominence, but with rhythmical stress, and often quality/quantity, prominence.

Stress and pitch variations combined may, therefore, be said to constitute a complex which is most powerful in signalling the situation and degree of the accent in a word.

(3) *Sound quality.*—The actual sequence of phonemes constituting a word also contributes to the listener's impression of an accentual

pattern, i.e. to the relative prominence of sounds and syllables. In a sequence of phonemes (said on a monotone with equal stress and length), vowels will normally be more prominent than consonants; among the vowels, prominence increases as the vowel becomes more open; among the consonants, those which are vowel-like, e.g. /m, n, ŋ, l, r/, stand out from the remainder, while fricatives have a higher prominence than plosives. Thus, if a nonsense word composed of English consonants and short vowels, such as [ɪlɒlelæ], is presented to English listeners without pitch, length, or stress variations, it usually happens that [ɒ] and [æ] are judged to be the points of greatest prominence. However, it should be noted that a different sound inserted in a repetitive sequence of similar sounds may tend to stand out from its neighbours, although its 'inherent' sonority is less than that of its neighbours, e.g. [ɪ] in such a sequence as [ænænænɪnænæ], where the contrasting feature of [ɪ] is not so much its quality as its difference from the environment.

In addition to the prominence of sounds, due to their nature or the character of the context in which they occur, certain English phonemes are particularly associated with unaccented situations.[1] Thus RP /ə/ does not normally occur in accented syllables; and /ɪ, ʊ/, though both may receive full accentual prominence, have a high frequency of occurrence in unaccented syllables. The other English vowels may also occur in syllables which do not receive the primary accent (see §7.13), but they may be associated in the speaker's and listener's minds with some degree of secondary accent (especially /æ, ɒ/ and the long vowels and diphthongs) by virtue of their greater qualitative prominence (and also, when separated from a primary accent by one or more unaccented syllables, for reasons of rhythm)—compare, for example, the accentual prominence of the last syllables in *never* /ˈnevə/ and *nephew*/ /ˈnevjuː/, *wrecker* /ˈrekə/ and *record* /ˈrekɔːd/; or of the first syllables of *contain* /kənˈteɪn/ and *canteen* /kænˈtiːn/, *aghast* /əˈgɑːst/ and *august* (adj.) /ɔːˈgʌst/.

This association of vowel quality and prominence leads sometimes to variation on the speaker's part both as to the qualities used and to the situation of the pitch prominence. Thus, especially in syllables preceding the primary accent, 'strong' and 'weak' vowels may occur according to the speaker's feeling of strong or weak stress (a feeling of weak stress resulting in secondary accent or lack of accent), e.g. /uː/, /ʊ/, or /ə/ in the first syllable of *July*, /əʊ/, [o], or /ə/ in the first syllable of *November*, *proceed*, /e/ or /ə/ in the first syllable of *September*. Alternatively, especially in disyllables each of which may contain a strong vowel, e.g. in *contact* (v.) /ˈkɒntækt/, *adult* /ˈædʌlt/, there may be hesitancy as to the situation of the pitch prominence

---

[1] For a full treatment, see G. F. Arnold, *Stress in English Words*, 1957.

denoting primary accent; if the prominence is placed on the second syllable, there is likely to be weakening of the first vowel, e.g. /kən'tækt/, /ə'dʌlt/. It is to be noted that, despite relatively weak stress, there is often no choice between strong and weak vowel, when the vowel occurs in the syllable immediately following the primary stress, e.g. *phoneme, insect, syntax, placard, diphthong, record* (n.), *perfume, hubbub, expert, female, hero, convoy,* etc., all retain a strong vowel in the final syllable, however weakly stressed by the speaker.

It is also to be noted that in those types of English, e.g. Northern regional, where the first syllable of such words as *obtain, contain, continue, expect,* has a strong vowel rather than the /ə/ or /ɪ/ used in RP, an impression of unusual accentuation on the first syllable is given to RP listeners.

Quantity.—If the nonsense word [ɪlɒlelæ] is presented to English listeners, with no pitch variation but with vowels of different length, those vowels which have the greatest length will be judged most prominent despite their quality. Thus, [ɪ], of relatively weak prominence in quality alone, may stand out from the other vowels of the word if pronounced [ɪː].

The RP long vowels and diphthongs (particularly in their non-reduced forms) will always, therefore, be associated with prominence, especially by a listener, however weakly stressed by the speaker they may be, and despite the fact that a long vowel or diphthong in a relatively unaccented syllable does not have the same length that it would have in an accented syllable. This is the case of the vowels in the final (post-tonic) syllable in such words as *phoneme* /iː/, *placard* /aː/, *foreword* /ɜː/, *railway* /eɪ/, *compound* /aʊ/, *invoice* /ɔɪ/, etc.; for most speakers, in the pre-tonic syllable of *idea* /aɪ/, *sarcastic* /aː/; and, more particularly, when a rhythmic stress is associated with such vowels in a syllable remote from the tonic, e.g. finally in *pedigree* /iː/, *photograph* /aː/ (or /æ/), *telescope* /əʊ/; initially, in *parliamentary* /aː/, *perpendicular* /ɜː/, *photographic* /əʊ/. A vowel in an unaccented syllable may in fact be longer than that in an adjacent accented syllable, without depriving the latter of its prominence, e.g. /ɪ/ and /əʊ/ in *pillow*, /æ/ and /aɪ/ in *ally*, /ʌ/ and /ɪə/ in *frontier*, etc.

(5) *Conclusion.*—It will be seen that any or all of these four factors may play a part in rendering a sound or syllable prominent. In speech, however, it is pitch variation which is the most commonly used and efficient cue of prominence for the listener. Pitch prominence is not, however, necessarily associated with the syllable having the highest pitch; thus, in *examination*, said questioningly and querulously as ˙ • ˙ • ˙ , the accented syllables achieve their prominence from their outstandingly low pitch.

Length variation is also a strong contributory factor both as regards the association of vowel quantity with accentuation and also as a feature of prominence in its own right (note, in this respect, the use of length to replace pitch in the intoning of prayers in church, e.g. in 'and the blessing of God be upon you' with the lengthening of the short vowels of *bless, God, upon* /ɒ/). Sound qualities also contribute to an impression of prominence, but mainly through the characteristic relationship of certain qualities with unaccented syllables and others with accented syllables.

Stress, strictly defined in terms of energy of articulation for the speaker and of loudness for the listener, is the least effective means of conveying prominence. Indeed, the syllable uttered with the greatest intensity may not be the one with the greatest accent or prominence; thus, *insult* (n.), said in questioning and indignant fashion as $\bullet$ $\overset{\bullet}{}$, may have more energy expended on /sʌlt/ than on /ɪn/, but /ɪn/ remains for the speaker and listener the accented syllable. It should be noted, however, that stress has a particular reality for the speaker which is not communicated directly to the listener. The speaker feels a rhythmic beat in uttering a word, which is associated with his mental (linguistic) usage of the word and extended to the variation of energy used in the articulation of the word. This subjective, rhythmic, pattern may evoke an equivalent response in the listener's perception of the word, but rather through the listener's linguistic recollection (in terms of the system which he shares with the speaker) than through the exchange of signals susceptible of acoustic analysis. It is in this sense that an accented syllable may be felt as stressed by the speaker and interpreted thus by the listener though it has no physical existence; for example, in the case given by Daniel Jones,[1] *Thank you* may be realized as /ˈkkjuː/, where the stressed and accented syllable consists of silence.

9.3   Word Accentual Patterns[2]

Since certain syllables of a word are more prominent than the others for any of the reasons mentioned above, it may be said that a word has a characteristic accentual or rhythmic pattern for speaker and listener alike. This basic pattern, which is as much a part of a word's identity as its sound sequence, may, however, be somewhat modified by the general accentual pattern of the longer utterance in which it occurs (see §11.2). In the following selection of patterns for polysyllabic *simple* words (i.e. excluding words composed of separable root morphemes

---

[1] *Outline of English Phonetics*, §909, footnote.
[2] See also R. Kingdon. *The Groundwork of English Stress*, Longman, 1958; and G. F. Arnold, op. cit.

or words, but including those containing an affix), the accentual elements are marked thus:—

> ❯ —syllable receiving potential primary (tonic, nuclear) accent;
> ● , ○ —syllable receiving potential secondary (pitch prominent or rhythmic) accent; in pre-nuclear syllables, such secondary accent is frequently manifested by actual or potential pitch prominence,[1] in post-nuclear syllables, secondary accent may be manifested, when adjacent to tonic, merely by qualitative or quantitative prominence—marked as ○, or, when remote from tonic, together with a rhythmical beat— marked ●.
> · —unaccented syllable (associated usually with the 'weak' vowels /ə, ɪ, ʊ/ or with syllabic /m, n, l/).

Pattern	*Examples*

2 syllables

- ● ❯ —unknown, Chinese, idea, antique, thirteen, canteen, cashier, chastise
- · ❯ —alone, machine, arrive, behind, invent, reform
- ❯ ○ —profile, placard, female, invoice, programme, window
- ❯ · —over, under, husband, valley, rhythm, cotton, table

Pattern	*Examples*

3 syllables

- ● · ❯ —understand, cigarette, magazine, entertain, personnel, seventeen, afternoon
- ❯ · · —quantity, yesterday, innocence, bachelor, wanderer
- ❯ · ● —appetite, pedigree, photograph, cataract, telephone
- · ❯ · —important, encounter, excessive, relation, eleven
- ● ❯ · —uncertain, re-entry, foreknowledge
- · ❯ ○ —tobacco, tomato, embargo, prehensile (or ● ❯ ○)

Pattern	*Examples*

4 syllables

- · ❯ · · —remarkable, impossible, affirmative, establishment, photography
- ● ❯ · · —rhinoceros, unfortunate, diocesan

[1] Note that this type of syllable carries the main accent of a word manifesting 'stress shift'. (See §11.2).

. ˋ . • —acetylene, acclimatize, enumerate
• . ˋ . —unimportant, insufficient, circulation, diplomatic, photographic
ˋ . . . —cowardliness, melancholy, caterpillar, criticism
ˋ . • . —telescoping, appetizing, educated, helicopter
ˋ . . • —counterattack, capitalize
• . . ˋ —aquamarine, photogravure
. • . ˋ (or • . . ˋ)—misrepresent, misunderstand

Pattern	Examples
5 syllables	

. • . ˋ . —affiliation, consideration, apotheosis
• . . ˋ . —antimacassar, circumlocution, interdependence
• . ˋ . . —satisfactory, objectivity, aristocracy
• . ˋ . • —rehabilitate, inexactitude, incapacitate
. ˋ . . . —catholicism, administrative, empiricism

Pattern	Examples
6 syllables	

. • . ˋ . . —inferiority, impossibility, convertibility
• . . ˋ . . —characteristically, variability, meteorological
• . ˋ . . . —uncooperative, ceremoniously, indistinguishable
• . . . ˋ . —palatalization, nationalization, autobiographic (or with • . • . ˋ .)
. • . . ˋ . —personification, identification, electrification

Pattern	Examples
7 or 8 syllables	

• . ˋ . . . . —unilateralism
• . • . ˋ . . —unreliability
. • . ˋ . . . —enthusiastically (/-kəlɪ/)
. • . . . ˋ . —industrialization
. • . . ˋ . . —impenetrability
• . • . . . ˋ . —internationalization

The stress patterns of some of the derived forms listed here are predictable, as certain general rules apply with regard to suffixing. When certain suffixes are added to a word, the root retains its original primary accent; such stress-neutral suffixes include *-ness* and *-ism*. Thus po'lite, po'liteness; 'cowardly, 'cowardliness; A'merican,

A'*mericanism*; '*token*, '*tokenism*. Other suffixes such as *-esque* and *-ette* are stress-attracting ('autostressed'), the accentual pattern of such words as *pictu*'*resque* and *launde*'*rette* manifesting stress on the suffix; whilst others such as *-ity* are 'pre-stressed', the primary accent of words such as '*rapid*, *re*'*liable* being replaced in the derived forms *ra*'*pidity* and *relia*'*bility* by accents on the syllable immediately preceding the suffix.[1] See §9.7.

It will be seen from the selection of English word accentual patterns given above that there is a certain rhythmic tendency towards alternation of accented and unaccented syllables. Such a regular rhythmic pattern is often, however, disturbed by the meaningful prominence given to a prefix, e.g. *mis-*, *un-*, *in-*, etc., or by the retention of a strong vowel quality or the presence of a long vowel or diphthong in what might rhythmically be expected to be an unaccented syllable. The conflict between considerations of rhythm and other factors giving an impression of accentual prominence results in numerous cases of pattern instability (see §9.4).

Compound words (i.e. words composed of separable root morphemes, whether or not the compound is hyphenated in the spelling) normally contain a single primary (nuclear, tonic) accent on one element of the compound, the other element or elements carrying secondary accent. The most common type of compound has the primary accent on the first element. In the case of *disyllabic* compounds of this kind, the secondary prominence of the second element is usually mainly qualitative or quantitative (i.e. lacking the rhythmic beat which may fall on syllables remote from the nucleus):—

❯ ○ —air-raid, bandstand, backache, blackbird, blackmail, bird-cage, bookcase, bridesmaid, bulldog, cardboard, catmint, chain-gang, clothesbrush, coal-mine, crossword, duckpond, earthquake, flowerpot, footprint, gas-mask, greenfly, heartburn, highbrow, knee-cap, lifeboat, mail-bag, nightdress, offprint, route-march, tail-coat, teapot, washstand, windscreen

(In some cases of such compounds, the second element is unaccented and has the weak vowel /ə/, e.g. 'boatswain, coalman, chairman, footman, postman, saucepan'.)

In *three-syllable* compounds, the pattern may be ❯ ○ • (with qualitative or quantitative prominence on the second syllable) or ❯ • • (with rhythmic and qualitative/quantitative prominence on the third syllable), e.g.:—

❯ ○ • —air-worthy, bluebottle, dance-music, dog-collar, forerunner,

---

[1] For a full account of affixes and stress, see Erik Fudge, *English Word Stress*, Allen and Unwin, 1984.

> gold-digger, grasshopper, grandfather, handwriting, housekeeper, landlady, lawnmower, manslaughter, newspaper, postoffice, shopkeeper, steam-roller, step-ladder, stock-piling, take-over, tape-measure

➘ . ● —booby-trap, borderline, bowling-green, butterscotch, buttonhole, chambermaid, chatterbox, chimney-sweep, copyright, drawing-pin, fire-brigade, gingerbread, honeymoon, ladybird, mortar-board, office-boy, waterspout, waiting-room

Other word patterns may be illustrated as follows:—

➘ . ● . —antechamber, booking-office, carpet-sweeper, dinner-jacket, engine-driver, knuckleduster, lighthouse-keeper, organ-grinder, power-station, season-ticket, tape-recorder

➘ . . ● —musical-box, catherine-wheel, labour-exchange

. ➘ ○ . —dispatch-rider, machine-minder

➘ . ● . . —fire-extinguisher

➘ . . ● . —cabinet-maker

In other types of compound the first element does not bear the primary (nuclear) accent, but has normally a secondary accent deriving from potential pitch and rhythmic prominence, e.g.:—

● ➘ —back-fire, beam-ends, black-lead, downstairs, first-class, free-wheel, full-grown, ground-floor, henceforth, knee-deep, mincepie, north-west, short-term

● ➘ . —archbishop, blackcurrant, churchwarden, coldblooded, cross-question, downhearted, field-marshal, flat-footed, good-looking, half-volley, horse-chestnut, lawn-tennis, pig-headed, pot-bellied, safekeeping, shop-window, short-sighted, well-meaning

● . ➘ —country-house, double-cross, ginger-beer, secondhand

● . ➘ . —broken-hearted, easy-going, indiarubber, mass-production, sergeant-major

● ➘ . . —post-graduate, vice-chancellor

● ➘ . ● . —hot-water-bottle, waste-paper-basket

Compounds of this latter kind are sometimes said to have 'double' or 'level stress', but it should be noted that, although both elements may show a nuclear pitch change, e.g. *free-wheel* ➚➚ or ⌣⌣ , such a falling or rising pitch change is more usually associated with the second element ₒ➚ or ●⌣ . The effect of the association of pitch prominence of some kind with both elements is, however, to make both elements of the compound stand out, with corresponding meaningful prominence. Compounds of the first kind, e.g. *crossword* ➚ ₒ , with most of the prominence and meaningful weight concentrated on the first element, are often referred to as carrying a 'single stress', which unifies rather than opposes the elements.

It will be noticed from the examples listed that there is a tendency for noun + noun compounds to have a different stress pattern from adjective + noun compounds. Most commonly in noun + noun (A + B) compounds, it is the first element that takes the primary accent. Thus *grapefruit* ➘ ○ . However, if B is made of A, the second element is more likely to be accented. Thus *lemon squash* ● . ➘ (squash made of lemons) but *mineral water* ➘ . ● . (not water made of minerals), this again examplifying the most usual pattern for noun + noun compounds.[1]

9.4 Word Pattern Instability

The accentual patterns of words are liable to change. Considerable changes of this kind have taken place within the last three hundred years, in addition to the large-scale accentual shifts affecting French importations in ME. Thus, in the seventeenth century, and still in American English, a secondary accent with a strong vowel fell on the penultimate syllables of such words as *necessary*, *adversary*, *momentary*; the noun and verbal accentual opposition between, for example, *abuse* (n.) ● . and *abuse* (v.) . ● has been lost, though in this pair of words a qualitative/quantitative distinction is maintained in the second syllable; we no longer place the primary accent on the second syllable of *revenue*, *illustrate*, *confiscate*, *character*, etc., or on the first syllable of *humidity*, *convenient*, *prosperity*, etc.

Hesitancy and variation of pattern occurring at the present time are the result of rhythmic and analogical pressures, both of which entail in addition considerable changes of sound pattern in the word.[2]

(1) *Rhythmic changes.*—In some words containing more than two syllables there appears to be a tendency to avoid a succession of weak syllables, especially if these have /ə/ or /ɪ/. Thus, in words of three syllables, there is variation between ➘ . . and . ➘ . patterns, e.g.[3] *exquisite* */ˈekskwɪzɪt/ or /ɪksˈkwɪzɪt/, *deficit* */ˈdefɪsɪt/ or /dɪˈfɪsɪt/, *integral* */ˈɪntɪɡrəl/ or /ɪnˈteɡrəl/, *mischievous* */ˈmɪstʃɪvəs/ or

---

[1] A detailed account of the construction-type and stress is given in Fudge *op. cit.*

[2] These remarks apply mainly to RP and to the patterns of isolate words rather than those variants occurring in connected speech (see §11.2); they do not take into account patterns used in other speech forms, e.g. in Scottish English, *enquiry* /ˈenkwɪrɪ/, *realize* /rɪəˈlaɪz/, *advertisement* /ˌædvərˈtaɪzmənt/.

[3] Where there is an accepted 'correct' pattern, it is marked here with * in the transcription; the marks ˈ and ˌ indicate primary (➘) and secondary (● or ○) accent respectively, but see §§6.3.3 and 6.3.4 above.

/mɪsˈtʃiːvəs/   (vulg. /mɪsˈtʃiːvɪəs/). *inculcate* */ˈɪŋkʌlˌkeɪt/   or
/ɪŋˈkʌlˌkeɪt/; note, too, *acumen* /ˈækjʊmen/ or /əˈkjuːmen/, *sonorous*
/ˈsɒnərəs/ or /səˈnɔːrəs/, *precedence* /ˈpresɪdns/ or /prɪˈsiːdns/, where
❧ . . increasingly replaces the traditional . ❧ . pattern, and the
pattern instability of such words as *importune* */ɪmˈpɔːtju n/ or
/ˌɪmpɔːˈtjuːn/, *premature* /ˈpremətjʊə/ or /ˌpreməˈtjʊə/.

Similarly, in words of four syllables, there is variation between the
patterns ❧ . . . or ❧ . . ● and ● ❧ . . or ● ❧ . ●
e.g. *controversy* */ˈkɒntrəvəsɪ/ or /kənˈtrɒvəsɪ/, *hospitable*
*/ˈhɒspɪtəbl/ or /həˈspɪtəbl/, *despicable* */ˈdespɪkəbl/ or /dɪˈspɪkəbl/,
formidable */ˈfɔːmɪdəbl/ or /fəˈmɪdəbl/, *capitalist* */ˈkæpɪtəlɪst/ or
/kəˈpɪtəlɪst/, *aristocrat* */ˈærɪstəˌkræt/ or /əˈrɪstəˌkræt/. Note, too,
variation between . ❧ . . and ● . ❧ . in such words as *centri-
fugal* */se (or /ə/) nˈtrɪfjʊgl/ or /ˌsentrɪˈfjuːgl/, *centripetal*
*/senˈtrɪpɪtl/ or /ˌsentrɪˈpiːtl/, *metallurgy* */mɪˈtælədʒɪ/ or
/ˌmetəˈlɜːdʒɪ/ or /ˈmetəˌlɜːdʒɪ/. A relatively new word such as *television* now appears to have the pattern ❧ . . . predominantly, the
variant ● . ❧ . being less common.

Longer words, too, often exhibit a tendency towards the alternation
of accented and unaccented syllables with various rhythmic patterns,
e.g. *tuberculosis* /ˌtjuː bəkjʊˈləʊsɪs/ or tjʊˌbɜːkjʊˈləʊsɪs, *articulatory*
/ˌɑːtɪkjʊˈleɪtərɪ/, /ɑː(or /ə/)ˌtɪkjʊˈleɪtərɪ/ or /ˌɑː(or /ə/)ˈtɪkjʊlətrɪ/,
inexplicable */ɪnˈeksplɪkəbl/ or /ˌɪnɪkˈsplɪkəbl/.

(2) *Analogical changes.*—It sometimes happens that a word's
accentual pattern is influenced not only by rhythmic pressure but also
by the accentual structure of a similar word of frequent occurrence.
Thus, the analogy of the root forms *apply* /əˈplaɪ/, *prefer* /prɪˈfɜː/,
compare /kəmˈpeə/, is responsible for the realization of *applicable*,
preferable, *comparable*, as /əˈplɪkəbl, prɪˈfɜːrəbl, kəmˈpærəbl/ instead
of */ˈæplɪkəbl, ˈpref(ə)rəbl, ˈkɒmp(ə)rəbl/. Again, the existence of *contribution*, *distribution* /ˌkɒntrɪˈbjuːʃn, ˌdɪstrɪˈbjuːʃn/ may account for
the pronunciation /ˈkɒntrɪˌbjuːt, ˈdɪstrɪˌbjuːt/ (*contribute*, *distribute*)
instead of the more usual ('correct') */kənˈtrɪˌbjuːt, dɪsˈtrɪˌbjuːt/,
where the first syllable is totally weakened and the last retains only a
certain qualitative prominence. The case of such a word as *dispute* (n.),
with the form /ˈdɪˌspjuːt/ instead of the more usual /dɪˈspjuːt/,
exemplifies an analogous form comparable with the accentual oppositions of verb and noun in disyllables (see following section), i.e.
/ˈdɪˌspjuːt/ (n.) as against /dɪˈspjuːt/ (v.), cf. *discount* /ˈdɪˌskaʊnt/
(n.), /dɪˈskaʊnt/ (v.). Primary accent is also unstable in such
compounds as *shop-steward* (❧ ○ or ● ❧), *weather-forecast*
(❧ . ● . or ● . ❧ .).

9.5 Distinctive Word Accentual Patterns

The accentual pattern of a word establishes the contrastive relationship of its parts; it may also have a distinctive function in that it opposes words of comparable sound structure (and identical spelling). Such word oppositions (for the most part disyllables of French origin) may or may not involve phonemic changes of quality.

(1) A relatively small number of words[1] exhibit oppositions of accentual pattern which are manifested mainly by a *shift of pitch or stress prominence*, with slight variations of quantity. In situations where the prime signal of prominence—pitch—is not operative, the oppositions are either totally lost or are inefficiently marked by stress alone, or are maintained by an exaggeration of the quantity variation. Thus, there being no significant qualitative change, the noun and verb forms of the following words are normally distinguished primarily by the situation of the pitch-prominent syllable; *discount, import, impress, incense, increase, inlay, insult, offset, overhang*—pitch prominence on the first element for nouns, on the second element for verbs. In other cases, some speakers may make a reduction or obscuration of the vowel quality in the first syllable in the case of the verbal form, e.g.:—

	Noun/Adjective	*Verb*
abstract	/ˈæbˌstrækt/	/ˌæbˈstrækt/ or /əbˈstrækt/
accent	/ˈækˌsent/ or /ˈæksnt/	/ˌækˈsent/ or /əkˈsent/
digest	/ˈdaɪˌdʒest/	/ˌdaɪˈdʒest/ or /dɪˈdʒest/
torment	/ˈtɔːˌment/	/ˌtɔːˈment/ or /təˈment/
transfer[2]	/ˈtrɑːnsˌfɜː/	/ˌtrɑːnsˈfɜː/ or /trænsˈfɜː/
transport[2]	/ˈtrɑːnsˌpɔːt/	/ˌtrɑːnsˈpɔːt/ or /trənsˈpɔːt/

(2) More commonly, the change in accentual pattern is manifested mainly by a shift in pitch prominence together with a related variation of quality. Often, the qualitative change takes the form of a reduction of the unaccented vowel of the first element of the verbal form to /ə/ or /ɪ/; less frequently, by a reduction of the vowel in the second element of the noun/adjective form, e.g.:—

---

[1] The small number of disyllables involved in such accentual oppositions is shown by L. Guierre, *L'accentuation en anglais contemporain* (unpublished doctoral thesis), Paris, 1979. Out of a corpus of more than 10,000 disyllabic words, only 85 exhibited changes of verb, noun or adjective function by means of a shift of accented syllable: 72 words oppose *v.* ᔓ *n.* (e.g. *convict*)—whereas in 186 cases (e.g. *profit*) functions were not distinguished by means of accent; 9 words opposed *n/adj.* ᔓ *v.* (e.g. *present*) through accent, while other oppositions of function through accent were exhibited in *compact* (*n.* ᔓ *v./adj.*), *absent, direct, prostrate* (*adj.* ᔓ *v.*).

[2] Also with /træn-/.

	Noun/Adjective	*Verb*
absent	/ˈæbsənt/	/əbˈsent/
combine	/ˈkɒmˌbaɪn/	/kəmˈbaɪn/
compress	/ˈkɒmˌpres/	/kəmˈpres/
concert	/ˈkɒnsət/	/kənˈsɜ t/
conduct	/ˈkɒnˌdʌkt/	/kənˈdʌkt/
consort	/ˈkɒnˌsɔ t/	/kənˈsɔ t/
contract	/ˈkɒnˌtrækt/	/kənˈtrækt/
contrast	/ˈkɒnˌtrɑ st/	/kənˈtrɑ st/
convict	/ˈkɒnvɪkt/	/kənˈvɪkt/
desert	/ˈdezət/	/dɪˈzɜ t/
export	/ˈekˌspɔ t/	/ɪkˈspɔ t/
frequent	/ˈfri kwənt/	/frɪˈkwent/
object	/ˈɒbdʒɪkt/	/əbˈdʒekt/
perfect	/ˈpɜ fɪkt/	/pəˈfekt/
*permit**	/ˈpɜ mɪt/	/pəˈmɪt/
present	/ˈpreznt/	/prɪˈzent/
proceeds	/ˈprəʊˌsi dz/	/prəˈsi dz/
produce	/ˈprɒˌdju s/	/prəˈdju s/
progress	/ˈprəʊˌgres/	/prəˈgres/
project	/ˈprɒˌdʒekt/	/prəˈdʒekt/
protest	/ˈprəʊˌtest/	/prəˈtest/
rebel	/ˈrebl/	/rɪˈbel/
record	/ˈreˌkɔ d/	/rɪˈkɔ d/
refuse	/ˈreˌfju s/	/rɪˈfju z/[1]
segment	/ˈsegmənt/	/ˌsegˈment/
subject	/ˈsʌbdʒɪkt/	/səbˈdʒekt/
*survey**	/ˈsɜ ˌveɪ/	/səˈveɪ/
August	/ˈɔ gəst/ (n.)	/ˌɔ ˈgʌst/ (adj.)
minute	/ˈmɪnɪt/ (n.)	/ˌmaɪˈnju t/ (adj.)

(* In these words, the opposition of /ɜ / and /ə/ in the first syllable amounts to an opposition of vowel quantity; it is to be noted that the verb *to survey* may have the same accentual pattern as the noun in the particular sense of 'to carry out a survey'.)

Several disyllables do not conform to the general noun/verb accentual pattern distinction or exhibit instability, e.g. *comment* /ˈkɒment/ for both noun and verb; *contact* /ˈkɒnˌtækt/ (n.) and /ˈkɒnˌtækt/, /ˌkɒnˈtækt/ or /kənˈtækt/ (v.); *detail* /ˈdi ˌteɪl/ (n.) and /ˈdi ˌteɪl/ or /ˌdi ˈteɪl/ (v.); *contrast* has a verbal form /ˈkɒnˌtrɑ st/ in addition to the more usual form given above. In all these cases, and in that of

---

[1] The noun and verb forms of *refuse* differ also in the final consonant and the resulting variation of vowel length of /u: /.

dispute, already mentioned, the noun form is tending to supersede the verbal pattern.

Words containing more than two syllables also exhibit distinctive accentual patterns associated with pitch, stress, and quality cues, e.g.:

	Noun/Adjective	Verb
alternate	/ˌɔːlˈtɔːnət/ /əlˈtɜːnət/	/ˈɔːltəˌneɪt/
associate	/əˈsəʊsjət, -sɪət, -ʃjət/	/əˈsəʊsɪˌeɪt, əˈsəʊʃɪˌeɪt/
attribute	/ˈætrɪˌbjuːt/	/əˈtrɪˌbjuːt/
envelope	/ˈenvəˌləʊp/ /ˈenvələp/	/ɪnˈveləp/
reprimand	/ˈreprɪˌmaːnd/	/ˌrepriˈmaːnd/
interchange	/ˈɪntəˌtʃeɪndʒ/	/ˌɪntəˈtʃeɪndʒ/
compliment	/ˈkɒmplɪmənt/	/ˌkɒmplɪˈment/ /ˈkɒmplɪˌment/
supplement	/ˈsʌplɪmənt/	/ˌsʌplɪˈment/ /ˈsʌplɪˌment/
estimate	/ˈestɪmət/	/ˈestɪˌmeɪt/
intimate	/ˈɪntɪmət/	/ˈɪntɪˌmeɪt/
moderate	/ˈmɒdərət/	/ˈmɒdəˌreɪt/
prophesy	/ˈprɒfəsɪ/	/ˈprɒfɪˌsaɪ/
separate	/ˈsepərət/	/ˈsepəˌreɪt/
invalid	/ˈɪnvəlɪd/ ('sick') /ˌɪnˈvælɪd/ ('void')	

9.6 Elision

Since OE, it has always been a feature of the structure of English words that the weakly accented syllables have undergone a process of gradation, i.e. loss of phonemes or obscuration of vowels (see also §§7.9.12, 7.13). The same process of gradation, with resultant contraction, may be observed in operation in PresE. It is important, however, to distinguish between cases of elision which have been established in the language for some time (although the spelling may still reflect an earlier, fuller form) and those which have become current only recently. In these latter cases, the forms exhibiting elision and syncope are typical of rapid, colloquial speech, whereas more formal speech tends to retain the fuller form under the preservative influence of the spelling. The examples of elided word forms in colloquial speech which are given below are independent of the type of reduction affecting particular words and syllables under weak accent in connected speech (see §10.4). They are also to be distinguished from the reduced forms in various types of regional and popular speech, which the educated speaker might characterize as vulgar, e.g. *recognize* as /ˈrekəˌnaɪz/, *satisfactory* as

/ˌsæsˈfæktrɪ/, *cigarette* as /sɪˈgret/, *possible* as /ˈpɒsbl/, *Waterloo* as /ˌwɔːˈluː /, *lovely* as /ˈlʌlɪ/, etc.

(1) *Vowels*[1]

(*a*) *Established*—Loss of vowels under weak accent within the word has occurred at various stages of the language's development and is now established, e.g.—initially, *state, scholar, sample*; medially, *Gloucester, marriage, halfpenny, evening, chimney, curtsey, forecastle* /ˈfəʊksl/, *gooseberry, Salisbury* /ˈsɔːlzbrɪ/; in a final syllable, *time, name, loved, hands* (< *handes*), *eaten, written, cousin*.

(*b*) *Present colloquial*.—In PresE such elision is likely to take place especially in a sequence of unaccented syllables, in respect of /ə/ and /ɪ/. Thus, in post-nuclear (post-tonic) positions, the sequence consonant + /ə/ + /r/ + weak vowel, e.g. in *preferable*, tends increasingly to lose the /ə/ of the second syllable, /fər/ being reduced to /fr/; similar reductions affect /ər/ following other consonants, e.g. in *repertory, temperature, comparable, territory, lavatory, temporary* /ˈtemprərɪ/, *anniversary, vicarage, category, factory, robbery, labourexchange* /ˈleɪbrɪksˌtʃeɪndʒ/, *murderer* /ˈmɜːdrə/, *customary, camera, honourable, scullery, suffering, beverage, rhinoceros, nursery, Nazareth, fisheries, treasury, natural* /ˈnætʃrəl/, *dangerous, utterance, history, ordinary*. Though labelled here as 'colloquial' these elisions may occur regularly within the speech of an individual, the fuller version not forming a part of his idiolect. In the same way, there may be an elision of a weak vowel following a consonant and preceding /l/, or the reduction of syllabic /l̩/ to syllable marginal /l/, in *grappling, doubling, fatalist, paddling, bachelor, specialist, usually, insolent, easily, carefully, buffalo, novelist, family, panelling, chancellor*, etc. Note, too, frequent loss of post-nuclear /ə/ or /ɪ/ in *university* /ˌjuːnɪˈvɜːstɪ/, *probably* /ˈprɒbblɪ/, *difficult* /ˈdɪfklt/, *national* /ˈnæʃnl/, *fashionable* /ˈfæʃnəbl/, *reasonably* /ˈriːznəblɪ/, *parliament* /ˈpɑːlmənt/, *government* /ˈgʌvmənt/. A similar process may apply with the loss of syllabicity in the present participles of verbs such as *flavour, lighten* and *thicken* where the /ə/ may be elided or the syllabic consonant /r̩/ or /n̩/ replaced by a non-syllabic consonant marginal to the syllable. Thus /ˈfleɪvrɪŋ/, /ˈlaɪtnɪŋ/ and /ˈθɪknɪŋ/ in place of /ˈfleɪvərɪŋ/, /ˈlaɪtənɪŋ/ and /ˈθɪkənɪŋ/ respectively. It may be noted that some speakers make a regular distinction between the participle with three syllables and the noun of two syllables exhibiting elision.

In pre-nuclear positions, /ə/ or /ɪ/ of the weak syllable preceding the primary accent is apt to be lost in very rapid speech, especially when the

---

[1] For absorption of the 2nd element of a diphthong before another vowel (smoothing), see §7.11.

tonic syllable has initial /l/ or /r/,[1] e.g. *police, Palladium, parade, terrific, correct, collision, believe, balloon, barometer, direction, delightful, gorilla, galoshes, ferocious, philology, veranda, voluptuous, saloon, solicitor, syringe, charade*, etc.; also, with a continuant consonant preceding and a consonant other than /l/ or /r/ following, in *phonetics, photography, thermometer, supporter, suppose, satirical, circumference, perhaps* /p'hæps/, etc. Note, too, the elision of /ɪ/ (common amongst schoolchildren) in *geometry* /'dʒɒmətrɪ/, *geography* /'dʒɒgrəfɪ/.

(2) Consonants

(*a*) *Established*—Apart from such consonants as have been lost through vocalization, e.g. OE *hlaford* > *lord*, OE *wealcan* > *walk* /wɔːk/, or have lost allophones in certain situations, e.g. /h/ = [x, ç] in *brought, night*, the reduction of many consonant clusters has long been established, e.g. initial /wr, kn, gn, hl, hr, hn/ in *write, know, gnaw, loaf, ring, nut*; medial /t/ + /n/ or /l/ in *fasten, listen, often, thistle, castle*; and final /mb, mn/ in *lamb, hymn*, etc.

(*b*) *Present colloquial.*—In PresE simplification of clusters continues to take place, especially involving the loss of the alveolars /t, d/ when medial in a cluster of three consonants. In the following examples, retention of the alveolar plosives is characteristic of careful speech: *exactly, facts, mostly, handsome, windmill, handbag, wristwatch, friendship, kindness, landlord, lastly, restless, landscape, Westminster, coastguard, dustman, perfectly* (and more rarely /t/ in such words as *attempts, prompts*). /θ/ is normally elided from *asthma* and *isthmus* but, like /f/ and /θ/, may sometimes be omitted from *months, twelfths, fifths, cloths*; and in rapid speech elision of /k/ in *asked* and /l/ in *only* may occur.

[ɫ] is apt to be lost when preceded by /ɔː/, which has a resonance similar to that of [ɫ], e.g. *always* /'ɔːwɪz/, *already* /ˌɔːˈredɪ/, *although* /ˌɔːˈðəʊ/, *all right* /'ɔːˈraɪt/, *almanac* /'ɔːməˌnæk/ (cf. established loss of [ɫ] in *walk, talk*, etc.).

/p/ may be lost in clusters where its position is analogous to that of an epenthetic plosive e.g. *glimpse* /glɪms/.

Whole syllables may be elided in rapid speech, especially in the vicinity of /r/ or where there is a sequence of [r] sounds, *library* /'laɪbrɪ/, *February* /'febrɪ/, *literary* /'lɪtrɪ/, *meteorological* /ˌmiːtrəˈlɒdʒɪkl/.

---

[1] Such elisions in word initial syllables are more likely when the preceding word, belonging to the same group, ends in a vowel, e.g. *the police* /ðəˈpliːs/, *I believe* /aɪ ˈbliːv/, but *local police* /ˈləʊkl pəˈliːs/, *can't believe* /ˈkɑːnt bəˈliːv/.

9.7   Word Accent—Advice to Foreign Learners

The rhythmic pattern of a word, and especially the situation of the syllables carrying the primary (tonic, nuclear) accent and the pretonic secondary accent, should have as much importance attached to it as to the sequence of phonemes composing the word. Despite the fact that an English listener will tend to interpret a distorted sound or accentual pattern (as when a foreigner pronounces *develop* as /ˈdevələp/) in terms of his own (correct) pattern and is aided in this adjustment by the meaning of the total context, it may nevertheless happen that a word pronounced with the correct sound sequence may well be misunderstood if the relative prominence of the syllables is incorrect. Learners should be careful to make the appropriate reduction of unaccented vowels and are recommended to use a form with total elision of a weak vowel in such possible cases as are given in the preceding sections. They should pay particular attention to the role of variation of quality in those words which are distinguished from others by a shift of accent (see §9.5) without, however, extending such variation of accentual patterns indiscriminately to all disyllables, e.g. *report*, *delay*, *select*, *reserve*, *account*, etc., have the same pattern in both verb and noun/adjective functions.

Moreover, the accentual pattern of an extended word form should not necessarily be associated with that of the root upon which it is based: compare, for instance, *photograph* /ˈfəʊtəˌgrɑːf/ with *photography* /fəˈtɒgrəfɪ/; *nation* /ˈneɪʃn/ with *national* /ˈnæʃnəl/, *nationality* /ˌnæʃˈnælɪtɪ/, *nationalistic* /ˌnæʃnəˈlɪstɪk/; *origin* /ˈɒrɪdʒɪn/ with *original* /əˈrɪdʒənəl/.

It is possible to give rules governing the relationship of accentuation and the spelling of English polysyllabic words (see, for instance, Kingdon, 1958; Chomsky and Halle, 1968; Guierre, 1979), but these are of necessity extremely complex if they are to have general validity. The foreign learner will no doubt become accustomed to learning the accentual patterns of words as he meets them for the first time, but there are certain relatively simple rules (see Guierre, 1970; Fudge, 1984), involving the influence of word endings on accentuation, which, though not without exceptions, have sufficient general applicability to serve as a useful guide to a learner.

For instance, in the case of the following endings, the primary accent falls on the preceding syllable:

-ity: ˈquality, natioˈnality, uniˈversity, etc.

-ion, *-ian*: diˈscussion, inˈtention, perˈfection, maˈgician, negotiˈation, phoneˈtician, etc.

-ic: draˈmatic, emˈphatic, phoˈnetic, hiˈstoric, etc. (Note, however, the exceptions such as ˈArabic, ˈcatholic, etc.)

-ify (*v.*): ˈterrify, ˈjustify, iˈdentify, etc.

-ible: in⟨'⟩credible, ⟨'⟩terrible, i⟨'⟩llegible, etc.
-igible: ⟨'⟩negligible, ⟨'⟩dirigible, in⟨'⟩telligible, etc.
-ish (*v.*): ⟨'⟩finish, ⟨'⟩publish, ⟨'⟩flourish, etc.

Again, verbs of 3 or more syllables ending in *-ate*, throw the main accent back two syllables, e.g. ⟨'⟩penetrate, ⟨'⟩indicate, ne⟨'⟩gotiate, etc.; whereas verbs of 2 syllables ending in *-ate* place the accent on *-ate*, e.g. in⟨'⟩flate, trans⟨'⟩late, de⟨'⟩bate, dic⟨'⟩tate, etc.

9.8   Phonotactic Possibilities[1]

English does not exploit, in the word and the syllable, all the possible combinations of its phonemes. For instance, long vowels and diphthongs do not precede final /ŋ/;[2] /e, æ, ʌ, ɒ/ do not occur finally; the types of consonant cluster permitted are subject to constraints. *Initially*, /ŋ/ does not occur; no combinations are possible with /tʃ, dʒ, ð, z/; /r, j, w/ can occur in clusters only as the non-initial element; such initial sequences as /fs, mh, stl, spw/ are unknown, etc. *Finally*, only /l/ may occur before non-syllabic /m, n/; /h, r, j, w/ do not occur in the type of phonemic analysis here used; terminal sequences such as /kf, ʃp, lð, ʒbd/ are unknown, etc.

The Tables in §9.9 show the way in which consonants (singly and in clusters) combine with the vowel phonemes of English in initial and final positions of the word. Many more consonant sequences will naturally occur medially at syllable boundaries in polysyllabic words, but a knowledge of the tolerated word initial and final sequences will usually give a guide to the point of phonological syllable boundary where onset of accent or other phonetic features do not supply the solution. Thus, in the pronunciation /ˈnætʃrəlɪ/ (*naturally*), it is reasonable to assume that the syllable boundary falls between /tʃ/ and /r/, since /-ætʃ/ and /rə-/ are possible word final and initial sequences, whereas word final /-æ/ and initial /tʃrə-/ do not occur.

However, although the general pattern of word initial and final phoneme sequences is plain, there are certain problems which have to be considered before comprehensive tables can be established.

(1) It is necessary to decide upon the size and the nature of the word list which is to be analysed. In particular, a decision must be taken concerning the extent to which rare, archaic or foreign words and proper names are to be included. A difficulty arises only when such words provide examples of unusual combinations of phonemes. Then it is a matter of deciding whether the word is of such currency that it must be allowed to establish the possibility of a particular sequence of

---

[1] See O'Connor and Trim (1953), and Hultzén, Allen, Miron (1964.)
[2] It should be noted that such combinations do occur as a result of assimilation. See §11.3.5.

phonemes, even though it may furnish the unique example. The Tables given below are based generally on the items contained in the *Everyman English Pronouncing Dictionary* (Dent, 1977). But the decision is often arbitrary, depending upon the native feeling for the 'Englishness' or otherwise of the sequence. Thus, *Gwen* and *Sarah* are used as examples of /gwe-/ and /sɛə-/ but the variant pronunciation /lɔːns/ for *Launce* is excluded as an example of final /-ɔːns/; *voodoo* is allowed to exemplify /vuː-/, but *fenks* (which would provide an instance of final /-eŋks/) and *zoril* (/zɒ-/) are excluded on the grounds of rarity; both *Schweppes* and *schnapps* are discarded as unique evidence of /ʃw-/ and /ʃn-/ because of their restricted use, nor do *tsar, tsetse* illustrate initial /ts-/ since both have variant pronunciations with /z-/ or /s-/ and /t-/ respectively which conform to the more usual English patterns.

(2) It frequently happens that a word has more than one accepted pronunciation. Usually, as in the common variation between /ə/ and /ɪ/ in certain unaccented syllables, the variants conform to the general pattern of combinatory possibilities. Occasionally, however, one such variant pronunciation will provide a unique example of a phoneme combination. Thus, the choice of /ʊ/ or /uː/ in *groom* provides the single instance of /grʊ-/ (if *Grundig* is excluded); /grʊ-/ is included in the Tables as tolerable in the pattern of English /gr + V/ sequences. On the other hand, *width, breadth, hundredth* have variants with /-tθ/ or /-dθ/; but the latter is excluded in favour of the (more common) former, since these words are the only cases of /V/ + /t-d/ + /θ/. Again, words such as *French, range* may be said with either /-ntʃ/ and /-ndʒ/ or /-nʃ/ and /-nʒ/. Since the former seem to be most common, the latter are excluded as final CC clusters. On the other hand, though many speakers would not distinguish the final clusters in *prince* /-ns/ and *prints* /-nts/, the distinction is sufficiently widespread for both /-ns/ and /-nts/ to be considered as possible final clusters (see also §8.4.4).

(3) Phoneme sequences have different values according to their frequency of occurrence in normal discourse. Thus, /gl- / occurs before most vowels in a large number of common words, whereas /gj-/ is highly restricted (e.g. in the rare *gules*); similarly, /-ld/ is extremely common after most vowels, whereas /-lm/ occurs only after /ɪ, e, ʌ/ (the single example of /-ɪlm/, *film*, having a high likelihood of occurrence, the sole case of /-ʌlm/, *culm*, being comparatively rare).

(4) Final sequences which include a syllabic consonant, e.g. in *rhythm* /-ɪðm/, *mutton* /-ʌtn/, *cattle* /-ætl/, *muddled* /-ʌdld/, have the syllabic analysed as /ə + C/ for the purpose of the Tables.

(5) The greater complexity of final consonant clusters (as compared with those occurring initially) is largely accounted for by the fact that final /t, d, s, z/ often represent a suffixed morpheme, e.g. *-ed, -s, -'s*, as in *parked, plagued, dukes, leagues, chef's* etc.

9.9 Tables of Word Initial and Final Phoneme Sequences

(1) *V*

The following ten vowels constitute monosyllabic words: /iː/ *E*, /ə/ *a*, /ɑː/ *are*, /ɔː/ *or*, /ɜː/ *err*, /eɪ/ *A*, /aɪ/ *I*, /əʊ/ *owe*, /ɪə/ *ear*, /ɛə/ *air*. In addition, /iː/ and /uː/ occur as reduced forms for *he* and *who*, and /ɔɪ/ may occur in the exclamation *Oy!*

(2) *Initial V*

All vowels occur initially, with the exception of /ʊ/ and /ʊə/.[1]

(3) *Initial CV-(Table I)*

/ŋ/ does not occur initially. /ʒ/ occurs initially before /ɪ/, /iː/, /æ/ and /ɑː/ in such foreign words as *gigolo, gigue, Zhivago, jabot, genre*. The other consonants generally occur before all vowels, though marked deficiencies are evident before /ʊə, ʊ, ɔɪ/. The following show more than 3 empty vowel slots: /z/ (12), /ð/ (9), /θ/ (6).

(4) *Initial CCV- (Table II)*

(*a*) Initial CC clusters pattern as follows:—

```
p + l, r, j
t +    r, j, w
k + l, r, j, w
b + l, r, j
d +    r, j, w
g + l, r, j, w
m +       j
n +       j
l +       j
f + l, r, j
v +       j
θ +    r, j, w
s + l,    j, w, p, t, k, m, n, f
ʃ +    r
h +       j
```

(*b*) /Cj/ occurs only before /uː/ or /ʊə/ or occasionally /ʊ/. Initial /tw, dw, gw/ occur before only a restricted set of vowels; /hw/ is excluded as an initial RP sequence, the variant /w/ being more common. Only /sp/ occurs before all vowels; only CC + /uː/ (6) has

---

[1] However, there are well-established pronunciations of such foreign proper names as *Uppsala* /ʊpˈsɑːlə/ and *Urdu* /ˈʊəduː/.

Table I Word Initial CV-

	ɪ	e	æ	ʌ	ɒ	ʊ	ə	iː	ɑː	ɔː	uː	ɜː	eɪ	aɪ	ɔɪ	əʊ	aʊ	ɪə	eə	ʊə
p	+	+	+	+	+	+	+	+	+	+	+	+	+	+	+	+	+	+	+	+
t	+	+	+	+	+	+	+	+	+	+	+	+	+	+	+	+	+	+	+	+
k	+	+	+	+	+	+	+	+	+	+	+	+	+	+	+	+	+	+	+	+
b	+	+	+	+	+	+	+	+	+	+	+	+	+	+	+	+	+	+	+	+
d	+	+	+	+	+	+	+	+	+	+	+	+	+	+	+	+	+	+	+	+
g	+	+	+	+	+	+	+	+	+	+	+	+	+	+	+	+	+	+	+	+
tʃ	+	+	+	+	+		+	+	+	+	+	+	+	+	+	+	+	+	+	
dʒ	+	+	+	+	+	+	+	+	+	+	+	+	+	+	+	+	+	+	+	
m	+	+	+	+	+	+	+	+	+	+	+	+	+	+	+	+	+	+	+	+
n	+	+	+	+	+	+	+	+	+	+	+	+	+	+	+	+	+	+	+	+
l	+	+	+	+	+	+	+	+	+	+	+	+	+	+	+	+	+	+	+	+
r	+	+	+	+	+	+	+	+	+	+	+	+	+	+	+	+	+	+	+	+
f	+	+	+	+	+	+	+	+	+	+	+	+	+	+	+	+	+	+	+	+
v	+	+	+	+	+		+	+	+	+	+	+	+	+	+	+	+	+	+	
θ	+	+	+	+	+		+	+	+	+		+	+	+		+	+	+	+	
ð	+	+	+	+	+		+	+	+	+		+	+	+		+	+	+	+	
s	+	+	+	+	+	+	+	+	+	+	+	+	+	+	+	+	+	+	+	+
z	+	+	+	+	+		+	+	+	+	+	+	+	+		+	+		+	
ʃ	+	+	+	+	+	+	+	+	+	+	+	+	+	+		+	+	+	+	+
ʒ	+	+	+	+	+		+			+		+							+	
h	+	+	+	+	+	+	+	+	+	+	+	+	+	+	+	+	+	+	+	+
j	+	+	+	+	+		+	+	+	+	+	+	+	+		+			+	+
w	+	+	+	+	+	+	+		+	+		+	+	+		+		+	+	+

Note.—The following items are included: *kursaal* /kʊə-/, *July* /dʒʊ-/, *lure* /lʊə-/, *Ruritania* /rʊə-/, *voodoo*, *Thetis*, *Thark*, *thane*, *sourdine* /sʊə-/, *Sarah*, *Zambia*, *jalousie*, *genre*, *houri*, *Yare*.

less than 10 empty slots, whereas /ɛə, ɔɪ, ɜː, ɪə, ə, ɑː, aʊ, ʊə/ are deficient in more than 20 places.

(5) *Initial CCCV- (Table III)*

(*a*) Initial CCC clusters pattern as follows:—

$$s + p + l, r, j$$
$$+ t + \quad r, j$$
$$+ k + l, r, j, w$$

(*b*) /s/ is the essential first element of CCC clusters; the second element is a fortis stop; the third element must be one of /l, r, j, w/. Of the 12 potential CCC sequences /spw-, stl-, stw-/ do not occur. /CCj/ occurs only before /uː/ or /ʊə/; /skl-/ occurs only before /ɪə/, though the item *sclerosis* admits the variants /skle-, sklɪ-, sklə-/.

(*c*) The name of the bird *smew* provides a single example of the initial sequence /smj-/.

(6) *Final -V*

All vowels except /e, æ, ʌ, ɒ/ occur finally. /ʊ/ occurs word finally in *to* before a word beginning with a vowel or in pre-pausal position (as well as in certain pronunciations of a word like *statue*). No short vowels occur in stressed open syllables.

(7) *Final -VC (Table IV)*

/r, h, j, w/ do not occur finally in the present phonemic analysis of RP. /ʒ/ occurs finally only after /iː, ɑː, uː, eɪ/ in words of recent French origin; /ŋ/ only after /ɪ, æ, ʌ, ɒ/; /ð/ only after /ɪ, iː, uː, eɪ, aɪ, əʊ, aʊ/; /g/ only after /ɪ, e, æ, ʌ, ɒ, iː, ɜː, ɑː, ɔː, uː, eɪ, əʊ/. Only /d/ occurs after all vowels. No vowel occurs before all consonants; /ʊə/ (17), /ɛə/ (16), /ɪə/ (15), /ɔɪ/ (12), /ʊ/ (12) show more than 10 empty slots.

Table II Word Initial CCV-

	ɪ	e	æ	ʌ	ɒ	ʊ	ə	iː	ɑː	ɔː	uː	ɜː	eɪ	aɪ	ɔɪ	əʊ	aʊ	ɪə	eə	əʊ
pl	+	+	+	+	+		+	+	+	+	+		+	+	+	+	+	+		+
pr	+	+	+	+	+		+	+	+	+	+		+	+	+	+	+		+	+
pj	+	+	+	+	+		+	+	+	+	+		+	+	+	+	+			+
tr	+	+	+		+			+	+	+	+		+	+	+	+	+			+
tj											+									
tw	+	+	+		+	+	+	+	+	+	+		+	+	+	+	+			
kl	+	+	+	+	+	+	+	+	+	+	+	+	+	+	+	+	+	+	+	+
kr	+	+	+	+	+	+	+	+	+	+	+	+	+	+	+	+	+	+		+
kj			+			+								+						
kw	+	+	+		+		+	+	+	+	+	+	+	+	+	+	+	+		
bl	+	+	+	+	+	+	+	+	+	+	+	+	+	+	+	+	+	+	+	+
br	+	+	+	+	+	+	+	+	+	+	+	+	+	+	+	+	+	+		+
bj	+	+	+	+	+	+	+	+	+	+	+		+	+	+	+	+	+		+
dr	+	+	+	+	+		+	+	+	+	+		+	+	+	+	+	+		+
dj	+	+	+							+	+			+						
dw	+	+												+						
gl	+	+	+	+	+		+	+	+	+	+		+	+		+		+	+	+
gr	+	+	+	+	+	+	+	+	+	+	+		+	+	+	+	+	+		+
gj	+	+									+									
gw		+									+			+						
mj	+										+									+
nj						+					+									+

Table II Word Initial CCV - *continued*

	ɪ	e	æ	ʌ	ɒ	ʊ	ə	iː	ɑː	ɔ	uː	ɜː	eə	aɪ	ɔ	əʊ	aʊ	eɪ	ɛə	ɪə
lj	+	+	+	+	+	+	+	+	+	+	+									
fl	+	+	+	+	+		+	+	+	+	+	+	+	+	+	+	+		+	+
fr	+	+	+	+	+			+	+	+	+		+	+	+	+	+			+
fj	+					+		+			+			+		+				
vj								+			+									
θr	+	+	+	+	+		+	+	+	+	+		+	+		+	+		+	+
θj											+									
θw			+		+	+		+		+				+		+				
sp	+	+	+	+	+	+	+	+	+	+	+	+	+	+	+	+	+	+		
st	+	+	+	+	+	+	+	+	+	+	+	+	+	+		+	+	+	+	
sk	+	+	+	+	+		+	+	+	+	+	+	+	+		+	+		+	
sm	+	+	+	+	+	+		+	+	+	+	+	+	+	+	+	+	+		
sn	+	+	+	+	+			+	+	+	+		+	+	+	+	+	+		
sf	+	+	+	+	+					+	+		+	+		+	+	+		
sl	+	+	+	+	+			+	+	+	+	+	+	+		+	+			
sj						+									−					
sw	+	+	+	+	+			+	+	+	+	+	+	+		+	+	+	+	+
ʃr	+	+			+			+			+					+	+			
hj	+	+						+			+					+				+

Note:—The following items are included: *pleonastic* /plɪə-/, *Prague*, *Blore* /blɔː/, *Blois* /blɔɪs/, *Brereton* /brɪə-/, *Brer* /brɜː/, *Drury, Dwight, Clare, Croydon, gules, Gwynne, Gwen, mulatto* /mjʊ-/, *Floyd* /flɔɪd/, *Freud* /frɔɪd/, *Thrace, threepence* /θrɪ-/, *Thule* /θjuː-/, *Thwaite, sputnik, Smeaton, Smaile, Shropshire.*

Table III Word Initial CCCV-

	ɪ	e	æ	ʌ	ɒ	ʊ	ə	iː	ɑː	ɔː	uː	ɜː	eɪ	aɪ	ɔɪ	əʊ	aʊ	ɪə	eə	ʊə
spl	+	+	+	+	+			+				+	+	+						
spr	+	+	+	+	+			+		+			+	+			+			
spj											+									+
str	+	+	+	+	+			+	+	+	+		+	+		+	+			
stj											+									
skl																		+		
skr	+		+	+	+			+		+	+		+	+		+	+			
skj											+									
skw	+	+			+			+				+	+	+				+	+	+
smj											+									

Note:—The following items are included: *Stroud, sclerosis* /sklɪə-/, *squamose, Squeers.*

Table IV Word Final -VC

	ʊə	eə	ɪə	aʊ	əʊ	ɔɪ	aɪ	eɪ	ɜː	uː	ɔː	ɑː	iː	ə	ʊ	ʌ	ɒ	æ	e	ɪ
p					+		+	+	+	+	+	+	+			+	+	+	+	+
t				+	+	+		+	+	+	+	+	+			+	+	+	+	+
k	+			+	+	+	+	+	+	+	+	+	+		+	+	+	+	+	+
b					+		+	+	+	+	+	+	+			+	+	+	+	+
d		+	+	+	+	+	+	+	+	+	+	+	+		+	+	+	+	+	+
g					+			+	+	+	+	+	+		+	+	+	+	+	+
tʃ				+				+		+	+	+	+		+	+	+	+	+	+
dʒ				+	+		+	+		+	+	+	+			+	+	+	+	+
m					+		+	+	+	+	+	+	+			+	+	+	+	+
n		+	+	+	+	+	+	+	+	+	+	+	+			+	+	+	+	+
ŋ																+	+	+		+
l	+		+	+	+	+	+	+	+	+	+	+	+		+	+	+	+	+	+
f					+	+	+	+	+	+	+	+	+			+	+	+	+	+
v					+		+	+	+	+		+	+			+	+	+	+	+
θ					+		+	+	+	+		+	+	+		+	+	+	+	+
ð					+		+	+		+		+	+			+	+	+	+	+
s	+	+	+	+	+	+	+	+	+	+	+	+	+			+	+	+	+	+
z	+	+	+	+	+	+	+	+	+	+	+	+	+			+	+	+	+	+
ʃ								+		+	+	+	+		+	+	+	+	+	+
ʒ										+										

Note:— The following items are included: *yoick, gowk, Prague, morgue, fugue, putsch /-ʊtʃ/, hooch, doge /dəʊdʒ/, Ian, tairn, coif, gaff, rev, hath, doth, vermouth /-əθ/, bourse /-ʊəs/, fez, tarboosh, douche, gauche.*

Table V Word Final -VCC

	ɪ	e	æ	ʌ	ɒ	ʊ	ə	iː	ɑː	ɔː	uː	ɜː	eɪ	aɪ	ɔɪ	əʊ	aʊ	ɪə	eə	ʊə
pt	+	+	+	+	+		+	+	+	+	+	+	+	+		+				
pθ		+																		
ps	+	+	+	+	+		+	+	+	+	+	+	+	+		+				
tθ	+	+					+	+												
ts	+	+	+	+	+	+	+	+	+	+	+	+	+	+	+	+	+			
kt	+	+	+	+	+	+	+		+	+	+	+	+	+		+	+			
ks	+	+	+	+	+	+			+	+	+	+	+	+		+				
bd	+	+	+	+	+		+		+	+	+	+	+	+		+				
bz	+	+	+	+	+	+	+		+	+	+	+		+		+				
dz	+	+	+	+	+			+							+	+	+	+	+	+
gd	+	+	+	+	+			+		+			+							
gz	+	+	+	+	+			+	+	+		+	+			+	+			
tʃ/t	+	+	+	+	+			+	+		+	+	+			+	+			
dʒd	+	+	+	+								+	+	+						
mp	+	+		+																
md	+	+	+	+		+	+	+	+	+	+	+	+	+						
mf				+						+	+					+				
mθ										+										
mz	+	+	+	+	+		+	+	+	+	+	+	+	+	+	+	+			
nt	+	+	+	+	+		+		+	+		+	+	+	+	+	+			+
nd	+	+	+	+	+		+	+	+	+	+	+	+	+		+				
ntʃ	+	+		+					+	+										

Table V Word Final -VCC *continued*

	ɪ	e	æ	ʌ	ɑ	ʊ	ə	iː	ɑː	ɔː	uː	ɜː	eɪ	aɪ	ɔɪ	əʊ	aʊ	eə	ɛ	ɪə
ndʒ	+	+	+	+			+										+			+
nθ	+	+	+	+			+	+						+						
ns	+	+	+	+	+		+		+											
nz	+	+	+	+	+		+	+	+	+	+	+	+	+	+	+	+	+	+	+
nd	+		+	+	+															
ŋk	+		+	+	+															
ŋz	+		+	+	+															
lp	+		+	+																
lt	+	+	+	+						+						+				
lk	+	+	+	+						+										
lb	+		+	+			+													+
ld	+	+		+	+		+	+	+	+	+	+	+	+	+	+	+	+		+
ltʃ	+	+		+																
ldʒ	+			+																
lm	+	+				+														
ln	+			+							+									
lf	+	+	+		+	+														
lv		+	+	+	+															
lθ		+		+						+										
ls	+	+								+										
lz	+	+	+	+	+		+	+	+	+	+	+	+	+	+	+	+	+		+
lʃ		+																		

Table V Word Final -VCC *continued*

	ɪ	e	æ	ʌ	ɒ	ʊ	ə	iː	ɑː	ɔː	uː	ɜː	eɪ	aɪ	ɔɪ	əʊ	aʊ	ɪə	eə	ʊə
ft	+	+	+	+	+			+	+	+	+	+	+	+						
fθ	+	+	+	+	+			+	+	+	+	+	+	+						
fs	+	+	+	+	+			+	+											
vd	+	+	+	+				+	+	+	+	+	+	+	+	+				
vz	+	+	+	+				+	+	+	+	+	+	+		+				
θt		+						+	+	+	+	+								
θs	+	+	+		+			+	+	+			+			+	+			
ðd					+		+		+				+	+		+	+			
ðz								+	+		+		+	+		+	+			
sp	+		+	+	+		+	+	+											
st	+	+	+	+	+		+	+	+	+	+	+	+	+	+	+	+			
sk	+	+	+	+	+		+	+	+											
zd	+	+	+	+	+			+	+	+	+		+	+	+	+	+			
ʃt	+	+				+	+	+	+											
ʒd								+	+		+									

Note:—The following items are included: *macadamed* /-əmd/, *triumph* /-ʌmf/, *amaranth* /-ænθ/, *aeons* /ˈiənz/, *megilp, culm, coolth, revved, revs, breathed* (in the special phonetic sense as /breθt/), *kiosk*.

(8) *Final -VCC (Table V)*

(*a*) Final CC clusters pattern as follows:—

```
p +    t,                          θ, s
t +                                θ, s
k +    t,                           s
b +            d,                       z
d +                                     z
g +            d,                       z
tʃ +   t
dʒ+            d
m +  p,        d,              f,   θ,   z
n +    t,      d, tʃ, dʒ,           θ, s, z
ŋ +        k,  d,                       z
l  + p, t, k, b, d, tʃ, dʒ, m, n, f, v, θ, s, z, ʃ
f +    t,                           θ, s
v +            d,                       z
θ +    t,                            s
ð +            d,                       z
s + p, t, k
z +            d
ʃ +    t
ʒ +            d
```

(*b*) In the present analysis of RP /r, h, j, w/ do not combine with other consonants in final positions. /g, ŋ, ð/ do not occupy final position in a final CC cluster. /pθ/ occurs only after /e/, /mθ/ only after /ɔ:/, /ln/ only after /ɪ/, /lʃ/ only after /e/, /fθ/ only after /ɪ/. Only /dz/ occurs after all vowels; /nz, lz/ occur after all but 2 vowels. All other CC clusters show considerable restrictions in their ability to combine with preceding vowels.

Vowels also show deficiencies in their ability to combine with the 59 possible final clusters; none combines with all clusters. The following combine with less than half of the final CC clusters: /ɪə/ (with only 2), /ɛə/ (2), /ʊə/ (5), /ʊ/ (8), /ɔɪ/ (10), /aʊ/ (17), /ə/ (23), /ɜ:/ (25), /aɪ/ (25), /əʊ/ (26), /i:/ (27), /u:/ (27), /eɪ/ (28), /ɔ:/ (28). The highest rate of combination with CC is shown by /ɪ, e, ʌ/.

Table VI Word Final -VCCC

	ɪ	e	æ	ʌ	ɒ	ʊ	ə	iː	ɑː	ɔː	uː	ɜː	eɪ	aɪ	ɔɪ	əʊ	aʊ	ɪə	eə	ʊə
pts	+	+	+	+	+															
pst	+		+									+	+							
pθs	+	+																		
tst	+	+					+						+							
tθs	+			+																
dst	+																			
kts	+	+	+		+															
kst	+	+	+		+		+									+				
ksθ	+																			
mpt	+	+	+	+	+															
mps	+	+	+	+	+															
mfs				+																
ntθ							+													
nts	+	+	+	+	+		+		+	+			+	+	+		+			
ndz	+	+	+	+	+		+	+	+		+			+			+			
ntʃt	+	+		+					+	+										
ndʒd	+	+		+									+				+			
nθs	+	+	+	+	+			+						+						
nst	+	+	+	+					+								+			
nzd		+		+																
ŋst			+																	
ŋkt	+	+	+	+																
ŋkθ	+			+																
ŋks			+	+	+															
lpt		+	+	+																
lps		+	+	+																

Table VI Word Final -VCCC *continued*

	ɪ	e	æ	ʌ	ɒ	ʊ	ə	iː	ɑː	ɔː	uː	ɜː	ɪə	aɪ	ɔɪ	əʊ	aʊ	eɪ	eə	ʊə
lts	+	+	+	+																
lkt	+	+		+						+										
lks	+	+	+	+						+										
lbz	+		+	+						+						+				
ldz	+	+						+		+		+								
ltʃt	+	+		+																
ldʒd	+			+																
lmd	+	+																		
lmz	+	+		+		+														
lnz	+	+																		
lfs	+	+	+	+	+	+														
lfθ	+	+																		
lvd	+	+			+															
lvz	+		+		+															
lθs	+	+							+											
lst	+	+		+	+					+				+						
fts	+	+		+					+											
fθs	+																			
spt	+			+					+											
sps	+			+					+											
sts	+	+	+	+	+		+	+	+	+	+	+	+		+	+	+			
skt	+	+		+	+				+											
sks	+			+	+															

Note.—The following items are included: *traipsed, blitzed, flummoxed, flanged, coelacanths, mulct, calx, albs, waltzed* (/wɔːlst/), *cusps, kiosks.*

(9) *Final -VCCC (Table VI)*

(*a*) Final VCCC clusters pattern as follows:—

```
p +    t,      θ⎫                    p + s          ⎫
t +            θ⎪                    t + s          ⎪
k +    t        ⎪                    k + s          ⎪
m + p,       f  ⎪                    d + s          ⎪
n +    t,      θ⎬+ s                 m +    p        ⎬+ t
ŋ +       k     ⎪                    n + s,     tʃ   ⎪
l + p, t, k, f, θ⎪                   ŋ + s,   k      ⎪
f +    t,      θ⎪                    l + s, p, k, tʃ ⎪
s + p, t, k    ⎭                     s +    p, k    ⎭

n +    d      ⎫                      n + dʒ,     z ⎫
l + b, d, m, n, v⎬+ z                l + dʒ, m, v   ⎬+ d

                 k +      s ⎫
                 n + t      ⎪
                 ŋ +   k    ⎬+ θ
                 l +      f ⎭
```

(*b*) Only /nts/ (12), /ndz/ (11), /sts/ (15) cluster with more than half the possible preceding vowel phonemes. CCC clusters follow predominantly short vowels. 11 of the 49 CCC final clusters occur after only one vowel (5 after /ɪ/, 4 after /e/, 1 after /ʌ/, 1 after /ə/).

(10) *Final -VCCCC*

Final CCCC clusters occur only rarely as a result of the suffixation to CCC of a /t/ or /s/ morpheme, e.g. /-mpts/ *prompts*, *exempts*, /-mpst/ *glimpsed*, /-lkts/ *mulcts*, /-lpts/ *sculpts*, /-lfθs/ *twelfths*, /-ksts/ *texts*, /-ksθs/ *sixths*, /-ntθs/ *thousandths*.

(11) With a vowel inventory of 20 items and the possible initial and final consonant clusters given in the Tables above, it is clear that a large number of potential combinations are not utilized. Thus, such unused monosyllabic words as the following conform to an already existing pattern: /faʊd, saɪdʒ, mɒmp, bruːtʃ, pliːk, splʌk, stredʒ/. If, in addition, deficiencies in the Tables are made good on the grounds of general patterning, it would be possible to construct words of an English phonological character with, for instance, initial /tʃʊ-, rɜː-, glɔɪ-, skɪə-, sprəʊ-/ or final /-ɔːg, -aɪtʃ, -uːnt, -ɑːndʒ, -ʌkst/, etc.

9.10   Suffix Formation

A limited amount of information has already been given (§9.3) on the effect on a word's stress-pattern of the addition of certain suffixes.

These examples mostly concern derivatives and frequently involve changes in word-class. Inflectional endings (which do not normally affect stress) follow certain rules which affect segmental aspects of pronunciation. The following regularities may usefully be listed here.

(1) *Past tense formation*

For regular verbs in which the past tense is signalled by the addition of an *-ed* ending, the following rules of pronunciation apply:
  (a) If the stem ends in /t/ or /d/, add /ɪd/
  e.g. *exclude* /ɪkˈskluːd, ɪkˈskluːdɪd/; *guard* /gɑːd, ˈgɑːdɪd/; *rot* /rɒt, ˈrɒtɪd/; *target* /ˈtɑːgɪt, ˈtɑːgɪtɪd/
Otherwise
  (b) If the stem ends in any lenis sound (apart from /d/), add /d/
  e.g. *buzz* /bʌz, bʌzd/; *hammer* /ˈhæmə, ˈhæməd/; *kill* /kɪl, kɪld/; *listen* /ˈlɪsn̩, ˈlɪsn̩d/
  (c) If the stem ends in any fortis consonant (apart from /t/) add /t/
  e.g. *arch* /ɑːtʃ, ɑːtʃt/; *immerse* /ɪˈmɜːs, ɪˈmɜːst/; *kick* /kɪk, kɪkt/; *sniff* /snɪf, snɪft/

(2) *Plural formation*

(and 3rd person singular of present tense of verbs)
  (a) If the stem ends in a sibilant (a sound in which there is some element of fricative grooving), add /ɪz/
  e.g. *address* /əˈdres, əˈdresɪz/; *arch* /ɑːtʃ, ˈɑːtʃɪz/; *graze* /greɪz, ˈgreɪzɪz/; *judge* /dʒʌdʒ, ˈdʒʌdʒɪz/; *rush* /ˈrʌʃ, ˈrʌʃɪz/
Exceptionally, the voicing of the fricative in *house* changes: /haʊs, ˈhaʊzɪz/.[1]
  Otherwise
  (b) If the stem ends in any non-sibilant lenis sound, add /z/
  e.g. *blow* /bləʊ, bləʊz/; *pattern* /ˈpætn̩, ˈpætn̩z/; *regard* /rɪˈgɑːd, rɪˈgɑːdz/; *thrill* /θrɪl, θrɪlz/
  (c) If the stem ends in any non-sibilant fortis consonant, add /s/
  e.g. *laugh* /lɑːf, lɑːfs/; *pick* /pɪk, pɪks/; *resort* /rɪˈzɔːt, rɪˈzɔːts/

(3) *Present participle formation*

In all cases, add /ɪŋ/
  e.g. *kill* /ˈkɪl, ˈkɪlɪŋ/; *laugh* /lɑːf, ˈlɑːfɪŋ/; *sing* /sɪŋ, ˈsɪŋɪŋ/; *trim* /trɪm, ˈtrɪmɪŋ/
  For cases where the stem ends with orthographic /r/, see (6) below.
  For stems ending in syllabic /n̩/ or /l̩/, the syllabic nature of the nasal or lateral is frequently retained, e.g. *handle* /ˈhændl̩, ˈhændl̩ɪŋ/;

---

[1] In all comparable cases, such alteration is reflected in the spelling.

widen /ˈwaɪdn̩, ˈwaɪdn̩ɪŋ/. However, some speakers may insert a /ə/, retaining the same number of syllables, thus /ˈhændəlɪŋ, ˈwaɪdənɪŋ/; whilst for others the nasal or lateral may lose its syllabic function, thus /ˈhændlɪŋ, ˈwaɪdnɪŋ/. It should be noted that in such cases, the quality of the /l/ is altered, the dark [ɫ] of [ˈhændɫ] being replaced by a clear [l]. (See also §9.6.)

(4) *Comparison of adjectives*

For those adjectives whose comparative and superlative degrees are formed by the suffixing of *-er* and *-est* respectively, the pronunciation of the stem remains unchanged except in the case of stems ending in /ŋ/ or /r/ (see (5) and (6) below). Thus /ə/ and /ɪst/ are regularly added, as in *easy* /ˈiːzɪ, ˈiːzɪə, ˈiːzɪɪst/; *great* /greɪt, ˈgreɪtə, ˈgreɪtɪst/; *big* /bɪg, ˈbɪgə, ˈbɪgɪst/.

(5) *Stems ending in /ŋ/*

When the comparative and superlative suffixes are added to stems ending in /ŋ/, a /g/ is inserted, e.g. *long* /lɒŋ, ˈlɒŋgə, ˈlɒŋgɪst/.

In all other cases, the /ŋ/ is followed immediately by the suffix, e.g. participle *-ing* as *longing* /ˈlɒŋɪŋ/, adjectival modifier *-ish* as *longish* /ˈlɒŋɪʃ/, or agentive *-er* as *hanger* /ˈhæŋə/, *singer* /ˈsɪŋə/.

It should be noted that monomorphemic words (*not* formed of a stem and affix) exhibit the sequence /-ŋg-/ intervocalically, e.g. *anger* /ˈæŋgə/, *finger* /ˈfɪŋgə/.

(6) */r/- links in suffix formation* [1]

In the case of words which end with orthographic *r*, an /r/-link is regularly inserted between the final vowel of the stem /ə, ɜ:, ɑ:, ɔ:/ and any initial vowel of the suffix.

e.g. present participles *blur* /blɜ:, blɜ:rɪŋ/; *secure* /sɪˈkjʊə, sɪˈkjʊərɪŋ/; *stare* /steə, ˈsteərɪŋ/; *store* /stɔ:, ˈstɔ:rɪŋ/; comparative and superlative adjectives (stem + /ə,ɪst/) *clear* /klɪə, ˈklɪərə, ˈklɪərɪst/.

This process applies to derivational as well as to inflectional suffixes, e.g. adjectival *-y*, e.g. *star* /stɑ:, ˈstɑ:rɪ/; agentive noun *-er*, e.g. *murder* /ˈmɜ:də, ˈmɜ:dərə/; verb-forming *-ize*, e.g. *familiar* /fəˈmɪlɪə, fəˈmɪlɪəraɪz/.

9.11   Variability in the Phonemic Structure of Words [2]

In connected speech, English words exhibit variations of accentual pattern and changes of a phonemic or phonetic kind, involving assimi-

---

[1] This does not apply to past tense *-ed* (see 1(b) above.)

[2] See my 'A note on the variability of the phonemic components of English words', *Brno Studies in English*, vol. 8, 1969.

lation and elision, especially at word boundaries (see Chapter 11). There is also often a remarkable latitude in the choice of phonemes used in words when said in isolation by RP speakers. Even with the exclusion of cases of differing phonemic inventories—e.g. the choice between using /ʍ/ or /w/ for *wh* words or /ɔː/ or /ɔə/ in words of the *bore* type—there remains a high degree of variability within the same variety of pronunciation. The permissible variations concern mainly vowels, but cases of a choice of consonant also occur. The following are examples:—

(1) *Vowels*

/iː/ ~ /ɪ/ 'acetylene, economy'; ~ /c/ 'economics, premature'; ~ /eɪ/ 'deify, detour'; ~ /aɪ/ 'Argentine, iodine'
/ɪ/ ~ /e/ 'alphabet, orchestra'; ~ /aɪ/ 'privacy, dynasty'; ~ /eɪ/ 'magistrate, holiday'; ~ /ə/ 'believe, system, adequate'
/e/ ~ /eɪ/ 'again, maintain'; ~ /ə/ 'accent, emblem'
/æ/ ~ /ɑː/ 'graph, translate'; ~ /eɪ/ 'patriot, amoral'; ~ /ɛə/ 'larynx, pharynx'; ~ /ə/ 'agnostic, vapidity'
/ʌ/ ~ /ɒ/ 'constable, combat'; ~ /ə/ 'bankrupt, dandruff'
/ɒ/ ~ /ɔː/ 'salt, wrath, Australia'; ~ /ə/ 'obscure, obligatory'
/ɔː/ ~ /ʊə/ 'sure, poor'
/ʊ/ ~ /uː/ 'room, groom'
/uː/ ~ /juː/ 'suit, supreme, allusion'
/eɪ/ ~ /ɑː/ 'data, esplanade'
/əʊ/ ~ /ə/ 'allocate, phonetics'

(2) *Consonants*

/t/ ~ /tj/ ~ /tʃ/ 'amateur'; /tj/ ~ /tʃ/ 'actual, Christian'; /dj/ ~ /dʒ/ 'educate, grandeur'; /dʒ/ ~ /ʒ/ 'garage'; /g/ ~ /dʒ/ 'gibberish, pedagogic'; /ntʃ/ ~ /nʃ/ 'French, branch'; /ndʒ/ ~ /nʒ/ 'revenge, strange'; /k/ ~ /kw/ 'quoit'; /ŋk/ ~ /ŋ/ 'anxious'; /ŋg/ ~ /ŋ/ 'English'; /sj/ ~ /sɪ/ ~ /ʃɪ/ 'associate'; /sj/ ~ /ʃ/ 'issue, sexual'; /zj/ ~ /ʒ/ 'usual, azure'; /ʃ/ ~ /ʒ/ 'magnesia, Asia'; /s/ ~ /z/ 'usage, unison'; /f/ ~ /p/ 'diphthong, naphtha'.

10

Connected Speech

10.1 Accent

Connected speech, i.e. an utterance consisting of more than one word, exhibits features of accentuation that are in many ways comparable with those found in the polysyllabic word. Thus the character of a connected utterance may be said to be determined both by a changing pattern of successive qualities and quantities and also by the relationship of its parts, i.e. of the words composing the continuum. Some parts of the connected utterance will be made to stand out from their environment, in the same way that certain syllables of a polysyllabic word are more prominent than their neighbours; in both cases, accentuation has a contrastive function. Accentuation in connected speech differs, however, from the usual case of a polysyllable in that the situation of the accent in connected speech is determined largely by the meaning which the utterance is intended to convey. The meaningful, distinctive, function of accent in words is, on the other hand, of restricted application (§9.5). The following selected examples illustrate some of the similarities and differences of accentual patterns in the word and in connected speech:—

She can may be ❯ ₒ	/ˈʃiː ˌkæn/ or . ❯ /ʃɪˈkæn/ (cf. the varying patterns of *insult* as verb or noun),
but not ❯ .	/ˈʃiː kən/, as in *beacon*.
She can go may be ❯ . •	(cf. *telephone*)
. ❯ ₒ	(cf. *tobacco*)
• . ❯	Or . . ❯ (cf. *cigarette*)
but not ❯ . .	(cf. *bachelor*).
How can she? may be ❯ . .	(cf. *quantity*)
• ❯ .	(cf. *uncertain*)
but not . ❯ .	(cf. *encounter*).
How can she do it? may be • . . ❯ .	(cf. *interdependence*)
• . ❯ . .	(cf. *aristocracy*)
but not . ❯ . . .	(cf. *administrative*).
We put the case in the hall may be . • . • . . ❯	

260

❭ . . ● . . ●
 . ❭ . ● . . ●
 . ● . ❭ . . ●
 . ❭ . ❭ . . ❭
 . ● . ● ❭ . ● . , etc.,

but not . ● . . . ❭ . (cf. *industrialization*)
with no accent on *case* and *hall*.

He understands the importance of practising—where *understands*, *importance*, *practising*, must have an accent of some kind on their appropriate syllables, whether or not *he*, for instance, is accented.

Such examples suggest that:—

(1) Although accentual patterns of connected speech are freer than those of the word and are largely determined by the meaning to be conveyed, some words are predisposed by their function in the language to receive accent. These *content* or *lexical* words are typically main verbs, adverbs, nouns, adjectives, demonstrative pronouns, etc. Other categories of words, such as auxiliary verbs, conjunctions, prepositions, pronouns, relative pronouns and articles (*form* or *grammatical* words), are more likely to be unaccented, although they, too, may be exceptionally accented if the meaning requires it.

The examples given above illustrate the freedom of accentual patterning in utterances taken without a context. But the meaning of any utterance is largely conditioned by the situation and context in which it occurs. Thus, it must be expected that the freedom of accentual patterning of the utterance and, in particular, of the situation of the primary (tonic) accent will be considerably curtailed by the constraints imposed by the contextual environment. In the case of an opening remark, or when a new topic is introduced into a conversation, there is greater scope for variations of meaning pointed by accentuation. Or again, it happens that some accentual freedom is possible in responses; thus, in response to the statement *She came last week* (. ● ● ❭), an incredulous reaction *Last week!* might have the pattern ❭ ○ [1] (i.e. 'Wasn't it the week before?') or ● ❭ (i.e. 'Don't you mean last month?'); or, in response to *What was the weather like?*, the reply *It rained every day* might have the pattern . ● ● . ❭ (emphasizing the continuous nature of the rain) or . ❭ ○ . ● (where the fact of raining is emphasized). But, in the following dialogue, such constraints are placed upon the accentuation, both by the context and by the nature of the content words, that little variation is possible (those words likely to be most strongly accented being printed in italics):—

[1] Note that the sign ❭ here shows the place of the primary, tonic accent. It may be marked by the onset of a falling or, as here, a rising change of pitch direction.

'Did you have a good *holiday*?'
'*Yes, very* good.'
Was the *weather* all right?'
'It was *fine* for the *first* part, but for the *rest* of the time it was pretty *mixed*. We *enjoyed* ourselves though. We had the *car*, so we were able to do some *sight-seeing*, when it was too *wet* to go on the *beach*.'

(2) Many monosyllabic form words are subject to qualitative variation according to whether they receive the accent or not. Nevertheless, weakening of an unaccented form word may be inhibited by its position, e.g. *can* /kən/ or /kn/ in unaccented initial and medial positions in the utterance, but /kæn/ in an unaccented final position. On the other hand, monosyllabic content words in relatively weakly accented positions (adjacent to a strong accent) retain their full vowel value and the prominence associated with it, e.g. *how* in *How can she?* (• ➘ .); or again, in *We put the case in the hall*, *case* and *hall* will always receive a secondary accent, wherever the primary accent is concentrated, because of the qualitative prominence of their full, strong vowels (and, frequently for the rhythmic beat which they carry), whereas *put* with its relatively weak vowel /ʊ/ may lose all accentual prominence, e.g. in the second pattern given for this sentence on p. 261.

(3) More than one word in an utterance may receive a primary (tonic, nuclear) accent. A deliberate, emphatic, or excited style of speaking often exhibits a proliferation of primary, tonic accents; a more rapid and matter-of-fact delivery is likely to show fewer primary and more secondary accents.

(4) Polysyllabic words, containing one accented syllable when said in isolation, carry an accent (primary or secondary) on that syllable in connected speech.

(5) In an extended dialogue in normal conversational style, the number of weak syllables (unaccented) tends to exceed that of those carrying an accent (primary or secondary).

10.2   Manifestation of Accent in Connected Speech

The same factors which we saw to be responsible for achieving a pattern of prominences in the word, i.e. variations of pitch, length, stress, and quality, contribute to the manifestation of the accented parts of connected speech. Just as in the case of the word, it is necessary to distinguish those factors which are significant realities only for the speaker from those which, being perceived and interpreted by the listener, are significant in the function of speech as an act of communication.

10.3 Stress and Rhythm

The speaker is aware of the occurrence in the utterance of a number of strong stresses or beats corresponding to those parts of the utterance to which he wishes to attach particular accentual meaning and on which he expends relatively great articulatory energy; the remaining words or syllables are weakly and rapidly articulated. The number of syllables stressed by the speaker depends largely upon the nature of the words composing the utterance. Thus, an utterance containing a high percentage of content words is likely to receive more stresses than one with the same number of syllables but a higher proportion of form words: compare, for example, two sentences of eight syllables:—

The first six have all won a prize—. • • • • • • ❱
There were prizes for six of them—. • • • • ❱ • •

Stress of this kind constitutes a reality for the speaker, but is not, by itself, an efficient means of communicating accent in connected speech.

Nevertheless, the syllables uttered with the greatest stress constitute, for the speaker, hubs with which unstressed syllables will be associated to form rhythmic groups.[1] It is a feature of English that the utterance is delivered as a series of close-knit rhythmic groups, which override in importance on the phonetic level the significance of the word on the linguistic level. Compare the rhythmic groups, based on a strongly accented syllable, which are likely to occur in the following sentences:

They couldn't have	chosen a	better	time for their	holiday

I want to	I want	to go	I want	to go	now

I want	to go	to-morrow

Mary and	George	specially	want	to go	to-morrow

It is noticeable that the rhythmic beats of an utterance occur at fairly equal intervals of time.[2] As a result of this, the speed at which the

[1] See W. Jassem, 'Stress in Modern English,' *Bulletin de la Société Polonaise de Linguistique*, Cracow, 1952; *Intonation of Conversational English*, Wroclaw, 1952; 'Indication of speech rhythm of educated southern English,' *Le Maître Phonétique*, no. 92, 1949.
[2] It should be emphasized that such *isochrony* is of a very approximate kind, J. D. O'Connor has shown ('The perception of time intervals,' *Progress Report*, 1965, Phonetics Laboratory, University College, London) that even when a speaker is

unstressed syllables are uttered—and the length of each—will depend upon the number occurring between the strong beats. All the unaccented syllables occurring between two strong beats may not, however, be uttered with equal rapidity: those following the strong beat of a rhythmic group tend to occupy slightly more time than those which precede the strong beat. Thus, in the phrase *The authority | of the government | is in danger*, particular speed of utterance is associated with the unaccented *of the*, *is in*, compared with *-ity*, *-ernment*. The rhythmic grouping of unaccented syllables generally correlates with grammatical word-clusters; a rhythmic division will not normally fall within a word pattern, but several words may combine to form one rhythmic group. It often happens, however, that an unaccented word may equally well be assigned to either of two rhythmic groups, e.g. in *They couldn't have chosen*, the weak *have* /həv/ may be the last syllable of the first group or the first syllable of the second group.

Syllables carrying a strong stress are usually signalled to a listener by means of pitch prominence (see §§10.5, 10.5.1), but it frequently happens that a syllable stressed by the speaker has no pitch prominence. In this case, the syllable (or word) is given some accentual prominence for the listener by a combination of any of the factors of loudness (relating to stress), sonority (relating to the quality and length of the syllabic sound), and the nature of the word ('content' as opposed to 'form'). The following sentences illustrate the occurrence of stressed syllables said on a monotone within an utterance or, following a primary accent initiating a rise, within a rising post-tonic sequence of syllables; such stressed syllables, without pitch prominence, may be said to carry for a listener secondary accent of a rhythmic, qualitative/quantitative, or semantic kind:—

seems in	. ● . ⌐ . .
	it seems impossible
wants, have in	. ● . ● . ⌐
	he wants to have it now

deliberately attempting to produce isochrony in doggerel verse the real durations of groups vary between 488 and 566 msecs and that a listener's perception of equality of intervals between stimuli allows for considerable latitude. O'Connor also demonstrates ('The duration of the foot in relation to the number of component sound segments,' *Progress Report*, 1968) that, in a constant frame with a variable item having different numbers of segments, the frame items do not accommodate appreciably to the length of the variable. The variable shows greater length according to the number of its segments, though the duration is not evenly proportional to the number of segments. All that can be said is that there is a tendency towards compression and isochrony as the number of segments increases.

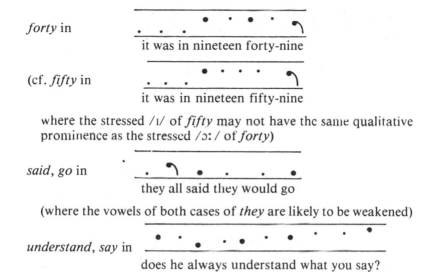

forty in

it was in nineteen forty-nine

(cf. *fifty* in

it was in nineteen fifty-nine

where the stressed /ɪ/ of *fifty* may not have the same qualitative prominence as the stressed /ɔː/ of *forty*)

said, go in

they all said they would go

(where the vowels of both cases of *they* are likely to be weakened)

understand, say in

does he always understand what you say?

(For variations of word accentual patterns in connected speech, see §11.2.)

10.4 Quantity and Quality

(1) *Accented words.*—Vowels and continuant consonants in accented syllables which form the hub of a rhythmic group are shortened according to the number of unaccented syllables (especially following) in the group. Thus, the /aɪ/ of /taɪd/ (*tide*) shows progressive shortening in such rhythmic groups as *tidy, tidily, she tidied it*, etc.; the /ʌ/ and /m/ of /kʌm/ (*come*) are similarly shortened in *comfort, comfortable, come for me, circumference*. Or again, a comparable phonemic sequence will have slight variations of sound length according to the division into rhythmic groups: cf. *aboard a liner* /ə'bɔːd ə'laɪnə/ and *a border-liner* /ə'bɔːdə ˌlaɪnə/—/ɔː/ being slightly shorter in the second case; *minor official* /'maɪnər ə'fɪʃl/ and *mine are official* /'maɪn ərə'fɪʃl/—/aɪ/ being longer in the second case. Such variation of rhythmic grouping, involving changes of quantity, constitutes a reality for the speaker, but it is doubtful whether slight modifications of this kind are markedly significant to a listener, since the choice of meaning for such similar phoneme sequences is normally determined by the context, such cues as are provided by rhythmic variation of quantity being redundant.

(2) *Unaccented words.*—A more marked effect is that which characterizes the quantity and quality of unaccented words. Content words (monosyllables and polysyllables) generally have in connected speech the qualitative pattern of their isolate form and therefore retain some

measure of qualitative prominence even when no pitch prominence is associated with them and when they are relatively unstressed, e.g.:—

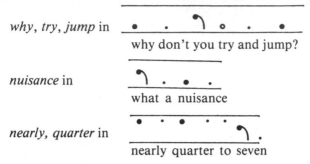

why, try, jump in

why don't you try and jump?

nuisance in

what a nuisance

nearly, quarter in

nearly quarter to seven

But many form words have two or more qualitative and quantitative patterns according to whether they are unaccented (as is usual) or accented (in special situations or when said in isolation). As compared with the accented realizations of these words (the 'strong' forms), the unaccented ('weak' form) varieties of these words show reductions of the length of sounds, obscuration of vowels towards /ə, ɪ, ʊ/, and the elision of vowels and consonants. The following list of examples presents the most common of these words, first in their unaccented (normal) weak forms and secondly in their less usual[1] accented strong form:—

	Unaccented	*Accented*
a	/ə/	/eɪ/
am	/m, əm/	/æm/
an	/n, ən/	/æn/
and	/ənd, nd, ən, n/	/ænd/
are	/ə/ + consonant	/ɑː/
	/ər, r/ + vowel	/ɑːr/
as	/əz/	/æz/
at	/ət/	/æt/
be	/bɪ/([bi])	/biː/
been	/bɪn/	/biːn/ (also /bɪn/ for some speakers)

---

[1] The following 42 items occur in the first 200 most common words in connected speech: *the, you, I, to, and, a, that, we, of, have, is, are, for, at, he, but, there, do, as, be, them, will, me, was, can, him, had, your, been, from, my, or, she, by, some, her, his, us, an, am, has, shall*. It is significant that of these the following 19 have over 90% unaccented occurrences with a weak form: *at, of, the, to, as, and, or, a, his, an, but, been, for, her, we, be, shall, was, them*. Other items of rarer occurrence, such as *than*, only exceptionally occur with the strong form.

	Unaccented	Accented
but	/bət/	/bʌt/
can (aux.)	/kən, kn/	/kæn/
could	/kəd, kd/	/kʊd/
do (aux.)	/dʊ, də, d/	/duː/
does (aux.)	/dəz, z, s/	/dʌz/

(e.g. What's (= does) he like? /ˈwɒts iː ˈlaɪk/,
When's (= does) he arrive? /ˈwenz iː əˈraɪv/)

	Unaccented	Accented
for	/fə/ + consonant /fər, fr/ + vowel	/fɔː/ /fɔːr/
from	/frəm/	/frɒm/
had (aux.)[1]	/həd, əd, d/[2]	/hæd/
has (aux.)[1]	/həz, əz, z, s/[2]	/hæz/
have (aux.)[1]	/həv, əv, v/[2]	/hæv/
he	/hɪ, iː, ɪ/[2] ([hi])	/hiː/
her	/hə, ɜː, ə/[2]	/hɜː/
him	/ɪm/	/hɪm/
his	/ɪz/[2]	/hɪz/
is	/s, z/	/ɪz/
me	/mɪ/ ([mi])	/miː/
must	/məst/[3]	/mʌst/
not	/nt, n/	/nɒt/
of	/əv, v, ə/	/ɒv/
Saint	/sənt, snt, sən, sn/	/seɪnt/
shall	/ʃəl, ʃl/	/ʃæl/
she	/ʃɪ/ ([ʃi])	/ʃiː/
should	/ʃəd, ʃd/	/ʃʊd/
Sir	/sə/ + consonant /sər/ + vowel	/sɜː/ /sɜːr/
some (unspecified quantity)	/səm, sm/	/sʌm/
than	/ðən, ðn/	/ðæn/ (rare)
that (conj. and rel. pron.)[4]	/ðət/	/ðæt/ (rare)

---

[1] The distinction between auxiliary *have* and the main verb may be illustrated by examples such as *He considered what he* /həd/ *left* (weak form of auxiliary verb = what had been left by him) and *He considered what he* /hæd/ *left* (main verb, non-weakenable = what he still possessed).

[2] A weak form with /h/ would normally be used when unaccented but following a pause.

[3] *Often* /məs/ with elision of /t/. See §11.3.6.

[4] *That* as a demonstrative adjective or pronoun is always accented, e.g. *that man* /ˈðæt ˈmæn/, *that's the one* /ˈðæts ðə ˈwʌn/.

	Unaccented	*Accented*
the	/ðɪ/ ([ði]) + vowel	/ðiː/
	ðə/ + consonant	ʹʹ
them	/ðəm/ *also* /əm, m/	/ðəm/
there (indef. adv.)[1]	/ðə/ + consonant	/ðɛə/ (rare)
	/ðər/ + vowel	/ðɛər/ (rare)
to	/tə/ + consonant	/tuː/
	/tʊ/ + vowel	ʹʹ
us	/əs, s/	/ʌs/
was	/wəz/	/wɒz/
we	/wɪ/ ([wi])	/wiː/
were	/wə/ + consonant	/wɜː/
	/wər/ + vowel	/wɜːr/
who	/hʊ, uː, ʊ/ ([hu])[2]	/huː/
will	/l/	/wɪl/
would	/wəd, əd, d/	/wʊd/
you	/jʊ/ ([ju])	/juː/

It should be noted that verb forms such as *am, are, be, can, could, do, does, had, has, have, is, must, shall, was, were, will, would* retain a strong form when they occur finally even though they are unaccented, e.g. *Who's coming?* ʹ*I am* /æm/; *Who's got it?* ʹ*I have* /hæv/.

Similarly, prepositions, e.g. *to, from, at, for*, apart from having a strong form when receiving a primary (nuclear, tonic) accent, also have a qualitative prominence when final and unaccented, e.g. *Where have they gone to?* (/tuː/, also /tʊ/, but not /tə/); *Where's he come from?* (/frɒm/ rather than /frəm/); *What are you laughing for, at?* (/fɔː, æt/). This applies, too, when prepositions and auxiliary verbs occur finally in a rhythmic group including at a 'deletion site' where the following item is understood, e.g. *He* ʹ*looked at* /æt/ *and* ʹ*solved the* ʹ*problem*; or ʹ*people who can af*ʹ*ford* /tuː/ (sc. *do so*) ʹ*buy* ʹ*luxuries* cf. ʹ*People who can af*ʹ*ford* /tə/ ʹ*buy* ʹ*luxuries,* ʹ*do so*. When a preposition occurs before an unaccented pronoun, either the strong or the weak form may be used for the preposition, e.g. *I gave it to you* (/tə/ or /tuː/); *I've heard from him* (/frəm/ or /frɒm/); *I waited for you* (/fə/ or /fɔː/); *I looked at her* (/ət/ or /æt/).

Note, too, that certain form words, not normally possessing an alternative weak form for unaccented occurrences, may show such reductions in very rapid speech, e.g. *I* (/ə/) *don't know*; *What's your* (/jə/) *name?*; *I go by* (/bə/) *bus*; *Do you know my* (/mə/) *brother?*; *for*

---

[1] As a demonstrative adverb, *there* will be accented, e.g. *there's the book* /ʹðɛəz ðə bʊk/.

[2] A weak form with /h/ would normally be used when unaccented but following a pause.

love nor (/nə/) *money;*[1] *two or* (/ə/) *three;*[1] *ever so* (/sə/) *many.*[1] In the case of the disyllables *any, many*, a qualitative prominence may be retained on the first syllable under weak accent—/enɪ, menɪ/, but fully reduced, unaccented forms may be heard in rapid speech, e.g. *Have any more come?* /ˈhævnɪ ˈmɔː ˈkʌm/; *How many do you want?* /ˈhaʊ mnɪ djuː ˈwɒnt/. Other monosyllabic form words normally retain their strong vowels in relatively unaccented positions, e.g. *on, when, then, one*, but again, in very rapid speech, reduced vowel forms may be heard, especially when the word is adjacent to a strongly accented syllable, e.g. *What on* (/ən/ or /n̩/) *earth!*; *When* (/wən/) *all's said and done*; *Then* (/ðən/) *after a time*; *one* (/wən/) *always hopes.*

It may be said that the more rapid the delivery the greater the tendency to reduction and obscuration of unaccented words. Even monosyllabic content words may be reduced in rapid casual speech, if they occur in a relatively unaccented situation adjacent to a primary accent, and especially if they contain a short vowel, e.g. /ɪ/, *You sit over here* /ˈjuː s(ə)t ˌəʊvə ˈhɪə/; /ʊ/, *He put it there* /ˈhiː p(ə)t ɪt ˌðɛə/; /ʌ/, *He'll come back* /ˈhiːl k(ə)m ˌbæk/; /e/, *Don't get lost* /ˈdəʊnt g(ə)t ˈlɒst/; less frequently with the more prominent short vowels /æ, ɒ/, e.g. /æ/, *They all sat down on the floor* /ðeɪ ˈɔːl sət ˈdaʊn ən ðə ˈflɔː/; /ɒ/, *We want to go* /ˈwiː wənt tə ˌgəʊ/; and, finally, the diphthong /əʊ/, with its dominant central [ə] element, is readily reducible to /ə/ under weak accent, e.g. *You can't go with him* /jʊ ˈkɑːnt gə ˈwɪð ɪm/; *He's going to do it* /ˈhiːz gənə ˌduː ɪt/.

10.5 Intonation[2]

The meaning of an English utterance, i.e. the information it conveys to a listener, derives not only from its changing sound pattern and the contrastive, accentual prominences already referred to, but also from associated variations of pitch. Such rises and falls in pitch level, or patterns of *intonation*, have two main functions:—

(1) *Accentual.*—Intonation changes are the most efficient means of rendering prominent for a listener those parts of an utterance on which the speaker wishes to concentrate attention; pitch change is especially significant as a cue for signalling the word or words carrying primary (nuclear) accent. It should be remembered, however, that the accentual pattern of a response is often largely conditioned by constraints imposed by the context (see §10.2).

---

[1] These weak forms seem to be restricted to a limited number of phrases and, in the case of *or*, particularly occur in linking two forms as in the example given here.

[2] For a more complete treatment of intonation in these terms, see J. D. O'Connor and G. F. Arnold, *The Intonation of Colloquial English*, 1973, Longman, and works referred to in the bibliography under Palmer, Kingdon, Schubiger, Jassem, Lee, Crystal, Cruttenden.

(2) *Non-accentual.*—In addition, intonation is used as a means for distinguishing different types of sentence, e.g. the same sequence of words may, with a falling intonation, be interpreted as a statement or, with a rising intonation, as a question.[1] Moreover, a listener derives from a speaker's intonation information as to the latter's emotional attitude (to the listener or to the topic of a conversation) or personality, e.g. his intonation might reveal a patronizing attitude to the listener, an incredulous attitude to the topic or a querulous disposition. Furthermore, intonation has a complex linking function in dialogue and within the speech of a single speaker.

In so far as a listener interprets correctly those parts of an utterance upon which the speaker wishes to concentrate attention, or is aware of the speaker's attitude to him, or makes judgments upon the personality of the speaker, the pattern of intonation used may be said to constitute a linguistic system which has a communicative function within a particular community. There seems no doubt that intonation in its accentual function and in that non-accentual function concerned with the distinction of sentence types, does constitute a linguistic reality of this kind. Since, however, we sometimes misinterpret the emotional attitude as conveyed by intonation, it may be said that non-accentual intonation patterns of this kind are less perfectly systematized, or that such linguistic systems are more numerous and applicable to smaller communities (regional or social) than phonological systems, so that a faulty judgment of emotional attitudes conveyed by intonation cues may derive from an interpretation of these cues in terms of our own, different, intonation usage in showing such attitudes (cf. the interpretative adjustments needed on the phonological level between speakers of two different types of English).

10.5.1   The Accentual or Emphatic Function of Intonation

The various degrees of accentuation in an utterance may be signalled by means of intonation in the following way:—

- (a) *Primary* (*nuclear*) *accent*—by means of a change of pitch *direction* initiated by the syllable receiving the accent (marked ˎ , ˋ , ˏ , ˊ , ˇ , ˆ).
- (b) *Secondary* (*pitch prominent*) *accent*—by means of a change of pitch *level* (higher or lower) on the accented syllable (marked ˈ).
- (c) *Secondary accent without pitch prominence*[2]—secondary accent on some words may be manifested by qualitative, quantitative, or rhythmic prominence, without pitch prominence (marked ˌ).

---

[1] It should be noted that this is not meant as a generalization about the intonation of questions: as such it would be an over-simplification. See §10.5.3.

[2] Such accentuation is regarded by some as *stress* rather than *accent*.

(*d*) *Unaccented syllables*—do not normally have pitch or other prominence and are unmarked (see, however, §10.5.4).

10.5.1.1 Realization of Primary Accent

The primary accent (or accents) in a sentence is shown by initiating a change of pitch direction, with the *nucleus* (carrying a falling or rising tone or a combination of the two) on the appropriate syllable of the word (or words) on which attention is particularly to be concentrated. The *situation* of the nucleus or nuclei is, therefore, of prime importance in conveying meaning, e.g. compare the meanings of the following sentence according to the shift of nucleus:—

(*a*) `Jack ˌlikes ˌfish (i.e. not George, but Jack)

(*b*) ˌJack `likes ˌfish (i.e. there is no question of his *hating* fish)

(*c*) ˌJack ˌlikes `fish (i.e. not meat or poultry, etc.)

or again, the meanings of (*a*) and (*c*) may be combined in

`Jack ˌlikes `fish

In the sense that the nuclear syllable stands out from amongst its neighbours (both accented and unaccented syllables), the nucleus and its situation may be said to have a special contrastive function, a function of emphasizing a particular part of an utterance and thus focusing attention on it. But it may happen that special contrastive prominence is not attached to any of ·the accented syllables of a sentence—this is more common in reading than in normal speech, in which it is usual for one or more words in a sentence to be 'pointed'. Where no word is specially contrasted, the nuclear change of pitch direction will be initiated by the last accented syllable, e.g.:-

By the ˈtime we ˈgot to the ˌhouse, we were ˈall ˈwet ˌthrough.

In a more animated style, more typical of conversation, the same sentence might have nuclear pitch changes on several accented syllables, e.g.:—

By the `time we `got to the ˆhouse, we were `all ˌwet `through.

The way in which the change of pitch direction is realized depends on the type of change involved and on the nature and extent of the phonological sequence covered.

10.5.1.2   Types of Nuclear Tone

(1) *The falling nuclear tone* (ˏ, ˋ).—The falling glide may start from the highest pitch of the speaking voice and fall to the lowest pitch (in the case of the *high-fall*), or from a mid pitch to the lowest pitch (in the case of the *low-fall*), or with variation of starting point according to the intonation context. The falling glide is most perceptible when it takes place on a syllable containing a long vowel or diphthong or a voiced continuant (e.g. /m, n, ŋ, l, z/, etc.), e.g.:—

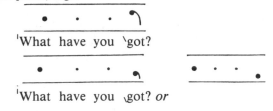

ˋNo.   He ˈcouldn't be ˏseen.   It was ˋraining.

When a fall occurs on a syllable containing a short vowel with its limits formed by fortis, voiceless consonants (especially the stops /p, t, k/), the glide, particularly of a low-fall, is so rapid that it is not easily perceptible, or may be realized merely as a low level pitch in relation to a preceding higher pitch, e.g.:—

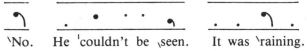

ˈWhat have you ˋgot?

but   ˈWhat have you ˏgot? *or*

Again, when syllables follow the nucleus—the *tail*—the fall may be realized as the juxtaposition of relatively high pitch on the nuclear syllable and low pitches on the syllables of the tail, e.g.:—

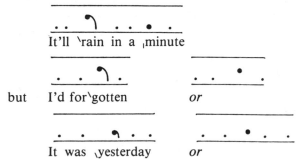

It'll ˋrain in a ˌminute

but   I'd forˋgotten   *or*

It was ˏyesterday   *or*

(2) *The rising nuclear tone* (ˏ, ˊ).—In the same way, a rising glide, which may extend from low to mid, or from mid to high, or with other variations of starting and end points between low and high, is more easily perceptible when it occurs on a syllable containing a long vowel or diphthong or a voiced continuant consonant, e.g.:—

ˏNo. ˈCan you ˏsee? He's ˌnot ˏill.

When a low-rising glide occurs on a short syllable, it must necessarily be accomplished much more rapidly, or may merely consist of a relatively high level pitch in relation to a preceding low pitch, or even of a slightly lowered level pitch in relation to a preceding mid or high pitch, e.g.:—

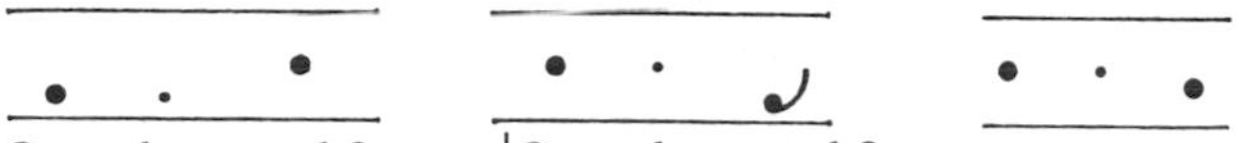

ˌCan she ˏcook? ˈCan she ˏcook? *or*

With a tail, the rise is achieved by means of a relatively low pitch on the nuclear syllable with an ascending scale on the following syllables, e.g.:—

ˈIs it ˏraining? ˈAre you ˏcomfortable?

(3) *The falling-rising nuclear tone* (ˇ).—The fall and rise may be confined within one syllable, the glide beginning at about mid level and ending at the same level (or slightly above or below); in the case of a short syllable, the dip in pitch is made extremely rapidly and may be realized as an instant of 'creaky' voice or even of cessation of voice, e.g.:—

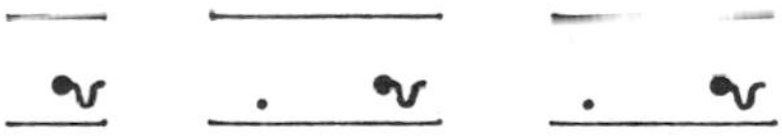

ˇNo. It's ˇtrue. It's ˇshut.

When an unaccented tail follows the nuclear syllable, the fall occurs on the nuclear syllable and the rise is spread over the tail, e.g.:—

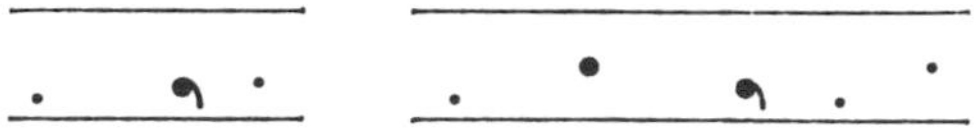

It's ˇraining. It's ˈquite ˇcomfortable.

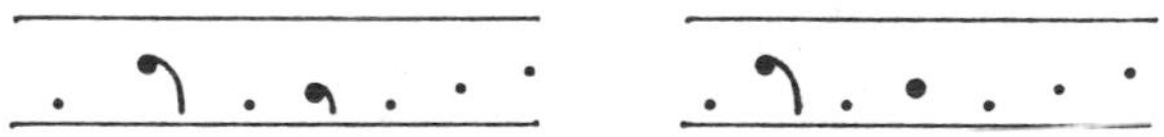

It's ˋnot a ˇcaterpillar *or*

When a secondary accent follows the primary (nuclear) accent, the fall takes place on the nuclear syllable and the rise is initiated on the syllable carrying the secondary accent, e.g.:—

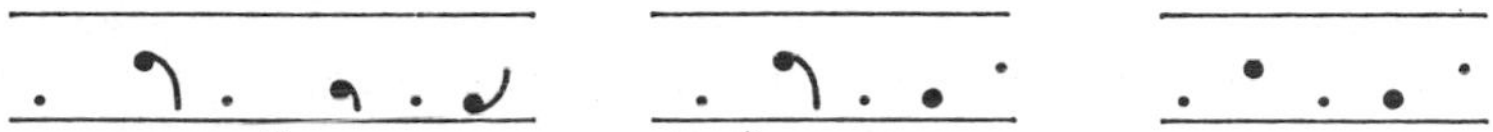

He ˋdidn't ˇtelephone. He's ˇeducated *or*

In a longer utterance, the rise begins on the last stressed syllable of the tail. What amounts to the same pattern may occur where, within the same group, a word containing a falling syllable is followed by a word containing a rising syllable, both syllables carrying a primary accent, e.g.:—

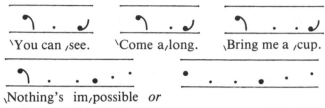

ˋYou can ˌsee.   ˋCome aˌlong.   ˌBring me a ˌcup.

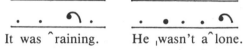

ˌNothing's imˌpossible   *or*

(4) *Rising reinforcement of a fall* (ˆ).—A fall may be reinforced by an introductory rise, especially on a long syllable containing voiced continuant consonants (which may be given extra length), e.g.:—

It was ˆraining.   He ˌwasn't aˆlone.

A reinforced short syllable followed by a tail may be realized as a low accented nuclear syllable followed by a fall on the tail, e.g.:—

You'd   ˆbetter.   It was ˆyesterday.

When such reinforcement occurs on the falling part of a divided fall-rise (i.e. when the rise is situated on a later word), it has the effect of focusing attention on the falling nucleus, e.g.:—

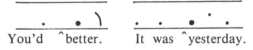

ˆYou can ˌsee   *or*

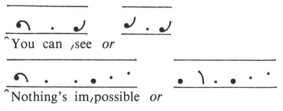

ˆNothing's imˌpossible   *or*

(5) In a running dialogue, more than half of the nuclear tones may be expected to be of the falling type, followed in frequency by the fall-rise or divided fall-rise, and finally the rises. The actual proportion of tone types will, of course, depend to a certain extent upon the style of the conversation and the emotional attitudes of the speakers. See §11.6.

10.5.1.3 Realization of Secondary Accent

(1) *Pre-nuclear.*—Syllables preceding the nucleus may have *pitch prominence* (secondary accent, marked ') through being given a high level pitch when initial or a high level pitch in relation to preceding syllables, e.g.:—

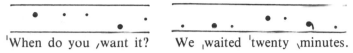

'When do you ,want it?   We ,waited 'twenty ,minutes.

The first pre-nuclear accented syllable has been called the *head* (a 'high head' if given pitch prominence as above); any syllables occurring between the head and the nucleus are then said to constitute the *body*. Alternatively, many would define the *head* as the stretch of speech from the first accented syllable up to (but not including) the nucleus. The term *body* would then be discarded. Accented syllables within the body (or further syllables within the head) may be given pitch prominence by means of a step down in pitch, e.g.:—

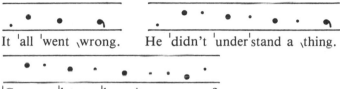

It 'all 'went ,wrong.   He 'didn't 'under'stand a ,thing.

'Can you 'let me 'have it to,morrow?

Additional pitch prominence may also be given to an accented syllable in the body,[1] in a sequence of such accented syllables, by means of a step up (marked"), thus constituting in effect a supplementary head, e.g.:—

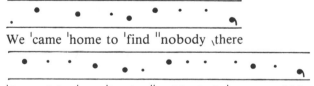

We 'came 'home to 'find "nobody ,there

'One of the 'two 'lorries "suddenly be'gan to , skid.

Such a pattern of pitch accentuation would have the effect of giving special prominence to *nobody* and *suddenly*. Alternative intonation patterns would divide these sentences into two groups:—

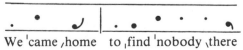

We 'came ,home   to ,find 'nobody ,there

---

[1] i.e. within the head in most terminology.

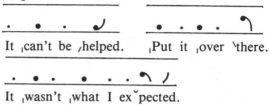

'One of the 'two ˌlorries 'suddenly beˈgan to ˌskid.

Pre-nuclear syllables may also be accented *without pitch prominence*, i.e. they are accented only for reasons of rhythmical stress, quality, or quantity, or because of the content nature of the word (marked ˌ, whether high or low in pitch). They may be the only accented syllables before the nucleus and be said on a relatively low level pitch (a 'low head'), e.g.:—

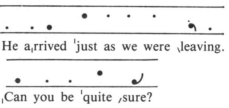

It ˌcan't be ˌhelped.   ˌPut it ˌover ˈthere.

It ˌwasn't ˌwhat I exˇpected.

If such syllables precede a high head, they are relatively low and level, e.g.:—

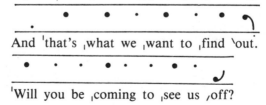

He aˌrrived 'just as we were ˌleaving.

ˌCan you be 'quite ˌsure?

(the high head on *just* and *quite* giving these words special prominence).

If such syllables occur within the body (or head), they are kept on about the same pitch as the preceding pitch-prominent syllable, e.g.:—

And 'that's ˌwhat we ˌwant to ˌfind ˈout.

'Will you be ˌcoming to ˌsee us ˌoff?

(2) *Post-nuclear.*—After a falling nucleus, a secondary accent is manifested by rhythmic, qualitative, or quantitative prominence, the pitch remaining low (marked ˌ), e.g.:—

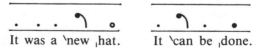

It was a ˈnew ˌhat.   It ˈcan be ˌdone.

After a rising nucleus, however, syllables carrying secondary accent (also marked ˌ) continue on a rising pitch, e.g.:—

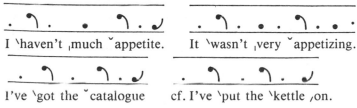

'Did you ,see him ,yesterday?   ,I didn't ,think it was ,funny.

When final, they may have a certain additional pitch prominence, e.g.:—

'Does he ,like ,dogs?   'Did you 'see how ,pale he ,looked?

cf. 'Have you 'put the ,kettle ,on? *and* 'Have you 'got the ,catalogue?

In the case of a falling-rising nucleus (whether on a single word where a secondary accent falls on the final syllable or in cases where the rise takes place on a following word), the pitch prominence (consisting of a rise) is very considerable, e.g.:—

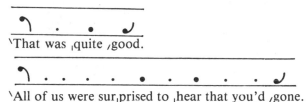

I ˋhaven't ,much ˇappetite.   It ˋwasn't ,very ˇappetizing.

I've ˋgot the ˇcatalogue   cf. I've ˋput the ˋkettle ,on.

(3) *Secondary accent between fall and rise.*—Syllables carrying secondary accent, without pitch prominence, may occur between a fall and a rise; in this case, the unaccented syllables and those carrying secondary accent have a relatively low level pitch, e.g.:—

ˋThat was ,quite ,good.

ˋAll of us were sur,prised to ,hear that you'd ,gone.

10.5.1.4 Realization of Unaccented Syllables

Unaccented syllables, in addition to the fact that they are said very rapidly and usually undergo some obscuration of their quality, do not normally have any pitch prominence. They may occur before the head, before the nucleus, or after the nucleus.

(1) *Pre-nuclear.*—Unaccented syllables occurring before a nucleus (without a head), like syllables carrying secondary accent without pitch

prominence, are normally relatively low, whether the nucleus is a fall or a rise, e.g.:—

It's ˋnot.   There were ˋtwo of them *or*

And ˌthen, —.   There were eˌleven.   And ˌwhen we aˌrrived, —.

Unaccented syllables before a high head are usually said on a relatively low pitch, the head having contrastive prominence in relation to them, e.g.:—

He's ˈalways ˌlate.   It was ˈafter ˌdinner, —.

If pre-nuclear unaccented syllables, their weak quality remaining, are said on a relatively high pitch (marked ⁻), the effect is more emphatic and animated than if they are low in pitch; the utterance may have a specially bright, lively, encouraging character before a rise, or an indignant, quarrelsome note before a fall,[1] e.g.:—

(lively)   ⁻It ˌis.   ⁻There were ˌnine of us.

(indignant)   ⁻It ˋis.   ⁻There were ˋnine of us.

(2) *After first accented syllable.*—Within the body, unaccented syllables remain on almost the same pitch as the preceding accented syllable, e.g.:—

ˈAll of us ˈwanted to ˌhelp him.   ˈPut it ˈon the ˌtable.

ˈWill you be ˈable to ˈcome toˌmorrow?

If the unaccented syllables are on a higher pitch than the preceding accented syllables, a special impression of liveliness, eagerness, impatience, or encouragement is again produced, e.g.:—

---

[1] But over-generalization is to be avoided.

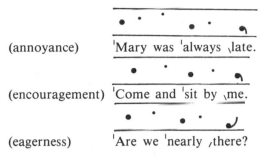

(annoyance) 'Mary was 'always ˌlate.

(encouragement) 'Come and 'sit by ˌme.

(eagerness) 'Are we 'nearly ˌthere?

It is to be noted that in these cases the accented syllables within the body receive extra relative pitch-prominence, the pattern being equivalent to a series of rising nuclei.

(3) *Post-nuclear.*—Unaccented syllables following a falling nucleus remain on a low level, e.g.:—

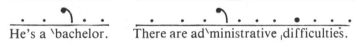

He's a ˋbachelor.   There are adˋministrative ˌdifficulties.

After a rising nucleus, unaccented syllables continue (or effect) the rise (the last syllable of all having a short rising glide sometimes, which gives it an extra prominence without contrastive significance), e.g.:—

'Put it 'on the ˌtable.   It's ˌnot imˌpossible.

ˌHas he ˌgot a soˈlicitor?

The rise of a falling-rising nucleus may be spead over the following unaccented syllables, e.g.:—

He 'doesn't 'like ˇcriticism.

Between a fall and a rise, unaccented syllables remain relatively low, e.g.:—

ˋYesterday was ˌfine.

10.5.2   The Grammatical and Attitudinal Functions of Intonation

As was pointed out in §10.5, intonation, in addition to its function of providing a means of accentuation (or emphatic focus), may also serve to distinguish sentence types (e.g. statement and question) and to indicate the emotional attitude of the speaker. Such functions apply equally to utterances consisting of more than one word and to those of a single word (of one or more syllables). In these cases, it is not so much the situation of the nucleus which is of importance, but rather the type of nuclear tone employed, i.e. whether a fall, rise-fall, rise, or fall-rise is used. Thus, a statement form of words may be made into a question if a rise is used instead of a fall, e.g. 'He's ˈnot ˌthere' (statement) *v.* 'He's ˌnot ˈthere?' (question); or, in such a case as that quoted by H. E. Palmer,[1] the sentence 'He doesn't lend his books to anybody' may have two meanings according to whether *anybody* is said with a falling nucleus (i.e. he lends them to nobody) or with a falling-rising nucleus (i.e. he does lend them to some people). This semantic function of intonation (typified by the last example) occurs less frequently than that which shows the speaker's emotional attitude: compare, for instance, 'It's ˈall ˌright' (a plain statement of fact), 'It's ˈall ˌright' (an encouragement), and 'It's ˌall ˌright' (a grudging or petulant agreement). In this connection, in addition to the type of nuclear tone used, the pitch of that part of the utterance preceding the nucleus (the head) is also of great importance (and sometimes the pitch of unaccented syllables— see §10.5.1.4(1)).

In the examples given in the following sections, an attempt is made to assign generalized verbal descriptions to the attitudes conveyed by intonation patterns in respect of various types of utterance; the main types of utterance are:—

(*a*) assertions
(*b*) questions containing an interrogative word (X-questions, also called wh-questions or open questions)
(*c*) questions expecting 'Yes' or 'No' as an answer (Yes/No questions, also called closed questions)
(*d*) question tags
(*e*) commands, requests, etc.
(*f*) exclamations, greetings, etc.

The examples are given as isolated utterances, but it should be remembered that the attitudinal meaning of an utterance must always be interpreted within a context, both of the situation (see also §10.5.3 below) and also of the speaker's personality. It may well happen that an intonation which is neutral in one set of circumstances might be, for instance, offensive or patronizing when used by another person or in other circumstances.

----

[1] See H. E. Palmer, *English Intonation with systematic exercises*, Heffer, 1922; also W. R. Lee, *An English Intonation Reader*, Macmillan, 1960.

10.5.2.1 Falling Nuclear Tones

A falling nuclear tone, whether ˎ or ˋ, is generally matter-of-fact, separative, and assertive, the higher the fall the more vigorous the degree of finality implied. No explicit appeal is made to the listener, yet the pattern is not necessarily impolite; a conversation amongst people who are intimately acquainted might, for instance, exhibit a preponderance of falling intonations, without the exchange being querulous or lacking the social courtesies of speech.

(1) *Low-falling nuclear tone*

Pattern—nucleus (tail)

(*a*) ˎNo. ˎYesterday (detached, unexcited)

(*b*) ˎWhen? (curt) ˎHow are you ˌgoing to ˌdo it? (weak insistence on *how*)

(*c*) ˎAre you ˌcoming?[1] ˎDoes he ˌwant to?[1] (curt, impatient, testy)

(*d*) (He ˎdoes,) ˎdoesn't he? (ˎLovely,) ˎisn't it? (calmly presupposing agreement)

(*e*) ˎCount them. ˎGet it ˌthen (calm, detached, peremptory)

(*f*) ˎTragic! (quietly sympathetic; or distant and unmoved, especially if the fall does not reach the lowest level); ˎMorning (perfunctory)

Pattern—high head, nucleus (tail), the high pre-nuclear pattern showing a degree of lively interest.

(*a*) The ˈparcel aˈrrived on ˎThursday (matter-of-fact, but interested)

(*b*) ˈWhat do you ˈwant to ˎdo? (blunt to strangers, but a common unemotional form amongst intimates)

(*c*) ˈAre you ˎgoing? (peremptory, impatient)

(*e*) ˈPut it ˈover ˎthere (polite, neutral)

(*f*) ˈWhat a ˎmess (phlegmatic, mild)

ˈ(ˉ) Good ˎmorning (the high pitch on *good*, whether it is an accented head or an unaccented high pre-nuclear syllable, makes the greeting pleasant, though routine)

Pattern—low head, nucleus (tail); the low pre-nuclear pattern throws the nucleus into greater prominence and often shows lack of interest.

(*a*) It's ˌall we could exˎpect (surly, uninterested)

(*b*) ˌWhat are we ˌgoing to ˎdo? (resigned, bored)

(*c*) ˌHave you ˌgot the ˎtickets? (uninvolved, perfunctory)

(*e*) ˌLeave it ˌon the ˎtable (preoccupied, expecting to be obeyed as a matter of course)

---

[1] The insistence or curtness here is caused partly by the placement of the nucleus on the auxiliary verb. It should be noted that nucleus placement and choice of nuclear tone are separable variables.

(*f*) ˌHow aˎnnoying (bored, unconcerned, sarcastic)
ˌGood ˎmorning (routine, perfunctory greeting)

(2) *High-falling nuclear tone.*—Animated; may be strongly contrastive or contradictory; often showing strong indignation or excitement; very common in ordinary colloquial speech.

Pattern.—(pre-head), nucleus (tail).
(*a*) ˋNo. It ˋwas. Of ˋcourse it ˌisn't (vigorous agreement or contradiction)
(*b*) ˋWhy? ˋHow ˌcan she? (surprise, indignation, incredulity)
(*c*) Do ˋyou ˌlike it? You're ˋsure? (insistence, demands as answer)
(*d*) (She ˋdoesn't), ˋdoes she? (He ˋdoes), ˋdoesn't he? (demands agreement)
(*e*) ˋDrop it. ˋCancel it ˌthen (energetic, angry command)
(*f*) ˋWhat a surˌprise! (strong surprise, indignation)
ˋGood ˌmorning (hearty greeting)

Pattern.—low head, nucleus (tail); a high-falling nuclear tone usually depends for its effect on a relatively low pattern of any preceding syllables, all the accentual force being concentrated in the nucleus; the following sentences said with high heads (and bodies) would have less contrast associated with the nuclear word.
(*a*) ˌNot at ˋall. I ˌquite aˋgree.
(*b*) ˌWhy do you ˋwant it?
(*c*) ˌCan we ˌhave it ˋnow?
(*e*) ˌGo and ˋfind it.
(*f*) ˌWhat a ˌstupid misˋtake!
ˌGood ˋmorning (a bright, cheerful greeting)

(3) *Rising-falling nuclear tone.*—The initial rise may reinforce the meaning of any high fall, often with additional warmth, indignation, sarcasm, etc. A preceding head will usually be relatively low.

Pattern—(low head) nucleus (tail).
(*a*) ˆYes. It was aˆpalling. Aˌbout ˆtime (all may show enthusiastic agreement or enthusiasm; but 'ˆYes', said slowly, expresses doubt, /ˆpɔːl/, prolonged, shows horror, and 'ˆtime' may reveal sarcasm or indignation)
(*b*) ˌWhat does his ˆfather ˌdo? (suspicious, indignant interest)
(*c*) ˌCan you be ˆsure (mocking, knowing, suspicious)
(*d*) ˆIs she? ˆDoesn't he? (incredulous, mocking, indignant)
(*e*) ˌGet aˆnother one (pert, haughty, sulky, indignant)
(*f*) ˌOh, inˆdeed. ˌHow ˆnice for you (sarcastic)
ˌGood ˆmorning (portentous, ironical greeting)

10.5.2.2 Rising Nuclear Tones

(1) *Low-rising nuclear tone.*—Essentially unfinished and continuative, often with overtones of politeness, encouragement, pleading, diffidence, suspicion, etc.

Pattern—nucleus (tail).
- (*a*) ˌNo. ˌPossibly (tentative, grudging, encouraging). Note also the introductory usage: 'ˌThen,—,' and adverbially after a main clause: '(We were aˋlone), ˌluckily.'
- (*b*) ˌHow did you ˌdo it? (insistence on 'How'—the lower the starting point of the rise, the greater the insistence)
- (*c*) ˌAre they ˌcoming? (insistence on 'Are')
  ˌIs he? (doubtful, indifferent)
- (*d*) (He's ˋgot one), ˌhasn't he? (It isn't ˋthere), ˌis it? (doubtful, asking for information)
- (*e*) ˌWait. ˌHold it (gentle command or request)
- (*f*) ˌWell (introducing a topic, or an uninterested question form)

Pattern—high head, nucleus (tail); a relatively high pre-nuclear pattern gives an effect of a fresh thought, lively interest, appeal, encouragement, etc.
- (*a*) It's ˈall ˌright. It ˈdoesn't ˌmatter. She ˈwon't be ˌlong (reassuring statements). Also dependent clauses occurring before the main clause, e.g. 'ˈWhen we aˌrrived, (they'd alˈready ˏgone)'; following a main clause containing a falling nucleus, the pre-nuclear pattern of this dependent clause is likely to be low, e.g. '(They'd alˈready ˏgone), ˌwhen we aˌrrived'.
- (*b*) ˈWhat's the ˌtime? (polite inquiry)
- (*c*) ˈCan you ˌcome? (polite, interested)
- (*e*) ˈSit ˌdown. ˈCome over ˌhere (pleasant, encouraging invitation)
- (*f*) ˈAllˈthe ˌbest. ˈGood ˌluck (cheerful good wishes). ˈGood ˌmorning (cheerful, friendly greeting)

Pattern—low head, nucleus (tail); a relatively low pre-nuclear pattern often signifies complaint, suspicion, veiled threat, lack of interest or enthusiasm, etc.
- (*a*) It's ˌall ˌright. It's ˌnot imˌportant (resigned, disgruntled, long-suffering, bored). Also in dependent clauses, before or after the main clause, e.g. "If ˌJack's ˌhome, (we'll ˌcome at ˋeight)'; '(We'll ˌcome at ˋeight), if ˌJack's ˌhome'; in the first case, 'ˌJack' has not the contrastive accentual force which would be associated with 'ˈJack'.
- (*b*) ˌWhat have you been ˌdoing? (unsympathetic, menacing, threatening)
  ˌWhat's your ˌname? (peremptory, routine cross-examination)
- (*c*) ˌCan you ˌcome ˌnext ˌweek? (uninterested, disgruntled, bored)

(*e*) ˌTry aˌgain (routine request, peremptory)
    ˌDon't ˌleave the ˌdoor ˌopen (long-suffering, complaining)
(*f*) ˌGood ˌmorning (polite but perfunctory greeting)

(2) *High-rising nuclear tone.*—This nuclear tone, rising to a high pitch, is associated essentially with questions, e.g.:—

(i) An elliptical question (showing eagerness, brightness, enthusiasm, or asking for a repetition):—
ˌCoffee? (= 'Will you have some more coffee?' or 'Did you say coffee?')
ˌLike it? (= 'Do you like it?')
ˌMonday? (= 'What about Monday?' or 'Did you say Monday?')
ˌJohn? (= 'I'm calling you—are you there?' or 'Is that you, John?' or 'Did you say "John"?')
ˌWhen? (= 'Would you repeat what you said?')

(ii) A question showing great eagerness, excitement, concern, indignation, etc.:—
It ˌis? ˈYou ˌdid? (surprise, incredulity)
ˌCan you ˌcome? (eager expectancy)
You ˌactually ˌsaw him? ˌWhat ˌme? (indignation, surprise, horror)
ˌCan we aˌfford it? (concern, expectancy, apprehension)
It ˈwasn't ˌyours! (dismay, surprise, indignation)

10.5.2.3 Falling-Rising Nuclear Tones

The falling-rising nuclear tone combines the dominant effect of the fall (contradictory, contrastive) with any of the emotional or meaningful attitudes (not expressed verbally) associated with the rise. Both fall and rise may occur within one word, e.g.:—

Pattern—(accented or unaccented pre-nuclear syllables), nuclear word (tail).
(*a*)   ˇNo (doubtful or encouraging)
        He ˇcould (forcefully reproachful)
        ˇSometimes (encouraging)
        I ˈhaven't ˈmuch ˇappetite ('but I'll join you to be polite'; if the pre-nuclear pattern is low, the effect is less agreeable—disgruntled)
        I'm ˇwaiting ('so do hurry up')
        ˇLately, (it's been ˌtoo ˈwet) (lively, introductory, continuative)
        If he ˇcould, (we'd be delighted) (forceful dependent clause)
(*b*)   ˇWhen? ˇHow? (forceful, encouraging, prompting)

(*e*), (*f*) ˇJohn! ˇLook! (an appealing, inviting summons)
    ˇGently! (encouraging, soothing, warning)

or the fall and the rise may occur on different, accented, words, e.g.:—

Pattern—(accented or unaccented pre-nuclear syllables), word containing fall (intervening syllables, with or without accent), word containing rise (tail)

(*a*) ˎHe ˏcould ('but I doubt whether *you* could')
    It ˌwasn't ˎyour ˏfault (reasoning, sympathetic)
    ˎThat's the ˌway to ˏdo it (encouraging, pleasant)
    (He'll ˎhave to), ˎone ˏday (insistence on *one*, followed by the rise of the dependent clause)
    On ˎSaturday ˏmorning, (we'll be ˌgoing ˎout) (contrastive fall on *Saturday* followed by continuative, introductory rise)

(*b*) ˎWhen can you ˏcome? (a polite questioning rise, preceded by a fall on *when* to insist on the precise time)

(*c*) Will ˎyou be ˌcoming on ˏSunday? (a polite questioning rise, preceded by a fall on *you* to focus attention on *your* intended action)
    ˎCan ˏyou? (insistence on your *ability* to do something associated with the polite questioning rise)

(*e*) ˎDo ˌsit ˏdown. ˎSee if you ˏcan (pressing request)
    ˎMind ˌhow you ˏgo (strong but sympathetic warning)

(*f*) ˎWell ˏdone! (warm, sympathetically appreciative)

10.5.2.4 Multi-nuclear Patterns

It often happens that, in addition to the composite nuclear patterns consisting of a fall + a rise, a number of nuclei occur in a single syntactic group. Such a series of nuclear syllables, often occurring rhythmically at equal intervals of time, may produce an effect of a categoric, downright, hectoring, insistent, self-assertive way of speaking. Nevertheless, such multi-nuclear patterns are extremely common in ordinary conversation and often serve no other purpose than to produce a lively, animated effect and to focus attention on the important words of an utterance, e.g.:—

(1) *A series of falling nuclear tones preceding a fall.*—An emphatic equivalent of a head (+ body) + falling nucleus.

(*a*) We ˎnever ˎthought he ˎhad a ˎchance
    It was ˎall we could ˎdo to ˎstop him

(*b*) ˎWhat do you ˎthink we can ˎdo?

(*c*) ˎCan she ˎdo the ˎwork?

(e) ˋDon't be ˋsuch a ˋfool
ˋGo and ˋtry aˋgain.
(f) ˋWhat an ˋawful ˋmess. ˌGood ˋafterˋnoon

(2) *A series of falling nuclear tones preceding a rise.*—An emphatic equivalent of a head (+ body) + rising nucleus (or fall-rise).
(a) I ˋalways ˋthought he ˌwould
I was ˋmost imˋpressed that ˋthey should ˌwant to
It ˋlooks as ˋblack as ˋnight ˌoutˇside
(b) ˋHow many ˋseats were you ˋable to ˌget?
(c) Are you ˋsure that ˋGeorge and ˋMary ˌknow?
(e) ˋMind you ˋput your ˋhat and ˋcoat ˌon
ˋCome and ˋsee us ˋwhen you ˇcan
(f) ˋWhat a ˋvery ˋsilly ˌlittle ˌboy!

(3) *A series of rising nuclear tones preceding a fall.*—An emphatic, impatient, or patronizing equivalent of a head (+ body) + falling nucleus.
(a) And ˌnow you ˌboth must ˌgo to ˋbed (decisive, but humouring)
It's ˌonly ˌin your ˌown ˋinterests (strongly persuasive, somewhat impatient)
(b) ˌWhat on ˌearth do you ˌthink you're ˋdoing?
(c) ˌCan you exˌpect them to ˌdo it aˋlone?
(e) ˌDon't be ˌsuch a ˌsilly ˋfool!
(The last three examples showing impatience, exasperation.)

(4) *A series of rising nuclear tones preceding a rise.*—A repetitive indication of the attitudes associated with a rising nuclear tone (appeal, complaint, sarcasm, etc.), being the equivalent of a head (+ body) + low rise.
(a) You ˌknow we ˌonly ˌwanted to ˌhelp (patronizing, grudging)
(b) ˌWhen were you ˌthinking of ˌpaying it ˌback? (patronizing, sarcastic)
(c) ˌWill you be ˌcoming to ˌsee us on ˌMonday? (apprehensive, unenthusiastic)
(e) ˌDon't ˌmake ˌsuch a ˌnoise! (quietly pleading, the appeal being stronger as a result of the succession of rises)
The same sentences said with a series of higher rises would give an effect of greater animation, excitement, urgency, etc.

10.5.2.5 Other Devices for Signalling Attitudes

Many other devices exist for expressing in sound the mood of a speaker in addition to the actual words which he uses. A rapid rate of delivery, for instance, may express irritation or urgency, whereas a slower rate may show hesitancy, doubt, or boredom in statements, or sympathy or encouragement in questions and commands; a repeated alveolar click denotes discontent; an egressive voiceless air-stream with friction at the rounded lips and a falling pitch (produced by the adjustment of the mouth cavity by movement of the tongue) expresses surprise, admiration, relief, whereas an ingressive air-stream of the same type may, in addition, be used to signify pain or pleasurable anticipation; and the utterance may be punctuated by sighs, denoting boredom, impatience, or sorrow. The intonation of a sentence, however, may indicate attitudes of the speaker other than those associated with the type of nucleus used or the choice of a relatively low or high pre-nuclear pattern of syllables:—

(1) *Range of intonation.*—The degree of enthusiasm, liveliness, interest, in those tunes where the pre-nuclear pattern is relatively high will be greater the higher the pitch of the head, e.g. with an extra-high pitch on the syllable italicized in the following examples and a consequent greater pitch separation of any accented syllables between the head and nucleus:—

(*a*) It's 'aw*fully* ˌgood
'*Eve*ryone 'thought it was ˌmarvellous
It's '*not* as 'bad as you ˌthink
(*b*) '*What's* the ˌtime?
(*c*) '*Are* you ˌsure?
(*e*) '*Look* at ˌthat
(*f*) '*Well* I ˌnever
'*Good* 'afterˌnoon

(2) *Continuous level pitch.*—In certain situations (excluding the monotonous chant of prayers sometimes heard in church), a continuous level pitch may be used to express a curt, detached, preoccupied attitude, which may give the impression of overbearing superiority if the pitch is relatively high, or of surly impatience if the pitch is relatively low:—

ˌThat'll be ˌall.   It's ˌnot a ˌbit of ˌgood
ˌWhat do you ˌwant?   ˌAre you ˌcoming?
ˌCome ˌin.   ˌHow do you ˌdo?
(The accented syllables are here marked with ˌˌ, since, whether they are high or low, they do not have pitch prominence.)

10.5.3 The Discourse Function of Intonation[1]

As was pointed out in §10.5, intonation has a complex linking function in dialogue and within the extended connected speech of a single speaker. To some extent this function may be seen as overlapping with the grammatical function, differing syntactic structures which consist

---

[1] This is too large a topic to go into in detail here. Much research is currently being carried out in the field: see entries in the bibliography under Brazil, Couper-Kuhlen, Gussenhoven, House, Ladd.

of the same sequence of words tending to display different intonation patterns, e.g. 'He re'signed ˌsadly' (= the speaker is sorry to report someone else's resignation) *v.* 'He re'signed ˋsadly' (= the man who resigned was sad to do so). However, varying intonation is a matter not only of syntax but also of pragmatics which is concerned with the interpretation of utterances. So, for instance, it may be true on occasion that 'He's ˋfinished' (with a falling nuclear tone) is a statement whilst 'He's ˌfinished' (with a rising nuclear tone) has the force of a question. However, in some particular conversational context, the version with a rising nuclear tone might be a defensive statement: 'He's ˌfinished' (so why are you complaining?).

10.6   Advice to Foreign Learners

Of all the features of accent in connected speech, the foreign learner should pay particular attention to:—

(1) The choice of words upon which the speaker's stress and accent (primary and secondary) fall and the situation of the nucleus. This placing of the accent in connected speech will usually be determined by the meaning which is to be conveyed, subject to the constraints imposed by the context and total situation.

(2) The rhythmic nature of connected English. The accented syllables follow each other at roughly equal intervals of time; any intervening unaccented syllables are said rapidly, the greater the number of such syllables the more rapidly they are uttered; unaccented syllables are associated with the hub of an accented syllable, so that an utterance is divisible into a series of rhythmic groups, themselves closely related usually to syntactic groups.

(3) The related weakening of unaccented words, e.g. the appropriate use of weak forms. A strong form in what is intended to be an unaccented position will give an impression of accent to the English ear. Thus, *He was late*, pronounced /hiː wɒz ˈleɪt/ instead of /hɪ (or [hi]) wəz ˈleɪt/, gives undue prominence to *was* and may appear to contradict some such statement as *He wasn't late*.

He should also be aware of the attitudinal implications of pitch variation. Frequently, the tunes used in English to distinguish sentence types will, in their broad pattern, be similar to those of his own language; but he should note, for instance, the high frequency of occurrence among English RP speakers of falling-rising tunes (often within a single word), which are less commonly encountered in other languages. He should be acquainted, too, with the English usage of falls and rises to signify the mood of the speaker, so that any over-use of rises will not give an unintentional impression of, for example, diffidence or complaint, and too many falls create an unwitting effect of impolite assertiveness.

11

The Word in Connected Speech

11.1 Every utterance is a continuous, changing pattern of sound quality with associated (prosodic) features of quantity, pitch, and stress. The word (consisting of one or several morphemes) is, like the phoneme, an abstraction from this continuum and must be expected to be realized in phonetically different ways according to the context, cf. the various allophonic (phonetic) realizations of the abstract unit known as the phoneme. The word constitutes, however, a separable linguistic reality for the speaker. Whether it has a simple or a complex morphemic structure, it is an element of language which is commutable in an utterance with other members of its class, i.e. nouns for other nouns, verbs for other verbs, etc. It is, moreover, often capable of constituting an utterance by itself. It must, therefore, be considered as an abstraction on a higher level than the phoneme, its separable identity having been recognized in the sophisticated written form of English by the use of spaces between words. If however, the word is admitted as an abstracted linguistic unit, it is important to note the differences which may exist between its concrete realization when said (often artificially) in isolation and those which it has when, in connected speech, it is subject to the pressures of its sound environment or of the accentual or rhythmic group of which it forms part. Those word forms which are typical of connected speech are often known as *special context forms*. The variations involved may affect the word as a whole, e.g. weak forms in an unaccented situation or word accentual patterns within the larger rhythmic pattern of the complete utterance; or may affect more particularly the sounds used at word boundaries, such changes involving a consideration of the features of morpheme and word junctures, junctural assimilations, elision, and liaison forms. In addition, it will be seen that the extent of variation depends largely upon the speed of utterance, the slower or more careful and formal the delivery the greater the tendency to preserve a form nearer to that of the isolate word.

11.1   Neutralization of Weak Forms

We have seen already (§10.4(2)) that a number of form words may have different pronunciations according to whether they are accented (or said in isolation) or, more typically, are unaccented. Such is the reduction and obscuration of the unaccented forms that words which are phonetically and phonemically separate when said in isolation may be neutralized under weak accent. Such neutralization causes no confusion because of the high rate of redundancy of meaningful cues in English; it is only rarely that the context will allow a variety of interpretation for any one cue supplied by an unaccented word form. The examples of neutralization which follow might occur in rapid, familiar RP:—

/ə/ = unaccented *are, a* (and, less commonly, *her, or, of*)
      The 'plays *are* ˌpoor
      He 'plays *a* ˌpoor ˌman
      She 'wants *a* ˌdog
      She 'wants *her* ˌdog (less rapidly, with reduced /ɜː/ for *her*)
      'One *or* 'two *of* them *are* ˌcoming (or /ɔː/ for *or*, /əv/ for *of*)
      'Two 'books *are* ˌmine
      'Two 'books *of* ˌmine (or, less rapidly, /əv/ for *of*)

/əv/ = unaccented *have* (aux.), *of*
      'Some *of* ˌone, . . .
      'Some *have* ˌwon, . . .
      The 'boys *of* 'Eton ˌfish
      The 'boys *have* 'eaten ˌfish
      (The last two utterances being identical, the meaning is clear only from the larger context.)

/ər/ = unaccented *are, or*
      'Ten *or* ˌunder (less rapidly, /ɔː/ for *or*)
      'Ten *are* ˌunder

/ðə/ = unaccented *the, there*
      There 'seems a ˌchance
      The 'seams are ˌcrooked

/s/ = unaccented *is, has, does*
      'What's ('*s* = *does* or *is*) he ˌlike?
      'What's ('*s* = *has*) he ˌlost?

/z/ = unaccented *is, has, does*
      'Where's ('*s* = *has*, less commonly *does*) he ˌput it?
      'Where's ('*s* = *is*) he ˌgoing?

/ɔz/ = unaccented *as, has*
　　　'How 'much *has* he ˌdone?
　　　As 'much *as* he ˌcan

/ən/ = unaccented *and, an*
　　　'On *and* ˌoff
　　　'On *an* ˌoff-ˌchance

/n̩/ = unaccented *and, not*
　　　'Did*n't* he ˌdo it? /'dɪdn̩ː/
　　　He 'did *and* he ˌdidn't /hɪ 'dɪd n̩ iː ˌdɪdnt/

/d/ = unaccented *had, would*
　　　I'd ('*d* = *had, would*) 'put it ˌhere

11.2　Variation of the Word's Accentual Pattern; Stress Shift

The accentual (rhythmic) pattern of a word generally remains constant whatever the environment, retaining its rhythmic identity in the total rhythmic grouping of the longer utterance (§§10.3, 10.4). Although a word may lose, in connected speech, the nuclear pitch change which it has in isolation, the relation of primary and secondary accents is not changed, e.g.:—

be'hind; ˌget be'hind me; be'hind the 'book ˌcase
'wind ˌscreen; 'wind ˌscreen ˌwiper; the 'wind ˌscreen was 'smashed;
　　he ˌbought a 'new 'wind ˌscreen
'yesterday; I ˌsaw him 'yesterday; 'yesterday 'morning
'post ˌoffice; 'post ˌoffice ˌclerk; 'near the 'post ˌoffice

But it happens that when a word (simple or compound) pattern consists in isolation of a primary accent preceded by a secondary accent, e.g. ● ＼ , ● ＼ ‧ ‧ , ● ‧ ＼ , etc., the primary accent may be thrown back to the syllable carrying secondary stress in isolation, if, in connected speech, a strong accent follows closely, e.g.:—

'thir ˌteen, *but* 'thir ˌteen 'shillings
'West 'minster, *but* 'West ˌminster 'Abbey
'full 'grown, *but* a 'full ˌgrown 'man
'after 'noon, *but* 'after ˌnoon 'tea

It will be noted, too, that, when a strongly accented syllable closely precedes, the potential pitch-prominent secondary accent may be reduced to one of quality, quantity, or rhythm, without pitch-prominence, e.g.:—

'eight ˌthir 'teen; 'near ˌWest 'minster; 'not ˌfull 'grown; 'Friday ˌafter 'noon

Moreover, when the primary accent is shifted back, in the case of a strong accent following, the secondary accent which falls on the syllable having primary accent in isolation frequently has no pitch-prominence, and may, if the quality of the syllable permits, receive no accentual prominence of any kind, e.g. 'West₁minster ˅Abbey *or* 'Westminster ˅Abbey.

Although because the primary accent may be regarded as being 'shifted back' this process is often referred to as *stress shift*, it might be more accurate to say that the primary accent of the first word is lost whilst the secondary accent (on the earlier syllable) remains. Syllables capable of retaining such secondary accent are exemplified in §9.3 with the representation •. It may already have been seen from those examples that English tends to the alternation of accented and unaccented syllables.

It is in order to avoid the placing of primary accents on adjacent syllables that stress shift occurs in phrases such as 'Chinese ˅restaurant (but ₁Chi˅nese), 'outside ˅world (but 'out˅side), 'aquamarine ˅necklace. Cf. ₁aquama'rine ti˅ara, ₁diplo'matic ˅incident, where the stress-shifted forms are optional ('aquamarine ti˅ara, 'diplomatic ˅incident), the accents not occurring on adjacent syllables in either case.

It may be added that this tendency to the alternation of accented and unaccented syllables is so strong that the stress may be shifted in the case of certain words whose citation form contains only one, later, stress, e.g. or˅nate but 'ornate ˅carvings; u˅nique but 'unique ˅features; and di˅rect but 'direct ˅access (this latter, in those idiolects which pronounce /də˅rekt/, necessitating a change of vowel phoneme /'daɪrekt ˅ækses/). The alternation tendency extends into longer utterances and may be seen in examples such as i˅dea but *the* 'idea ˅pleases me; 'recom˅mend but *I can* 'recommend ˅several; and in phrasal verbs such as 'come ˅out, 'get ˅in, e.g. *The* 'pictures 'didn't come ˅out, but *They* 'came out ˅well; and 'What 'time will 'you get ˅in? but 'What 'time will you 'get in from ˅work?

11.3   Phonetic Variations at Word or Morpheme Boundaries

We have seen (Chapter 5) that our basic linguistic units (the phonemes) are derived by a process of abstraction from connected speech. If the phoneme /t/ is given a convenient, generalized label—a fortis voiceless alveolar plosive—it is nevertheless true that the actual phonetic realization of this consonant depends on the nature of the context, e.g. /t/ is aspirated when associated with accent (except after /s/), and dental, rather than alveolar, when adjacent to /θ/ or /ð/. Phonetically, we are dealing with a sound and articulatory continuum rather than with discrete units: features of sound segment A may be found in a following segment B, and features of B in A (cf. 'transitions' of consonants, §8.2.2). If, therefore, the utterance is analysed in terms of a sequence of phonemes, account must be taken of the phonetic continuity and merging of qualities by describing the mutual influence which contiguous elements exert upon each other; in other words, tendencies towards 'assimilation' have to be noted. The tendencies outlined below are valid for colloquial English RP but may not be characteristic of other languages.

Variations of articulation may be of an allophonic kind, either within a word or at word boundaries; or, at word and morpheme boundaries, they may be of such an extent that a change of phoneme is involved, as between the pronunciation of a word in isolation and that which it may have in context. The fact that the phonemic pattern of a word is subject to variation emphasizes the *potential* nature of phonemic oppositions. The meaning of a word derives as much from the situation and context in which it occurs as from its precise phonemic shape, the high redundancy of English tolerating considerable confusion at the phonemic level. The mutual influence of contiguous phonemes in English may function predominantly in a *regressive* or *anticipatory* direction, i.e. features of one phoneme are anticipated in the articulation of the preceding phoneme; or it is *progressive* or *perseverative*, i.e. one phoneme markedly influences the following phoneme; and, sometimes, a fusion or *coalescence* of phonemes may take place.

11.3.1 Allophonic Variations

Since the realization of any phoneme differs according to the context in which it occurs, it is necessary to give examples only of those variants which exhibit striking changes of phonemic features. The influence of the phonetic features of a segment on the production of an adjacent segment is a matter of *co-articulatory effects*. The same types of allophonic variation, involving a change of place of articulation, voicing, lip position, or position of the soft palate, may be found within the word and also at word boundaries:—

(1) *Place of mouth articulation*
 (a) *within word*:—
 /t/—post-alveolar in *try* (influence of [ɹ])
   dental in *eighth* (influence of [θ])
 /k/[1]—advanced (pre-velar) in *key* (influence of [iː])
 /n/—dental in *tenth* (influence of [θ])
 /m/ or /n/—labio-dental in *nymph*, *infant* (influence of [f])
 /ʌ/—retracted in *result* (influence of [ɫ])

---

[1] Note the combinative OE [c, ɟ] > [tʃ, dʒ] before a front vowel, involving a considerable phonetic shift in the nature of the phoneme.

/u:/—centralized in *music* (influence of [j])
(*b*) *at word boundaries*:—
/t/—dental in *not that* (influence of [ð])
/d/—dental in *hide them* (influence of [ð])
/n/ or /m/—labio-dental *ten forks, come for me* (influence of [f])
/s/—retracted in *this road* (influence of [ɹ])

(2) *Voice*—usually devoicing of continuants following a fortis consonant.
(*a*) *within word*:—
/r/—devoiced in *cry*; /l/—in *plight*; /w/—in *quite*
/j/—in *queue*
/m, n, ŋ/ are slightly devoiced in such words as *smoke, snow, mutton, open* (when pronounced /ˈəʊpm̥/), *bacon* (when /ˈbeɪkŋ̥/)
(*b*) *at word boundaries* (such variations being restricted to cases where a sequence of words forms a close-knit entity—a phrasal word or rhythmic group):—
/l/—in *at last* [əˈtl̥ɑːst]; /r/—in *at rest* [əˈtr̥est]; /w/[1]—in *at once* [əˈtw̥ʌns]; /j/—in *thank you* [ˈθæŋk̥ju].
Note also the devoicing of word final lenis fricative or plosive consonants before silence, and the fricatives when followed by a fortis consonant, and of word initial lenis fricative or plosive consonants when preceded by silence, e.g. in *What can you give?* ([ɣ̥]); *Can you breathe?* ([ð̥]); *It's his* ([z̥]); *Near the bridge* ([d̥ʒ̥]); *they've* ([ɣ̥]) *come*; *with* ([ð̥]) *some*; *He's* ([z̥]) *seen it*; *George* ([d̥ʒ̥]) *can*; ([ɣ̥]) *very good* ([d̥]); ([ð̥]) *there*; ([z̥]) *zinc does* ([z̥]).

(3) *Lip position*—under the influence of adjacent vowels or semi-vowels. (*a*) *within word*:—

	lip-spread	lip-rounded[2]
/p/	*pea, heap*	*pool, hoop, upward*
/t/	*tea, beat*	*two, boot, twice, outward*
/k/	*keep, speak*	*cool, spook, quite, backward*
/m/	*mean, seem*	*moon, loom, somewhat*
/n/	*knee, seen*	*noon, onward*
/l/	*leave, feel*	*loom, fool, always*
/r/[3]	*read*	*rude*
/f/	*feel, leaf*	*fool, roof*

---

[1] Note also the devoicing /w/ < /ʊ/ in *to* followed by a vowel, e.g. *see to it* [ˈsiː tw̥ ɪt].
[2] This will apply only for those speakers who have appreciable rounding of the vowel.
[3] For some speakers /r/ has inherent labialization and will not be lip-spread even before a lip-spread vowel.

/s/ *seat, geese* *soon, goose, sweep*
/ʃ/ *sheet, leash* *shoot, douche, dishwasher*
/h/ *he* *who* etc.

(b) *at word boundaries* (any marked labialization being dependent upon the close-knit nature of the group): e.g. /t, k, n, ŋ, l, s/ are somewhat labialized in such cases as *that one, thick one, thin one, wrong one, shall we, this way,* the syllables with initial /w/ carrying no accent; a rounded vowel in an adjacent word does not seem to exert the same labializing influence, e.g. /uː/ does not labialize /s/ markedly in *Who said that?* nor /ɔː/ in *This ought to.*

(4) *Nasal resonance*—resulting particularly from anticipatory but also from prolonged lowering of the soft palate in the vicinity of a nasal consonant.

(a) *within word*: nasalization of vowel preceding /m/ in *ham* and /n/ in *and*, of vowel between nasal consonants in *man, men, innermost*, and of short vowels on each side of the nasal consonant in *any, sunny, summer, singer*; also /l/ in such situations as in *helmet, wrongly*; and possible slight nasalization of vowel following /n/, as in *now.*

(b) *at word boundaries*: vowels may sometimes be nasalized somewhat by the boundary nasal consonant of an adjacent word, especially when an adjacent nasal consonant also occurs in the word containing the vowel, e.g. the first /ə/ in *bring another,* or /ɪ/ in *come in,* and also, without an adjacent nasal consonant in the word containing the vowel (usually unaccented), e.g. /ə/ in *come along, wait for me,* /ɪ/ in *every night,* etc.; or again, a frictionless continuant consonant may be nasalized, e.g. /l/ in *tell me.*

11.3.2 Phonemic Variations

In a synchronic view of the present state of the language, in which a word's *internal* phonemic pattern is established and largely invariable, there can be no question of assimilation involving phonemic change (as against allophonic variation). Nevertheless, different pronunciations of the same word (either between two speakers or between different styles of speech in the same speaker) sometimes exhibit a different choice of internal phoneme depending on the degree of assimilatory pressure of the word environment felt by the speaker, e.g. *length* may be /leŋθ, leŋkθ/, or /lenθ/, *encounter* may have /ɪn/ or /ɪŋ/ in the first syllable, *disgrace* may have final /s/ or /z/ in the first syllable, *absolutely* may have final /b/ or /p/ in the first syllable, *and* issue may have medial /sj/ or a coalesced form /ʃ/. From a diachronic point of view, a phonemic change within a word may sometimes be attributable to the combinatory pressures exerted on a phoneme by the word environment, e.g. by labialization /wa(ː)/ > /wɒ/ or /wɔː/ (*swan, water*); /ɪr, er, ʊr/ coalesced into /ər/ (later /ɜː/) under the influence of the post-vocalic /ɹ/ (*first, earth, curse*); /s/ or /z/ and /j/ combined their phonetic characteristics to give /ʃ, ʒ/ (*mansion, vision*), etc.

But, in the contemporary language, it is at *word boundaries* in connected speech that most cases of phonemic change occur (i.e. change as compared with the phonemic pattern of the isolate word form). Such phonemic variation is found in changes within the pairs of fortis/lenis phonemes and, more particularly, in changes involving modification of the place of articulation, or a combination of voicing and place.

11.3.3   Fortis/Lenis Variations

Word final lenis fricatives followed by a word initial fortis consonant may with some speakers be realized as the corresponding fortis fricative, if the two words form part of a close-knit group. Thus, isolate final /ð/ of *with* may be replaced by /θ/ in *with thanks*; /z/ of *was* by /s/ in *he was sent*; /v/ of *of, we've*, by /f/ in *of course, we've found it*. Such a change to a fortis fricative is an extension of the allophonic devoicing of such consonants mentioned in §11.3.1(2). The phonemic change may be complete in that a preceding long vowel or diphthong may be realized in the reduced form appropriate to a syllable closed by a fortis consonant, e.g. in *breathe, these, we've, chose*, in the examples given above, but this is relatively rare.

The weak form of *is* or *has* is /s/ or /z/ according to the final consonant of the preceding word, e.g. *the cat has* or *is* with /s/ (= the plural or possessive morpheme in *cats, cat's*), cf. *the dog has* or *is* with /z/ (= the plural or possessive morpheme in *dogs, dog's*).

It is unusual in RP for word final /b, d, g/ to be influenced in the same way by following fortis consonants, though voiceless forms may be heard in such contexts in northern speech, e.g. the /d/ of *good time* and the /g/ of *big case* may be realized as /t, k/.

It is to be noted that word or morpheme final fortis consonants in English rarely show tendencies to assimilate to their lenis counterparts: such pronunciations of *nice boy, black dress, half-done, they both do, wishbone, birthday*, as /ˈnaɪz ˌbɔɪ, ˈblæg ˌdres, ˈhɑːvˌdʌn, ðeɪ ˈbəʊð ˌduː, ˌwɪʒˌbəʊn, ˌbɜːðˌdeɪ/ are typical of many foreign learners.

11.3.4   Nasality and labialization

Phonemic assimilations involving *nasality* (i.e. anticipation or prolongation of the lowered soft palate position) would be likely to show /b/ (or /v/) > /m/, /d/ (or /z/ or /ð/) > /n/, /g/ > /ŋ/, such changes being based on roughly homorganic mouth articulations; nasalization of other sounds, e.g. /l/ or vowels, is never phonemic, there being no nasalized counterpart with approximately homorganic mouth articulation. Such phonemic nasalization as does occur concerns mainly the alveolars, especially adjacent to the negative *'nt* /n(t)/, and is characteristic of very rapid speech, often as a popular form unacceptable in RP (marked * in the examples below), e.g.:—

> /d > n/—*He wouldn't do it* /hɪ ˈwʊnn(t) ˌduː ɪt/
> *good news* /ˈgʊn ˌnjuːz/
> /d > g > ŋ/—*He wouldn't go* /hɪ ˈwʊŋŋ(k) ˌgəʊ/
> /d > b > m/—*Good morning* /ˌgʊm ˈmɔːnɪŋ/
> /v > m/—*You can have mine* /jʊ kŋ ˌhæm ˈmaɪn/

(In the above examples, the nasalized assimilated form may be elided together.)

> /z > n/—*He doesn't know* /hɪ ˈdʌnn(t) ˌnəʊ/*
> /ð > n/—*He wasn't there* /hɪ ˈwɒnn(t) ˌneə/*
> *to win the race* /tə ˈwɪn nə ˌreɪs/*

The extension of *labialization* produces no changes of a phonemic kind, since lip-position is not a distinctive feature opposing any two phonemes in RP. /ɒ/ and /ɑː/ come nearest to having an opposition of lip action, but the lip-rounding for /ɒ/ is very slight and open and, in any case, there is some difference of tongue position and considerable difference of length. Where /w/ precedes a vowel of the /ɑː/ type (and, therefore, might be expected to exert a rounding influence), either labialization has become established at an earlier stage of the language's development (e.g. in *was*, *what*, *war*, *water*, etc.) or two pronunciations are to-day permitted, e.g. *qualm* /kwɑːm/ or /kwɔːm/, *quaff* /kwɒf/ or /kwɑːf/. Labialization of /ɑː/ involving a phonemic change to /ɒ/ or /ɔː/ does not extend beyond word boundaries, e.g. in *two arms* or *the car won't go*. Some confusion may, however, occur between a strongly centralized form of /əʊ/ and /ɜː/ in a labial context, cf. *they weren't wanted* and *they won't want it*; also, with the influence of a strongly labialized form of /r/ in such a pair as *they weren't right*, *they won't write*.

11.3.5 Variations of Place: Assimilation

The assumption by a word-final phoneme (in the isolate form) of the phonetic characteristics of a following phoneme in connected speech is a frequent result of assimilatory tendencies, usually regressive (anticipatory) or coalescent, involving a variation in the place of articulation. Though such changes are normal in colloquial speech, native speakers are usually unaware that they are made. The phenomenon is essentially the same as that resulting in non-phonemic assimilation of place. (See §§8.2.5(2), 8.6.2(2).)

Regressive (or Anticipatory) Assimilation: Instablity of final alveolars [1]

Word final /t, d, n, s, z/ readily assimilate to the place of the following word initial consonant, i.e. whilst retaining the original voicing, /t, d, n/ are replaced by bilabials before bilabial consonants and by velars before velar consonants; /s, z/ are replaced by palato-alveolars before consonants containing a palatal feature:

/t/ → /p/ before /p, b, m/, e.g. *that pen, that boy, that man* /ˈðæp ˌpen, ˈðæp ˌbɔɪ, ˈðæp ˌmæn/;

     → /k/ before /k, g/, e.g. *that cup, that girl* /ˈðæk ˌkʌp, ˈðæk ˌgɜːl/;

     but /p/ does not show similar changes before /t, d, n, k, g/

     nor /k/ before /t, d, n, p, b, m/.

/d/ → /b/ before /p, b, m/, e.g. *good pen, good boy, good man* /ˈgʊb ˌpen, ˈgʊb ˌbɔɪ, ˈgʊb ˌmæn/;

     → /g/ before /k, g/, e.g. *good concert, good girl* /ˈgʊg ˌkɒnsət, ˈgʊg ˌgɜːl/;

     but /b/ does not show similar changes before /t, d, n, k, g/,

     nor /g/ before /t, d, n, p, b, m/.

/n/ → /m/ before /p, b, m/, e.g. *ten players, ten boys, ten men* /ˈtem ˌpleɪəz, ˈtem ˌbɔɪz, ˈtem ˌmen/

     → /ŋ/ before /k, g/, e.g. *ten cups, ten girls* /ˈteŋ ˌkʌps, ˈteŋ ˌgɜːlz/.

     (As a result of word final assimilations, /ŋ/ may be preceded by vowels other than /ɪ, e, æ, ɒ, ʌ/. Thus /ŋ/ can occur after long vowels as a result of assimilation (cf. §9.8), e.g. *I've been* /ˈbiːŋ/ *gardening, She'll soon* /ˈsuːŋ/ *come, his own* /ˈəʊŋ/ *car,* etc.)

     Assimilations of /m/ to /n/ before /t, d, n/ and to /ŋ/ before /k, g/ or of /ŋ/ to /m/ before /p, b, m/ and to /n/ before /t, d, n/ are abnormal or occur in speech characterized generally as slipshod.

/s/ → /ʃ/ before /ʃ, tʃ, dʒ, j/, e.g. *this shop, cross channel, this judge, this year* /ˈðɪʃ ˌʃɒp, ˈkrɒʃ ˌtʃænl̩, ˈðɪʃ ˌdʒʌdʒ, ˈðɪʃ ˌjɪə/

     However, /s/ shows no phonemic change before other consonants, e.g. /ˈðɪθ ˌθɪŋ/ (*this thing*) is abnormal; /f, ʃ/, too, are not influenced to any marked extent by a

---

[1] See also A. C. Gimson, 'The instability of English alveolar articulations,' *Le Maître Phonétique*, no. 113, 1960.

following consonant, but, in very rapid and informal speech, final /θ/ may assimilate to /s/ before /s/, e.g. *both sides* /ˈbəʊs ˌsaɪdż/.

/z/→ /ʒ/ before /ʃ, tʃ, dʒ, j/ or sometimes → /ʃ/ (change to fortis) before /ʃ/, e.g. *those young men* /ˈðəʊʒ ˈjʌŋ ˌmen/, *cheese shop* /ˈtʃiːʒ ʃɒp/, *those churches* /ˈðəʊʒ ˌtʃɜːtʃɪz/, *hus she?* /ˈhæʒ ʃɪ/ or /ˈhæʃ ʃɪ/.

However, /z/ does not show similar changes before other consonants. The place of articulation of /v, ʒ/ is not usually influenced greatly by a following consonant but, in very rapid and informal speech, final /ð/ may assimilate to /z/ or /s/ before /s, z/, e.g. *I loathe singing* /aɪ ˈləʊz ˌsɪŋɪŋ/, and word initial /ð/—especially in the article *the*—may assimilate to /s, z/ following /s, z/, e.g. *What's the time?* /ˈwɒts zə ˌtaɪm/, *Has the post come?* /ˈhæz zə ˌpəʊs ˌkʌm/, in very rapid speech.

In this connection, it is to be noted that the alveolars have a relatively high frequency of word final occurrence, especially when inflexional, and are particularly apt to undergo neutralization as redundant oppositions in connected speech. As always, phonemic oppositions having been neutralized, the sense of an utterance may be determined by the context, e.g. /ˈræŋ ˌkwɪklɪ/ (*ran* or *rang quickly*), /ˈraɪp ˌpeəz/ (*right* or *ripe pears* or *pairs*), /ˈlaɪk ˌkri m/ (*like* or *light cream*), /ˈhɒp məˌnjʊə/ (*hot* or *hop manure*), /ˈpærɪʃ ˈʃəʊ/ (*Paris Show* or *parish show*), /ˈwɒtʃ jɔː ˌweɪt/ (*what's* or *watch your weight*),[1] or, with a neutralization to a labio-dental articulation, /ˈgreɪp ˌvaɪn/ (*great* or *grape vine*), [ˈrʌŋ fə jɔː ˌmʌnɪ] (*run* or *rum for your money*).

When alveolar consonants /t, d, n/ are adjacent in clusters or sequences susceptible to assimilation, all (or none) of them will undergo the assimilation, e.g. *Don't* /ˈdəʊmp/ *be late, He won't* /ˈwəʊŋk/ *come, I didn't* /ˈdɪgŋk/ *go, He found* /ˈfaʊmb/ */both, a kind* /ˈkaɪŋg/ *gift, red and black* /ˈreb m̩ ˈblæk/.

(2) *Coalescence of* /t, d, s, z/ *with* /j/
The process which has led to earlier /t, d, s, z/ + /j/ giving /tʃ, dʒ, ʃ, ʒ/ medially in a word (*nature, grandeur, mission, vision*—§8.3.1) may operate in contemporary colloquial speech at word boundaries, e.g.:—

/t/ + /j/—*What you want* . . . /ˈwɒtʃʊ ˌwɒnt . . ./
/d/ + /j/—*Would you?* /ˈwʊdʒʊ/
/s/ + /j/—*In case you need it* /ɪŋ ˈkeɪʃʊ ˌniːd ɪt/
/z/ + /j/—*Has your letter come?* /hæʒɔː ˌletə ˌkʌm/
                 as yet /əˈʒet/

[1] If the utterance is reduced to /ˈwɒtʃɔː ˌweɪt/, there is also the possibility of the interpretation *watch or wait*.

The coalescence is more complete in the case of /t, d,/ + /j/ (especially in question tags, e.g. *didn't you?, could you?*, etc.); in the case of /s, z/ + /j/, the coalescence into /ʃ, ʒ/ may be marked by extra length of friction, e.g. *Don't miss your train* /ˈdəʊmp ˈmɪʃʃɔː ˌtreɪn/, cf. *I can't be sure* /aɪ ˈkɑːmp bɪ ˌʃɔː/.

In very careful speech, some RP speakers would use somewhat artificial, uncoalesced, forms within words, e.g. /ˈneɪtjə, ˈkwestjən, ˌʌnˈfɔːtjʊnət, ˈsəʊldjə/ (*nature, question, unfortunate, soldier*), etc. Such speakers would also avoid coalescences at word boundaries; other, careful, speakers who use the normal coalesced forms within words, would consciously avoid them at word boundaries. But see §11.6.

(3) *Progressive (or Perseverative) Assimilation* is relatively uncommon. It may occur when a plosive is followed by a syllabic nasal and the nasal undergoes assimilation to the same place of articulation as the preceding plosive, e.g. /n/ → /m/ after /p, b/, *happen, urban* /ˈhæpm̩, ˈɜːbm̩/; and /n/→ /ŋ/ after /k, g/ in *second chance, organ* /ˈsekŋ̩ ˈtʃɑːns, ɔːgŋ̩/.

11.3.6   Elision

Apart from word internal elisions (see §9.6) and those associated with weak forms, sounds may be elided in rapid, colloquial speech, especially at or in the vicinity of word boundaries.

(1) *Vowels (a) Allophonic variation.*—As in the case of consonants, variations in the production of vowels may be insufficient to cause a change of phoneme. When one syllable ends with a closing diphthong (i.e. one whose second element is closer than its first, in RP /eɪ, aɪ, ɔɪ, əʊ, aʊ/) and the next syllable begins with a vowel, the second element of the diphthong may be elided. Word internal examples of the type discussed in §8.2.5 (e.g. *hyaena* /haɪˈiːnə/ smoothed to [haˈiːnə]) may result in neutralization, thus *layer* /ˈleɪə/ with smoothing = *lair* [leə], *mower* /ˈməʊə/ with smoothing = *myrrh* [məə] interpretable as /mɜː/. Similar smoothing occurs across word boundaries, e.g. *go away* [ˌgɜː ˈweɪ], *I may as well* [aɪ ˌmeəz ˌwel], *I enjoy it* [aɪ ɪnˈdʒɒ ɪt], *try again* [ˌtra əˈgen] or [ˌtraː ˈgen].

(b) *Phonemic elision.*—Initial /ə/ is often elided particularly when followed by a continuant and preceded by a word final consonant (compensation for the loss of /ə/ frequently being made by the syllabicity of the continuant), e.g. *not alone* /ˈnɒtl̩ ˈləʊn/, *get another* /ˈgetn̩ ˈnʌðə/, *run along* /ˈrʌnl̩ ˈlɒŋ/, *he was annoyed* /hɪ wəzn̩ ˈnɔɪd/; or again, when final /ə/ occurs with following linking /r/ (see §11.3.7) and word initial vowel, /ə/ may be elided, e.g. *after a while* /ˈɑː ftrəˈwaɪl/, *as a matter of fact* /əz ə ˈmætrəv ˌfækt/, *father and son* /ˈfɑ ðrən ˈsʌn/, *over and above* /ˈəʊvrən əˈbʌv/.

(2) *Consonants.*—In addition to the loss of /h/ in pronominal weak forms and other consonantal elisions typical of weak forms,[1] the alveolar plosives are apt to be elided. Such elision appears to take place most readily when /t/ or /d/ is the middle one of three consonants and has the same voicing[2] as the first consonant of the sequence. Any consonant may appear in third position, though elision of the alveolar plosive is relatively rare before /h/ and /j/. Thus elision is common in the sequence voiceless continuant + /t/ or voiced continuant + /d/ (e.g. /-st, -ft, -ʃt, -nd, -ld, -zd, -ðd, -vd/) followed by a word with an initial consonant e.g. *next day, raced back, last chance, first light, west region, just one; left turn, soft centres, left wheel, drift by, soft roes; mashed potatoes, finished now, finished late, pushed them; bend back, tinned meat, lend-lease, found five, send round, dined well; hold tight, old man, cold lunch, bold face, world religion; refused both, gazed past, caused losses, raised gently; loathed beer; moved back, loved flowers, saved runs, served sherry,* etc. Similarly, word final clusters of voiceless plosive or affricate + /t/ or voiced plosive or affricate + /d/ (e.g. /-pt, -kt, -tʃt, -bd, -gd, -dʒd/) may lose the final alveolar stop when the following word has an initial consonant, e.g. *kept quiet, helped me, stopped speaking, jumped well; liked jam, thanked me, looked like, looked fine, picked one; reached Paris, fetched me, reached Rome, parched throat; robbed both, rubbed gently, grabbed them; lagged behind, dragged down, begged one; changed colour, urged them, arranged roses, judged fairly,* etc. (In the sequence /-skt/, /k/ rather than /t/ is often elided, e.g. *risked prison, asked them.*) Elision of final /t/ or /d/ is rarer before initial /h/, e.g. the alveolar stops are more regularly retained in *kept hold, worked hard, East Ham, reached home, gift horse, rushed home, grabbed hold, round here, bald head, jugged hare, changed horses, raised hands, moved house,* etc. Final sequences /-nt, -lt/ tend to keep either /t/ or [ʔ], the appropriate reduction of preceding sounds being retained as a result of the final fortis plosive, e.g. in *sent back, count them, can't fail; felt bad, built near, salt lake,* etc. Final /t, d/ followed by a word beginning with /j/ are usually kept in a coalesced form with /j/, i.e. /tʃ/ or /dʒ/, e.g. *helped you, liked you, lost you, left you, grabbed you, lend you, told you,* etc. It will be seen that in many cases, e.g. in *I walked back, they seemed glad,* elision of word final /t/ or /d/ eliminates the phonetic cue of past tense, compensation for which is made by the general context. Such is the instability of the alveolar plosives in such a position of apparent inflexional significance that it can be assumed that the context

---

[1] See also §8.2.5.
[2] The negative contraction /-nt/ is an exception to this voicing rule. (See later in this paragraph).

regularly carries the burden of tense distinction. Where the juxta-position of words brings together a cluster of consonants (particularly of stops), elision of a plosive medial in three or more is to be expected, since, because of the normal lack of release of a stop in such a situation, the only cue to its presence is likely to be the total duration of closure.

The /t/ of the negative /-nt/ is often elided, particularly in disyl-lables, before a following consonant, e.g. *you mustn't lose it* /ju ˋmʌsn ˇluːz ɪt/, *doesn't she know?* /ˈdʌzn ʃɪ ˌnəʊ/, and sometimes before a vowel, e.g. *wouldn't he come?* /ˈwʊdn ɪ ˌkʌm/, *you mustn't over-eat* /jʊ ˋmʌsn ˌəʊvər ˇiːt/. Less common is the omission of the stops in the negative /-nt/ component of monosyllables, e.g. *he won't do it* /hɪ ˈwəʊn ˌduː ɪt/; in this latter case, there is a tendency for /əʊ/ to have full rather than reduced length because of the omission of the syllable-final fortis stop. Clusters of word final /t/ and word initial /t/ or /d/ are sometimes simplified in rapid informal speech, e.g. *I've got to go* /aɪv ˌɡɒtə ˋɡəʊ/, *what do you want?* /ˈwɒdə jʊ ˌwɒn̩t/, and less commonly /d/ before /t/ or /d/, e.g. *we could try* /wɪ kə ˇtraɪ/, *they should do it* /ˋðeɪ ʃə ˌduː ɪt/. The elision of one of a boundary cluster of two con-sonants sometimes occurs in very rapid speech, but is usually charac-terized as a vulgarism, e.g. *he went away* /hɪ ˈwen ə˱weɪ/, *I want to come* /aɪ ˋwɒnə ˌkʌm/ (< /aɪ ˋwɒntə ˌkʌm/, which frequently occurs), *give me a cake* ˈɡɪ mɪ ə ˌkeɪk/, *let me come in* ˈlemɪ ˌkʌm ˌɪn/, *get me some paper* /ˈɡemɪ sm ˌpeɪpə/, as well as the most reduced forms of *I'm going to* /aɪm ɡənə, aɪŋənə, aɪŋnə/.

11.3.7　Liaison

As has been mentioned in §8.8(2)(*a*), RP retains word final post-vocalic /r/ as a *linking form* when the following word begins with a vowel, i.e. in those cases where an [r] sound existed in earlier forms of RP, as the spelling indicates. The vowel endings to which an /r/ *link* may, in this sense, justifiably be added are /-ɑː, -ɔː/ and those single or complex vowels containing final [ə] (/ə, ɜː, ɪə, eə, ʊə/), e.g. in *far off, four aces, answer it, fur inside, near it, wear out, secure everything.* By analogy, this /r/ linking usage is extended to all /ɑː, ɔː, ə/ endings, even when there is no historical (spelling) justification. Such *intrusive* /r/s are to be heard particularly in the case of /ə/ endings, e.g. *Russia and China* /ˈrʌʃər ən ˈtʃaɪnə/, *drama and music* /ˈdrɑːmər ən ˈmjuːzɪk/, *idea of* /aɪˈdɪər əv/, *India and Pakistan* /ˈɪndɪər ən ˌpɑːkɪˈstɑːn/, *area of agree-ment* /ˈeərɪər əv əˈɡriːmənt/, etc. Less frequently, analogous links (unjustified by the spelling) are made with final /ɑː, ɔː/ e.g. *Shah of Iran* /ˈʃɑːr əv ɪˈrɑːn/, *law and order* /ˈlɔːr ənd ˈɔːdə/, *awe-inspiring* /ˈɔːr ɪn̩spaɪərɪŋ/. It is clear that the RP system of linking /r/s strongly encourages the creation of analogous links in similar phonetic contexts. Spelling consciousness remains an inhibiting factor, but the present general tendency among RP speakers is to use intrusive /r/ links after final /ə/, even—unconsciously—among those who object most strongly. Words containing final /ɑː/ or /ɔː/, without an earlier form with /r/, are less common than those with /ə/. The pressure of analogy to use an intrusive /r/ might in consequence appear to be greater; but the comparative rarity of the cases of such intrusive /r/s tends to make speakers more aware of the 'correct' forms; thus *I saw it* /aɪ 'sɔː r ɪt/, *drawing*, /'drɔːrɪŋ/, are generally disapproved of, though it is likely that many RP speakers have to make a conscious effort to avoid the use of such forms. The focusing of attention on this particular type of analogous formation as an undesirable speech habit has led to the use by some speakers of a pause or glottal stop in such critical cases of vowel hiatus, with the result that, in avoiding 'intrusive' /r/s, they have also abandoned justifiable linking /r/s in favour of a vowel glide or glottal stop, e.g. in *secure it, I'm sure it does, War and Peace, winter evening*. If such a situation had arisen in a freer stage of the development of the language, i.e. when spelling forms were not so fixed or influential as at present, it is possible that the intrusive /r/s would have been adopted as regular usage and the spelling modified. As might be expected, in those regions where post-vocalic /r/ is pronounced and *pour, paw* identified as separate word forms in isolation, the tendency to introduce analogous linking /r/s is less marked than in RP or in RP-influenced types of speech.

It should be noted that, in synchronic terms, the same process is in operation whether the /r/ link inserted is historically justified (linking) or not (intrusive). The examples below demonstrate that the environment is phonetically comparable whether the /r/ link is inserted before a suffix or before a separate word and whether it is linking or intrusive.

stir	*stirring*	*stir it in*		
/stɜː/	'stɜːrɪŋ	'stɜːr ɪt 'ɪn/		
dear	*dearer*	*my dear Anna*	*idea of it*	
/dɪə/	'dɪərə	maɪ 'dɪər 'ænə	aɪ'dɪər əv ɪt/	
roar	*roaring*	*roar angrily*	*raw egg*	*strawy*
/rɔː/	'rɔːrɪŋ	'rɔːr 'æŋgrəlɪ	'rɔːr 'eg	'strɔːrɪ/
star	*starry*	*a star in the sky*	*the spa at Bath*	*schwaish*
/stɑː/	'stɑːrɪ	ə 'stɑːr ɪn ðə 'skaɪ	ðə 'spɑː r ət ˌbɑː θ	'ʃwɑːrɪʃ/

There appears, however, to be some gradation in the likelihood of occurrence as follows:

(1) Where a word ends in a non-high vowel, the insertion of /r/ is *obligatory* before a *suffix* beginning with a vowel. (See §9.10.)

(2) Before another word the insertion of such an /r/ is *optional*. However, it occurs in the vast *majority* of cases where a historically justified *linking* /r/ is possible.

(3) Where the /r/ link is *intrusive*, speakers tend to use it after /ə/ (e.g.

vanilla essence /vəˈnɪlər ˈesəns/, *vodka and tonic* /ˈvɒɡkər ən ˈtɒnɪk/)
more readily than
(4) after /ɑː/ or /ɔː/ (e.g. *nougat and chocolate* ˈnuːɡɑːr ən ˈtʃɒklɪt/,
straw in the wind /ˈstrɔːr ɪn ðə ˈwɪnd/).

There is considerable resistance to

(5) the insertion of intrusive /r/ before a suffix (e.g. *strawy* /ˈstrɔːrɪ/.
   Such avoidance occasionally leads to the omission of the normal
(citation form) /r/ in a word such as *assurance*, giving rise to a from
form /əˈʃɔːəns/ which may be regarded as *hypercorrection*. When the
fear, with some speakers, of using the intrusive /r/ inhibits liason
across word boundaries, a vowel glide or a glottal stop may be used, e.g.
the door opened /ðə ˈdɔːwəupənd/ or [ðə dɔː ˌʔəupənd].
   Finally, it may be added that it is usual (and not stylistically significant) in connected speech for the linking /r/ form of words to be used
before a vowel, e.g. *thanks for everything* /fər/, *my father and mother*
/ˈfɑːðər/, *the weather ought to improve* /ˈweðər/, *here and there*
/hɪər/, *I don't care if they do* /kɛər/.
   Phonetically (as well as historically) the resulting /r/ closes the
syllable rather than being initial in the next, e.g. the /r/ of *more ice*
/ˈmɔːr ˈaɪs/ is shorter than that of *more rice* /ˈmɔː ˈraɪs/, the latter also
being associated with stress onset and possible pitch change. (cf.
§11.3.8.)
   It is unusual for a word final consonant to be carried over as initial in
a word beginning with an accented vowel, the identity of the words
being retained (see §11.3.8). Thus, *run off*, *give in*, *less often*, are rarely
/ˌrʌ ˈnɒf, ˌɡɪ ˈvɪn, ˌle ˈsɒfn/; more particularly, the fortis plosives do not
acquire aspiration such as would accompany their shift to an accented
syllable-initial position, e.g. *get up*, *look out*, *stop arguing*, are not
usually [ˌɡe ˈtʰʌp, ˌlu ˈkʰaʊt, ˌstɒ ˈpʰɑːɡjʊɪŋ]. One or two phrases in
common use do, however, show such transference, e.g. *at home*, *not at
all*, often pronounced [ə ˈtʰəum, ˌnɒt ə ˈtʰɔːɬ]; they may be considered as
constituting, in effect, composite word forms.

11.3.8   Juncture

Despite the fact that the word may have its isolate-form identity considerably modified by its immediate phonemic and accentual context,
both as regards its constituent sounds and its accentual or rhythmic
pattern, phonetic features may be retained in the speech continuum
which mark word or morpheme boundaries. Thus, the phonemic
sequence /piːstɔːks/ (with secondary accent on the syllable containing
/ɔː/) may mean *pea stalks* or *peace talks* according to the situation of
the word boundaries (i.e. /iː-st/ or /iːst-tɔː/). In this case, if the
boundary occurs between /s/ and /t/, the identity of the words *peace*
and *talks* may be established by the reduced /iː/ (in a syllable closed by

a fortis consonant) and by the slight aspiration of /t/ (initial in a syllable carrying a secondary accent); on the other hand, if the boundary occurs between /iː/ and /s/, this may be signalled by the relatively full length of /iː/ (in an open word-final syllable) and by the unaspirated allophone of /t/ (following /s/ in the same syllable), as well as by the stronger /s/. Such phonetic differentiation depends upon the speaker's consciousness of the word as an independent entity. Or, alternatively, distinctive function of phonetic features in the continuum may be said to be associated with the type of *juncture* (close or open) which occurs; thus, in *pea stalks*, open (i.e. as before a pause) juncture relates /iː/ to /s/ and close (i.e. as within a word) juncture relates /s/ to /t/, whereas in *peace talks*, close juncture relates /iː/ to /s/ and open juncture /s/ to /t/, with the relevant phonetic cues. If the two utterances were not distinguished in such terms, it would be necessary to postulate, for instance, a phonemic opposition between the full and reduced forms of /iː/ and between the aspirated and unaspirated types of /t/. A phonemic transcription which follows the orthographic convention in showing spaces or hyphens between words retains the identity of the word but obscures the continuous, unbroken nature of connected speech. The following examples illustrate various ways in which phonetic cues may mark word boundaries

/əneɪm/—*a name* (relatively long /n/, associated with stress onset and possible pitch change)
　　　an aim (relatively short /n/, stress and pitch change beginning on /eɪ/)
/ðætstʌf/[1]—*that stuff* (unaspirated /t/, strong /s/)
　　　that's tough (aspirated /t/, weaker /s/)
/ðəweɪtəkʌtɪt/[1]—*the waiter cut it* (reduced /eɪ/, rhythmic groups /ðə'weɪtə-'kʌtɪt/)
　　　the way to cut it (long /eɪ/, rhythmic groups /ðə'weɪ-tə'kʌtɪt/)
/aɪskriːm/—*I scream* (long /aɪ/, strong /s/, relatively little devoicing of /r/)
　　　ice-cream (reduced /aɪ/, weaker /s/, devoiced /r/)
/haʊstreɪnd/—*how strained* (long /aʊ/, strong /s/, little devoicing of /r/)
　　　house trained (reduced /aʊ/, weaker /s/, devoiced /r/)
/waɪtʃuːz/—*white shoes* (reduced /aɪ/, long /ʃ/)
　　　why choose (long /aɪ/, short [ʃ] element of /tʃ/ affricate)

---

[1] Examples from Daniel Jones, 'The word as a phonetic entity,' *Le Maître Phonétique*, no. 36, 1931, and 'The hyphen as a phonetic sign', *Zeitschrift für Phonetik*, 1956.

Similarly, simple word entities may be distinguished from words composed of separable morphemes:—

/haɪnɪs/[1]—*highness* (/aɪ/ and /n/ in close juncture, rhythmical
    shortening of /aɪ/)
    high-ness (/aɪ/ and /n/ in open juncture, full length of
    /aɪ/)
/naɪtreɪt/[2]—*night-rate* (/t/ and /r/ in open junctural relationship,
    little devoicing of /r/)
    nitrate (/t/ and /r/ close junctured, devoiced /r/)

It is to be noted, however, that such junctural cues are only potentially distinctive and, in any case, merely provide cues to word identification additional to the large number already contained in any utterance. Junctural oppositions are, in fact, frequently neutralized in connected speech or may have such slight phonetic value as to be difficult for a listener to perceive; they may, therefore, be said to be on a lower plane of relevance than the phonemic units conveyed by qualities and the various accentual patterns.

11.4   Frequency of Occurrence of Monosyllabic and Polysyllabic Words

In a running text of a conversational kind, the following approximate percentages of occurrence of words containing different numbers of syllables are to be expected: 1 syllable—81%; 2 syllables—15%; 3 syllables—3%. The remaining 1% of words have 4 syllables or more, those with 5 or more syllables accounting for a minute proportion of the total word list. If the 1,000 most common words used are examined,[3] it has been calculated that some 15% admit of the kind of phonemic variability mentioned in §9.11. Half of such words permitting phonemic variation are monosyllables whose phonemic structure depends upon the degree of accent placed upon them.

11.5   Advice to Foreign Learners

The foreign learner need not attempt to reproduce in his speech all the special context forms of words mentioned in the foregoing sections. He

---

[1] From Daniel Jones, 'The hyphen . . .,' op. cit.
[2] From Trager and Bloch, 'The syllabic phonemes of English,' *Language*, 17, 1941; also Trager and Smith, *An Outline of English Structure*, 1951; I. Lehiste, 'An acoustic-phonetic study of internal open juncture', University of Michigan, 1959.
[3] See my 'Note on the variability of the phonemic components of English words,' (1969), op. cit.

must, however, observe the rules concerning weak forms, should cultivate the correct variations of word rhythmic patterns according to the context, and should make a proper use of liaison forms (German speakers, in particular, should avoid an excess of pre-vocalic glottal stops). In addition, he should be aware of the English assimilatory tendencies governing words in context, so as to avoid un-English assimilations such as *I like that* /aɪ ˈlaɪg ˌðæt/ (incorrect voicing) or *I was there* /aɪ wəð ˈðɛə/ (incorrect dental modification of the place of articulation). If his speech is to be a perfect reproduction of that of the native speaker, he must use the special assimilated and elided word forms used in context which have been described above. In any case, whether or not he uses such forms himself, he must know of their existence, for otherwise he will find it difficult to understand much of ordinary colloquial English. This knowledge is particularly important because a second language is often learned on a basis of isolate word forms; in the speech of the native, however, the outline of these words will frequently be modified or obscured, as has been seen.

The foreign learner is recommended to aim at a careful colloquial style of English in his own speech and, at the same time, to be aware of the features which characterize the rapid colloquial (or familiar) style he is likely to hear from native speakers. The following dialogue illustrates some of the differences which may be found between the two styles, (1) being careful colloquial and (2) rapid familiar:—

A. What do you think we should do this evening?
(1) ˈwɒt du ju ˈθɪŋk wi(ː) ʃʊd ˌduː ðɪs ˌiːvnɪŋ
(2) ˈwɒdʒʊ ˈθɪŋk wɪ ʃəd ˌduː ðəs ˌiːvnɪŋ

B. How many of us will there be?
(1) ˈhaʊ ˌmenɪ ˈɒv əs wɪl ðə ˌbiː
(2) ˈhaʊ mnɪ əv əs l ðə ˌbiː

A. There are the two of us, and probably the two girls
(1) ˌðer ə ðə ˈtuː əv ˌʌs, ənd ˈprɒbəblɪ ðə ˈtuː ˈɡɜːlz
(2) ðər ə ðə ˈtuː əv ˌʌs, m ˈprɒbblɪ ðə ˈtuː ˈɡɜːlz

    from next door. That'll be four of us already
(1) frəm ˈnekst ˌdɔː ˌðætl bɪ ˇfɔːr əv əs ɔːlˈredɪ
(2) frm ˌneks ˌdɔː ˌðætl bɪ ˇfɔːr əv əs ɔːˈredɪ

    I think they're a nice young couple, don't you?
(1) aɪ ˌθɪŋk ˌðeɪ ər ə ˈnaɪs ˌjʌŋ ˌkʌpl, ˈdəʊnt ˌjuː
(2) a(ɪ) ˌθɪŋk ˌðeər ə ˈnaɪʃ ʃʌŋ ˌkʌpl, ˈdəʊnˌtʃuː

B.   I've only talked to them once, but they seemed nice
(1) aɪv ˌəʊnlɪ ˈtɔːkt tə ðəm ˈwʌns, bət ðeɪ ˈsiːmd ˌnaɪs
(2) a(ɪ)v ˌəʊnɪ ˈtɔːk tə ðm ˌwʌns, bət ðe(ɪ) ˈsiːm ˌnaɪs

     I wonder if we should go to the theatre
(1) aɪ ˈwʌndər ɪf wɪ ʃʊd gəʊ tə ðə θɪˌetə
(2) a(ɪ) ˈwʌndr ɪf wɪ ʃg ˌgəʊ tə ðə θɪˌetə

     I can try and book some seats round the corner
(1) aɪ kən ˈtraɪ ən ˌbʊk səm ˌsiːts ˌraʊnd ðə ˈkɔːnə
(2) a(ɪ) kŋ ˈtraː m ˌbʊk sm ˌsiːts ˌɽaʊn ðə ˈkɔːnə

11.6 Stylistic Variation

It should be stressed that all the features of connected speech discussed in this chapter are common in the normal, fluent speech of native speakers of English and that the lack of such features would be abnormal and artificial. As throughout the rest of this book, the descriptive emphasis has been on RP which, it may be seen, is not a monolithic accent but which displays considerable variation. Many factors influence this variation and one which may usefully be singled out is style of discourse.

It is important to avoid equating 'casual' and 'rapid', since slow speech is possible in a casual situation and rapid utterances can occur in more formal circumstances. It should also be borne in mind that the average rate of delivery differs from speaker to speaker regardless of style of speech. Thus the degree of formality and the rate of utterance are independent variables. The generalizations which follow are based on data drawn from twenty hours of tape-recorded spontaneous conversation concentrating on the speech of six RP speakers.[1] Rate of utterance was not found to be a function of style, nor was style defined in terms of pace.[2] Rather, social situations were set up that were designed to be markedly formal (e.g. an undergraduate in conversation with a professor who was a stranger to her) or markedly casual (e.g. a man in conversation with his wife). All speakers were recorded in both formal and casual situations and the speech of all of them exhibited the same trends to differing degrees.

(1) *Stress and intonation*

In all styles of speech, simple falls in pitch (whether from a high or a mid starting point) account for the majority of nuclear tones, between 60% and 70% in most conversation. The falling-rising nuclear tone accounts

---

[1] For details of this research, see Ramsaran (1978).
[2] The slowest rate of utterance recorded in conversation was 189 sylls/min (3·1 sylls/sec, 7·6 segs/sec) and the fastest was 324 sylls/min (5·4 sylls/sec, 13·4 segs/sec).

for roughly 20% on average. Thus it may be seen that speech exhibiting a large number of rises or rise-falls would be conspicuous in this respect. In general, intonation patterns show no marked distribution in casual speech. However, formal speech shows some concentrations of one pattern, whether repetitions of fall-rise nuclear tones or a stretch of speech with repeated rising nuclear tones, e.g. *If you pull them ˌoff | and put them in a glass of ˌwater | they ˋgrow littˌle roots | and ˌthen | you plant them in ˌsoil | and they ˌgrow | and then you've got another ˌspider plant.*

Casual speech has longer intonation groups and contains fewer stressed syllables than formal speech.

(2) *Weak forms*

The use of strong and weak forms does not appear to be a matter of style except insofar as the more frequent occurrence of strong forms in more formal situations results from the additional stresses of formal rhythms. The alternation of strong and weak forms is entirely regular in both formal and casual styles of speech: weak forms occur unless the grammatical word is stressed. Since stresses are more frequent in the intonation groups of formal speech, strong forms may occur more often.

(3) *Linking /r/*

As with weak forms, linking /r/ is frequent in all styles of speech, though an /r/ link is not necessarily used on every occasion where such an insertion would be possible. (See §11.3.7.) Its occurrence is of no stylistic significance. (The avoidance of intrusive /r/ results from a deliberate carefulness shown by some speakers in more formal speech.)

(4) *Assimilation*

Assimilations occur in all styles of speech. However, unassimilated forms occur more often than assimilated forms which tend to increase in frequency in the more casual style of speech, regardless of pace.

The fact that rate of utterance has no direct effect on the use of assimilation may be illustrated by examples taken from the conversation of a single speaker who has /dʒʌʃ ʃʌtɪŋ/ for *just shutting* (also exhibiting elision of /t/) when speaking at a medium pace in a comparatively formal situation, but /hɔːs ʃəʊ/ for *horse show* when speaking very rapidly in a casual situation.

In general, although all types of anticipatory de-alveolar assimilation do occur, speakers use palato-alveolar assimilations (of the kind /speɪʃ ʃʌtl̩/ for *space shuttle*) and bilabial assimilations (of the kind

/ðæp pɜːsn̩/ for *that person*) far less commonly than they use velar assimilations (of the kind /ʃɔː k kʌt/ for *short cut*). Such velar assimilation is also more common than coalescent assimilations (such as /d/ + /j/ → /dʒ/ as in /nəʊtɪdʒɒtsmən/ for *noted yachtsman* or /z/ + /j/ → /ʒ/ as in /bɪkəʒuː/ for *because you must*). However, coalescence is frequent in common phrases such as the auxiliary verbs + pronouns of *did you, can't you* etc. /dɪdʒuː, kɑːntʃuː/ and occur even in very formal conversation, e.g. *Would you like a cup of tea?* /ˈwʊdʒuː ˈlaɪk ə ˈkʌp əv ˌtiː/.

(5) *Elisions*

Elisions do show some correlation with pace. In all styles they become more frequent as the rate of utterance increases; but, whereas in formal speech they are almost entirely regular (e.g. alveolar plosives may be elided interconsonantally, /ə/ in pre-nuclear unstressed syllables, and /h/ in unstressed non-initial grammatical words), in casual speech they are less rule-bound. Casual speech may contain unpredictable elisions such as those of /l/ and /ð/ in *Well, that's all right* /we ˈæts ɔːˌraɪt/.

(6) *Co-occurrence of phonemic features of connected speech*

It should be noted that the occurrence of /r/ links, elisions and assimilations is optional in the sense that when the appropriate phonetic environments occur, these processes may or may not operate. The preceding sections (1)–(5) indicate some tendencies in the likelihood of occurrence. If, then, such processes do operate, they will follow the regular patterns described in §§11.3.5–7. Disregarding the occasional irregular elisions that may occur in casual speech, it should be added that an utterance not uncommonly contains instances of both assimilation and elision in conjunction with each other, since alveolar consonant clusters are not infrequent in word-final position: after the elision of a final /t/ or /d/ the remaining fricative or nasal may be assimilated to the place of articulation of the initial consonant of the following word, e.g. *closed shop* /kləʊzd ʃɒp → kləʊz ʃɒp → kləʊʒ ʃɒp/, *hand made* /hænd meɪd → hæn meɪd → hæm meɪd/ and *just shutting* /dʒʌst ʃʌtɪŋ → dʒʌs ʃʌtɪŋ → dʒʌʃ ʃʌtɪŋ/. The conjunction *and* has a common weak form with /d/ elided and the /ə/ may also be elided, leaving the nasal to function syllabically, particularly after plosives. The resulting syllabic /n̩/ is itself susceptible to assimilation, which accounts for such pronunciations as /ˈwʊg ŋ̍ ˈglɑːs/ (*wood and glass*).

(7) *Plosive release*

One of the most stylistically significant variables concerns a non-phonemic variation in the release of plosives, particularly the fortis series. Not only is this a matter of allophonic realization, but it also cuts across phonemic boundaries in that it applies to /p, t, k/ and, to a lesser extent, /b, d, g/. As is explained in §8.2.3(2), a plosive usually has an inaudible release when followed by another stop consonant. However, in the most formal social situations, there is a marked increase in the number of audibly released plosives in such a context, e.g. [ˈaɪ lʊktʰ ˈkwɪzɪkəl].

Summary

No feature is unique to a variety, but some features are distributionally marked. In particular, pre-consonantal plosives may be audibly released when speech is formal, whereas assimilations increase in frequency as speech becomes more casual. Elision is the only feature that bears a definite relation to pace, occurring more frequently as pace increases, however formal the situation may be. There is more fluctuation of pace in casual speech.

Since assimilations, elisions and /r/ links occur with some frequency in all situations whether formal or casual, it is clearly important that foreign learners should cultivate these features in their speech.

Appendix: 12

Teaching the Pronunciation of English

12.1 The Place of Pronunciation

In the preceding chapters, the chief features of English pronunciation (especially of RP) have been set out in some detail. Clearly a foreign learner who requires an adequate performance in the language for the practical purposes of everyday communication will not need to master all the variants described. Nevertheless, any teacher or learner must consider how much of the time given to the acquisition of another language should be devoted to pronunciation and what level of performance is necessary for efficient communication.

12.1.1 It can be claimed that speech, like writing, constitutes no more than the transmission phase of language, providing a signalling system for the language's more essential store of items defined in the lexicon and of syntactic rules contained in the grammar. Yet high adequacy in lexis and grammar can be negated by incompetence in the signalling phase, when the prime medium is speech. Thus, unless a learner expects to deal with English only in its written form, there is no escape from the acquisition of at least the rudimentary elements of English pronunciation. Such a conclusion implies that in any course of English a realistic amount of time should be devoted to practice in the spoken language.

12.1.2 However, the teaching of pronunciation presents particular difficulties. Grammatical structures can be ordered and taught in sequence; a vocabulary compiled on a basis of frequency of occurrence can be utilized for the presentation of early grammatical structures, with the addition of special sets of lexical items as situations or special purposes require. Pronunciation, on the other hand, does not permit such progressive treatment, since all phonetic/phonological features are potentially present from the very first lesson, unless vocabulary items are artificially introduced. Nevertheless, the teacher must deal systematically with the teaching of pronunciation, even though he may be forced to postpone the correction of some mistakes which occur in the early stages. In organizing his teaching he will require answers to such questions as:

What form of pronunciation is to be taken as model?
What level of performance is to be aimed at?
Can the difficulties of English pronunciation be ordered?
What general principles should underlie the teaching of pronunciation?

12.2 The Choice of Models of Pronunciation

This is a matter of special importance as far as English is concerned because of the world-wide use of the language and because of the profusion of differing spoken forms existing not only in such mother-tongue areas as Britain, North America and Australasia but also in those vast regions of India and Africa where English is used as an adopted *lingua franca* (see §6.3.5).

12.2.1 The Native Speaker

In normal circumstances, the Englishman or the American, for instance, will by early adulthood be making habitual use of one speech form determined mainly by his family background and by his social environment. Such variations in his pronunciation as occur are likely to be the result of differences in situation. It will no doubt be possible to identify the phonetic and phonological features which characterize his pronunciation when he is making a formal speech or when he is talking to children or when he is influenced by anger or tenderness, and so on. Such phonetic indices are of course accompanied by appropriate lexical and grammatical variations of usage. The pronunciation effects of stylistic variation are shown particularly in changes of tempo and intonation and in the use made of elision and assimilation (see §12.7.3). In addition, some speakers will tend (often unwittingly) to adapt their own speech to some extent to that of their interlocutor, e.g. by making concessions to the other's social or regional accent. Thus, in speaking to an American, an Englishman might use the pronunciations /ˈskedjuːl, praɪˈmerəlɪ/ for *schedule, primarily* in preference to his usual /ˈʃedjuːl, ˈpraɪmərəlɪ/. Or again, even amongst his own countrymen he may feel that his usual /dɪˈspjuːt/ for *dispute* (*n.*) is inappropriate in the company of those engaged in industrial strikes for whom /ˈdɪspjuːt/ is the (recent) preferred form.

However, although the native speaker generally has a basic stability in his habits of speech production, he has considerable ability in the reception and comprehension of other forms of English which show marked divergencies in their phonetic and phonological characteristics. There can be no doubt that such receptive efficiency has been brought about by half a century of aural exposure through radio and television in particular to most of the important spoken forms of the language.

Thus, the Londoner will now have little difficulty in understanding the commoner forms of American English, although he may experience some difficulty with the more extreme, popular types of, say, Glasgow or Belfast speech.

12.2.2 The Foreign Learner

It is rare for the foreign learner, usually acquiring English in an artificial and intermittent fashion, to approach the native's receptive and productive competence. Indeed, it can be argued that only exceptionally is it necessary to have such an aim. But, whatever abilities the learner may acquire in the later stages of learning English, he will be well advised at the beginning to model his productive performance on but one type of spoken English, without any conscious attempt to alter his pronunciation according to style or situation in the way that the native speaker does, but restricting himself to what has been called a 'careful, colloquial' style (see §11.5). As he gains confidence, productive precision and fluency in the single style, he can for the purposes of widening his receptive competence gradually be exposed to other important regional types. If his introduction to English is via a British spoken form, he might, when this production habit is firmly established, be given opportunities to gain experience in receiving a widely accepted form of American English such as may be heard from newsreaders on the national networks (see §12.9.5).

12.3 Choice of Basic Model

Faced with the great diversity of English accents, the foreign learner might wish that there existed a neutral, all-purpose, international pronunciation of English. It is claimed by some that as a result of the great improvement in communications in this century the present divergencies in English as it is spoken throughout the world (see also §6.3.5) will gradually be eliminated and there will emerge a universally intelligible pronunciation of English which all can use. The present evidence suggests, if the total English-speaking population of the world is taken into account, that this natural and desirable process as yet makes no advance. If there is to be an acceptable international pronunciation of English in the foreseeable future, it seems likely that it will have to be artificially formulated and disseminated[1] (§12.8). There are some formidable difficulties which beset the acceptance of a solution of this kind, not least of which is the native speaker's inability to use a type of

---

[1] I have attempted in 'Towards an international pronunciation of English', pp 45–53. *In Honour of A. S. Hornby* (Oxford University Press, 1978) to present some theoretical examples of such artificial pronunciation systems for English.

hybrid English pronunciation which only partially resembles his own.

The more realistic, immediate solution lies in the choice of one of the main natural forms of English as the basic model, e.g. a representative form of British or American pronunciation, with the possibility of the selection for geographical reasons of such other (numerically minor) forms as Australian or South African. The advantage of such choices is that these forms (in a standard variety) are without difficulty mutually intelligible. The decisive criteria in the choice of any teaching model must be that it has wide currency, is widely and readily understood, is adequately described in textbooks and has ample recorded material available for the learner. It is clear that, if these criteria are admitted, British RP is an important candidate as a basic model which has considerable prestige and is already taught throughout the world.

12.4 A Wider-based RP

The emergence of RP as a standard pronunciation has already been given some treatment (§6.3.2), together with a preliminary assessment of the present-day situation. It is not sufficient, however, for the foreign learner to be presented with a general account of British attitudes to a standard of pronunciation. He requires, on the one hand, advice as to which English speech form is appropriate for him and, on the other, wherever this is possible, guidance as to the acceptable tolerances within the form.

RP must be regarded as an evolving mode of pronunciation in its phonological system, its phonetic realization and the incidence of its phonemes. Certainly the specification of RP as the property of a single social class within a restricted geographical location is no longer valid.[1] It is now realistic to allow considerable dilution in the original concept of the RP speaker, with the consequent admission into the permitted speech forms of certain variants until recently regarded as regional. Nevertheless, the essential regional base (historically) of the pronunciation regarded as 'standard' or 'received' remains the educated speech of the South East of England, as described in the preceding chapters. It is this system which is recommended in general terms to the foreign learner, though certain optional items such as /hw/ (§8.9.2) may be firmly excluded and the incidence of /ə/ and /ɪ/ less rigidly prescribed (see §12.7.1(b)). Where a choice is related to the usages of different generations, the learner is always advised to adopt the form commonly found amongst speakers of the middle generations, i.e. the type of RP referred to in earlier chapters as 'general'. Similarly, the learner can be permitted some latitude in the phonetic realization of the RP

---

[1] See the 'Introduction' to the *English Pronouncing Dictionary* (14th edition, Dent, 1977) where I have sought to provide a less restrictive definition.

phonemes, especially as far as vowel articulations are concerned (see §12.7). The extent of permitted phonetic and phonemic latitude will depend upon the level of performance at which learners, with their differing needs, will be aiming.

It can of course be claimed that the traditional concept of RP suffers such dilution as a result of the tolerances suggested that a new label should be applied to the model. 'General British' (GB) has been used[1] and may in time supersede the abbreviation RP. But so widespread in Britain and abroad is the use of the term RP that it is retained in this discussion.

12.5   Performance Targets

Factors which will obviously determine the learner's aims are concerned with his age and his natural ability, and with his motivation and the use to which he intends to put the language. He may succeed merely in speaking English with the phonetic and phonological system of his own language, in which case he is likely to be totally unintelligible to most native English listeners or, at best, comprehensible only to the extent that a small number of information points can be decoded as a result of the general context of the situation. If an attempt is made to approximate to native English speech forms, the achievement may lie somewhere between two extremes. The lowest requirement can be described as one of *minimum general intelligibility*, i.e. one which possesses a set of distinctive elements which correspond in some measure to the inventory of the RP phonemic system and which is capable of conveying a message efficiently from a native English listener's standpoint, given that the context of the message is known and that the listener has had time to 'tune in' to the speaker's pronunciation. At the other extreme, the learner may be said to achieve a performance of *high acceptability*, i.e. a form of speech which the native listener may not identify as non-native, which conveys information as readily as would a native's and which arrives at this result through precision in the phonetic (allophonic) realization of phonemes and by confident handling of accentual and intonational patterns.

It must be admitted that the great majority of foreign learners will have a severely practical purpose for acquiring English and will perceive no important benefit in approaching the performance of the native speaker. Indeed, the learner may derive some advantage in retaining a clearly foreign image in his dealings with English speakers, e.g. the waiter or the taxidriver, whose discourse with a native speaker is likely to be limited and stereotyped, is unlikely to need to progress beyond a

---

[1] For instance, by J. Windsor Lewis in his *Concise Pronouncing Dictionary of British and American English* (Oxford University Press, 1972).

level of basic intelligibility. Too much should not be made of phonetic and phonological niceties if this is the goal. Such is the redundancy present in natural languages that, within a defined context and with an adequate stock of words and basic syntactic patterns, considerable intelligibility can be achieved even though the pronunciation is seriously deformed. (For instance, at a dinner table, someone who asks for the *potatoes*—pronounced as [bəˈdeːdoːz]—is likely to be understood without difficulty, though it should be noted that an accentually divergent form such as [ˈbɒdeːdoːz] might well perplex.)

There will however be many learners who, for academic reasons or because their work requires them to deal on equal terms with native speakers in Britain or abroad or even as tourists, wish to communicate easily without signalling too blatantly their foreign origin. For them, a mastery of English pronunciation and a ready understanding of a variety of English accents will not be enough; they must also expect to have a comprehensive command of syntax, including everyday elliptical structures, a wide-ranging vocabulary (containing new or fashionable locutions) and a deep acquaintance with English culture. The *foreign teacher* of English constitutes a special case. He has the obligation to present his students with as faithful a model of English pronunciation as is possible. In the first place, and particularly if he is dealing with young pupils, his students will imitate a bad pronunciation as exactly as they will a good one; and, secondly, if he is using illustrative recorded material, his own pronunciation must not diverge markedly from the native model.

There remains one further and separate category of competence in pronunciation which seeks neither to imitate a natural model nor to have any international validity: it may be termed a level of *restricted intelligibility*. However undesirable such a level may be thought to be when the efficacy of English as a world language is in question, there is no doubt that for most of those who use English as a second language— as a lingua franca within their own country having a number of indigenous languages none of which is acceptable as a national language— this is a reality, especially within the continents of Africa and India. Such forms of English conform in all important features of lexis and grammar to the native language of Britain or America and may thus in their written form pose no problems of international intelligibility. It is in the spoken form of transmission that phonetic and phonological interference from the indigenous languages may erect a formidable barrier for listeners from communities where English is a native language. If the interference is such that no attempt is made to do other than use the sound system and prosody of the indigenous language, however effective this may be within the country concerned, communication with native English speakers may break down.

12.6   Priorities

The various elements of English pronunciation will offer differing degrees of difficulty according to the linguistic background of the learner. Teaching should obviously be concentrated on those features of English which are not found in the learner's native language. There are, however, certain basic characteristics of pronunciation which seem sufficiently specific to English to constitute a priority for the great majority of learners.

12.6.1   Accentuation

The stress-timed rhythm of the English utterance (be it a single word or connected speech) with the related obscuration of weak syllables is the prime distinguishing feature of the language's pronunciation, with no exact parallel in any other language. In fact, in connected speech, unaccented syllables considerably outnumber those carrying primary or secondary accents. For some learners, e.g. with French or an Italian language or an African tone language as background, the problems of English accentuation are especially great and will require prolonged emphasis. For all learners, accentuation must provide the foundation on which any pronunciation course is built. The great variety of accentual patterns in English words must, of course, be given an important and early place in any teaching programme. However, it is worth keeping in mind that, in ordinary connected speech, monosyllables account for more than 80% of words occurring, with words of two syllables coming next with 15%, three-syllable words with nearly 3% and longer words occurring comparatively rarely.

12.6.2   Segmental systems

(a) It should be noted that in running English speech vowels account for some 40% and consonants 60% of the phonemes uttered (§§7.4, 8.10). The fact that RP /ə/ and /ɪ/ have a frequency of occurrence of 10·74% and 8·33% respectively, whereas /ɔɪ/ and /ʊə/ are comparatively rare, may assume some importance in the construction of drills. Similarly, it is noteworthy that among the consonants the alveolar phonemes occur most frequently, whereas /ʒ/ is relatively rare. Although the fact that /ð/ occurs ten times more frequently than its fortis counterpart /θ/ can be accounted for by the frequent occurrence of such grammatical items as *the* or *that* (as pointed out in §8.10), the discrepancy may seem to indicate the relative weight which should be given to /ð/ in teaching. On the other hand, /θ/ occurs more frequently in accented (and therefore prominent) positions than /ð/.

   (b) Whatever the relative frequency of actual occurrences of the items contained in the phoneme inventories, the full systems (20V and

24C) must be regarded as complex compared with the systems of many other languages. In particular, the opposition of the close vowels /iː/ ∿ /ɪ/, /uː/ ∿ /ʊ/, the existence of a central long vowel /ɜː/ and the delicately differentiated front vowel set of /iː/ ∿ /ɪ/ ∿ /e/ ∿ /æ/ + /ʌ/, together with the significant or conditioned variations of vowel length, will pose problems to many foreign learners. Similarly, in the consonant system, English has a comparatively rare complexity in its set of fricative places of articulation—labio-dental, dental, alveolar, palato-alveolar and glottal (§8.4(1)). Again, although English shares with many languages a system of plosives of the sort /p, t, k, b, d, g/, the conventions of realization will not always be the same, English preferring presence or absence of aspiration as a crucial distinctive feature whereas many other languages, e.g. Romance or Slav, more typically make use of voicing (§8.2.11). Finally, as far as consonants are concerned, English characteristically permits a large number of consonant clusters (§9.8). Consonant clusters occur, of course, in many other languages, e.g. German and Polish, but the combinations permitted may differ from those of English. There are nevertheless other languages whose possibilities of consonant clustering are much more limited, e.g. Spanish or Italian, or whose syllables regularly have a simple CV shape, e.g. many Oriental and African languages. It is clear that in such cases much practice in English two- and three-consonant clusters will be needed to avoid the insertion of intrusive vowels—not only initially and finally in the word (where clustering as opposed to single consonants has only a 20% occurrence) but also across word and morpheme boundaries.

(c) The choice of phonemes must, of course, coincide with that of native speakers using the same type of pronunciation. It has already been pointed out (§9.10) that there exists in many cases a free choice of phonemes without a denotion of a particular generation or style, e.g. /e/ or /eɪ/ in *again*; /iː/ or /e/ in *Kenya, zebra*; /ɔː/ or /ɒ/ in *salt*; /ʊ/ or /uː/ in *room*; /sj/ or /ʃ/ in *issue*; /g/ or /dʒ/ for the last consonant in *pedagogy*, etc. There are other choices (§12.7.3) which may be determined by considerations of generation or style. In all cases of doubt, the learner is advised to consult a dictionary[1] which gives several RP variants and to use the variant which, having some advantage in frequency of occurrence, is placed first.

12.6.3 Sounds in context

English has its own specific habits as regards both assimilation and elision (§§9.6, 11.3, 11.3.7), but how far these are adopted by the foreign learner will depend on the performance target which he has set

[1] The *English Pronouncing Dictionary*, (14th edition, Dent, 1988) is the most comprehensive for British English.

himself (§12.7.3). Particularly affected are the alveolar articulations which exhibit notable instability.

12.6.4   Intonation

Although nearly all non-tone languages share certain characteristics of intonation, e.g. a tendency to use generally falling tunes for declarative statements and commands, whereas ultimately rising patterns are often associated with questions and non-finality, there are some tunes (as well as certain usages as regards the pitch of unaccented syllables) which are specific to English. It should be remembered that intonation makes a most important contribution to the accentuation patterning of English (pitch variation serving to make salient those information points to which the speaker wishes to draw attention). To that extent, intonation may be taken to fall within the priority category (12.6.1) above. In addition, the attitudinal implications of intonation become increasingly important if a high level of achievement is desired. However, in the early stages of learning English, although the intonation patterns presented by the teacher should always be authentic, attention should be concentrated on the role of pitch in accentual oppositions, especially as regards the location in the utterance of pitch-prominent syllables. Once this basic level is achieved, variations in tone shape can be introduced.

12.7   RP High Acceptability

If high acceptability in RP is defined as a level of attainment in production which, for the native listener, is as readily intelligible as that of a native RP speaker and which is not immediately identifiable as foreign, and as a level of receptive ability which allows the foreign listener to understand without difficulty all varieties and styles of RP as well as the other important forms of English, it is to be expected that the learner will be familiar with the features of current English described in Chapters 7–11. His productive performance must be related to one specific type of RP. However, just as no two RP speakers of the same generation (nor the same RP speaker on different occasions) speak in precisely the same way, the learner may be permitted certain tolerances in his pronunciation, provided that his speech retains an internal consistency, i.e. avoids the incongruity of a mixture of regional or generation styles. Some native speakers are consciously apt to adopt unhabitual speech forms, e.g. by attempting to use an American pronunciation, when they hope to create a special effect in a particular situation. The foreign learner, however proficient he has become, is well-advised not to attempt such an effect, in the same way that he should be wary in his use of slang or non-standard grammar. The latitude which can be admitted concerns rather the phonetic realization of the segmental phonemes, i.e. the choice of allophonic variants (and in particular those of the vowels). In the following sections, the important essentials are listed and suggestions made as to possible tolerances compatible with a goal of high acceptability.

12.7.1 Vowels

(a) *Essentials* As mentioned in §12.6.2(b), the learner must have at his disposal the 20 vowel phonemes (12 monophthongs and 8 diphthongs), together with the appropriate durational variations (§7.4), especially when these latter are significant in such oppositions as *seed* ⌣ *seat, heard* ⌣ *hurt, road* ⌣ *wrote,* etc. Special attention must be paid to the quality/quantity complexes involved in such series as *bead, beat, bit* (§7.9.2(5)) or *food, boot, good* (§7.9.9(5)), these items illustrating the occurrence respectively of long tense /iː/, reduced tense /iː/ = [i], short lax /ɪ/ and long tense /uː/, reduced tense /uː/ = [u], short lax /ʊ/. Although oppositions of only two phonemes are involved here, it is important in teaching to identify the three phonetic complexes so as to ensure that the vowels of, for instance, *beat* and *boot* are not given undue length.

(b) *Tolerances* Provided that the oppositions are retained, i.e. that the realizations of phonemes in the same context do not overlap, some latitude in performance is possible. Thus, for instance, in the series /iː, ɪ, e, æ/, the qualities produced may be somewhat more open than those indicated by the mark • in the diagrams of Chapter 7. Permissible *areas* (as opposed to points) of production encompassing several of the variants given in Chapter 7, are shown in Fig. 46.

/iː/ and /uː/, which are usually pronounced in General RP with a slight glide from a more open, centralized position to a closer, more fronted position, may be given a pure vowel articulation with a close front or back position respectively, similar to the qualities commonly associated with vowels of this type in other languages. Though there is a danger that such pronunciations may sound hypercorrect to the native listener, especially if the vowels used are cardinal in quality, they are to be preferred to gliding vowels whose starting point is so open that it falls within the area typical of popular regional speech—thus introducing unwittingly a comic incongruity if the remainder of the system conforms to the RP model.

The theoretical areas of tolerance for /ɑː/ and /ɔː/ are extensive, the limitations being imposed by the presence of /æ/ = [æː], e.g. in an opposition such as *cad* ⌣ *card,* and of /uː/, e.g. in *food* ⌣ *ford.* The variations shown in §§7.9.6, 7.9.8 may be permitted. Similarly, the variants for /ɜː/ shown in §7.9.11 may be safely used, provided that they do not overlap with the realization of /ɑː/, e.g. if an open variety of /ɜː/ is used in a word such as *burn,* this will necessitate a more retracted /ɑː/ in *barn.*

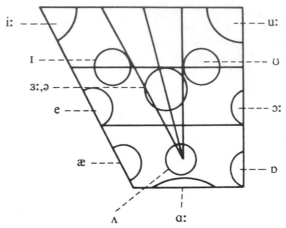

FIG. 46.—RP monophthongs: acceptable areas.

The diphthongization sometimes associated with RP /ɪ, e, æ/ mentioned in Chapter 7 seems to be growing less common and need not be adopted. However, the increasing use of a close vowel (i.e. a short /iː/ for final /ɪ/) amongst middle and young generation speakers justifies its use by foreign learners, if it is found to be easier than the traditional /ɪ/, in such cases as *happy*, *easy*, etc. In the case of final /ə/, there is no need for a specially open variant to be used (§7.9.12(2)), an excessively open variant often being judged comic.

As stated in §7.9.2, there is often free variation in the use of /ə/ or /ɪ/ in some unaccented syllables. The pronunciation /ə/ appears to be increasingly preferred, e.g. for the penultimate vowel in the termination -*ity* in such as word as *quality* (/-ətɪ/ rather than /-ɪtɪ/), -*ily* (especially after /r/) as in *merrily* (/-əlɪ/ rather than /-ɪlɪ/), -*ate* as in *fortunate* (/-ət/ rather than /-ɪt/). Again, /ə/ or /ɪ/ are equally acceptable in the terminations -*less*, -*ness*, -*ace*, e.g. *hopeless*, *goodness*, *palace*, with /ə/ gaining ground; but it still seems preferable to retain /ɪ/ in -*et* as in *carpet* and essential to have /ɪ/ in -*age* as in *cabbage*, as well as in the inflexion -*es*, -*ed* as in *horses*, *waited*.

As for the 8 RP diphthongs, the area of the first element is more important than the second element, which is only lightly touched on and has little prominence. These areas of onset may acceptably be extensive but should not overlap (see Figs. 47, 48). The regional connotations of the quality of the starting points (as described in §§7.10–7.12) should be borne in mind: if, for instance, /eɪ/ is said with a starting point more open than cardinal [ɛ], the impression given may be that of popular London speech.

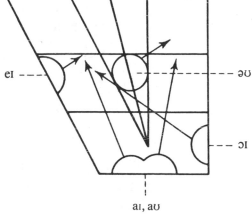

FIG. 47.—RP falling diphthongs: acceptable onset areas.

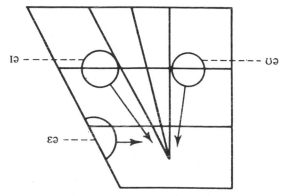

FIG. 48.—RP centring diphthongs: acceptable onset areas.

In the case of /aɪ, aʊ/, there may be a common (open central) starting point (§§7.10.2, 7.10.5); the levelling of /aɪə, aʊə/, though it has long been common in Southern England, is not essential for the foreign learner. It should also be noted that /ʊə/ is increasingly replaced by /ɔː/ not only in such words as *poor*, *sure*, but also in *moor*, *tour*, etc. (§7.12.3(3)). As for /əʊ/ (§7.10.4), although the general RP form [əʊ] is most widespread and should thus be recommended, the more conservative form with a somewhat more retracted first element [o̞] is not inadmissible; but learners are advised to avoid the diphthong having a fronted onset [ë], this variant now being regarded as excessively affected.

12.7.2   Consonants

(a) *Essentials*   The full inventory of 24 consonant phonemes must be available to the speaker.

At this high level of performance, it is essential that the aspiration of fortis /p, t, k/ in accented positions (§8.2.1) should be maintained as the major factor distinguishing these phonemes from lenis /b, d, g/, i.e. constituting a more potent differentiating feature than presence or absence of voicing. Learners whose mother tongue relies on voicing as the prime feature of opposition (e.g. most Romance and Slav language speakers) must take particular care. If, for instance, *pat* is realized as [pæt] rather than [pʰæt], an English listener is likely to understand *bat*, the absence of aspiration suggesting /b/ to an English ear. Similarly, /l/ and /r/ following accented /p, t, k/ (and to a lesser extent /j/ and /w/ since oppositions involving preceding fortis/lenis plosives are rare) must be devoiced, as if thus signalling aspiration, so that *plead* and *bleed* are distinguished primarily by [l̥] in *plead* or *pray* and *bray* primarily by [r̥] in *pray*.

The articulation of /t, d/ must be clearly alveolar (§8.2.5(5)), and when followed by the homorganic syllabics /n/ and /l/, as in *button*, *sudden*, *little*, *middle*, the release must be nasal or lateral respectively without an intrusive vowel (§8.2.3(4, 5)).

It is also characteristic of highly acceptable RP that the first plosive of stop sequences should have no audible release (§8.2.3(2)), e.g. in *actor*, *black tie*, *rugby*, *big dog*. Intrusive vowels should be avoided in clusters of other consonants, e.g. between /s/ and /p, t, k/ as in *sport*, *strike*, *school* or in such final sequences as /lmz/ (*films*) or /lnz/ (*kilns*).

Alveolar /s, z/ must remain clearly distinct from dental /θ, ð/ and palato-alveolar /ʃ, ʒ/ (§8.4).

The /l/ phoneme should have the qualities and correct distribution of allophones mentioned in §8.7.1, i.e. [l, ɫ, l̩]. Similarly, /r/ should have a post-alveolar approximant or frictionless continuant articulation rather than any kind of trill (§8.7.1). High performance RP will make use of the linking /r/, e.g. for *far away* /ˈfɑː r əˈweɪ/ is more typical than /ˈfɑː əˈweɪ/; and for *pour out* /ˈpɔː r ˈaʊt/ is preferred to /ˈpɔː ˈaʊt/. On the other hand, 'intrusive' /r/, as in *vanilla* /r/ *ice*, is best avoided by all but the most competent, lest the usage be extended to those other cases, e.g. *I saw* /r/ *it*, *draw* /r/ *ing room*, which are often stigmatized by RP speakers (§11.3.7).

(b) *Tolerances*   Certain of the variants or allophones described in Chapter 8 may be disregarded without detriment to an impression of highly acceptable performance. For instance, the devoicing of lenis consonants /b, d, g, dʒ, v, ð, z, ʒ/ in post- or pre-pausal position is not crucial: full voicing is permissible provided that a [ə] off-glide is not added finally to a word such as *big* ([ˈbɪɡᵊ]) so that it is decoded as *bigger*.

Final (i.e. pre-pausal) plosives, although usually without audible release, as in *lit*, *lid*, may be given an explosive last stage, the resultant impression being one of careful speech. The use of [ʔ] (§8.2.7) or glottal reinforcement (§8.2.3(3)) in connection with the fortis plosives and affricate is never necessary; nor is the affrication or weakening of plosives mentioned in §8.2.3(6).

Although, as mentioned in previous sections, it is important to gain articulatory skill in producing the numerous RP consonant clusters, it should be remembered that sequences of more than two consonants with simple words are comparatively rare; a greater test of articulatory skill occurs at morpheme and word boundaries, e.g. in *corkscrew, fixed price, pitched battle, sobbed bitter*, etc.

12.7.3   Sounds in context

(a) *Elision*   The examples of post-nuclear vowel elision in the words quoted in §9.6(1, b), e.g. loss of /ə/ in *comparable, factory, dangerous, carefully*, etc., must be regarded as optional, the retention of the weak vowel being entirely acceptable. In pre-nuclear positions, e.g. in *polite, solicitor*, the foreign learner is best advised to avoid elision of the weak vowel, a practice which is characteristic of rapid, casual speech.

On the other hand, the alveolar consonant elisions mentioned in §9.6(2, b) can be adopted by the foreign learner, especially those involving the simplification of a three consonant cluster by the elision of a medial /t/ or /d/, e.g. in *restless*, *kindness*, where retention of the alveolar stop can be regarded as unusually careful.

In connected speech, considerable elision of both vowels and consonants is characteristic of a colloquial style (§11.3.6). It is not necessary, however, for the foreign learner (even with a high acceptability target) to seek to adopt all these native speaker habits. Once again, he may restrict himself to the elision of alveolar stops occurring medially in clusters of three consonants (especially when /t/ or /d/ is followed by another stop) brought together at word boundaries, e.g. in *left turn, mashed potatoes, jogged by, wind down*, etc.

(b) *Assimilation*   It is assumed that the competent foreign learner will make most of the allophonic contextual assimilations mentioned in §11.3.1, these usually resulting from the inevitable accommodation which takes place between two articulations in the speech continuum. Certain changes which may provide cues to meaning, e.g. the devoicing of /l/ and /r/ after accented /p, t, k/ mentioned in 12.7.2, (a) above, are essential. In the case of assimilations involving changes of phoneme (§§11.3.2–5), especially at word boundaries, it should be remembered that these are important because they have stylistic implications. Thus, if a native speaker elides medial /t/ and /d/ in consonant clusters, it is likely that he will also assimilate word final /t, d, n, s, z/ at word boundaries as suggested in §11.3.5. It is therefore consistent for the highly competent foreign learner to adopt similar habits. He must always be careful that in seeking to adopt an informal, colloquial style of English speech he does not introduce assimilatory habits which are characteristic of his own native language but not of English (§11.5).

However, what is more important than the development of productive skills in either elision or assimilation is the cultivation of the ability to receive and decode the highly elided and assimilated speech produced by native English speakers. Such speech must be regarded as the norm in all ordinary circumstances. The foreign student must therefore spend a considerable amount of time listening to normal colloquial English in order to acquire skill in identifying information points in an utterance (making full use of all contextual and syntactic cues and probabilities), when apparently crucial sounds are absent or when the isolate form of a word has become greatly changed in context, e.g. /ʃwɪ/ is a frequent telescoped form of /ʃəlwɪ/ (*shall we*). The native speaker is, of course, usually unaware that he makes reductions of this sort.

12.7.4 Accentuation

It has already been pointed out (§12.6.1) that the accentual features of English must form the base for the teaching of the language's pronunciation. These include the correct reduction of unaccented grammatical items (weak forms—§10.4(2)). In connected speech, the weak forms of the most common grammatical items occur overwhelmingly more frequently than the strong forms, and, from this point of view, may be considered the usual pronunciation. However, if a native speaker is asked to pronounce such common words as *and, but, at, of,* etc. he will naturally give the rare citation (accented) forms /ænd, bʌt, æt, ɒv/ rather than the more common /ənd, bət, ət, əv/. He is genuinely unaware that he regularly reduces such words when unaccented in connected speech and will often deny that he would normally pronounce a phrase such as *And there was a knock at the door* as /ən ðə wəz ə ˈnɒk ət ðə ˈdɔː/, describing such a speech style as careless. It follows that it is wiser to listen to the way in which the native speaks rather than to ask his opinion. Similarly, most dictionaries understandably record the strong pronunciation of these grammatical words, without always giving the weak alternatives. The foreign learner—at any level—must regard the strong forms as being 'marked', i.e. having a special meaning compared with the 'unmarked' sense of the usual weak forms: thus, the oppositive, emphatic meaning of *I ˈcan* /kæn/ *come, I'm going ˈto* /tuː/ *London* with associated stress accent may be compared with the same phrases said neutrally with /kən/ and /tə/. However, the uncommon reduced forms, heard only in very rapid speech and of which some examples are given in the last part of §10.4(2), need not be imitated by foreign learners, even those with the highest target. The use of /jə/ or /mə/ in such phrases as *your mother, my father* has social connotations and, if employed inappropriately by a learner, could appear comically incongruous.

The proficient learner will, however, make use of those variations in the accentual patterns of words which are the result of the general rhythmic pressures of extended speech as opposed to the patterns of isolate words (§11.2). Such variation affects particularly adjectives or the adjectival element of a noun phrase, the predicative pattern (corresponding to the isolate form given in dictionaries) being regarded as normal, whereas the attributive pattern displays the variant, e.g. compare the patterns in citation or predicative situations as in *My car's secondhand* [ˌ--ˈ-], *This is Waterloo* [ˌ--ˈ-] and the attributive variants *A secondhand* [ˈ---] *car, Waterloo* [ˈ---] *Station*. Such variation, 'stress-shift', is essential for high acceptability.

12.7.5 Intonation

The intonation of English has been studied in greater detail and for longer than that of any other language. No definitive analysis, classifying the features of RP intonation, has yet appeared (though that presented by O'Connor and Arnold (1973) provides the most comprehensive and useful account from the foreign learner's point of view). Difficulties arise not so much in the accentuation role of intonation, i.e. the use of pitch as a prime factor in making a syllable or word prominent amongst its neighbours, or in the association of tone patterns with general grammatical structure (§10.5.1ff). It is rather in the assignment of emotional (attitudinal) colouring to one or other tone pattern that disagreement still exists, even when discussion is restricted to a single type of pronunciation such as RP. One reason for such disagreement is that there cannot be said to be a simple one-to-one correlation between a particular tone pattern and a particular attitude, the tone pattern which manifests an attitude depending very much upon the intonational environment; moreover, the attitude itself is not easily defined in discrete terms. Thus, not all speakers would agree upon what constitutes a perfunctory or detached attitude in making a statement nor upon which tune should be chosen to signal such an attitude. Similarly, a listener may misinterpret a speaker's attitude because his (the listener's) intonation habits are somewhat different, although the two segmental systems do not differ.

Nevertheless, there is sufficient common ground in the correlation of attitude and tone pattern for the highly competent student to be confident in making use of this other function of intonation, in addition, of course, to the essential role of signalling the location of nucleus and accented syllables. He should be skilled, for instance, in the use of the falling-rising pattern (§10.5.2.3), occurring both on a single word and spread over two or more words. This pattern is extremely common in RP and is important for conveying many nuances of doubt, encouragement, unspoken implications, etc., which in other languages might require more explicit lexical or syntactic cues. The learner should also note the frequent use of emphatic falls on pre-nuclear accented syllables (capable also of being identified as multi-nuclear patterns as in §10.5.2.4) which are a common feature of natural discourse—as opposed to much reading aloud.

Despite the encouragement of many textbooks to use rising intonation patterns for Yes/No questions and falling patterns for X-questions (i.e. those containing an interrogative word), the learner should note that a rising intonation is at least as common for the latter type, especially when the enquiry is polite or appealing. The intonation for question-tags should also be correctly used: a falling tune expecting *confirmation* of a statement (e.g. \`*isn't it*?), whereas a rising tune indicates a request for *information* (e.g. ‚*isn't it*?).

Finally, the learner aiming at the highest achievement should be aware of the attitudinal importance of the general pitch level of the intonation head and body preceding the nucleus, a high level usually indicating enthusiasm, interest, liveliness compared with a low level which may give an impression of a perfunctory, uninterested, surly or suspicious attitude.

12.8 Minimum General Intelligibility

This type of performance has been described in §12.5 as one which preserves the chief elements of the RP system and is capable of conveying a message with some ease (in a given context) to a native English listener. It is not necessarily related specifically to any one form of English. It is regarded as essential that the accentual characteristics of English (including rhythmic features and the associated obscuration of weak syllables[1]) should be retained, as well as the ability to produce the common consonant clusters. It is in fact possible to reduce the segmental inventory of English very considerably and still retain a good level of intelligibility.[2] For instance, the vowel system can be reduced to a central pair /ə:/ and /ə/. If this is done the sentence /ˈwən də jə ˈθəŋk ðə ˈtʃəldrən wəl gət ˈhə:m frəm ˈskə:l?/ is not too difficult to interpret as 'When do you think the children will get home from school?', especially if the situation predisposes the listener to understand 'children' and 'school'. The disadvantage of such a reduction is that it produces a form of English unlike any natural speech, with the attendant problem that native speakers would have difficulty in teaching it.

---

[1] Minimally reduced forms can be employed if they are thought to be easier, e.g. /ənd/ for *and* rather than /ən/, /nd/ or /n/; *he*, *his*, etc. can retain the /h/.

[2] See *In Honour of A. S. Hornby, op. cit.*

It follows that any simplified form of pronunciation should have features with most of the major natural forms. In addition, the model should have three requisites:—

1. It should be at least as easy for the foreign student to learn as any natural model.
2. It should be readily intelligible to most native speakers of English.
3. It should provide a base for the learner who has acquired it to understand the major natural varieties of English.

Given that the accentual features common to all natural forms of English must be retained, it is in the segmental phonemes that simplification may be expected. An amalgam of British RP and a generally accepted form of American pronunciation would seem an ideal solution, representing the great majority of native English speakers. The result would also show a more obvious affinity to the orthography of the language than does RP. (It is undoubtedly true that English orthography, though often maligned for its apparent lack of correlation with present pronunciation, does exhibit underlying regularities applicable to a number of forms of English.) The preservation of the pronunciation of post-vocalic /r/ in words like *farm*, *heard* is an example of closer adherence to orthography which may in fact reflect a majority pronunciation and which might be helpful to some learners who do not wish to identify their English pronunciation with any one accent. However, apart from this potential presence of post-vocalic /r/ (and the recommended omission from the system of /hw/), the major forms of English exhibit considerable homogeneity in their consonant systems, which offer no further possibilities of simplification if they are to retain some resemblance to a natural system.

12.8.1 Vowels

The vowel system may be simplified in both phonemic and phonetic respects, while still keeping an acceptable level of intelligibility.

(a) The centring diphthongs /ɪə, ɛə, ʊə/ (§7.12.1), for instance, are of comparatively rare occurrence (1·5% of vowels; 0·7% of all phonemes in connected speech). They can always be interpreted as V + /r/ when appropriate, e.g. *peer* as /piːr/; *pair* as /peɪr/; and *poor* as /puːr/ (though in the latter case it would be more economical to replace RP /ʊə/ by ɔː/). Where there is no *r* in the spelling, e.g. in *idea*, *skua*, /iː/ or /ɪ/ + /ə/ and /uː/ or /ʊ/ + /ə/ would be used.

(b) Similarly, many cases of long vowels can be made to conform to the orthography by the retention of post-vocalic /r/, *farm*, *four*, *heard* might well have V + /r/, though such words as *calm* and *saw* would retain their /r/-less form. The unique case of /ɜː/ without *r* in *colonel* could conform to V + /r/ by analogy, as often in American English.

(c) Finally, it would doubtless be simpler for many foreign learners if certain phonetic adjustments in the realization of vowel phonemes were made, by using Cardinal Vowel values (§4.4.2) wherever possible. Thus, /iː, uː, ɔː/ would have cardinal values; /eɪ/ and /əʊ/ would be realized as long cardinal [e] and [o] (as they are in many forms of English); /e/ and /æ/ would be pronounced as cardinal [ɛ] and [a]; /ɑː/ would be long cardinal [a]; /ʌ/ and /ə/ would have the quality of accented and unaccented mid central [ə], with a long counterpart of similar quality; /ɪ, ʊ, ɒ/ would remain as now; /aɪ/ and /aʊ/ would have a similar (front) starting point. The resulting 16 vowel inventory would be as follows:—

6 *short monophthongs*: /ɪ/ (*sit*); /ɛ/ (*set*); /a/ (*sat*); /ɒ/ (*sot*); /ʊ/ (*soot*); /ə/ (*another*) /əˈnəðər/

7 *long monophthongs*: /iː/ (*bee, beer*); /eː/ (*pay, pair*); /aː/ (*calm, car*); /ɔː/ (*paw, pour, poor*); /oː/ (*home*); /uː/ (*do, dour*); /əː/ (*bird*)

3 *diphthongs*: /aɪ/ (*buy*); /aʊ/ (*cow*); /ɔɪ/ (*boy*)

(The vowel relationships are shown in the diagrams given in Figs. 49, 50.)

The following transcription demonstrates the use of such a vowel system with a full RP consonant inventory:—

aɪ ˈdoːnt ˈjuːʒəlɪ kəm ˈhiːr baɪ ˈkaːr—ðə ˈtreːnz ə ˈɡʊd ˈdiːl ˌmoːr kənˈviːnjənt wɛn wiːr ˈspɛndɪŋ ə ˈfjuː ˈaʊərz ɪn ˈtaʊn wɪð ðə ˈbɔɪz. juː ˈhaf tə biː ˈso ˈəːrlɪ ɪf juː ˈwɒnt tə ˈfaɪnd ə ˈpaːrkɪŋ ˌpleːs. aɪ ˈθɪŋk ˈmoːst ˈɡaraːdʒɪz ˈtʃaːrdʒ ˈfaːr tuː ˈmətʃ fər ˈpuːr ˈfoːk laɪk ˈəs. ðə ˈreːlfeːrz ˈtʃiːpər—so ˈʃal wiː ˈmiːt ət ðə ˈsteːʃən?[1]

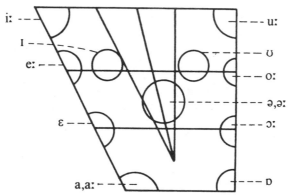

FIG. 49.—Monophthongs: simplified system.

[1] In orthography: 'I don't usually come here by car—the train's a good deal more convenient when we're spending a few hours in town with the boys. You have to be so early if you want to find a parking place. I think most garages charge far too much for poor folk like us. The rail fare's cheaper—so shall we meet at the station?'

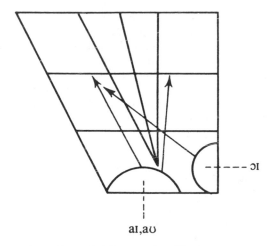

ɔɪ

aɪ,aʊ

FIG. 50.—Diphthongs: simplified system.

Note.—It is also conceivable, if minimum intelligibility is the target, that the variations of vowel length (e.g. the significant reduction of /iː / in *feet* as opposed to the same vowel in *feed*) might be disregarded—the fully long variety being used in all contexts. The loss of such an important cue to meaning throws even greater weight on to the sense-defining function of the context.

12.8.2 Consonants

As far as consonants are concerned, it is important that all phonemic oppositions should be maintained, though the optional /hw/ (§8.9.1(4, 5)) may be omitted. Nevertheless, certain phonetic tolerances may be permitted:—

(a) In the phonemic series /p, t, k, b, d, g/ (where presence or absence of aspiration is typically significant in initial accented positions in most native forms of English) voicing may be used as the distinguishing cue, if only the most basic type of intelligibility is the aim: thus, *pie* would be distinguished from *buy* by the presence of voice in /b/ and its absence in /p/ (as is the case in the plosive systems of many languages such as those of the Romance and Slav families). Again, the loss of such an important cue implies great dependence on the context for the definition of meaning.

Less communicative harm is done if the articulation point of /t, d/ is dental rather than alveolar. Most languages use a dental contact point for this type of stop, and to do so in English entails no loss of intelligibility, though the phonetic deviation is usually immediately apparent to an English ear. It is much less permissible (from the point of view of communication) to replace, as many speakers of Indian languages tend to do, /t, d/ by retroflex [ʈ, ɖ] and /θ, ð/ by dental aspirated [t̪ʰ, d̪ʰ].

(b) The sound [ŋ] may lose its phonemic status, in the sense that, besides occurring regularly before /k/ (as in *think*), it will retain a following voiced velar plosive element elsewhere, e.g. *sing, singer* [sɪŋg, ˈsɪŋgə], where RP omits [g]. [ŋ] is then a conditioned variant of /n/ before velar plosives. Thus, *hanger* and *anger* with /ŋ/ and /ŋg/ respectively in RP may both have [ŋg] if found to be easier at the rudimentary level of achievement. Such a usage corresponds to that of several British English regional forms (§8.6.2). No two English words are distinguished in meaning by the opposition of /ŋ/ and /ŋg/.

(c) The complex English fricative system must be retained, but some relaxation of the articulation of the dental /ð/ is allowable in weak positions (§8.4.3(3)), especially in the case of *the* following /s/ or /z/, e.g. in 'What's the time?' or 'Is there any left?'. In such positions, it is difficult in rapid, casual speech to articulate with any precision a truly dental sound immediately after an alveolar one. The English often replace it with a dentalized [z̪]; if a foreign learner uses a [z] sound in such positions of weak prominence, it may be hardly noticeable.

(d) The complex realizations of RP /l/ (§8.7) may be simplified; in particular, the 'clear' allophone may be used (as in some forms of Irish English) where the 'dark' [ɫ] is normal in RP, without loss of intelligibility. The devoiced [l̥] allophone following initial accented /p, k/, on the other hand, is an important carrier of meaning in an opposition such *plot* ∿ *blot*. It follows that, if voicing rather than aspiration is used as the distinguishing feature of /p, k/ *v.* /b, g/ as suggested in (a) above, the devoicing of /l/ after /ˈp, ˈk/ is less likely to occur; if this type of pronunciation is adopted, the listener's decoding of the message may again have to rely very heavily on the general context.

(e) There is little disturbance to comprehension if /r/ (§8.7.1) is realized as an alveolar tap or lingual roll (even in a post-vocalic position) rather than as the more typical RP post-alveolar frictionless continuant or approximant, since these variants occur in several British regional forms of speech. A uvular articulation, however, though interfering little with intelligibility once the listener has adjusted and though still occurring in the speech of some speakers in North-Eastern England, is always perceived as unusual. As with /l/ in (d) above, the devoiced allophone of /r/, the main cue distinguishing *pray* from *bray*, may be dispensed with, thus forcing the context to carry a heavy burden of information. There is no loss of intelligibility if the linking /r/ is not used (§§11.3.7, 12.7.2(a)).

(f) Although the use of syllabic /n, l/ is typical of RP, intelligibility does not suffer if /ə/ is inserted even after an alveolar consonant (cf. §12.7.2(a)), as in *mutton, hidden, fasten, little, middle*, etc. Following /t, d/, however, the insertion of /ə/ before /n, l/ will be perceived as strikingly unusual—and even childish.

12.8.3 Intonation

Since correct rhythm and accentuation (with the associated reduction of weak syllables) are regarded as indispensable for any level of spoken English (§12.6.1), all learners should be proficient in making use of pitch movements as important cues for signalling salient words or syllables. Those learners whose own language uses pitch variation for grammatical rather than for lexical (tone) purposes are likely to be able to transfer much of their own intonation usage into English without serious disturbance of intelligibility. (If, however, they ignore the specifically English attitudinal uses of intonation, they will run the risk of giving an unintended impression of, for instance, abruptness or boredom!) On the other hand, those learners whose mother tongue is a tone language may find the concept of intonation's functions as they occur in English and other European languages entirely novel. They must master, in addition to the essential pitch features related to accentuation, the basic intonation patterns which signal grammatical categories, e.g. the typically falling intonation for statements and the rising tunes so often used in questions. This is particularly important when, for instance, the native language makes use of such devices as particles for signalling questions, without any significant pitch variation.

12.8.4 Sounds in Context

At these lower levels of performance no attempt need be made to imitate native English habits of elision or assimilation.

The result of permitting all the concessions mentioned in §12.8, involving the acceptance of an amalgam of segmental and prosodic features which occur together in no one natural form of English, is likely to be a style of speech which, though sounding markedly artificial or foreign, will be generally intelligible to most native English speakers. The native listener will need to adjust his decoding habits in much the same way that he does when listening to a native speaker using a regional accent of English which differs considerably from his own. This rudimentary form of pronunciation is not, however, to be regarded as a teaching target, but rather as a minimum level of achievement consistent with some degree of intelligibility; severe problems of communication will be caused by any greater divergence from a natural model. A serious learner with the most modest aims, working with or without a teacher, should seek to match his pronunciation with a natural type of English.

12.9 Teaching Methods

Learners' situations and requirements present so many variables that it is difficult to give advice of general applicability. Is the learner a child or an adult? Is he learning in a class with a teacher or by himself with the help of recordings or broadcast lessons? Is he to learn English pronunciation as part of a course extending perhaps over several years or is he attempting to acquire the essentials in a much more limited time? Whatever the answers to these and other questions, it must be accepted that in nearly all cases he will be seeking to learn English in an artificial fashion, i.e. very differently from the natural way in which he acquired his mother tongue, with constant exposure to the language of his family environment and with strong (instinctive) motivation to learn an efficient verbal means of communication. Nevertheless, it is some five years before he attains proficiency in the basic skills of speech production and reception.

What is clear is that, in teaching pronunciation, we are concerned especially with imparting motor and auditory *skills* rather than with inculcating the kind of logical agility such as may be involved in the acquisition of a new grammar. It is true that the learner must assimilate rules for the distribution of allophones or for the assignment of intonation patterns to the appropriate grammatical or attitudinal context; he may even learn to apply rules for the derivation of word accentuation patterns from the orthography (most usefully with respect to the relation of the word accent and suffixation). But his knowledge of the rules is of little value if he is unable to transmit a rule in efficiently articulated speech.

Since it is generally the case that the acquisition of a second language's pronunciation becomes increasingly difficult after early adolescence, it is obvious that ideally it is desirable to teach pronunciation as soon as possible. With children it is often the case that the ability to mimic is retained to such a high degree that a demonstration of some feature of pronunciation, without further explanation, is sufficient (thus emphasizing how especially important it is that a teacher's own pronunciation should reach the highest level possible). When this ability is no longer present, as is the case with most adult learners, every effort must be made to overcome the interference from the sound system of the first language, through which the new, foreign (English) sounds are being filtered. Before attempting to produce English sounds, accentual or intonation patterns, it is invariably advisable to teach and establish certain basic *discriminatory skills*: the learner must be able (a) to distinguish with certainty between features of his own language and those of English; (b) to distinguish between the contrastive features of English.

The acquisition of such new auditory skills can be achieved by the use of extensive discrimination drills in which the learner is required to judge identities and differences in stimuli presented to him by a teacher or in a recording. Such 'ear training' is, of course, particularly important for those who aim at the higher levels of achievement in pronunciation where phonetic precision is essential. It is, however, not generally useful to expose a learner to a tape in a language laboratory without any preliminary instruction on the features which he is expected to perceive. The recorded material should be graded so that the discrimination tasks become progressively finer. The following sections illustrate possible procedures:[1]

12.9.1 Production: Vowels

Many learners of English have difficulty with the short vowel series exemplified by *pit, pet, pat, putt, pot, put*. The series should first be presented to them, either in words having a similar consonantal frame or, preferably, in isolation. After listening, the learner should be asked to identify the items presented in a number of randomly-ordered sets. (It is helpful if at this stage the learner is able to relate an English sound to a phonetic symbol or to a number, so that the success of his identification can be checked without reference to orthography, which can often be ambiguous.) In the next stage, the learner listens to examples of the same vowels (which by now he can identify correctly), but this time vowels of his own language are interspersed with the English ones. He must identify what is English and what is not. Finally, if maximum phonetic precision is the aim, in a similar test vowel qualities which are neither those of English nor of his own language are included. It is important in this case that he should succeed in identifying as non-English those qualities which deviate both from English and from his own language.

12.9.2 Production: Consonants

Similar exercises can be used in introducing possible difficult features of the English consonantal system. For instance, in the case of the importance of aspiration in distinguishing initial /p, t, k/ from /b, d, g/, it will be appropriate to present the English series for recognition (after describing the aspiration feature), and then to insert examples of strong but unaspirated [p, t, k] sounds to be identified as non-English by the student. When it is a question of drilling such non-continuant consonants, it is of course necessary for them to be articulated with a vowel sound following.

The emphasis placed on auditory discrimination drills is important in a more general sense. Particularly in the case of vowel articulations we monitor and adjust the quality of the sounds we produce very largely by means of the control provided by our own auditory feedback. The most

---

[1] See my *Practical Course of English Pronunciation: a Perceptual Approach* (Edward Arnold, 1975) in which drills of this kind are presented for use with or without a teacher.

successful way of correcting a vowel sound is to indicate the auditory relationships between similar sounds. There is little in the way of articulatory instruction that can be given, since the significant movements of the tongue, for instance, in the mouth are very slight. (An obvious exception to this generalization is the case of /ɜː/, for which it is useful to insist on the neutral (rather than rounded) position of the lips.) As for consonantal articulations, for most of which there is tactile sensation of contact or stricture, it is possible to give helpful articulatory instructions, e.g. as regards the alveolar rather than dental nature of /t, d, n, l/, etc.

12.9.3   Production: Accentuation

The perceptual approach used in teaching segmental phonemes can also be employed in the case of accentual features.[1] Learners (and especially those, such as tone language speakers, for whom the English concept of accentuation is quite new) must be taught to appreciate variation in the accentual patterns of English polysyllabic words, the varying rhythms of connected speech and the reduction of weak syllables in the utterance.

In the case of polysyllabic words, correct pattern identification (preferably by using such nonsense sequences as [ˈlɪ lɪ, lɪˈlɪ] or [ˈlɑː lə lə, ləˈlɑː lə] etc.) should precede drills involving differing patterns in English words, e.g. 'beˈhind' *v.* 'ˈunder'; or 'ˈyesterday' *v.* 'imˈportant' *v.* ˌmagaˈzine' *v.* 'ˈphotoˌgraph', etc. (see also §9.7).

Similarly, the learner should be presented with the different rhythmic patterns involved in such sequences as 'The car's come; the carpet's come; the carpenter's come', i.e. [• • • ;   • • • ;   • • • • •], before attempting to produce the varying rhythms himself. In the same way, he should listen to passages of connected speech in order to appreciate the compression and obscuration of weak syllables, e.g., in 'Two of the children were waiting at the corner of the road for a bus'. It should be insisted that, in performance, it is the prominent syllables /ˈtuː—ˈtʃɪl—ˈweɪt—ˈkɔː—ˈrəʊd—ˈbʌs/ which should be given most weight and that, if the intervening weak syllables are produced with a full form, the result will be loss of intelligibility for the English listener.

12.9.4   Production: Intonation

Learners may also by the same technique be led to appreciate the way in which pitch changes signal a shift of nucleus in a phrase where any word may carry primary accent.[2] In a sentence such as 'This is my book', the

[1] See my *Practical Course of English Pronunciation, op. cit.*, Section 4.
[2] *Ibid.*, Section 5.

nucleus may meaningfully be associated with any of the four words. Different versions should be presented to the learner until he is able to identify the nuclear placement with certainty. The more difficult exercises which must follow concern the recognition of the type of nuclear tone used (§10.5.1.2) and the appreciation of the pitch levels occurring before and after the nucleus (§§10.5.1.3−4). As in all other drills, correct recognition must precede attempts at production.

Learners with different linguistic backgrounds will, of course, experience different difficulties in appreciating the distinctive elements of English. It is for this reason that a teacher should be aware of the phonetic and phonological characteristics of the mother tongue of his students (and of their particular local variety of this first language). By contrasting the feature of the two languages, he will be able to predict the problems which will arise and on which he should concentrate his drills; he will also be able to make use of phonetic resemblances between the two languages which may not be readily evident to the learner.

Thus, a teacher of students whose language belongs to the Germanic or Slav families will not expect to encounter problems with the basic concept of word accentuation, which will almost certainly offer difficulty to speakers of, say, French or many Indian languages as well as to those who speak a tone language. On the other hand, as an example of the use of similarities, benefit may often be derived from relating English /ɪ/ to a vowel of the cardinal [e] type, which exists in many languages not possessing a centralized vowel such as English /ɪ/. Or again, many learners who cannot easily articulate the English 'dark' [ɫ] may in their own language have a vowel of the cardinal [o] quality, which is an excellent starting point (or even substitute) for English [ɫ] (and is indeed used by many native speakers for [ɫ]—§8.7(3)).

12.9.5 Reception

The importance of the receptive side of language learning as distinct from the productive aspect has already been touched upon (§12.2.2). Although it is normally sufficient for the foreign learner to become proficient in his production of but one type of English pronunciation, adequacy in the reception (i.e. comprehension) of more than one style of RP is essential if communication with native speakers is to be efficient. This can be ensured not only by exposing students to broadcasts and recordings of natural speech (in a variety of styles including the most rapid and those which are highly elliptical and accompanied by 'noise'), but also by means of dictation exercises of a more analytical kind. The learner will often find it rewarding to transcribe phonetically various utterances of differing degrees of formality and casualness, noting the stylistic markers.

As students become more proficient, it will certainly be necessary, if for instance their first approach to the language has been through RP, for them to acquire facility in understanding a representative type of American English. Other accents should be taught sparingly. The choice will depend upon the ability and the needs of the learner: an attachment to American films and television programmes will require an acquaintance with a wide range of American accents; or a visit to London may suggest that the acquisition of some receptive ability in popular London speech might be useful. Practice in reception and comprehension (whether it is by means of radio or television programmes or by specially recorded material) should however be supervised by a teacher who is able to judge how far the various styles of speech available are appropriate to a foreign learner's needs. It would obviously, for instance, be a mistake to accept unquestioningly as a model all that is broadcast on the home services of BBC radio. Apart from the speech of the newsreaders, who generally do not depart markedly from an RP norm, a great variety of accents, representative of different regions and cultures and of differing degrees of acceptability as far as the foreign learner is concerned, may be heard on the BBC: broadcast plays and comedy programmes are often given in regional accents, with a good proportion of slang and near-taboo vocabulary; commentaries on soccer matches are unlikely to be given in more than a modified form of RP, whereas cricket commentaries (less attractive or accessible to the foreigner) tend to have a higher percentage of RP voices. It is advisable, therefore, for the foreign learner, faced with such complexity of accents, to restrict his proficiency to the level of reception, not allowing his production model to be modified incongruously and unacceptably by indiscriminate exposure to non-standard pronunciation. It is often the more able student, especially sensitive to variations of accent, who may tend to be influenced by and to imitate whatever he hears, unless he receives guidance.

12.9.6 Assessment

There remains the problem of the assessment of a learner's performance, from the point of view of both reception and production.

(a) A learner's achievement in comprehension can obviously be tested and quantified by measuring the amount of information which he has derived from a passage of colloquial speech, e.g. by scoring the number of information points which have been correctly received (excluding those items such as proper names, etc., which may have been introduced to the listener for the first time). A score of this kind can be obtained either by questions on the text or by requiring the student to write down what he has heard. The test, when conducted with learners of high achievement, should involve passages in different pronunciation styles. The recognition of information points will, of course, be mainly concerned with the accented parts of an utterance and will be made easier by factors of redundancy and predictability. A test which involved the correct identification of intervening weak, grammatical items and inflexions would obviously be a measure of total comprehension; although this type of detailed decoding goes beyond that which a native speaker normally employs when listening to his own language, it is nevertheless a good analytic exercise for the learner.

(b) In the case of production, an assessment of efficiency is more difficult. An atomistic approach can be used, whereby the control of phonemic oppositions is tested through the reading aloud of word lists and short sentences containing crucial minimal pairs. Similarly, lists of words exemplifying a variety of accentual patterns will test this area of the learner's proficiency. Various types of sentence (the grammatical or attitudinal context being given) can also be used to assess appropriate sentence accentuation and choice of nucleus. If, however, read texts are used (even if, as lengthy passages or dialogues, they are specially contrived to exemplify the maximum number of features of segmental phonemes and connected speech), the artificiality of the procedure should be recognized and allowed for, since a certain unnaturalness of style is likely whether it is a native speaker or a foreign learner who is reading aloud.

At a higher level of achievement, phonetic quality must also be measured, the higher the level the more precise the phonetic specification in terms of the target model. Here the teacher's role is vital, since it is he who must judge (usually by ear) the extent to which the learner approaches the model. He will pay particular attention to the features of connected speech mentioned in §12.7.

The danger of an atomistic method of assessment meticulously applied is that departures from a norm will usually be found to be numerous, as much for the successful learner as for the one of lower ability. A simple aggregate of noted errors, undifferentiated in respect of their seriousness as far as communication is concerned, does not always provide a reliable indication of good or bad performance. A real assessment must be based on the intelligibility and acceptability of a learner's performance, in a situation of free discourse with a native speaker, when many of the so-called 'errors', not being perceived by the native listener, may be regarded as trivial and ignored.

THE INTERNATIONAL

		Bilabial	Labiodental	Dental, Alveolar, or Post-alveolar	Retroflex
CONSONANTS (pulmonic air-stream mechanism) — SONANTS	Nasal	m	ɱ	n	ɳ
	Plosive	p b		t d	ʈ ɖ
	(*Median*) Fricative	ɸ β	f v	θ ð s z	ʂ ʐ
	(*Median*) Approximant		ʋ	ɹ	ɻ
	Lateral Fricative			ɬ ɮ	
	Lateral (*Approximant*)			l	ɭ
	Trill			r	
	Tap or Flap			ɾ	ɽ
(non-pulmonic air-stream)	Ejective	pʼ		tʼ	
	Implosive	ɓ		ɗ	
	(*Median*) Click	ʘ		ʇ ʗ	
	Lateral Click			ʖ	

DIACRITICS

- ₒ Voiceless ṇ ḍ
- ˬ Voiced ş ţ
- ʰ Aspirated tʰ
- ̈ Breathy-voiced b̤ a̤
- ̩ Dental ţ
- ̠ Labialized ţ
- ̡ Palatalized ţ
- ˗ Velarized or Pharyngealized ɫ, ɫ
- ̩ Syllabic ṇ ḷ
- ˆ or ̭ Simultaneous s͡f (but see also under the heading Affricates)

- ˙ or . Raised e˙, ẹ, ẹ w
- ˎ or ̦ Lowered eˎ, ę, ę ɤ
- ₊ Advanced u+, u̟
- ˗ or ‑ Retracted i̱, i‑, ṯ
- ̈ Centralized ë
- ˜ Nasalized ã
- ˞, ˞, ʁ r-coloured a˞
- : Long aː
- ˙ Half-long aˑ
- ˘ Non-syllabic ŭ
- › More rounded ɔ›
- ‹ Less rounded y‹

OTHER SYMBOLS

- ɕ, ʑ Alveolo-palatal fricatives
- ʃ, ʒ Palatalized ʃ, ʒ
- ɼ Alveolar fricative trill
- ɺ Alveolar lateral flap
- ɧ Simultaneous ʃ and x
- ʃˢ Variety of ʃ resembling s, etc.
- ɪ = ɩ
- ʊ = ɷ
- ɜ = Variety of ə
- ɚ = r-coloured ə

PHONETIC ALPHABET (Revised to 1979)

Palato-alveolar		Palatal		Velar		Uvular		Labial-Palatal	Labial-Velar		Pharyngeal		Glottal	
			ɲ		ŋ	N								
		c	ɟ	k	ɡ	q	ɢ		k͡p	ɡ͡b			ʔ	
ʃ	ʒ	ç	j	x	ɣ	χ	ʁ			ʍ	ħ	ʕ	h	ɦ
			j		ɰ			ɥ		w				
			ʎ											
						R								
						R								
				k’										
					ɡ									

VOWELS

	Front	Back		Front	Back
Close	i ɨ	ɯ		y ʉ	u
	ɪ			ʏ	ɵ
Half-close	e	ɤ		ø	o
	ə				ɵ
Half-open	ɛ	ʌ		œ	ɔ
	æ ɐ				
Open	a	ɑ		Œ	ɒ
	Unrounded			*Rounded*	

STRESS, TONE (PITCH)

' stress, placed at beginning of stressed syllable :
, secondary stress : ‾ high level pitch, high tone : ˙
‿ low level : ′ high rising :
ˌ low rising : ` high falling :
ˌ low falling : ˆ rise-fall :
ˇ fall-rise.

AFFRICATES can be written as digraphs, as ligatures, or with slur marks ; thus ts, tʃ, dʒ : ʦ tʃ ʤ : t͡s t͡ʃ d͡ʒ.
c, ɟ may occasionally be used for tʃ, dʒ.

Bibliography

The following books and articles are either referred to in the preceding pages or are intended as a selected list of works for further reading and consultation. The titles of certain periodicals are abbreviated as follows:—

AJP	*American Journal of Psychology*
ES	*English Studies*
JASA	*Journal of the Acoustical Society of America*
JEP	*Journal of Experimental Psychology*
LS	*Language and Speech*
Mph	*Le Maître Phonétique*
Misc Ph	*Miscellanea Phonetica*
PMLA	*Publications of the Modern Language Association of America*
ZPh	*Zeitschrift für Phonetik*

Abberton, E. R. M. and Fourcin, A. J., 'Electrolaryngography', *Clinical Experimental Phonetics* ed. Code, C. and Ball, M., Croom Helm, 1984.

Abercrombie, D., *Problems and Principles*, Longmans, 1956.

—— 'Forgotten Phoneticians,' *Transactions of the Philological Society*, 1948.

—— 'Direct Palatography,' *ZPh*, vol. 10, 1957.

—— *English Phonetic Texts*, Faber, 1964.

—— *Studies in Phonetics and Linguistics*, Oxford Univ. Press, 1965.

—— *Elements of General Phonetics*, Edinburgh, 1967.

Abramson, A. S., 'Laryngeal timing in consonant distinctions', *Phonetica* 34, 1977.

—— and Lisker, L., 'A cross-language study of voicing in initial stops', *Word* 20, 1964.

—— and Lisker, L., 'Some effects of context on voice onset time in English Stops', *LS*, vol. 10, 1967.

—— and Lisker, L., 'Discriminability along the voicing continuum', *Proc. 6th Int. Cong. Phon. Sc.*, 1970.

Allen, W. S., *Phonetics in Ancient India*, Oxford Univ. Press, 1953.

Allen, W. Stannard, *Living English Speech*, Longmans, 1954.

Andrésen, B. S., '-*dier* and -*deer*; an experiment,' *MPh*, 108, 1957.

—— 'The Glottal Stop in the Received Pronunciation of English,' Universitetet i Bergen, Årbok, 1958.

—— *Preglottalisation in English Standard Pronunciation*, Oslo, 1968.

Armstrong, L. E., and Ward, I. C., *A Handbook of English Intonation*, 2nd ed., Heffer, 1949.

Arnold, G. F., *Stress in English Words*, North Holland Publishing Co., 1957.

—— Denes, P., Gimson, A. C., O'Connor, J. D., Trim, J. L. M., 'The Synthesis of English Vowels,' *LS*, vol. 1, April–June, 1958.

—— 'Strong and weak forms in Southern British English,' *MPh*, 113, 1960.

—— 'Concerning the theory of plosives,' *MPh*, 125, 1967.

—— and Gimson, A. C., *English Pronunciation Practice*, Univ. of London Press, 1965.

Bell, A. M., *Visible Speech*, 1867.

Berger, M. O., 'Vowel distribution and accentual prominence in modern English,' *Word*, vol. 11, 1955.

Blankenship, J., and Kay, C., 'Hesitation phenomena in English speech,' *Word*, vol. 20, 1964.

Bloch, B., and Trager, G. L., *Outline of Linguistic Analysis*, Linguistic Society of America, Baltimore, 1942.

Bloomfield, L., *Language*, Henry Holt and Co., New York, 1944.

Bolinger, D. L., 'A Theory of Pitch Accent in English,' *Word*, vol. 14, August–December, 1958.

—— 'Contrastive accent and contrastive stress,' *Language*, vol. 37, 1961.

—— 'Ambiguities in pitch accent,' *Word*, vol. 17, 1961.

Borden, Gloria J., and Harris Katherine S., *Speech Science Primer*: physiology, accoustics and perception of speech, Williams and Wilkins, Baltimore, 1984.

Brazil, D., Coulthard, M. and Johns, C., *Discourse Intonation and Language Teaching*, Longman, 1980

Broeders, Ton, and Hyams, Phil, 'The Pronunciation Component of an English-Dutch Dictionary' in R. R. K. Hartmann (ed.) *Lexeter 83 Proceedings*, Max Niemeyer Verlag, Tübingen, 1983.

Brosnahan, F. L., *The Sounds of Language*, Heffer, 1961.

Burgess, O. N., 'A spectrographic investigation of some Australian vowel sounds,' *LS*, vol. 11, 1968.

Calnan, J. S., 'The Surgical Treatment of Nasal Speech Disorders,' *Annals of the Royal College of Surgeons of England*, vol. 25, 1959.

Campbell, A., *Old English Grammar*, Oxford Univ. Press, 1959.

Catford, J. C., 'Phonation Types,' *In Honour of Daniel Jones*, Longman, 1964.

Chao, Y. R., *Language and Symbolic Systems*, Cambridge Univ. Press, 1968.

Chatman, S., *A Theory of Meter*, Mouton, 1965.

Chomsky, N., and Halle, M., *The Sound Pattern of English*, New York, 1968.

Christophersen, P., 'The Glottal Stop in English,' *ES*, vol. 33, 1952.

Cohen, A., *The Phonemes of English*, Martinus Nijhoff, The Hague, 1952.

Cook, V., *Active Intonation*, Longman, 1968.

Cooper, C., *Grammatica Linguae Anglicanae*, 1685.

—— *The English Teacher*, 1687.

Cooper, F. S., Delattre, P., Liberman, A. M., Borst, J. M., Gerstman, L. J., 'Some Experiments on the Perception of Synthetic Speech Sounds,' *JASA*, vol. 24, 1952.

—— Liberman, A. M., Harris, K. S., Grubb, P. M., 'Some Input-Output

Relations observed in Experiments on the Perception of Speech,'
Association Internatonale de Cybernétique, Belgium, 1958.

Couper-Kuhlen, Elizabeth, *An Introduction to English Prosody*, Edward
Arnold, 1986.

Cruttenden, Alan, *Intonation*, Cambridge University Press, 1986.

Crystal, D., 'A perspective for paralanguage,' *MPh*, 120, 1963.

—— and Quirk, R., *Systems of prosodic and paralinguistic features in English*,
Mouton, 1964.

—— *Prosodic Systems and Intonation in English*, Cambridge Univ. Press, 1969.

—— *The English Tone of Voice*, Edward Arnold, 1975.

Davidsen-Nielsen, N., 'English Stops after initial /s/,' *ES*, vol. 4, 1969.

Neutralization and Archiphoneme, Copenhagen, 1978.

—— 'Old English short vowels before nasals', in Ramsaran (forthcoming).

Delattre, P., 'The Physiological Interpretation of Sound Spectrograms,'
PMLA, vol. 66, September, 1951.

—— Liberman, A. M., Cooper, F. S., 'Voyelles synthétiques à deux formantes
et voyelles cardinales,' *MPh*, 96, 1951.

—— Cooper, F. S., Liberman, A. M., 'Some suggestions for language teaching
methods arising from research on the acoustic analysis and synthesis
of speech,' *(Institute of Languages and Linguistics*, Washington
D.C., Monograph Series, no. 2), September, 1952.

—— Liberman, A. M., Cooper, F. S., Gerstman, L. J., 'An experimental
study of the acoustic determinants of vowel color; observations on
one- and two-formant vowels synthesized from spectrographic
patterns,' *Word*, vol. 8, December, 1952.

—— Liberman, A. M., Cooper, F. S., 'Acoustic Loci and Transitional Cues
for Consonants,' *JASA*, vol. 27, 1955.

—— 'Les indices acoustiques de la parole,' *Phonetica*, vol. 2, 1958.

—— *Comparing the phonetic features of English, French, German and
Spanish*, Heidelberg, 1965.

—— 'From acoustic cues to distinctive features,' *Phonetica*, vol. 18, 1968.

Denes, P., 'The Effect of Duration on the Perception of Voicing,' *JASA*,
vol. 27, 1955.

—— 'A Preliminary Investigation of Certain Aspects of Intonation,' *LS*,
vol. 2, April–June, 1959.

—— and Pinson, E. N., *The Speech Chain*, Bell Telephone Laboratories, 1963.

—— 'On the Statistics of Spoken English,' *JASA*, vol. 35, 1963.

—— and Milton-Williams, J., 'Further studies in intonation,' *LS*, vol. 5, 1962.

Dobson, E. J., *English Pronunciation, 1500–1700*, Oxford Univ. Press, 1957.

Ellis, A. J., *On Early English Pronunciation*, 1869–89.

Fant, C. G. M., *Acoustic Theory of Speech Production*, Mouton, The Hague,
1960.

—— *Theory of Distinctive Features*, Speech Transmission Lab., K.T.H., 1966.

Firth, J. R., *Speech* and *The Tongues of Men*, reprint by Oxford Univ. Press,
1964.

Fischer-Jørgensen, E., 'Acoustic analysis of stop consonants,' *MiscPh*, vol. II,
1954.

—— *Trends in Phonological Theory: a historical introduction*, Copenhagen,
1975.

Fletcher, Harvey, *Speech and Hearing in Communication*, Princeton, D. Van Nostrand Co., 1953.

Fourcin, A. J., 'An aspect of the perception of pitch,' *Proc. Congress of Phonetic Sciences IV*, 1962.

—— and Abberton, E., 'First applications of a new laryngograph', *Medical and Biological Illustration*, vol. 21, 1971.

Fowler, M., 'Herdan's Statistical Parameters and the Frequency of English Phonemes,' *Studies to Josh Whatmough*, 1957.

Fry, D. B., 'The Frequency of Occurrence of Speech Sounds in Southern English,' *Archives Néerlandaises de Phonétique Expérimentale*, vol. xx, 1947.

—— 'Duration and Intensity as Physical Correlates of Linguistic Stress,' *JASA*, vol. 27, 1955.

—— 'Speech and Language,' *Journal of Laryngology and Otology*, July, 1957.

—— and Denes, P., 'The Solution of some Fundamental Problems in Mechanical Speech Recognition,' *LS*, vol. 1, January–March, 1958.

—— 'Experiments in the Perception of Stress.' *LS*, vol. 1, April–June, 1958.

—— 'The dependence of stress judgments on vowel formant structure,' *Proc. Congress of Phonetic Sciences V*, 1965.

—— 'Prosodic phenomena,' *Manual of Phonetics*, 1969.

—— *Homo Loquens*, Cambridge Univ. Press, 1977.

—— *The Physics of Speech*, Cambridge Univ. Press, 1979.

Fudge, E. C., 'Syllables', *Journal of Linguistics*, vol. 5, 1969.

—— *English Word-Stress*, Allen and Unwin, 1984.

Garde, P., *L'Accent*, Paris, 1968.

Gibbon, D. and Richter, H., *Intonation, Accent and Rhythm*, de Gruyter, Berlin, 1984.

Gil, A., *Logonomia Anglica*, 1619.

Giles, H., 'Patterns of evaluation of RP, South Wales and Somerset accented speech', *British Journal of Social and Clinical Psychology*, vol. 10, 1971.

Gimson, A. 'C., 'Implications of the Phonemic/Chronemic Grouping of English Vowels,' *Acta Linguistica*, v, 1945–49.

—— 'The Linguistic Relevance of Stress in English,' *ZPh*, vol. 9, 1956.

—— 'The Instability of English Alveolar Articulations,' *MPh*, 113, 1960.

—— 'Phonetic change and the RP vowel system,' *In Honour of Daniel Jones*, Longman, 1964.

—— 'A note on the variability of the phonemic components of English words,' *Brno Studies in English*, vol. 8, 1969.

—— 'British English Pronunciation—standards and evolution,' *Praxis*, vol. 17, 1970.

—— 'Phonology and the lexicographer', *Annals of the New York Academy of Sciences*, vol. 211, 1973.

—— *A Practical Course of English Pronunciation: a perceptual approach*, Edward Arnold, 1975.

—— 'Daniel Jones and standards of English pronunciation', *ES*, vol. 58, no. 2, 1977.

—— 'Towards an international pronunciation of English,' *In Honour of A. S. Hornby*, Oxford Univ. Press, 1978.

—— *English Pronouncing Dictionary*, 14th ed., Dent, 1977.
—— 'The pronunciation of English: its international intelligibility', *The Teaching of English in Japan*, Eichosha, Tokyo, 1978.
—— 'English RP: ancient or modern?', *Praxis*, vol. 1979.
—— 'The Pronunciation of English: its intelligibility and acceptability in the world', *Modern Languages*, vol. 62, no. 2, June 1981.
—— 'Pronunciation in EFL dictionaries', *Applied Linguistics*, vol. 2, no. 3, Autumn 1981.
—— and Ramsaran, S. M., *An English Pronunciation Companion to the Oxford Advanced Learner's Dictionary of Current English*, Oxford University Press, 1982.
Gleason, H. A., *An Introduction to Descriptive Linguistics*, Henry Holt and Co., New York, 1956.
—— *Linguistics and English Grammar*, New York, 1965.
Goldman-Eisler, F., *Psycholinguistics*, London, 1968.
Gray, G. W., and Wise, C. M., *The Bases of Speech*, Harper and Bros., New York, 3rd. ed., 1959.
Guierre, L., 'Secondary accent and segmentation in English,' *Langues Modernes*, 61, 1967.
—— *Drills in English Stress Patterns*, Longman, 1970.
—— *L'accentuation en anglais contemporain*, unpublished doctoral thesis, Paris, 1979.
Gussenhoven, C., *On the Grammar and Semantics of Sentence Accents*, Foris, Dordrecht, 1984.
Halle, M., Hughes, G. W., Radler, J. P. A., 'Acoustic Properties of Stop Consonants,' *JASA*, vol. 29, 1957.
—— 'On the bases of phonology,' *The Structure of Language* (ed. Fodor and Katz), Prentice-Hall, 1964.
Halliday, M. A. K., 'The Tones of English', *Archivum Linguisticum*, vol. xv, 1963.
—— 'Intonation in English Grammar', *Trans. Philological Soc.*, 1963.
—— McIntosh, A., Strevens, P., *The Linguistic Sciences and Language Teaching*, Longman, 1964.
—— *Intonation and Grammar in British English*, Mouton, 1967.
Harris, K. S., 'Cues for the Discrimination of American English Fricatives in Spoken Syllables,' *LS*, vol. 1, January–March, 1958.
—— Hoffman, H. S., Liberman, A. M., Delattre, P. C., Cooper, F. S., 'Effect of Third-Formant Transitions on the Perception of Voiced Stop Consonants,' *JASA*, vol. 30, 1958.
Hart, J., *An Orthographie*, 1569.
Hawkins, Peter, *Introducing Phonology*, Hutchinson, 1984.
Heffner, R. M. S., *General Phonetics*, Univ. of Wisconsin Press, 1949.
Herdan, G., *Type Token Mathematics*, Mouton and Co., The Hague, 1960.
Higginbottom, E. M., 'A study of the representation of English vowel phonemes in the orthography,' *LS*, vol. 5, 1962.
—— 'Glottal reinforcement in English', *Trans. Philological Society*, 1965.
Hill, L. A., 'Some Notes on Juncture,' *MPh*, 105, 1956.
—— 'The Effects of Clisis on the Occurrence of Clusters in English,' *ZPh*, vol. 10, 1957.

—— 'Stress marks and pitch marks,' *MPh*, 108, 1957.

—— 'Stress, pitch, prominence,' *MPh*, 114, 1960.

—— *Stress and Intonation Step by Step*, Oxford Univ. Press, 1965.

Hoard, J. E., 'Juncture and syllable structure in English,' *Phonetica*, vol. 15, 1966.

Hockett, C. F., *A Manual of Phonology* (*International Journal of American Linguistics*), 1955.

—— *A Course in Modern Linguistics*, Macmillan, New York, 1958.

Hoffman, H. S., 'Study of some Cues in the Perception of Voiced Stop Consonants,' *JASA*, vol. 30, 1958.

Honikman, B., 'Articulatory Settings,' *In Honour of Daniel Jones*, Longman, 1964.

House, Jill, 'Intonation Structures and Pragmatic Interpretation, in Ramsaran (forthcoming).

Huang, R., and Green, A. W. T., *Intonation in idiomatic English for Chinese students in S.E. Asia*, Hongkong, 1964.

—— *English Pronunciation*, Hongkong, 1965.

Hughes, G. W., and Halle, M., *'Spectral Properties of Fricative Consonants,'* *JASA*, vol. 28, 1956.

Hultzén, L. S., Allen, J. H. D., Miron, M. S., *Tables of transitional frequencies of English phonemes*, Univ. of Illinois, 1964.

Husson, R., *La Voix Chantée*, Paris, 1960.

International Phonetic Association, The Principles of the, University College, London, 1949.

Jakobson, R., Fant, C. G. M., Halle, M., *Preliminaries to Speech Analysis, Technical Report no. 13*, Acoustic Laboratory, Massachusetts Institute of Technology, 1952.

Jassem, W., 'Indication of Speech Rhythm in the Transcription of Educated Southern English,' *MPh*, 92, 1949.

—— *Intonation of Conversational English*, Wroclaw, 1952.

—— 'Stress in Modern English,' *Bulletin de la Société Polonaise de Linguistique*, xi, Kraków, 1952.

—— 'A note on plotting pitch curves,' *MPh*, 111, 1959.

—— 'The formants of fricative consonants,' *LS*, vol. 8, 1965.

Jespersen, O., *A Modern English Grammar*, Part I, Heidelberg, 1909.

Johnson, Samuel, *A Dictionary of the English Language*, 1755.

Jones, Daniel, *An Outline of English Phonetics*, 9th ed., 9th ed., Cambridge Univ. Press, 1975.

—— *The Pronunciation of English*, 4th ed., Cambridge Univ. Press, 1972.

—— *An English Pronouncing Dictionary*, 13th ed., Dent, 1967.

—— *The Phoneme; its Nature and Use*, Cambridge Univ. Press, 1976.

—— 'Some Thoughts on the Phoneme,' *Trans. of the Philological Society*, 1944.

—— 'The Word as a Phonetic Entity,' *MPh*, 36, 1931.

—— 'Chronemes and Tonemes,' *Acta Linguistica*, iv, 1944.

—— 'The Hyphen as a Phonetic Sign,' *ZPh*, vol. 9, 1955.

—— 'Falling and Rising Diphthongs in Southern English,' *MiscPh II*, 1954.

—— *In Honour of*, Longman, 1964.

Joos, M., *Acoustic Phonetics, Language* Monograph no. 23, 1948.

Kaiser, L. (ed.), *Manual of Phonetics*, Amsterdam, 1957.

Kaplan, H. M., *Anatomy and Physiology of Speech*, McGraw-Hill, 1960.

Kenyon, J. S., *American Pronunciation*, 9th ed., Wahr, Ann Arbor, 1945.

Kingdon, R., *Groundwork of English Intonation*, Longman, 1958.

—— *Groundwork of English Stress*, Longman, 1958.

Kökeritz, H., *Shakespeare's Pronunciation*, Yale Univ. Press, 1953.

Kurath, H., *A phonology and prosody of modern English*, Ann Arbor, 1964.

Ladd, D. R., *The Structure of Intonational Meaning*, Indiana University Press, Bloomington, 1978.

Ladefoged, P., 'The Classification of Vowels,' *Lingua*, vol. 2, 1956.

—— 'Use of Palatography,' *Journal of Speech and Hearing Disorders*, vol. 22, 1957.

—— Draper, M. H., Whitteredge, D., 'Syllables and Stress,' *MiscPh III*, 1958.

—— and Broadbent, D. E., 'Intonation Conveyed by Vowels,' *JASA*, vol. 29, 1957.

—— 'The Value of Phonetic Statements,' *Language*, vol. 36, 1960.

—— *Elements of Acoustic Phonetics*, Oliver and Boyd, 1962.

—— and Broadbent, D. E., 'Information conveyed by vowels,' *JASA*, vol. 29, 1957.

—— 'Stress and Pitch,' *MPh*, 115, 1961.

—— 'The nature of vowel quality,' Coimbra, 1962.

—— *Three areas of Experimental Phonetics*, Oxford Univ. Press, 1967.

—— *Preliminaries to linguistic phonetics*, Chicago Univ. Press, 1971.

—— *A course in phonetics*, New York, 1975.

Lass, Roger, *Phonology, An Introduction to Basic Concepts*, Cambridge University Press, 1984.

Laver, J. D. M., *The Phonetic Description of Voice Quality*, Cambridge University Press, 1980.

Lee, W. R., *An English Intonation Reader*, Macmillan, 1960.

Lehiste, I., *Acoustic-Phonetic Study of Internal Open Juncture*, Ann Arbor, 1959.

—— *Suprasegmentals*, MIT Press, 1970.

Lewis, J. Windsor, *A Guide to English Pronunciation*, Oslo, 1969.

—— *A Concise Pronouncing Dictionary of British and American English*, Oxford Univ. Press, 1972.

Liberman, A. M., Delattre, P., Gerstman, L. J., 'The Rôle of Selected Stimulus-Variables in the Perception of Unvoiced Stop Consonants,' *AJP*, vol. 65, 1952.

—— Delattre, P. C., Cooper, F. S., Gerstman, L. J., 'The Rôle of Consonant-Vowel Transitions in the Perception of the Stop and Nasal Consonants,' *Psychological Monographs*, no. 379 (*American Psychological Association*), 1954.

—— Delattre, P.C., Gerstman, L. J., Cooper, F. S., 'Tempo of Frequency Change as a Cue for Distinguishing Classes of Speech Sounds,' *JEP*, vol. 52, August, 1956.

—— 'Some Results of Research on Speech Perception,' *JASA*, vol. 29, 1957.

—— Harris, K. S., Hoffman, H. S., Griffith, B. C., 'The Discrimination of Speech Sounds within and across Phoneme Boundaries,' *JEP*, vol. 54, November, 1957.

—— Delattre, P. C., Cooper, F. S., 'Some Cues for the Distinction between Voiced and Voiceless Stops in Initial Positions,' *LS*, vol. 1, July–September, 1958.

—— Ingemann, F., Lisker, L., Delattre, P. C., Cooper, F. S., 'Minimal Rules for Synthesizing Speech,' *JASA*, vol. 31, 1959.

—— Harris, K. S., Kinney, J. A., Lane, H., 'The Discrimination of Relative Onset-time of the Components of certain Speech and Non-speech patterns,' *JEP*, vol. 61, May, 1961.

—— *Intonation, Perception and Language*, M.I.T. Research Monograph, 38, 1967.

Lisker, L., 'Closure Duration and the Intervocalic Voiced-Voiceless Distinction in English,' *Language*, vol. 33, 1957.

—— 'Minimal Cues for Separating /w, r, l, y/ in Intervocalic Positions,' *Word*, vol. 13, August, 1957.

—— 'Linguistic Segments, Acoustic Segments and Synthetic Speech,' *Language*, vol. 33, 1957.

—— and Abramson, A. S., 'A cross-language study of voicing in initial stops,' *Word*, vol. 20, 1964.

—— and Abramson, A. S., 'Glottal modes in consonant distinctions', *Proc. 7th Int. Cong. Phon. Sc.*, Mouton, 1972.

Lotz, J., Abramson, A. A., Gerstman, L. J., Ingemann, F., Nemser, W. J., 'The Perception of English Stops by Speakers of English, Hungarian and Thai; a Tape-cutting Experiment,' *LS*, vol. 3, April–June, 1960.

Lyons, J., *An Introduction to Theoretical Linguistics*, Cambridge Univ. Press, 1968.

MacCarthy, P. A. D., *English Pronunciation*, 4th ed., Heffer, 1952.

—— *English Intonation Reader*, Longman, 1956.

Malécot, A., 'Acoustic Cues for Nasal Consonants,' *Language*, vol. 32, 1956.

—— 'The effectiveness of intra-oral air-pressure parameters in distinguishing between stop consonants,' *Phonetica*, vol. 14, 1966.

Malmberg, B., *La Phonétique* (series *Que Sais-je*), Paris, 1960.

—— *Phonetics*, New York, 1963.

—— *Structural Linguistics and Human Communication*, New York, 1963.

——, ed., *Manual of Phonetics*, Amsterdam, 1968.

Martinet, A., *Phonology as Functional Phonetics*, Philological Society, London, 1949.

—— *Economies des Changements Phonétiques*, Berne, 1955.

Matthews, W., *Cockney Past and Present*, Routledge, 1938.

McIntosh, A., *Introduction to a Survey of Scottish Dialects*, Edinburgh: Nelson, 1952.

Miller, G. A., *Language and Communication*, McGraw Hill Book Co., New York, 1951.

Mitchell, A. G., *The Pronunciation of English in Australia*, Sydney, 1946.

Mitchell, A. G., *Spoken English*, Macmillan, 1957.

Mol, H., and Uhlenbeck, E. M., 'The Linguistic Relevance of Intensity in Stress,' *Lingua*, vol. 5, 1955–6.

Morton, J., and Jassem, W., 'Acoustic correlates of stress,' *LS*, vol. 8, 1965.

Nakata, K., 'Synthesis and Perception of Nasal Consonants,' *JASA*, vol. 31, 1959.

Newman, Stanley S., 'On the Stress System of English,' *Word*, vol. 2, 1946.

O'Connor, J. D., *New Phonetic Readings from Modern English Literature*, Berne, 1948.

—— Review of Trager and Smith, *Outline of English Structure, MPh*, 96, 1951.

—— 'RP and the Reinforcing Glottal Stop,' *ES*, vol. 33, 1952.

—— and Trim, J. L. M., 'Vowel, Consonant and Syllable: a Phonological Definition,' *Word*, vol. 9, August, 1953.

—— Gerstman, L. J., Liberman, A. M., Delattre, P. C., Cooper, F. S., 'Acoustic Cues for the Perception of initial /w, j, r, l/ in English,' *Word*, vol. 13, April, 1957.

—— 'Recent Work in English Phonetics,' *Phonetica*, vol. 1, 1957.

—— and Arnold, G. F., *Intonation of Colloquial English*, Longman, 2nd ed., 1973.

—— and Tooley, O. M., 'The perceptibility of certain word boundaries,' *In Honour of Daniel Jones*, Longman, 1964.

—— 'The perception of time intervals,' Progress Report, Phonetics Lab., Univ. College, London, 1965.

—— *Better English Pronunciation*, Cambridge Univ. Press, 1967.

—— 'The duration of the foot in relation to the number of component sound segments,' Progress Report, Phonetics Lab., Univ. College, London, 1968.

—— *Phonetics*, Penguin Books, 1973.

Orton, H., Dieth, E., *Survey of English Dialects*, Leeds, 1962.

Ostwald, P. F., *Sound making: the acoustic communication of emotion*, 1963.

Palmer, H. E., *English Intonation with Systematic Exercises*, Heffer, 1924.

Palsgrave, J., *Lesclarcissement de la Langue Francoyse*, 1530.

Peterson, G. E., and Lehiste, I., 'Duration of the syllable nuclei in English,' *JASA*, vol. 32, 1960.

Pike, K. L., *Phonetics*, Univ. of Michigan Press, 1943.

—— *The Intonation of American English*, Univ. of Michigan Press, 1945.

—— 'On the Phonemic Status of English Diphthongs,' *Language*, vol. 23, 1947.

—— *Phonemics*, Univ. of Michigan Press, 1947.

—— 'Grammatical Prerequisites to Phonemic Analysis,' *Word*, vol. 13, December, 1957.

Pitman, I., Ellis, A. J., *Phonotype*, 1847.

Pointon, G. E., *BBC Pronouncing Dictionary of British Names*, 2nd ed., Oxford University Press, 1983.

Potter, R. K., Kopp, G. A., Green, H. C., *Visible Speech*, D. Van Nostrand Co., New York, 1947.

Prator, C. H., *Manual of American English Pronunciation*, New York, 1957.

Pring, J. T., *Colloquial English Pronunciation*, Longman, 1959.

Puttenham, G., *Arte of English Poesie*, 1589.

Quirk, R., *The Use of English*, Longman, 2nd ed., 1963.

—— and Wrenn, C. L., *An Old English Grammar*, Methuen, 1955.

——, Greenbaum, S., Leech, G., Svartvik, J., *A Grammar of Contemporary English*, Longman, 1972.

Ramsaran, Susan, *Phonetic and Phonological Correlates of Style in English: a preliminary investigation*, Unpublished doctoral thesis, University of London, 1978.

—— *English Pronouncing Dictionary*, revised 14th ed. with supplement, Dent, 1988.

—— 'RP: fact *and* fiction,' in Ramsaran (forthcoming).

—— *Studies in the Pronunciation of English: A commemorative volume in memory of A. C. Gimson*, Croom Helm, forthcoming.

Roach, P., *English Phonetics and Phonology: a practical course*, Cambridge University Press, 1983.

Robins, R. H., *General Linguistics, an Introductory Survey*, Longman, 1967.

Saporta, Sol (ed.), *Psycholinguistics: a Book of Readings*, New York, 1961.

Saussure, F. de., *Cours de Linguistique Générale*, 4th ed., Paris, 1949.

Schubiger, M., *The Rôle of Intonation in Spoken English*, St. Gallen, 1935.

—— *English Intonation, its Form and Function*, Tübingen, 1958.

Scott, N. C., 'An Experiment on Stress Perception,' *MPh*, 67, 1939.

—— *English Conversations in Simplified Phonetic Transcription*, Heffer, 1942.

Sharf, D. J., 'Duration of post-stress intervocalic stops and preceding vowels,' *LS*, vol. 5, 1962.

Sharp, A. E., 'Falling-Rising Intonation Patterns in English,' *Phonetica*, vol. 2, 1958.

—— 'The analysis of stress and juncture in English,' *Trans. Philological Society*, 1960.

Sheridan, T., *General Dictionary of the English Language*, 1780.

Siertsma, B., 'Timbre, pitch and intonation,' *Lingua*, vol. 11, 1962.

Sivertsen, E., *Cockney Phonology*, Oslo Univ. Press, 1960.

Sledd, J., Review of Trager and Smith, *Outline of English Structure, Language*, vol. 31, 1955.

Smith, T., *De Recta et Emendata Linguae Anglicanae*, 1568.

Spencer, J., 'Received Pronunciation: Some Problems of Interpretation', *Lingua*, vol. vii, 1957.

Steele, J., *Prosodia Rationalis*, 1775–9.

Stetson, R. H., *Motor Phonetics*, 2nd ed., Amsterdam, 1951.

Strang, Barbara, *Modern English Structure*, 2nd ed., Edward Arnold, 1968.

Strevens, P. D., *Spoken Language*, Longman, 1956.

—— 'Spectra of Fricative Noise in Human Speech,' *LS*, vol. 3, January–March, 1960.

Sturtevant, E. H., *An Introduction to Linguistic Science*, Yale Univ. Press, 1947.

Swadesh, M., 'The Phonemic Principle,' *Language*, vol. 10, 1934.

Sweet, H., *History of English Sounds*, 1888.

—— *A Primer of Spoken English*, 4th ed., Clarendon Press, 1911.

—— *The Sounds of English*, 2nd. ed., Clarendon Press, 1929.

Thomas, C. K., *Introduction to the Phonetics of American English*, New York, 2nd ed., 1958.

Tibbitts, E. L., *Practice Material for the English Sounds*, Heffer, 1963.

Trager, G. L., and Bloch, B., 'The Syllabic Phonemes of English,' *Language*, vol. 17, 1941.

—— and Smith, H. L., *An Outline of English Structure* (*Studies in Linguistics*, Occasional Paper 3), Norman, Oklahoma, 1951.

—— 'Paralanguage: a first approximation,' *Studies in Linguistics*, 13, 1957.

Trim, J. L. M., 'Major and Minor Tone Groups in English,' *MPh*, 112, 1959.

—— 'English Standard Pronunciation,' *English Language Teaching*, vol. 26, 1961–62.

Trnka, B., *A Phonological Analysis of Present-day Standard English* (*Studies in English*, 5), Prague, 1935.

Troubetzkoy, N. S., *Principes de Phonologie*, transl. J. Cantineau, Paris, 1949.

Trudgill, P., *Sociolinguistic Patterns in British English* (ed.), Edward Arnold, 1978.

—— *Applied Sociolinguistics*, Academic Press, London, 1984.

Trudgill, P. and Hughes, A., *English Accents and Dialects*, Edward Arnold, 1979.

Twaddell, W. F., 'On Defining the Phoneme,' *Language, Monograph* 16, 1935.

Uldall, E., 'Attitudinal meanings conveyed by intonation,' *LS*, vol. 3, 1960.

—— 'Dimension of meaning in intonation,' *In Honour of Daniel Jones*, Longman, 1964.

Vachek, J., 'The Decline of the Phoneme /r/ in English,' *Sborník Prací Filosoficke Fakulty*, Brno, 1960.

—— 'On the Phonetic and Phonemic Problems of the Southern English WH Sounds,' *ZPh*, vol. 8, 1954.

—— 'Notes on the phonemic value of the modern English [ŋ] sound,' *In Honour of Daniel Jones*, 1964.

Vanvik, A. J., *On stress in present-day English*, Oslo, 1961.

Vassilyev, V. A., *English Phonetics: A Normative Course*, 2nd ed., Moscow, 1980.

—— *English Phonetics: a Theoretical Course*, Moscow, 1970.

Walker, J., *Critical Pronouncing Dictionary and Exposition of the English Language*, 1791.

Wallis, J., *Grammatica Linguae Anglicanae*, 1653.

Ward, I. C., *The Phonetics of English*, 4th ed., Heffer, 1948.

Wells, J. C., 'Local accents in England and Wales,' *Journal of Linguistics*, 1970.

—— *Accents of English*, vols. 1, 2, 3, Cambridge University Press, 1982.

—— and Colson, G., *Practical Phonetics*, Pitman, 1971.

Wells, R. S., 'The Pitch Phonemes of English,' *Language*, vol. 21, 1945.

Wiik, K., *Finnish and English Vowels*, Turku, 1965.

—— *Finish and English Laterals*, Turku, 1966.

Wilkins, D. A., *Linguistics in Language Teaching*, Edward Arnold, 1972.

—— *Second-Language Learning and Teaching*, Edward Arnold, 1974.

Wilkins, J., *Essay Towards a Real Character and a Philosophical Language*, 1668.

Wrenn, C. L., *The English Language*, Methuen, 1958.

Wyld, H. C., *A History of Modern Colloquial English*, 3rd ed., Blackwell, 1936.

Index

Index

Except where otherwise stated, references are to page numbers. Numbers in **bold** print refer to the page on which the definition of a term is to be found. Phonetic symbols are placed at the end of the appropriate letter section. Only those authors' names mentioned in the main text, and usually of historical interest, are included. For authors whose current work has been referred to, see Bibliography.